# American Rhetorical Excellence

## 101 PUBLIC ADDRESSES THAT SHAPED THE NATION'S HISTORY AND CULTURE

PERRY C. COTHAM

ARCHWAY
PUBLISHING

Archway Publishing books may be ordered through booksellers or by contacting:

Archway Publishing
1663 Liberty Drive
Bloomington, IN 47403
www.archwaypublishing.com
1 (888) 242-5904

ISBN: 978-1-4808-4454-4 (sc)
ISBN: 978-1-4808-4455-1 (e)

Library of Congress Control Number: 2017903542

Print information available on the last page.

Archway Publishing rev. date: 03/24/2017

# Contents

# The Gift of Rhetoric and Public Address: Some Introductory Thoughts

Public addresses make a difference—a huge difference! Whether we think of public addresses as orations, as speeches, or as persuasive written documents, so many of these public addresses are intricately linked to the kind of nation and society we experience in the United States in the early twenty-first century. This is the underlying, foundational premise of this book. There are many ways to study American politics, culture, religion, and reform, and public addresses provide a fascinating window to our shared past. The public addresses referenced in this work provide insights into our history and reflections of their times, but they are significant because they were strategic forces in actually shaping our history.

This study is about American rhetoric. And for the most part, American rhetoric is about oratory (public speaking). The sum of national public speaking has wielded a far greater impact on the course of American history than has the printed word. One might argue that the colonists talked themselves into a revolution, that the Founding Fathers clearly explained the need for a written constitution, that these same founders and political philosophers debated the nature and provisions of that important document, that they publicly argued for its ratification, and that political and reform speakers gave direction and shape—whether right or wrong, good or evil—to every important movement and dimension of the American life and character in every era of our history.

There is dynamic immediacy of the spoken message, including the speaker standing (or sitting, in some rare cases) in front of a live audience dealing with a vital issue or concern of the moment, and the stakes may be high. Nothing quite compares to that experience. Little wonder some of us enjoy the challenge of teaching public speaking and building self-confidence that translates into the speaking occasion—not simply to enable students to demonstrate their competence, control others, or gain extra attention but to instruct and coach students to employ those skills in advancing their own values and convictions. This makes a positive difference in the thinking and behavior of their listeners.

Of course, rhetoric does not require *oral* deliberation. We may think of oratory as public speaking, but there is written as well as spoken rhetoric. Indeed, there have been some published materials that truly changed the course of history, such as *Uncle Tom's Cabin* and *Common Sense*, to name two examples. We will cite at least two great written pieces of rhetoric in our listing of the top 101 public addresses in our history. And, in fact, one of those pieces of written rhetoric begins our listing of the top ten addresses.

How impossible it is to imagine that the influence of written rhetoric could, generally speaking, begin to compare to the cumulative impact of spoken rhetoric! Millions might view and listen to political debates in an election campaign year, and there is interest in the follow-up reviews and discussion after each debate. Could one imagine possible interest in a debate where the candidates all agreed to remain nonconfrontational and silent, simply released position papers, and asked the public to read them? Most of us would rather hear a speech than read one anytime!

Now here's the corollary: Oratorical literature deserves to be valued and studied at all levels of education. Obviously, students can learn much from these great speeches, as they shine a light on the past and the present. These speeches illuminate—with insight, wisdom, eloquence, wit, and sometimes sharp words—significant aspects of the national character and consciousness. Many speeches have such enduring value. There are many frequently studied addresses about freedom, and they can be studied with the same purpose as the study of major documents, such as the Magna Carta and Bill of Rights. Some of the most thought-provoking and influential expositions on the themes of "rights," "liberties," and "freedom" were first presented not in books or pamphlets but were advocated and debated from stumps, podiums, and grandstands in the form of nontranscribed oratory and public address.

"Freedom" and "liberty" are words we hear on the campaign trail and in press conferences—public officials appeal to the cause of freedom every day. The world of political and campaign oratory provides a living laboratory for studying the place of freedom and liberty within public discourse. (Of course, we recognize there are nuances and ambiguities inherent within the rhetorical use of such abstract concepts as freedom and liberty.) If nothing else, reading through this book can be an abbreviated course in American history, though admittedly there would be gaps and omissions in such an approach. Not every important event in American history inspired a great oration, memorable poem, or stirring song. Yet there can be more to be learned in terms of helping students to be better public speakers. I hope today's students can learn what works and what does not work with any specific audience. That is why I have attempted to write a brief contemporary application as a part of each of the major speeches discussed in this book.

Behind every great epic, whether poetry, narrative, or novel, there is a story as to what motivated the writer and what kind of story the writer seeks to tell. Behind every great song, there is a story that might well explain the meaning of the lyrics. Knowing that background, our understanding and appreciation for that song are enriched. One basic premise, then, of this book is that behind every great oration is a story, too. While a poem, narrative, novel, song, or musical piece might stand on its own and still be appreciated and enjoyed, it seems we only understand the great speeches in history by understanding the larger narrative or context.

## Understanding Rhetoric

A big, all-caps, headline in the front section of the Sunday, July 10, 2016, edition of *USA Today* caught my attention: **"RHETORIC NOT MEANT TO BE TAKEN LITERALLY?"** This lead article of the day, written by Rick Hampton, begins by citing voters who are "put off by some of the candidate's promises, like mass deportation of illegal immigrants and a ban on Muslim immigration." And then there is citation of the pledge to build a high, impenetrable border wall between the United States and Mexico. The idea, according to many political observers, is that there are numerous presidential campaign promises that are made in rhetorical flourish, but these promises are expected to be ignored, fudged, or just plain broken. The author cites some historical perspective.

- Franklin D. Roosevelt attacked Herbert Hoover for excessive spending, although later the New Deal spent sums vastly greater than Hoover could have imagined.
- Richard Nixon had a "secret plan to end the war in Vietnam," yet that war continued past his years in the Oval Office.
- George H. W. Bush proclaimed, "Read my lips. No new taxes!" Yet once in office, he signed a bill that increased taxes.
- The Clintons in 1993 promised to revamp health care but could not deliver on that pledge.
- Barack Obama never made good on a 2008 campaign pledge to close the Guantanamo Bay detention camp.

So all of these unattainable or vain promises and pledges are "mere rhetoric"?
The last people to embrace the change in meaning of a word or term, or even to

embrace a new spelling of some word or term, are the most intelligent, traditional-minded citizens. Some might be offended by the change, and others might resist such changes because they seem to be another step down the cultural ladder. University and college professors are among those most resistant to such change.

*Rhetoric* is one of those words that has changed in meaning over the centuries. One might argue the meaning of that word has devolved from something high and noble in logical and ethical persuasion down to mere language that is divorced from realities. We academic instructors in rhetoric and public address can insist on restoring the word to its original, classic meaning and connotation, but we are likely fighting a losing battle.

Not that *rhetoric* has disappeared in usage in Western society. Indeed, I have found the word used in *USA Today* headlines as well as other newspaper headlines. Every night as one watches any cable news broadcast, one is likely to hear the word uttered scores of times. In my folder of articles and cartoons on this subject is a cartoon in the *Tennessean* that has a most unflattering caricature of Donald Trump with the word "Campaign" across his famous hairstyle (with a dynamite stick wedged in his brain) and the word "Rhetoric" across the flames of fire shooting out his mouth.

Sometimes we hear expressions such as "The president's speech was nothing more than rhetoric." The idea in common usage is that rhetoric is all "empty talk" and "meaningless campaign promises" and, thus, easily divorced from actions. When a public person engages in fulsome talk and exaggeration, even falsehood, that message is sometimes dismissed as "mere rhetoric." It is difficult to find a nice-sounding word to communicate the same meaning as found for slang terms, such as *b. s.*, *malarkey*, *hogwash*, or *baloney*, to cite just a few. Yet the popular use of rhetoric carries almost the same negative meaning with contemporary listeners. I have sometimes used the term *bloviation* as a substitute word for *verbal nonsense*, but then again, many students may have no clue as to the meaning of such a word.

All too often, rhetoric is considered not simply as empty talk divorced from reality. The word now has a connotation of something much worse—a political weapon employed by one faction or candidate against political opponents. That is why we hear or read terms such as "irresponsible rhetoric," "hollow rhetoric," "angry rhetoric," "inflammatory rhetoric," "distractive rhetoric," "extremist rhetoric," "ugly rhetoric," "volatile rhetoric," "incendiary rhetoric," "bigoted rhetoric," "racist rhetoric," "polarizing rhetoric," "hateful rhetoric," "caustic rhetoric," "bellicose rhetoric," "nativist rhetoric," "reckless rhetoric," "harsh rhetoric," "authoritarian rhetoric," "xenophobic rhetoric," "divisive rhetoric," "hatchet rhetoric," "scary rhetoric," or even "acidic rhetoric." (And where did I find all those adjectives describing rhetoric cited in the previous sentence? Answer: They have all been used by the media to describe statements in speeches and debates of the 2016 presidential campaign.) At the top of my *USA Today* for Monday, July 18, 2016, a bold headline runs all across the page: "Obama urges politicians to temper rhetoric." In the story below, the President is quoted as making an appeal to tone down volatile rhetoric and focus on unity. "We don't need inflammatory rhetoric," Obama counseled. "Someone once wrote: 'A bullet need happen only once, but for peace to work we have to be reminded of its existence again and again and again.'"

So, it just might be that Donald Trump, as well as other political speakers (and especially demagogues), are quite effective in their use of rhetoric in the more contemporary connotation—as a political weapon or at least as empty, meaningless talk—yet most deficient in the use of rhetoric in the classical, Aristotelian sense. What do you think? Is it fair to say that whenever there is an adjective in front of the word "rhetoric" in today's popular usage, that adjective is always a negative one? Can you remember a time in which the adjective in front of the word "rhetoric" is a positive one (such as "positive rhetoric" or "meaningful rhetoric," or "healing rhetoric" or "conciliatory rhetoric" or "peaceful rhetoric"?) Clearly, words have enormous power to either unite or divide, to heal or wound.

So we academic instructors in rhetoric and public address can still teach the principles of the subject as laid out by Aristotle and a host of great teachers over the centuries, all the while reminding students of the original meaning of "rhetoric"—the use of words to persuade someone or others of something that is important to the speaker, who is using the best of logic and ethical credibility to convince the audience of a high and noble position or course of action. And while we make that point, the better part of wisdom acknowledges that hardly anyone else, other than we academic types, means anything noble and uplifting when the word "rhetoric" is used. Obviously, the foundational premise of this book is that rhetorical excellence does, indeed, exist and has existed throughout our history.

## Famous Speeches Make a Difference

Yes, rhetoric is an ancient art. Aristotle called rhetoric an art centuries ago. And rhetorical criticism is almost as ancient, too. Now the electronic era has seen such swift and dramatic changes in the playing field. Communication today can be instantaneous, and more visual than ever before. We have moved from Gutenberg to Apple. Social media seem to have changed everything. In modern times we may speak of visual rhetoric—videos and even still pictures can be more powerful, more emotionally gripping, than actual words. Some scholars of rhetorical theory believe that visual messages are so pervasive that they threaten to eclipse the influence of the spoken and written word in the twenty-first century. Images possess the power to stir deep emotions. A majority of adults, some contend, can readily discuss the last movie they viewed, but have trouble (if not find it impossible) to recall the last speech they heard in a live audience. Yet it seems inconceivable that rhetoric in the form of public address will ever fade from the scene.

Oratory today is, indeed, different from what it was in the past. There was a time when stump speaking was actually speaking on a stump, and no listener then could have imagined a radio or television that might transmit the voice and image of the speaker. There were times when families were willing to ride horse-drawn wagons and carriages several miles to sit outdoors, often on the hillside or flat ground, to listen to sermons lasting at least an hour or to political debates that might last five or six hours. Lincoln's greatest ceremonial speech is hailed for its brevity, while Daniel Webster could characteristically present a ceremonial address that would last three hours; of course, consider that, unlike Webster's featured appearances, Lincoln was not the keynote speaker at Gettysburg. (Incidentally, George Caleb Bingham's [1811-1879] classic painting *Stump Speaking* [1853] captures a Western political orator standing and speaking before an attentive outdoor gathering; the depiction is likely as authentic as anything we might imagine.)

The public addresses cited here made a difference in people's lives. All of them in some way both reflected and helped to shape our nation's political life and general culture. Among the U. S. presidents who cast a long shadow of influence over those who followed, some were great orators. David Gergen, former adviser to several presidents and now a regular political commentator for CNN, writes: "In the modern age...there is no weapon more powerful than persuasion by speech" (*Eyewitness to Power: The Essence of Leadership, Nixon to Clinton*. New York: Simon and Schuster, 2000, p. 210). As Winston Churchill once wrote: "Of all the talents bestowed upon men, none is so precious as the gift of oratory. He who enjoys it wields a power more durable than that of a great king. He is an independent force in the world" (*Ibid*).

The public speech or oration has, for centuries, altered the trajectory of history. Orators have been change agents in every institution in a free society, and even in societies not so free. Can you imagine Greece without Demosthenes or Rome without

Cicero? What would Germany have been like without the fiery oratory of Adolph Hitler in the 1930s and 40s? (The world would have been far better off, most of us might claim, without his murderous conquest of Europe and genocidal policy toward the Jewish population.) Can you imagine what Great Britain would have been like during the Second World War, especially the Nazi bombing of London in 1940, without the eloquent and passionate speeches of Prime Minister Winston Churchill? And in our own history, can we imagine the role in national destiny shaped by the rhetorical advocacy of speakers such as Patrick Henry, Daniel Webster, Abraham Lincoln, or Franklin D. Roosevelt? To be more specific, can you imagine the 1960 presidential election campaign without thinking about the Kennedy-Nixon debates? And now, can you imagine any U. S. presidential election campaign without nationally televised debates, even if some of those debates degenerated into name-calling and personal insults as happened in the fractured national campaign of 2016?

Sometimes just a single brief speech deeply jolts a large audience, making all listeners suddenly think of ideas and/or feel emotions in a new way. There are so many examples of such a phenomenon, but one of the best examples of such oratory occurred at the closing of the 1976 Republican National Convention. Incumbent President Gerald Ford had won the nomination over challenger, Governor Ronald Reagan of California. As the week's proceedings were being wrapped up, and Ford had delivered his acceptance address, Reagan supporters began chanting loudly his name, venting their disappointment their candidate did not win nomination. With seeming reluctance, the good-natured and smiling Reagan walked from his seat in the audience and made his way to the platform and then delivered the most stirring and effective oration of the entire convention. The speech, which seemed totally impromptu, displayed Reagan's superb oratorical skills and closed with his vision of what America should be and could be. One Republican leader was quoted as making a telling confession to fellow party leaders at the end of the speech: "My God, this party has just nominated the wrong man [Ford]!" Truth be known, Reagan's speech was simply a re-framed and adapted presentation of his basic stump speech, but this is not to take away from the great oratorical skills of the man who, four years later, would claim his party's highest prize and then go on to win the White House.

As an example of a stirring speech by someone who is not a professional orator and only speaks briefly, a recent one is poignant: At the 2016 Democratic National Convention, a Muslim-American father named Khizr Khan, with his wife standing silently beside him, addressed the large audience both in the Center and watching television at home. Khan spoke of their courageous son, Army Captain Humayun S. M. Khan, who was killed in 2004 by explosives while protecting other soldiers in his unit. The speech was delivered within the broader context of the Republican candidate Donald Trump having proposed (during his campaign) a ban on all Muslims entering the country. Khan courageously asked a pointed question directly to Trump: "Let me ask: Have you ever read the U. S. Constitution? I will gladly lend you my copy. [Then Khan pulled out a small pocket-sized copy of the Constitution and extended his hand while holding it.] Look for the words 'liberty' and 'equal protection of law.'" Though Khan spoke slowly and deliberately, there was no doubt about his passion and certainly no doubt about his point of view. "Have you ever been to Arlington Cemetery?" Khan asked on the last night of the convention. "Go look at the graves of the brave patriots who died defending America. You will see all faiths, genders, and ethnicities. You have sacrificed nothing and no one." The brief speech was a direct, incisive, impassioned, and courageous presentation that will be long remembered by all who heard it, even if Khan never makes a speech before a large audience again. (Trump's initial public response was to question why Khan's wife remained silent and suggested her silence may have been due to religious beliefs. The media focused on the story for several days.)

Entertainers seem to have a special platform for making brief political and reform speeches. At the January 2017 Golden Globes ceremony, Meryl Streep, whom *Time* called "the first lady of Hollywood," used her moment before the camera and a national audience to denounce with both charm and passion the President-elect Donald Trump. With nineteen Academy Award nominations for a wide range of movie performances, Streep had credibility and a diverse audience; understandably, the actor's presentation was as skillful and artful as any speech could possibly be. Her theme underscored the diversity of Americans and urged respect for all kinds of people. The speech garnered wide national attention along with a response from Trump calling the actress "over-rated." What might be considered by one segment of the population as a courageous moral statement might be adjudged by another segment of citizens as a shameless and disgraceful injection of partisan politics into an occasion intended only to honor and entertain.

The great changes and reform movements in our national experience have been powered by great speeches, delivered by one speaker to one particular audience at one particular time, and then many of these speeches reached a wider audience by television and/or print media. These mighty movements, both religious and political, that have shaped the destiny of the American nation surely began in small and obscure places from the talk and dialogue among intelligent though nameless men and women. As ideas took hold and were disseminated to larger groups, they gathered momentum and spread to other institutions and environments. Then, there emerged leaders who could give voice in both plain and eloquent language the needs, values, and hopes of ordinary people.

## Defining Presidential Greatness by Media Style

One way to define presidential greatness is how well our political leaders have seized the available technology of communication and used such technology to advance worthwhile causes and who successfully adapted their style with the shifting times. Abraham Lincoln was a gifted orator in an era when political rallies were both important civic events, but also a major source of popular entertainment. Theodore Roosevelt was a master of taking his cause directly to the people through the major medium available to him in his era. He understood the value of the expanding popular press along with the public podium it provided as a "bully pulpit" (a phrase he himself coined) to gain public support for his progressive reform and "trust busting" of large corporations, as well as for his military campaigns overseas. Franklin Delano Roosevelt, TR's Democratic cousin, was willing to seize radio and adapt his oral style, thus speaking conversationally to a national audience and offering information and reassurance during some of the darkest hours of national history. FDR's use of radio, particularly in his "fireside chats," broke new media ground to explain New Deal programs and gain public support.

John F. Kennedy elevated the media presidency to new heights with effective mastery of television. JFK felt secure enough to become the first president to permit televised press conferences; after all, he had already effectively debated his 1960 Republican opponent in a live televised format. The young president projected a media image of grace, charm, and wit; he also used television effectively in creating an image of himself as a tough Cold War warrior, vigorous athlete (despite serious chronic disabilities), and devoted family man (despite extramarital affairs). Perhaps no president could use the electronic media more effectively than Ronald Reagan, earning him the label "the great communicator." Reagan was the first professional actor elected to the American presidency. His seeming total ease in front of camera and microphone, whether in the oval office or at his party's national convention, permitted him to achieve a personal connection with his audience.

In the 1990s Bill Clinton went one step further, appearing on talk shows, MTV, and comedy programs, where he played his saxophone, discussed his family life, and answered personal questions on such topics as the style of underwear he wore. By the time of Clinton's election as president, the private lives and sexual conduct of politicians had become fair game for reporters, such a contrast to previous generations of presidents who could count on journalists and editorialists to honor certain boundaries, thus keeping these private behavioral choices undisclosed to the general public.

In recent times, modern electronic communication is ubiquitous and has truly altered the rapid speed of messages to citizens and the nature of the political message. Though the Internet is a little more than two decades old, just a blip on the radar screen of all history, it is clearly a major tool for all kinds of information and advocacy. An audience of millions can be reached by Twitter, Facebook, Instagram, texting, email, and many other electronic formats. Internet chatter can catapult an ordinary event or casual statement to a "news story." Republican Trent Lott, for example, eventually stepped down as U. S. Senate majority leader after casual comments he made at the celebration of Strom Thurmond's one hundredth birthday became a national issue. Donald Trump became notorious for his rapid-fire Twitter responses to just about anything and everything with which he objected or disagreed. One writer called Trump's rapid disdain or insult of anyone who dared to criticize or disagree with him as "Twitter torture," but the candidate's use of 140-character bursts kept his base fired up and the mainline media with a steady stream of new stories to report and discuss.

During his two-term tenure as president, Barack Obama turned to televised, one on one, interviews and social media, and thus have all major political candidates engaged the same rhetorical strategies—all inviting people to follow them on Twitter. Obama has been called "the first talk show president," making appearances on late night comedy shows. Flashing his broad smile often and naturally, he has been thought of as a comedic "natural," the best president ever at delivering a joke. Seems now that every politician needs to demonstrate he or she is a "regular guy or gal." And nothing says "real human being" like a sense of humor, especially a self-deprecating one. Ronald Reagan often quipped about his advanced age, once claiming to understand what the Founding Fathers intended in the Constitution because he knew them. You will see the names of all these speakers, as well as many more, cited in the pages ahead.

How sobering to think that the carefully crafted public address may be in a period of decline because of the electronic era! During this period of primary and general election campaigning, one may note that candidates campaign not so much for live audiences who long for an eloquent oration, but for television cameras. Rather than aiming to produce that eloquent oration, candidates seem to seek the pointed sound bite or clever figure of speech or "cute" pithy comment on Twitter that will get them a few seconds on television where they will be heard and seen by millions of viewers. This might represent the "busy-ness" of active American citizens or a "dumbing down" of the general public who think a complex issue can be reduced to a clever exclamation of only a few words dispensed electronically. It does mean political leaders and candidates are fully aware that video cameras are everywhere, some even secretly hidden, and that there is a twenty-four hour news cycle that must be constantly federal. Have the electronic media rendered great addresses and great books obsolete? Clearly, oratory in the twenty-first century is different from what it was two centuries ago, having shifted with the new forms and potentialities of media, but it would be a serious mistake to conclude the flame of American oratory has been reduced to a flicker.

## Selecting the Top 101 Speeches

Reducing rhetorical excellence to 101 public addresses is a task both formidable and humbling. Judgment must be made by any historian and rhetorical critic. Some speeches are obvious choices. In other cases, the speeches may be more representative of a person's speaking career than necessarily the best speech the person ever delivered. For example, it would be difficult to name the one most outstanding oration of speakers such as Wendell Phillips, Robert Ingersoll, or Robert LaFollette, to name three, and yet all three were outstanding orators whose effectiveness in public speaking was an integral part of their careers.

There is great variety in speeches that may be considered great pieces of rhetoric. Of course, if we are only selecting 101 addresses, we are zooming in on a miniscule portion of all the speeches that have made any kind of difference in our American society. As rhetorical critics we are forced to make judgment on what is great and effective and what is ineffective and a failure. Along the way we expect to find a good number of addresses that must be judged as eloquent. How do we go about making this selection, finding the "best of the best"? Sometimes an excellent speech fails to achieve its purpose, but still could be considered great if it sensitizes listeners to a point of view, challenges their thinking, and pushes listeners in the right direction.

There have been some mightily powerful and eloquent religious-moral addresses that have changed the course of American history. Eloquence, of course, is difficult to quantify, but it is the power to impact and move an audience to act or feel in some important way. Eloquence is not simply a matter of supreme self-confidence in front of an audience, the formal education of the communicator, or the speaker's flawless grammar and vocabulary. Eloquence is a dimension of persuasion wherein the right speaker, the right time, and occasion merge, and the speaker or writer presents a timely message with sincere passion, clarity, and forcefulness—and that message stirs a passionate response in the listener or reader!

Rhetorical critics are compelled to establish criteria or standards of excellence or greatness. Effective delivery is definitely important, and who among us does not enjoy listening to a spell-binding orator who rivets our attention for a period of time? Yet effective delivery alone may not render a speech great. William Jennings Bryan was an outstanding orator, perhaps the best of his generation. Yet in four nominations and hundreds, if not thousands, of campaign speeches for president, Bryan was never elected to the high office. There were some outstanding Southern orators in antebellum days who employed their delivery skills and eloquence in defense of slavery, even some preachers in slaveholding states made a persuasive biblical and moral case "justifying" slavery, but we would not call these political messages and sermons great because they did not advance noble ideas. Put succinctly, those speakers were on the wrong side of history.

On the flip side, a weak and unimpressive delivery does not necessarily negate the greatness of a speech so long as the ideas and words of the address are available to the wider audience. Thomas Jefferson was one of the most intelligent and thoughtful of all U. S. presidents, perhaps the most intelligent. His First Inaugural Address receives a high rating in this study, but Jefferson was definitely not renowned as a speaker; indeed, he was a reluctant orator, and his oral presentation of this speech was barely audible to those in attendance. And Abraham Lincoln was not a powerful orator, though, like Jefferson, he was a gifted writer and his ideas were profoundly expressed even in an unimpressive delivery. George Washington was a great president yet he believed he should express himself more through his actions than his few speeches. Washington, Jefferson, and Lincoln are all represented in this study, yet one characteristic they shared: They made almost no public speeches after entering the presidency.

Such a contrast from the president in office during the writing of this book—Barack Obama has delivered all kinds of addresses on almost every conceivable occasion: State of the Union Addresses annually, special policy addresses, special announcements, ceremonial speeches (especially memorial addresses), and numerous funeral eulogies.

In a July 12, 2016, address memorializing five Dallas police officers that were ambushed during a peaceful protest march, the President lamented he had been called on too many times to eulogize American victims of gun violence. In modern times, the U. S. president absolutely must speak both *to* and *for* the entire nation during periods of national sadness and perplexity. And, then, on January 10, 2017, Obama delivered his Farewell Address, the last public address of his presidency, in which he extolled the virtues of democracy, underscored his self-understanding of legacy, and promised a smooth transition of power to Trump (calling the cooperation a "hallmark of our democracy").

Do we look at the immediate response of a speech as a high standard of excellence? Consider that some speeches must be listed because of such a positive immediate response, whether strong emotional response or sustained applause, but that with the perspective of time historians deemed the speech to be self-serving, even demagogic. General Douglas MacArthur received strong positive response in his "Farewell Address to the Nation," and Richard Nixon also gained such immediate positive response and support after delivering his famous "Checkers Speech," yet neither address has garnered major respect from American political historians.

Eloquent speeches possess a number of traits, but one typical trait is the existence of a memorable phrase that encapsulates the entire address and, as Professor Kathleen Jamieson puts it, "serves as the hook on which we hang it in memory" (*Eloquence in an Electronic Age*, p. 90). Eloquent speakers can come up with a memorable phrase, one that serves as a synecdoche, where the part of the speech stands for the whole speech. The "synecdochic phrase," as Jamieson calls it, provides something memorable and eloquent that may characterize not only the address but perhaps even an entire administration or an entire generation (as in Churchill's "their finest hour" and his "blood, sweat, and tears" or Tom Brokaw's "the greatest generation").

At that point, few listeners, if any, really care if the memorable phrase was original with the speaker or that it might have been "stolen" from another source or written by a ghostwriter. We simply associate the memorable phrase with the man or woman who uttered it with no thought of its originality. (As an aside, most do care if an entire speech or a big portion of it was pilfered from another source without the slightest hint of attribution. Consider the brouhaha evoked by Melania Trump taking the stage at the Republican National Convention's opening night, July 18, 2016, and delivering a plagiarized section from an address by First Lady Michelle Obama some eight years earlier; shortly after the story broke, no one really seemed to care about this ethical breach.)

Interestingly, most famous speeches are not labeled by one official name. Because the apt, memorable phrase is so important in rendering any speech to be a great one, that phrase might become the title of the speech, though typically it would not be listed that way in any official program on the day of delivery. Thus we speak of King's best known speech as the "I Have a Dream Speech" rather than "The March on Washington Address." We speak of FDR's "Four Freedoms Address" rather than his "State of the Union Address." Nixon's "Confronting Allegations over Personal Use of Campaign Funds" will forever be known as the aforementioned "Checkers Speech." And who today really knows or cares what Patrick Henry's "Give Me Liberty or Give Me Death" speech might have been called prior to its delivery to the Virginia Convention?

## Rating the Top Ten American Public Addresses

This study attempts a listing of the top ten public addresses in our history. Other rhetorical critics would surely have a different listing. In my selecting and ranking, I have considered two major criteria: great ideas—ideas that advance the cause of truth and justice and which stand the test of time—and the positive, long range effectiveness of the speech. Some of these great speeches cast a vision for the future or establish a philosophy and agenda for the nation to follow. This is why an address such as Thomas Jefferson's First Inaugural Address or Lyndon B. Johnson's "We Shall Overcome" Address is included. Sometimes a single speech inspires an entire generation and may contain a famous line that is oft-quoted by future generations, thus JFK's Inaugural Address is included in our top ten public addresses.

Selecting the other ninety-one addresses surely comes down to judgment, and every critic has a slightly different judgment and opinion. Oratory is always expected at certain annual events, such as the president's State of the Union report to a joint session of Congress. Major party conventions have always provided a dynamic context for powerful, stirring political speeches. Indeed, one could make a case for including in this volume every one of the following orations: presidential Inaugural Addresses; major party nomination acceptance speeches; presidential ceremonial speeches; major nominee concession speeches; Farewell Addresses; and now even presidential candidates' spouse's address. So how do we choose? After all, how might we justify including the vice presidential nomination acceptance speech of Geraldine Ferraro in 1984 and not including the keynote address of Ann Richards at the Democratic National Convention in 1988? On what basis might we include a commencement address by Michelle Obama in Chicago, but exclude one by Barbara Bush at Wellesley or one by Tom Brokaw at Santa Fe? Our list of examples of American rhetorical excellence could easily become quite lengthy. Maybe by simply raising these questions the point is made that oratory has always been such an integral part of our political and cultural history.

In our history there have been millions upon millions of publicly uttered words by innumerable officials, educators, preachers, attorneys, campaigners, corporate and business leaders, labor leaders, trainers, reformers, satirists, and entertainers that have energized truth and challenged our thinking by inspiring, explaining, lecturing, preaching, advocating, uplifting, rallying, leading, challenging, and ennobling fellow Americans through the extraordinary event of the spoken word to a live audience—all molding and transforming in some way the national character of the past twenty-four decades, though we dare not dismiss the colonial rhetorical legacy!

Each of us will have personal favorites. You, as reader, can decide which addresses are the most important and which are least important. And you will have your reasons for your selections. We will not all concur in our listings, any more than we could agree on some ranking of the nation's best musical compositions, though typically there is much to be learned from most of our selections.

While we are simply including excerpts of the addresses here, some of these speeches are worth reading in their entirety and not just remembered by way of sound bites on special occasions. It is valuable to know what King's "Dream" actually entailed or what the Founding Fathers were actually thinking and hoping some "four score and seven years" prior to Lincoln's appearance at the Gettysburg battlefield and cemetery. Once past the first ten addresses, the speeches are listed generally in chronological order, thus enabling the reader to capture a flow of American history through different eras. I have had students in mind as this book is written, thus I have attempted a contemporary application of each of the 101 speeches delivered. I have attempted to hold the 101 essays to around a thousand words each with a uniform format, and sometimes there has been space to include an interesting fact or two.

## Ceremonial Speaking in the American Culture

In my top ten listing there is tacit understanding of the significant role of ceremonial speaking within the American democracy, not unlike its role in all other kinds of advanced societies and organizations. Seems that the ceremonial speaking occasion, what Aristotle called *epideictic* speaking, provides the best context for the highest levels of eloquence. Ceremonial speaking has also been called by other titles, too, such as panegyric, demonstrative, or declamation.

Obviously, ceremonial speaking has been around for centuries, case in point being the funeral oration of Pericles in extolling the "fallen sons" of a glorious ancient Greece. (Incidentally, we have no text of the great Greek speeches, but depend on the oratorical reconstruction of Thucydides in his *History of the Peloponnesian War* for any textual accuracy.) Aristotle explained the persuasive goal of *epideictic* speaking to be establishing honor or shame, that is, some leader or action or institution is to be praised or to be reviled. We know this category of speaking quite well, as we might recall the old-fashioned Fourth of July speeches and other national holiday orations. (Incidentally, the city of Boston declared that the Boston Massacre would be commemorated annually with speeches on the meaning of that unfortunate incident as it was considered to have national importance; in 1783 the city of Boston declared the Boston Massacre Address would be replaced by commemoration of Independence Day in which there would be a keynote address.)

Ceremonial speaking is not simply a tactic to fill time between musical numbers and introductions during special occasions. For this reason, four of the top ten speeches discussed here are ceremonial, beginning with Martin Luther King's eloquent speech at the March on Washington in August 1963. For decades before King's address, Lincoln's Gettysburg Address was considered the greatest speech in American history, and the latter was often required by school teachers to be memorized and recited by young students in the American classroom. One might argue that these and other such addresses constitute "sacred texts" in the canon of "Scriptures" for American civil religion.

Is there ever a sense in which silence can be rhetorical? Well, silence alone cannot be considered rhetoric any more than instrumental music alone could be considered rhetoric. Yet one rhetorical strategy is the "pregnant pause," a meaningful pausing somewhere in the oration to allow *pathos*, or emotion, to have its impact on an audience. And silence can, on certain speaking occasions, be more meaningful than words. This topic gives me the opportunity to cite an excerpt from a lengthy speech by James A. Garfield at the first Memorial Day ceremony. On May 30, 1868, Garfield was a Republican congressman and a former Civil War general at the time and eventually was slated to be elected president of the U. S. Addressing an audience of several thousand at Arlington National

Cemetery on what was then called Decoration Day, Garfield eloquently declared: "If silence is ever golden, it must be beside the graves of fifteen thousand men, whose lives were more significant than speech, and whose death was a poem the music of which can never be sung." Garfield was an effective speaker, but his assassination early in his term of office robbed him of any opportunity to deliver other stirring orations and establish any place among the nation's great speakers.

## The Nation's Most Prolific Ceremonial Speaker

Daniel Webster, it might be argued, was the most profound and eloquent ceremonial speaker in our nation's history. As a speaker, of course, Webster must be praised most for his eloquent defense of the Union and for his interpretation of the Constitution in the "great debate" in the Senate during the early national period. Yet there were a number of ceremonial speeches he delivered that were widely circulated in print and drawn upon by public school teachers and students alike: "First Settlement of New England" (December 22, 1820) marked the bicentennial of the landing of the pilgrims at Plymouth; "The Bunker Hill Monument," delivered open air (June 17, 1725), the fiftieth anniversary of the Battle of Bunker Hill before an audience of almost 100,000; and "Adams and Jefferson" (August 2, 1826), delivered at Boston's famed Faneuil Hall and celebrating the lives of two remarkable Founding Fathers who died on the same day—July 4, 1826, the fiftieth anniversary of the Declaration of Independence.

There were other remarkable Websterian special occasion orations, but they are cited here for the significance of such speaking: First, ceremonial speaking, gives a nation what is greatly needed—heroes, myths, symbols, shibboleths, and catch-phrases. These heroes may seem bigger than life, though only four of them are etched in stone at Mount Rushmore. And how often have we heard the phrases "Four score and seven years ago" or "I have a dream"? Second, when ceremonial speaking embraces greater truth and noble ideals, future national leaders can be instructed and inspired. In Webster's "Bunker Hill Address," for example, the speaker emphasized that the American political system was quite young and still remained an experiment, and some of his sentences seem to lie behind Lincoln's eloquence that was given voice at Gettysburg forty-three years later. We might note the continuity in themes throughout the decades in forty-four presidential Inaugural Addresses.

Let us take it as a "given" that the hundreds of names mentioned in this book as political, legislative, and reform communicators were sincere in their messages. Let us assume they sought to advance the cause of truth and justice as they understood that cause. They uttered words that enraged, delighted, inspired, chastened, reassured, and comforted Americans in days gone by. Sure, a few were misguided and perhaps misinformed or uninformed. Nonetheless, we may believe that their rhetorical efforts aimed to inspire men and women to learn the truth, be better citizens and, subsequently, to make this land a better nation and society.

Yes, there were some speakers and writers who used their gifts and skills as forces to fight and resist change and reform, who used eloquence in defense of the morally indefensible, or who simply used those skills in defense of the status quo. Those communicators who used fallacious reasoning or sacred texts to defend "the peculiar institution" of slavery serve as a clear example of speakers on the wrong side of history. Yet there is no need to deny their influence or, in most cases, even question their sincerity. We will discuss some of them in a later chapter, "The Hall of Shame."

Thankfully, there were other communicators who grasped the power of an idea whose time had come, whose eloquence advanced worthy causes on the right side of history. Those who most influenced our history and culture in the right direction were men and women of action who were also men and women of words, advocates who used words as instruments of power to stir people to think and then to act for a cause greater than themselves. As you read excerpts of some of their speeches, let your imagination place you in the middle of the audience so that you can feel the impact of the occasion and those words when first uttered and then imagine how those all around you may have been stirred and impelled to conviction and action!

## How This Book Originated

Risking to sound like an old man, ahem!, perhaps the beginning point for this study would have been a course in the history and criticism of American public address in the 1960s, as taught by Fred Walker, taken as a religion and speech major at Lipscomb University (then known as David Lipscomb College) in Nashville, Tennessee. My main interest at that point was pulpit oratory, or preaching, but the class introduced to me some of the nation's better-known speakers. As a text, we used A. Craig Baird's, *American Public Addresses, 1740–1952* (McGraw-Hill, 1956), and the speakers represented ran chronologically from Jonathan Edwards to Adlai Stevenson. Concerned about us students in homiletics not being overly exposed to biblical modernism, "Brother" Walker, as we called him, asked us to substitute Henry Ward Beecher's "Liverpool Address" for Beecher's sermon included in the volume entitled "The Two Revelations." Yet, Beecher fascinated me. All students in the class were required to select a speaker for a term project, presented in writing and orally for the class, and, as a ministry major, I selected Beecher. (In those days, alas, we had no PowerPoint presentation capability and rarely even attempted to use an overhead projector.)

After graduation I accepted a pulpit position in the Detroit metropolitan area. Soon encountering the sobering realities of a preaching minister and pastor, I decided to begin graduate studies in speech communication at Wayne State University. Before even completing my Masters, I began to enjoy the study of American history in general, and American public address specifically; consequently, I took as many courses in that area that were available. My major advisor was Professor George V. Bohman. His specialty was colonial public address and his dissertation on that subject, submitted for his doctorate at the University of Wisconsin, consumed some two thousand pages; he justifiably called the dissertation his *magnum opus*.

Dr. Bohman taught the courses in American public address. He seemed a wealth of knowledge on the subject and he knew a lot of trivia in that field, much of which might wind up as "identification" questions on his challenging exams. He could speak first-hand of a number of noted speakers in his time, including Franklin D. Roosevelt, though he sometimes told stories about the radio priest he called "Twelve Mile Charlie," who was Fr. Charles Coughlin, who pastored a parish in Royal Oak, Michigan, a suburb of Detroit off Woodward Avenue at Twelve Mile Road. I assumed a "directed study" for credit under Dr. Bohman by compiling an annotated bibliography, some fifty or so pages, for the study of American public address, and the chairman was quite pleased and gave my work a limited, private publication. After returning to Nashville and beginning my full-time professorship, Dr. Bohman mailed me his doctoral dissertation (only "hard copies" were available then) and asked me to edit the work and reduce it to around three hundred pages so that it would be appealing as a single volume. At the time, I felt his request was one more assignment than I should have been given, but I was honored that he trusted and respected my judgment and editorial skills.

The textbooks we used in Dr. Bohman's classes were the three volumes in the series *A History and Criticism of American Public Address* (McGraw Hill, 1943 and reprinted by Russell and Russell, 1960) prepared under the auspices of the Speech Association of America. The first two volumes were edited by William Norwood Brigance in 1943, and the third volume was edited by Marie Hochmuth Nichols in 1956. These volumes, along with Robert T. Oliver's *History of Public Speaking in America* (Allyn and Bacon, 1965), became my "Bible" as I prepared a compilation of notes on American public address to study in preparation for my "comps," our slang term for doctoral written comprehensive exams, and then my anticipated use in teaching this subject in future classes. (Incidentally, in the early years of teaching this subject, I used the Oliver book as my text, regretting the author ended his narrative with Woodrow Wilson's speeches rather than extending it at least to the speaking of FDR if not JFK.)

My compilation of notes on American public address while completing doctoral studies consumed over five hundred typed pages on my trusty Royal portable typewriter, and, as it turned out, was a volume that was borrowed by all my peers in the doctoral program as they were making their own preparation for "comps." This compilation might be seen as the first draft of this book and of course it has been updated by discussions of speakers in recent times. I have drawn from those dusty old notes while writing this volume, and then those notes were drawn from the above cited books as well as from notes I compiled later in the teaching of American history.

My doctoral dissertation was an attempt at a depth, historical-critical approach to one man's speaking career—Harry L. Hopkins, close adviser and friend of Franklin D. Roosevelt during the Great Depression and World War II. My real interest was in Roosevelt, but, being there were many dissertations and articles on Roosevelt's speaking, I felt another way to approach Roosevelt and the New Deal would be the rhetoric of Hopkins and other New Deal spokespersons.

As for the material in this book, I have drawn from the above sources as well as lecture notes in classes in public address, political communication, and American history. In the past decade or so in teaching Fundamentals of Communication at Middle Tennessee State University, I always incorporate a class session for students on the great speakers in both American and world history. I enjoy hearing what these students have to say about some of our national orators. I lead a discussion on what we can learn from the oratory of these famous speakers. I enjoy asking the class to vote on whom they believe to be the nation's greatest orator, and only once has any class voted for anyone other than Martin Luther King, Jr. (One class voted for John F. Kennedy.)

This book is being written in the midst of the 2016 presidential campaign, the most fractured and dysfunctional American political campaign I can remember. The word *rhetoric* is found in almost every daily newspaper and weekly newsmagazine, as well as in every news broadcast. As always, there are great challenges facing the nation and new ones will emerge as our history unfolds. And, most certainly, those challenges will be confronted, explained, debated, and resolutions will be advocated by means of public address. One can only imagine the eloquence that future generations will be blessed to read and hear!

A brief note of acknowledgment and appreciation to my wife Glenda who read this manuscript and searched for any typographical errors. I have been blessed with the opportunity to teach speech communication, public speaking, political communication, religious speaking, and American public address at various universities, including Middle Tennessee State University at the present time, yet also at Lipscomb University, Belmont University, Nashville State Community College, and Wayne State University. My goal here has been to present narratives and information for students, colleagues, friends, and general readers, and just hope most of them will be captured by the importance and relevance of the study.

And, finally, I am delighted to offer a statement of special gratitude to Stephanie Frame and Kayla Stobaugh of Archway Press for their very prompt, professional and congenial counsel and assistance during the submission and production stages of this book.

# PART ONE

## THE TOP TEN PUBLIC ADDRESSES IN AMERICAN HISTORY

# 1. Thomas Jefferson, Declaration of Independence, July 4, 1776

*Speaker/Author:* Thomas Jefferson was the principal author of the Declaration, though he labored on a committee composed also of John Adams, Benjamin Franklin, Roger Sherman, and Robert Livingston. Jefferson was chosen because he had already established a reputation for excellence in writing. In one sense, the entire Continental Congressional delegation might be viewed as "the speaker" and, as such, could not agree on whether the King should be held responsible for the slave trade. As for Jefferson, though a young man, he was already experienced in Virginia political life by serving in the colony's House of Burgesses. He had attended the College of William and Mary and was admitted to the Virginia bar in 1767. He became active in Virginia's independence movement, then later served the new nation as ambassador to France and, for two terms, as the third president of the new nation.

*Occasion:* True, this was not a public speech in the traditional sense of one speaker standing before a live audience in a one-time event. Yet the ideas and ideals of this address had surely been presented in various public addresses and sermons in various forums and settings throughout the colonies for months and years. Relations between the colonists and the mother country now seemed at a crisis point as there had already been fighting between the two sides in both the North and the South in 1775 and early 1776. There were two audiences for this rhetorical effort: Those colonists who still sided with Britain or were reluctant to support the patriot cause and, also, astute observers in the mother country and in other parts of Europe, especially France, who would be forming an opinion about the justice of the American patriot cause. Jefferson wrote that the Declaration was "an appeal to the tribunal of the world," and that the delegates possessed "….a decent respect for the opinions of mankind."

*Excerpt:* [The first section, after stating the gravity of the situation, memorably expressed the highest ideals of the delegates in a powerful and eloquent philosophical statement]: "We hold these truths to be self-evident, that all men are created equal, that they are endowed by their creator with certain unalienable rights, that among these are life, liberty, and the pursuit of happiness. That to secure these rights, governments are instituted among men, deriving their just powers from the consent of the governed. That whenever any form of government becomes destructive of these ends, it is the right of the people to alter or abolish it, and to institute a new government, laying its foundations on such principles, and organizing its powers in such form, as to them shall seem most likely to effect their safety and happiness."

*Little Known Facts:* Jefferson, a product of the Enlightenment, was reluctant to take the writing assignment for several reasons. Also, he was only thirty-three years old at the time of its drafting. The Continental Congress made significant changes in Jefferson's draft, most importantly removing—at the insistence of delegates from South Carolina and Georgia—his vigorous condemnation of King George III for permitting slavery and the slave trade in the colonies.

*Impact:* Because the Revolution was the single most important event in American history, this Declaration is important for stating its justification. In some ways, the Declaration is an *ex post facto* justification of American Revolution—it announced a condition or a status already established (of course later, the Continental Army waged war to secure that status). There are three major ways to analyze or understand the Declaration: (1) *Historically,* as one of the most important and influential documents in world history; (2) *Philosophically,* as a statement of political ideals drawn from English common law and natural law doctrine as advanced by English philosopher John Locke; and (3) *Rhetorically,* as a document intended to persuade an audience. While our excerpt above contains the noble ideals in the first section, most citizens are not aware of Jefferson's rhetorical strategy in building evidence to support his thesis that independence is justified. In the central section,

Jefferson reiterated the "long train of abuses and usurpations" on the part of King George that had led Americans to their drastic course. He does not mention Parliament, but personalizes the conflict in his references to the King. Jefferson is building his case and, like most persuaders, cites only evidence that supports the Patriot cause without reference to reasonable and patient British efforts to appease and accommodate the colonists. The immediate impact was positive as the Declaration was greeted in public and in private with every demonstration of delight and approval. It inspired the friends of the Revolution for their great task. The long-range impact of this address is immeasurable—it is often quoted by American citizens, especially minorities of all kinds, and by revolutionaries in various countries around the world. Wherever people have fought against totalitarian regimes, they have argued, using Jefferson's language, that governments derive "their just powers from the consent of the governed." One might contend the Declaration of Independence is the greatest single statement in the history of political thought.

*Contemporary Application:* Documents such as the Declaration of Independence and Martin Luther King's "Letter from a Birmingham Jail," to cite just two examples, provide clear evidence that written rhetoric to a specific audience can be just as persuasive and powerful as an actual speech presented orally to a live audience.

*Connection to Today:* The statement of noble ideals has continued to reverberate through all American history—the idea of equality as a natural right of all people has inspired the poor as well as the wealthy, women as well as men, blacks and Latinos and other ethnic populations as well as whites, and the gay and lesbian community. This rhetorical document lives and breathes even today. The stated ideals have always been open to interpretation, re-interpretation, and fresh application. Each generation re-interprets the Declaration of Independence so that it becomes a living expression of justice rather than an idiom of the eighteenth century.

# 2. Martin Luther King, Jr., The March on Washington for Jobs and Freedom Address, August 28, 1963

*Speaker:* There have been many outstanding black speakers, especially preachers, in American history, but most historians of culture are likely to rank the Reverend Martin Luther King, Jr. (1929–1968) at the top of the list. King was the son of a prominent Baptist preacher, educated at Morehouse College, entered the ministry, then pursued his doctorate in theology at Boston University. In 1955 the Rosa Parks bus incident occurred, sparking the modern Civil Rights movement, catapulting King into leadership for which he was well prepared. King was a preacher before he was a political and social reformer. Though often he lapsed into the oral style of the black folk preacher, in most ways his content was far stronger than typical African-American preachers. He drew heavily from intellectual sources (some critics say his use of sources too often neglected attribution), and he fashioned a rhetorical strategy for each major audience. He was best known for his calls for social justice and racial equality, to be reached through non-violence and passive resistance. Two additional themes were expounded in most addresses: An appeal to God and to "higher law" and the power of redemptive love and suffering.

*Occasion:* The centennial of the Emancipation Proclamation (1963) was another big year for protests and demonstrations for racial equality and social justice. A huge rally was planned for August 28, and supporters traveled from far and near, sometimes at great expense and inconvenience, to be among over 200,000 to march from the Washington Monument to the Lincoln Memorial. President Kennedy praised the "deep fervor and quiet dignity" of the well-disciplined demonstrators. Leaders of the movement voiced hope for equality and justice for all Americans, yet all anticipated the address by Dr.

Martin Luther King as the keynote speaker. This was the largest live audience in American history (at that time), a sympathetic and supportive gathering of largely African-American activists and supporters, sitting and standing outdoors in late summer heat, waiting to be encouraged and inspired by their moral leader. Millions more watched the speech from their homes or places of business through the national telecast of the event.

*Excerpt:* "I say to you my friends…even though we face the difficulties of today and tomorrow, I still have a dream. It is a dream deeply rooted in the 'American dream,' it is a dream that one day this nation will rise up and live out the true meaning of its creed: 'We hold these truths to be self-evidence, that all men are created equal.'…When we let freedom ring, when we let it ring from every village and every hamlet, from every state and every city, we will be able to speed up that day when all of God's children, black men and white men, Jews and Gentiles, Protestants and Catholics, will be able to join hands and sing in the words of the old Negro spiritual, 'Free at last! Free at last! Thank God Almighty, we are free at last!'"

*Impact:* King's address was a soaring success. Popularly known as the "I Have a Dream" speech, many critics as well as most university students deem the address to be the best speech in American history. The address was electrifying. Being telecast live nationally, it not only brought attention to the Civil Rights Movement, but provided white Americans with a model of African-American preaching and reform speaking at its best. The speaker referenced the Bible, the Declaration of Independence, and the U. S. Constitution. He used a homely analogy in declaring "In a sense we have come to our nation's Capital to cash a check," and, after referencing the Declaration and Constitution, that the Founding Fathers' "promissory note" had been defaulted upon by the nation, that "citizens of color" had been given "a bad check. But "the bank of justice" is not necessarily bankrupt, "so we have come to cash this check." In the style of the black preacher, King's soaring eloquence took flight. He fused religious rhetoric with familiar patriotic symbols, contending there was much work yet to be done in the movement. This speech belongs to the ages. In one sense, Martin Luther King is a "founding father," and this text is part of national sacred scripture. King himself likely did not realize the greatness of his oration at the time of delivery. For his leadership in the Civil Rights Movement, Martin Luther King was awarded the Nobel Peace Prize a year later. He was assassinated in 1968 on the eve of a strike on behalf of Memphis municipal workers.

*Little Known Fact:* As the address moved on with cumbersome wording and heavy thoughts, gospel singer Mahalia Jackson, positioned near the speaker, then exhorted: "Tell 'em about the dream, Martin." And soon words flowed from King, actually words he had employed previously in at least one earlier address in a mass rally at Detroit—words destined to find their place in the American canon of great oratorical literature that equaled any eloquence of Jefferson or Lincoln. The words are clearly identified with King by all Americans: "I have a dream."

*Contemporary Application:* More than a half century after this great speech, the main lesson is still true: The timely words of one person spoken at the right moment before an enormous crowd of admirers who simply need to be mobilized, encouraged, and inspired, can render that speech immortal and serve as a beacon for hope and change within society and the world at large.

*Connection to Today:* This speech became as famous and memorable in the latter twentieth century as Lincoln's much briefer Gettysburg Address became famous and memorable in the latter nineteenth century. The greatness lies in the fact that King was on the right side of history—the cause of social and racial justice is true and right both in the sight of a righteous God and in the very nature of enlightened reason. Sadly, the lives of both Lincoln and King were ended by an assassin.

# 3. Abraham Lincoln, Gettysburg Address, November 19, 1863

*Speaker*: Abraham Lincoln (1809–1865) knew the young nation was getting weary of war, and that as president he needed to inspire his fellow citizens to preserve a national government that boasted an ideal that all men are created equal. At this stage of the war, Lincoln had been pondering the deeper significance of such a terrible war. Lincoln's remarks were carefully crafted several days before he left Washington by train, but a romantic (though unlikely) version says Lincoln spotted an old envelope on the floor of the train, borrowed a pencil stub, and scribbled a few remarks, then dropped it to the floor looking disconsolate.

*Occasion*: During the first three days in July 1863, at Gettysburg, Pennsylvania, the most famous and most terrible battle on American soil was waged. The victory of Union troops on July 3 marked a crucial turning point in the Civil War. Yet, there was such an appalling loss of thousands of soldiers, imperfectly identified, and hastily buried. Seventeen acres on Cemetery Hill had been purchased for re-interment of these soldiers, and an estimated crowd of 15,000 gathered solemnly for its dedication. Edward Everett (a former senator, former secretary of state, and former Harvard president) delivered the main oration on this occasion, and the invitation to the President to present "a few appropriate remarks" was almost an after-thought by the planning committee.

*Excerpt*: "Four score and seven years ago our fathers brought forth on this continent, a new nation, conceived in liberty, and dedicated to the proposition that all men are created equal....This nation, under God, shall have a new birth of freedom—and that government of the people, by the people, for the people, shall not perish from the earth."

*Impact:* A huge irony exists: Both Lincoln and a number of others at the scene felt the speech a failure. And a number of newspapers reported the President's remarks were "silly" or "inappropriate" and deserved to be forgotten. After the President's martyrdom, there seemed almost universal consensus that the Gettysburg Address was the greatest and most eloquent speech in American history. With only 272 words and two minutes of time, Lincoln stated the essence of the Civil War and the high purpose served by those courageous soldiers who died on ground that had now become sacred. Though it celebrated a military victory, it is not martial in spirit. The speech can be read as a poem based on the metaphor of birth, death, and rebirth. William Jennings Bryan, perhaps the greatest political orator of his own time, did not exaggerate the greatness of Lincoln's tribute: "[The] Gettysburg Address is not surpassed, if equaled, in beauty, simplicity, force, and appropriateness by any speech of the same length of any language. It is the world's model in eloquence, elegance, and condensation." Generations of school children who never heard of Edward Everett as keynote speaker for the occasion, much less being able to locate a copy of his scholarly and lengthy address, have been expected to memorize the Gettysburg Address and recognize its eloquent opening immediately. "I shall be glad," wrote Everett to Lincoln the next day after the dedication, "if I could flatter myself that I came as near to the central idea of the occasion in two hours as you did in two minutes." Lincoln replied: "In our respective parts yesterday, you could not have been excused to make a short address, nor I a long one."

*Little Known Fact:* Brevity was a key trait of the speech, thus we have no official photograph of Lincoln delivering this speech. Before the photographer could complete set-up of his camera for an exposure and get a good angle, the President had completed the address. A dirge was sung and Doctor Baugher pronounced the benediction.

*Interesting Irony:* While it took one hundred and fifty years, the *Harrisburg Patriot-News* retracted a dismissive editorial penned by its Civil War-era predecessor, the *Harrisburg Patriot and Union*. The 1863 coverage described the speech as "silly remarks" that deserved a "veil of oblivion." The newspaper now (Nov. 16, 2013) says it regrets not seeing its "momentous importance, timeless eloquence, and lasting significance." The paper's retraction is clever: "By today's words alone, we cannot exalt, we cannot hallow, we cannot venerate this sacred text, for a grateful nation long ago came to view those words with reverence, without guidance from its chagrined member of the mainstream media."

*Contemporary Application:* A great address contains several unique features that render ceremonial speaking effective. One is brevity, especially important if there are other speakers on a program. Second, the style is simple but ornate. This address was a prose poem, now among great elegies and oratorical masterpieces. Third, Lincoln's tone was deliberately abstract and allowed listeners to fill in the specifics; he did not mention slavery, specific battles, or war strategy. Fourth, biblical language is adduced before an audience that knew well the contents of the Bible ("our fathers," "brought forth," and "resting place"). The opening line "Four score and seven years" has an Old Testament ring, just as "new birth" is of New Testament origin. The speech can be read as a poem based on the metaphor of birth, death, and rebirth. Four images of birth are embedded in its opening sentence ("conceived in liberty," "brought forth," "by our fathers," and "created equal"). Birth is followed by images of death—"final resting place," "who gave their lives," and "brave men, living and dead." After the nation's symbolic birth and death comes resurrection, "a new birth of freedom" and thus "not perish." Lincoln also used trilogy in phrasing ("government of the people, by the people, for the people" and "we cannot dedicate, we cannot consecrate, we cannot hallow this ground"). In essence, Lincoln could take the simplest words and bring out the beauty of the English language to serve his purpose of explaining what "this nation" is all about— equality as well as union. This is truly one of the world's greatest orations.

# 4. Franklin D. Roosevelt, First Inaugural Address, March 4, 1933

*Speaker:* Very few public men or women have exhibited greater respect for the power of the spoken word, or worked harder to use it effectively in the achievement of what each perceived to be the general social good, than Franklin D. Roosevelt (1882–1945). No previous president in American history had placed so much faith and importance in the power of oral persuasion; he spoke publicly upon every occasion he could arrange. During his long and unprecedented presidential career (he was elected president four times), he had used speechmaking to establish a tremendous rapport with the American people. FDR had established a tremendous sense of positive credibility, what Aristotle called *ethos*, with the American masses (of course, many die-hard Republicans opposed his policies and many detested him personally). Every important event, every important project, every significant act of his administration, is reflected in his speeches. He used these speeches to establish rapport with the American people. Because he had suffered polio and lost total leg strength as a young man, many felt that, despite birth into an aristocratic family, he understood human suffering and could empathize with hurting people. A complete listing of Roosevelt's speeches has been compiled by Gail Compton using private manuscript material at the Roosevelt Library in Hyde Park, New York. Compton has located and labeled 1,233 speeches of FDR between the years 1898 to 1945. The first speech is dated June 19, 1898, wherein young Franklin spoke in a Groton school debate on the issue of annexation of Hawaii. Address Number 1,233 is dated April 13, 1945, and was prepared for delivery over the radio at a Jefferson Day dinner. There is one script of this speech available in a long-hand draft. Sadly, Franklin Roosevelt never lived to deliver this speech. (We will say more about FDR as a speaker in another chapter.)

*Occasion:* The morning of Inauguration dawned a cold, overcast, windy and dreary day in Washington. Hopelessness and despair loomed throughout the land as the Great Depression had reached its lowest level and most dramatic stage. Around fifteen million Americans (about a quarter of the U. S. laboring force) were desperately seeking re-employment. The burgeoning burden of providing food, clothing, and shelter for all those people affected in some way by the depression and made heavier by the continued breakdown of state and local machinery. The efforts of the RFC had been insufficient to avert a banking crisis and two-thirds of the banks had been closed by official proclamation. Just thirty days earlier, Adolph Hitler had seized power in Germany. Uncertainty, even fear, about the future gripped the hearts and minds of a majority of American citizens. Never before had a change of presidents taken place against a background of despair so dramatic. Economic depression had also hit nations in Europe and elsewhere, too. The people throughout the length and breadth of forty-eight states gathered around their radios as their new leader stood on the steps of the Capitol to speak. The pressing task of the new president-elect was providing a realistic appraisal of the dire straits of the nation and then offering hope that measures to bring desperately needed relief would be taken immediately and successfully.

*Excerpt:* "This great nation will endure as it has endured, will revive and will prosper. So, first of all, let me assert my firm belief that the only thing we have to fear is fear itself….There are many ways in which it can be helped, but it can never be helped by merely talking about it. We must act and act quickly."

*Impact:* Some historians consider this to be Roosevelt's greatest speech. The stakes were high. Millions of citizens were listening for something hopeful and they found it. It was not because his program for recovery had major, new proposals; in fact, what Roosevelt did say was so vague that it was open to varying interpretation. Yet the confident ring in his voice, the facial expressions and other body language, his clarion call for sacrifice, discipline, and action all demonstrated a man confident in his new role as leader of the great nation.

American citizens were convinced they had elected a president who cared and was wise enough to act immediately. Not only in the United States, but the democracies of the world, listeners took hope and courage from this speech. This was perceived on both sides of the Atlantic as a new beginning for the crippled nation. In the U. S. during the next week, nearly a million Americans wrote their new leader to thank him or make additional comment. The speaker within just one public address created an impression that Hoover had never been able to make within years of high office—a man who knew how to lead and possessed the courage to do it with unrelenting faith in the future.

*Contemporary Application:* The speech confirms Aristotle's view that *ethos* can be the most persuasive form of proof, even in a ceremonial speech.

*Little Known Fact:* The speech's most memorable line—"The only thing we have to fear is fear itself"—was not a new platitude. Some historians believe the new president learned the admonition from a principal in elementary school. Outgoing President Herbert Hoover had stated essentially the same thing repeatedly for the previous three years. Yet given the crucially important speech context, the phrase and admonition will always be warmly associated with Franklin Roosevelt.

*Connection to Today:* The hope that was instilled in American citizens by this speech led to four months of the most brilliantly successful government operation in the nation's history—a fulfillment of what FDR had promised in an earlier campaign speech of "bold, persistent, experimentation." The legislation of the New Deal established a new role of government that survives until our present time. This speech was just the beginning. In our generation, we have seen Barack Obama, with his emphasis on "change" and "a new beginning," be compared favorably with Franklin Roosevelt.

# 5. Abraham Lincoln, Second Inaugural Address, March 4, 1865

*Speaker:* Despite being highly unpopular in the summer and fall of 1864, Lincoln even surprised himself by winning the presidential election over the Democratic candidate, General George B. McClelland, by some 500,000 votes. Victories by Union troops in the fall of 1864, especially the fall of Atlanta, had turned the tide, both in the field and in the ballot box. Here was a speaker who had endured some of the greatest stress and burden of leadership during a fratricidal war that any world leader could possibly carry. He had proven he could identify with both sides in this terrible conflict, even if both sides found reasons to detest him. While many have wondered about Lincoln's religion, especially his views about Jesus, the speaker clearly believed in a Divine Providence whose will needed to be humbly discerned by this terrible war experience: "The Almighty has his own purposes."

*Occasion:* Prior to election, both the President and his general (Grant) had been strongly criticized and dismissed by many in both parties as "failures." Between the election and March, conditions began to look more positive and clearly the Union forces would win the war. The big question—what was the President's view of Reconstruction? Already there were many in his party insisting the South be treated as conquered territories. Inauguration day began wet and windy. A larger crowd assembled for this Inaugural than might otherwise be expected: Approximately 50,000 gathered at the east portico of the Capitol. Bands played and flags were waved. Obviously, the setting was more festive compared to the previous Inaugural event which was somber. As the tall figure of the re-elected President arose to speak, the sun burst through the clouds and brightened the entire scene. Lincoln supposedly, even with his high-pitched and clear voice, was heard by all.

*Excerpt:* [In the peroration of the speech, the President borrows biblical language to enable his eloquence to take flight:] "With malice toward none, with charity for all, with firmness in the right as God gives us to see the right, let us strive on to finish the work we are in, to bind up the nation's wounds, to care for him who shall have borne the battle and for his widow and his orphan, to do all which may achieve and cherish a just and lasting peace among ourselves and with all nations."

*Impact:* This speech demonstrates Lincoln at his best: simple, forthright, honest, humble, and eloquent. The President proved he could "rise above" the pettiness of partisan politics and address the critical needs of the nation. He avoided blaming the war on any one group or faction and attempted to offset congressional pressure to punish the South for those states' secession from the Union. He knew the time had come to lay aside the ordeal of armed conflict, to reflect realistically on that ordeal, and to look to the future. His peroration sounded like a passage from Holy Scripture or a Greek tragedy. The speech ended with immense applause, Chief Justice Chase administered the oath of office, ending with Lincoln's emphatic "So help me God!" He then kissed that Bible, artillery boomed, the crowd cheered, and the second term—fated to be tragically brief—had begun! The address won universal praise from nearly all who heard or read it. Carl Schurz, a contemporary of Lincoln, exclaimed: "No American president had ever spoken words like these to the American people. Americans never had a president who found such words in the depths of his heart," and the London *Spectator* described the speech as "the noblest political document in history" that reflected "something of sacred and almost prophetical authority." Frederick Douglass, who attended with other invited guests the White House reception after the inauguration, pronounced the speech "a sacred effort."

*Interesting Facts/Ironies:* This address was one of the briefest Inaugural addresses in American history (703 words), yet one of the most memorable. The address was also remarkably impersonal. The speaker did not use the first-person-singular, nor did he reference any personal act or statement of the past four years. He cast neither praise nor blame. Lincoln did not accept any responsibility for the protracted nature of the war, but placed it all within divine providence in the mysterious purposes of a Higher Power. He offered no promises as to how long the war might last, stating that question fell within the purview of God's will. The emphasis on God's will seemed to absolve both the South and the North of guilt for the tragic, immense bloodshed.

*Contemporary Application:* This address was Lincoln's last public speech and it illustrates the tremendous role of both image and *ethos*, or source credibility, in a speaker's effectiveness. Lincoln had served as a war president, now he slips into a new role—"Father Abraham," the gentle man of faith and wisdom who chided his children for engaging in a terrible quarrel that reaped so much pain and death, but who also understood and forgave them. With this measure of *ethos*, plus the security of having won re-election, Lincoln courageously and subtly spoke against his opponents' radical philosophy of harshness against the vanquished.

*Connection to Today:* Over a century and a half have passed since the terrible and costly Civil War and the great eloquence of Abraham Lincoln. The President could not have known on this occasion that he had only a few weeks to live. Nor might he have imagined that a president so unpopular in his own time might later be viewed, by many historians, as the greatest of all U. S. presidents. We have noted that Lincoln was not an over-powering orator with a dynamic voice or an image that would project well on national television in our own time. Yet his life and oratory demonstrate that the right person at the right time on the stage of history can achieve greatness as a public servant and alter dramatically the trajectory of that nation's history.

# 6. Franklin D. Roosevelt, War Message to Congress, December 8, 1941

*Speaker:* By 1940, with the Hitler war machine conquering weaker nations all over Western Europe, American citizens were alarmed. The nation had gone through the experience of one great European war even within the lifetime of many citizens. The President had enhanced his credibility and power by winning an unprecedented third term to high office by soundly defeating isolationist Republican Wendell Willkie in the 1940 general election. As a speaker, the genius of Roosevelt was an ability to make the complex seem simple and to use language with clarity and simplicity. He had already committed the United States to becoming the "great arsenal of democracy," and now it remained to stockpile that arsenal. In his State of the Union Address on January 6, 1941, President Roosevelt described America's response to spreading world conflict. France had already fallen to Hitler's forces and Great Britain continued to resist the Nazi air attacks, but there was uncertainty as to how long the British could withstand aggression. By this time FDR was convinced the U. S. needed to enter the war on the side of the Allies. The January 1941 State of the Union Address has been called the "Four Freedoms Address." As an idealistic speech, it was instrumental in winning Congressional approval of the Lend-Lease program, but a majority in Congress seemed opposed, at least reluctant, to declare war on the Axis powers—that is, until eleven months later, Sunday, December 7.

*Occasion:* At 7:49 A. M., on the date the President declared would "live in infamy," the Japanese launched a surprise aerial attack on the American Naval base in Pearl Harbor in Oahu. Because the attack began early Sunday morning, the number of fatalities was maximized—almost 2,400 Americans were killed—and the destruction of ships and airplanes (188 planes and eighteen warships) constituted total destruction of the fleet. The American public was both stunned and outraged, and thus looked to their president for leadership. President Roosevelt had only a brief time to prepare one of the most important speeches in world history. A few hours after the attack, and having huddled with his advisers, FDR met privately with his personal secretary, Grace Tully, and carefully dictated the first draft of the address he would deliver to Congress the next day. Harry Hopkins had written a sentence to be inserted before the final paragraph, but otherwise there was almost no revision in that original draft. The speech would be heard around the world.

*Excerpt:* "Yesterday, December 7, 1941—a date which will live in infamy—the United States was suddenly and deliberately attacked by naval and air forces of the empire of Japan....Yesterday the Japanese government launched an attack against Malaya. Last night Japanese forces attacked Hong Kong. Last night Japanese forces attacked Guam. Last night Japanese forces attacked the Philippine Islands. Last night the Japanese attacked Wake Island. This morning the Japanese attacked Midway Island....With confidence in our armed forces—with the unbounding determination of our people—we will gain the inevitable triumph—so help us God. I ask that the Congress declare that since the unprovoked and dastardly attack by Japan on Sunday, December 7, a state of war has existed between the United States and the Japanese empire."

*Impact:* The President spoke in grave and somber tones. The assembly was hushed and silent. Both the moment and the address were historic. Lasting but six minutes, yet, in the context of international crisis, the address and subsequent vote brought a sudden termination to two decades of American isolationism. Upon completion, there was an ovation such as never heard during eight years of the Franklin Roosevelt presidency. The nation was unified as never before. There was no debate on the President's request, and he signed that formal declaration of war two and a half hours later. In the passage above, note how the skillful use of parallel structure and repetition adds to the dramatic and persuasive appeal of the message. The U. S. had now entered the war. Neither the nation nor the world would be the same.

*Contemporary Application:* When there is national crisis, citizens expect leadership to be wielded and words of authority, understanding, insight, and reassurance to be spoken. A crisis is a time for the wisest, most skilled national leadership, and that leadership is demonstrated many ways, but most importantly through the words that are spoken to the nation that explain or justify a call to action.

*Connection to Today:* Today's generation is most definitely impacted by the single biggest event of the twentieth century—World War II. This crisis affected more lives than any other in human history. The war has been analyzed by historians, and depicted, at times glamorized, by authors and film producers. Between 1937 and 1945 the world experienced slaughter and destruction on an unprecedented scale. New technologies brought large bombers carrying the means of destruction hundreds of miles beyond the front lines in Europe and Asia. Adolph Hitler was surely the one man who impacted the twentieth century more than any other person. While fighting his enemies, Hitler exploited industrial technology in an attempt to exterminate all European Jews in a genocide now known as the Holocaust. In the Pacific theater, there were both primitive means of combat (hand-to-hand) that was joined with sophisticated methods (aerial warfare launched from aircraft carriers), and then culminating in the dropping of two nuclear bombs on the Japanese civilian population. Civilian casualties outweighed military combat casualties. Immediately after the Second World War, new problems and challenges emerged. A Cold War ensued. This current generation of Americans is certainly impacted by the fact that President Roosevelt and other leaders brought the nation to war, and the majority felt our military commitment was morally justified and that the immense preparations and mobilization for war highly commendable. Nonetheless, our nation continues to be deeply impacted by that war and its consequences, and Americans' worldview and presidential rhetoric contributed mightily to the decision to enter the conflict.

# 7. Lyndon B. Johnson, "We Shall Overcome," March 15, 1965

*Speaker*: Lyndon Baines Johnson (1908–1973) catapulted into high office with the tragic assassination of John Kennedy in November 1963, accepting power at a time when an ominous cloud hung over the entire nation. Civil rights unrest especially contributed to the national sense of tension and uncertainty. Johnson had built a career in Congress as one of the shrewdest tacticians and most powerful Democrats in the Senate. As for his image as a communicator, the Senator from Texas contrasted sharply from his photogenic predecessor. He was a large man and at times seemed both crude and intimidating in interpersonal communication, knowing literally how to "collar" a would-be Senate voter; he could cajole, flatter, threaten, and intimidate as a political "insider." As a public speaker, Johnson came across as an old-fashioned politician. His manner seemed wooden and stilted, anything but dynamic. The Texan spoke with a deep Southern drawl which was neither appealing nor endearing. While he had been no friend of civil rights earlier in his career, as president of the entire nation he faced a new reality and, to his great credit, grabbed the reins of leadership and led Congress and the nation in pursuit of a "Great Society." Johnson first declared "War on Poverty." No citizen in the richest nation on earth should live in squalor, he believed. Yet no barrier to equal opportunity in the early 60s was greater than the color bar. As both an opportunist but also a new idealist, Johnson was able to lay aside his segregationist voting record (well received in Texas before the 60s) and become the most vocal proponent of racial equality ever to occupy the White House. Thus, on the subject of race, President Lyndon Johnson likely deserves more credit for being progressive than any white politician in American history.

*Occasion:* The struggle for rights and freedom among African-Americans had reached a boiling point in 1964, especially in the South. Only nineteen percent of voting-age blacks were on the rolls in Alabama, and in Mississippi that figure was a dismal six percent. Demonstrations were organized to alert the entire nation of these conditions. There had been several months of mounting tension with white opposition, and even occasions of white brutality, during these civil rights demonstrations. Voter registration drives, such as Freedom Summer in rural Mississippi, met opposition. Opponents claimed they were simply taking a stand for "law and order." Civil rights workers were under constant threat. The nation was polarized on the issue of race, for certain. The Civil Rights Act of 1964 fulfilled the implicit promise of the *Brown v. Board of Education* a decade earlier, yet more legislation was needed to assure voting rights. When Alabama police beat peaceful marchers on the Edmund Pettis Bridge outside Selma on March 7, 1965, horrifying so many citizens who were viewing the unfolding events on national television, Johnson seized the moment to address a joint session of Congress to push his Voting Rights Act.

*Excerpt:* "At times history and fate meet at a single time in a single place to shape a turning point in man's unending search for freedom. So it was at Lexington and Concord. So it was a century ago at Appomattox. So it was last week in Selma, Alabama….Even if we pass this bill, the battle will not be over. What happened in Selma is part of a far larger movement which reaches into every section and State of America. It is the effort of American Negroes to secure for themselves the full blessings of American life. Their cause must be our cause too, because it is not just Negroes but really it is all of us, who must overcome the crippling legacy of bigotry and injustice. And we shall overcome….This great, rich, restless country can offer opportunity and education and hope to all—all black and white, all North and South, sharecropper and city dweller. These are the enemies—poverty, ignorance, disease—they are our enemies, not our fellow man, not our neighbor. And these enemies too—poverty, disease, and ignorance—we shall overcome."

*Impact:* Lyndon Johnson spoke with an intensity rarely shown by him. He was a speaker with conviction and purpose that all viewers recognized. Having served in Congress for over two decades before becoming president, Johnson knew so many in his audience. This was no time for him to be vague or sentimental. Congress erupted in cheers. The speech was clearly a success. Dr. Martin Luther King, watching in Alabama, reportedly wept, and then telegrammed a message to the President calling the speech "moving, eloquent, unequivocal, and [a] passionate plea for human rights." This was an impassioned Johnson at his best, displaying a sense of courage and urgency for the whole nation, often eloquently appropriating the phrase "We shall overcome" from the Civil Rights Movement's theme song and anthem. Johnson's speech rallied such support for the Voting Rights Act that he won large majorities in both the House of Representatives (333 to 48) and the Senate (77 to 19) and signed it into law August 6, 1965.

*Contemporary Application:* The urgency of the times, combined with the intelligence and passion of the speaker, plus being on the right side of history—all combine to render the most non-charismatic speaker an effective, if not eloquent, orator.

*Connection to Today:* Interestingly, we Americans are all beneficiaries of the leadership, both the good and the bad, of Lyndon Johnson. This president was concerned about legacy, and he wanted to be remembered for his contributions to health, education, and welfare, but most of all to be respected for his courageous stand on race and civil rights. Sadly, he will be remembered as much or more for his escalation of the war in Vietnam, which consumed his time and energies and a large portion of the national budget. That burden was overwhelming. Johnson shocked the nation in March 1968 by stating he would not seek a second full term in the office of president.

# 8. Thomas Jefferson, First Inaugural Address, March 4, 1801

*Speaker:* Thomas Jefferson (1743–1826), much like Benjamin Franklin, was a person of diverse giftedness and interests—statesperson, political philosopher, excellent writer, creative inventor, linguist, scientist, attorney, and creative thinker about religion and philosophy in general. He served in the Virginia legislature and the Continental Congress, where he drafted the Declaration of Independence. Later, he was governor of Virginia, a diplomat in Europe, and George Washington's secretary of state. He did not participate in drafting the U. S. Constitution, about the only huge assignment he missed in his lifetime. In 1801 Jefferson was elected president, though the election was hotly contested. The election was a landmark event in that it marked the first time that control of the government passed from one political party, the Federalists, to another, the Republicans or Democratic Republicans. The election was decided in the House of Representatives as there was a tie between Jefferson and Aaron Burr in the Electoral College. Ironically, despite all his other talents, Jefferson was not a strong and powerful orator. While eloquent with the pen, a shy Thomas Jefferson delivered only two public speeches during his eight years in the presidency—his first and second Inaugural Addresses. The first one, of course, set the tone for his entire administration. Even this most important speech of his life was delivered in a quiet and unimpressive voice that was almost inaudible to those at a distance. Nonetheless, a carefully crafted and revised draft of the speech had been prepared for this important occasion.

*Occasion:* On the first Tuesday of March 1801, Thomas Jefferson left his room at Conrad and McMunn's boardinghouse and walked up Pennsylvania Avenue. Though he received military salutes along the way, he forbade the pomp and ceremony that had ushered George Washington into office. Accompanied by a few friends and an artillery company from the Maryland Militia (not Hamilton's professional military), Jefferson walked (refusing carriages) up the street into the unfinished capitol building. The ceremony was held in the newly finished Senate chamber, witnessed by the Vice President Burr, a number of members of government, and a few foreign diplomats. The President-elect took the oath of office from Chief Justice John Marshall, a distant relative and political opponent from Virginia. Thomas Jefferson's main purpose was to acknowledge the political discord that brought him to office and then make a plea for unity.

*Excerpt:* "Let us then, fellow citizens, unite with one heart and one mind.... Every difference of opinion is not a difference of principle. We have called by different names brethren of the same principle. We are all republicans; we are all federalists....Let us then, with courage and confidence, pursue our own federal and republican principles, our attachment to Union and representative government....I repair then, fellow citizens, to the post you have assigned me.... Relying then on the patronage of your good will, I advance with obedience to the work, ready to retire from it whenever you become sensible how much better choice it is in your power to make. And may that Infinite Power which rules the destinies of the universe lead our councils to what is best and give them a favorable issue of your peace and prosperity."

*Impact:* A new era in government had begun in the nineteenth century, just as Franklin Roosevelt ushered in a new era in the twentieth century. The new president effectively pled for unity, but made clear he and his opponents should not forget their ideological differences. Jefferson meant only to invite moderate Federalists into a broad Republican coalition that accepted a philosophy which held all powers belonged to the people and that maximum individual freedoms must be protected. He stated Americans were a free people with no need for a national state built on European models. He saw blessing in isolation from Europe and other lands and bountiful resources, thus only "a wise and frugal Government" is needed to insure individual liberty. Again, while Jefferson was no dynamic orator, this address is honored and remembered for its efforts to reduce factionalism and its succinct endorsement of a republican form of government. Jefferson was a far better writer than a public speaker, and this speech reads more like a political essay than an oration; likely, many listeners needed to access a printed copy to read the words again to catch a meaning they did not understand upon first hearing. Nonetheless, the speaker established a reputation and his philosophy of limited government is still highly respected today.

*Little Known Facts:* Jefferson's Inaugural Address was the first to be delivered by a president in Washington, D. C., where the new government had just moved from Philadelphia. Before his death in 1826, Jefferson chose this epitaph for his gravesite: "Here was buried Thomas Jefferson, author of the Declaration of Independence, of the statue of Virginia for religious freedom, and father of the University of Virginia." No mention is made in the epitaph of his presidency, but in 1800 Jefferson was elected to the first of two terms and momentous decisions were made during that tenure.

*Contemporary Application:* One need not be a powerful, spell-binding orator to wield influence over intelligent audiences—the validity and strength of the speaker's ideas ultimately constitute what is most important.

*Connection to Today:* The election marked the rise of the Republican Party and its ascendancy is sometimes called the "Revolution of 1800." In recent times, especially since the New Deal, those who have opposed big government and welfare legislation often reference Jeffersonian ideals as stated in this address. The good news is that Jefferson's stunning election did not trigger riots in the street, stir talk about secession from people in the states, and certainly no coup was attempted by Federalist sympathizers. There was a peaceful transfer of power for which this nation has become known even to this day. On the other hand, the young nation was deeply divided after the hard-fought campaign and strong disagreement over the principles that should shape the future of the nation.

# 9. Ronald Reagan, Address at Brandenburg Gate, June 12, 1987

*Speaker:* Ronald Reagan entered the White House determined to reassert U. S. leadership in international relations and not to lose the Cold War. His first six years in office saw a revival of Cold War confrontation. He did not consider the Soviets as a co-equal nation but, instead, labeled the U.S.S.R. an "evil empire." The President's views reflected those of conservative supporters—the Soviets constituted a monolithic and ideologically motivated foe bent on world conquest and domination. As a result, there was an escalation of weaponry, such as new missiles. Reagan announced the Strategic Defense Initiative (SDI), popularly known as "Star Wars program," in 1983 in order to deploy new defenses that could intercept and destroy ballistic missiles as they rose from the ground and arched through space. Few scientists thought that SDI could work. The Reagan Doctrine asserted America's right to intervene anywhere in the world to support groups fighting against Marxist governments. (More on Reagan as a speaker in another chapter.)

*Occasion:* The speech was delivered in the midst of a sudden thaw in U. S.-Soviet relations. The economic cost of super-power rivalry was burdening both nations. Moreover, Mikhail Gorbachev, who became general secretary of the Communist Party in 1985, was a new style Soviet leader who realized Russia needed economic growth and better industrial planning—not more weapons. Gorbachev withdrew troops from Afghanistan, reduced commitments to Cuba and Nicaragua, and proclaimed a policy of *glasnost* ("openness"), and began to implement *perestroika* ("economic liberalization") at home. These policies brought acclaim throughout the West. Summit meetings were arranged, one with Reagan in Reykjavik, Iceland. In this context of winds of international change blowing, this speech at the historic Brandenburg Gate was delivered during a commemoration of the 750<sup>th</sup> anniversary of Berlin. The Brandenburg Gate and the Berlin Wall separated Berlin into east and west sides, and the speech emphatically challenged the leader of the Soviet Union, Mikhail Gorbachev, to dismantle the wall that separated them. With this oration, Reagan was symbolically advocating greater freedom for the entire Eastern bloc.

*Excerpt:* "We welcome change and openness; for we believe that freedom and security go together, that the advance of human liberty—the advance of human liberty can only strengthen the cause of world peace. There is one sign the Soviets can make that would be unmistakable, that would advance dramatically the cause of freedom and peace. General Secretary Gorbachev, if you seek peace, if you seek prosperity for the Soviet Union and Eastern Europe, if you seek liberalization: Come here to this gate. Mr. Gorbachev, open this gate. Mr. Gorbachev—Mr. Gorbachev, tear down this wall!....[Peroration:] As I looked out a moment ago from the Reichstag, that embodiment of German unity, I noticed words crudely spray-painted upon the wall, perhaps by a young Berliner (quote): 'This wall will fall. Beliefs become reality.' Yes, across Europe, this wall will fall, for it cannot withstand faith; it cannot withstand truth. The wall cannot withstand freedom."

*Impact:* President Reagan's address, usually titled the "Brandenburg Gate Speech," was delivered to the people of West Berlin, but allegedly it was audible on the east side of the Berlin wall. As with President John Kennedy in an earlier speech in Berlin, each president offered a vision of a world beyond communism. Kenneth Duberstein, White House deputy chief of staff in 1987, says that after Reagan's speech, "it was inevitable the wall would come down" (*USA Today*, Nov. 9, 2014). Reagan's famous words uttered emphatically and authoritatively—"Mr. Gorbachev, tear down this wall!"—have been played innumerable times at Republican gatherings and historic remembrances. Indeed, it may be Reagan's best known words, akin to JFK's famous Inaugural plea that begins, "And so my fellow Americans, ask not what your country can do…". The address is definitely considered a highlight of Reagan's presidency and one of his most important speeches. This critic is rating the speech in the "top ten" listing for its directness and audacity, yet one factor must be considered: While Reagan called the Soviets' bluff and threw down the rhetorical gauntlet, Mikhail Gorbachev, more than Reagan, dismantled the Soviet empire. The walls were crumbling from within. Gorbachev saw the time was right and courageously acted to place his country on a new course.

*Little Known Fact:* White House speechwriter Peter Robinson was assigned to draft Reagan's address for this occasion, and he visited Berlin to gather material. He interviewed diplomats to learn what Reagan should not say that might provoke the Soviets. At a dinner party, Robinson heard someone lament he had not seen his sister in decades though she lived twenty miles away in East Berlin. A hostess became angry and exclaimed, "If Gorbachev is serious about reforming communism and reaching out to the West, he can prove it. He can get rid of this wall!" That, Robinson thought, sounds like Reagan. The State Department sent Reagan seven drafts, none including a request to tear down anything. When Reagan was riding to the venue and reading aloud his text one last time, he grinned and said, "The boys at State are going to kill me, but it's the right thing to do."

*Contemporary Application:* Courage and directness are sometimes required in an address where issues are clear-cut and moral action needs to be taken.

*Connection to Today:* We live in a world in which the old Soviet Union has been dissolved and U. S.-Russian relations are greatly improved, though not ideal, by any means. (Concern about Russians hacking into U. S. political figures' email and releasing these private messages to influence the 2016 presidential election is the most recent cause for alarm.) If there is fear about nuclear war in the U. S., those fears come from concerns about Iran or terrorist groups possessing weapons, and not the Russians. The wall finally fell at 10:30 p.m., November 9, 1989, with the peaceful opening of the gate at Bornholmer Strasse, and later that night at many other border crossings. Despite intervention in Korea, Vietnam, and Central America over the decades, the final phase of the Cold War ended without a shot. President Reagan courageously disregarded his own anti-communist rhetoric and kept the nation out of a major war.

# 10. John F. Kennedy, Inaugural Address, January 20, 1961

*Speaker:* John F. Kennedy (1917–1963) has the reputation for being one of the most popular presidents of the twentieth century, though not as highly rated by academics as by the general public. Part of that reputation is rooted in the charisma and charm Kennedy possessed as a young man, actually the youngest man ever to be elected U. S. president. Also, the sad and tragic assassination robbed all Americans of a chance to see just how great Kennedy might have become. JFK was born into a wealthy family in Brookline, Massachusetts, with several siblings as high achievers. During World War II he served in the U. S. Navy, and his heroism in commanding PT-109 and saving the lives of others is part of the Kennedy folklore. He served in the U. S. House of Representatives, 1946–52, and was elected to the U. S. Senate in 1952, unseating the well-known Henry Cabot Lodge; he won re-election to a second term in 1958. In the campaign of 1960, Kennedy defeated strong candidates in Hubert Humphrey and Lyndon Johnson to win the Democratic nomination. At the national convention in Los Angeles, JFK delivered his memorable "New Frontier" speech. In September, candidates Richard Nixon and Kennedy confronted each other in the first televised presidential debates, thus launching a tradition that is upheld in each campaign (though Nixon refused to debate in 1968 and 1972). The youthful senator projected an image of self-confidence, strong intelligence, and being well-informed; he emerged with a lead in the polls after the first debate. The image of John and Jacqueline Kennedy as a youthful "First Family" that connected with modern culture is one that remains despite some blemishes and mistakes made by his administration. Indeed, many romanticized it the "Camelot era."

*Occasion:* John Kennedy was sworn in as the thirty-fifth president on a bitterly cold day. While there was a cordial relationship between the outgoing President Eisenhower and the president-elect, Kennedy had won by a razor-thin margin and needed to gain popular support, ward off any sense of crisis, and develop a supportive mood toward goals he envisioned in the "New Frontier." He also needed to explain his understanding of the U. S. relationship with other nations, especially in the midst of the Cold War. Perhaps it is a bit ironic that Inauguration Day was bitterly cold, that the nation was in a Cold War with the Soviet Union, and the poet who experienced so much trouble reading his original poem for the occasion was Robert Frost.

*Excerpt:* "Let every nation know, whether it wishes us evil or ill, that we shall pay any price, bear any burden, meet any hardship, support any friend, oppose any foe to assure the survival and the success of liberty. This much we pledge— and more....In your hands, my fellow citizens, more than mine, will rest the final success or failure of our course....And so, my fellow Americans, ask not what your country can do for you—ask what you can do for your country."

*Impact:* Though quite brief (1,364 words), most rhetorical critics rate the speech highly, some (along with this critic) placing it within the top ten speeches in American history. Clearly, John Kennedy met the challenge of the occasion by further introducing himself to the nation and the rest of the free world as a credible and competent leader. Indeed, the speech does contain one of the most quoted lines ("Ask not....") in all American oratory, a line which illustrates stylistic devices of parallelism and antithesis. Seldom does the general public recall clearly some sentence from an Inaugural Address (FDR's "the only thing we have to fear is fear itself" being another memorable Inaugural declaration). The speech does develop the theme of a nation's power and its responsibilities. One can be nostalgic about another line in the speech: "Let the word go forth from this time and place, to friend and foe alike, that the torch has been passed to a new generation of Americans—born in this century, tempered by war, disciplined by a hard and bitter peace, proud of our ancient heritage."

Indeed, Kennedy was the first president born in the twentieth century and he seemingly was addressing younger people. On the other hand, what makes one Inaugural Address stand out above others (other than the times in which delivered)? One could easily argue that the pledge to "pay any price, bear any burden" represented the mindset that led to a costly investment (some would say "waste") of money and lives in the subsequent Vietnam War.

*Little Known Fact:* While his predecessor President Eisenhower allowed presidential press conferences to be filmed and shown later, Kennedy was the first president to ask for conferences to be broadcast live. JFK made good use of the electronic media and enjoyed an excellent, open relationship with the news media.

*Contemporary Application:* Inaugurations are rituals and not public policymaking situations and are intended to create social cohesion or national unity and even to encourage and inspire. Thus the ceremonial speech may employ effectively various stylistic strategies. The speaker's famous "Ask not…" line is cited almost universally in public speaking textbooks as a prime example of antithesis, a kind of parallelism that contrasts one idea with another; antithesis was employed elsewhere in other lines of the speech ("Let us never negotiate out of fear; but let us never fear to negotiate"). Kennedy sought connection with the best in leadership from the American heritage with the line "…that the torch has been passed to a new generation of Americans."

*Connection to Today:* Historians study the 60s as the decade transitioning the U. S. into an even more modern era—this event is the beginning of the turbulent decade. In the collective memory, John F. Kennedy is indisputably one of the greatest persuasive speakers of the twentieth century. His tragic assassination has surely contributed to his romanticized image.

# PART TWO

NINETY-ONE OTHER GREAT
AND/OR REPRESENTATIVE
PUBLIC ADDRESSES
IN AMERICAN HISTORY

# 11. Andrew Hamilton, Defense of Freedom of the Press, August 4, 1735

*Speaker*: Andrew Hamilton (1676–1741) was one of the most famous and prominent lawyers in the colonies. Born in Scotland, and no relation to Alexander Hamilton, he had migrated to Virginia as an indentured servant shortly before 1700. His professional life began by teaching school, then studying for admission to the bar, and later serving in the Maryland Assembly. After studying law in London, he settled in Philadelphia, where he became a prominent attorney and also served as attorney general of Pennsylvania. Undoubtedly, Hamilton was an effective speaker in general public address and a persuasive advocate in the legal setting.

*Occasion*: In 1732 a wealthy landowner, Lewis Morris, founded the *New York Weekly Journal*, thus enhancing the American newspaper tradition. Yet like other publications, this newspaper engaged in axe-grinding and mudslinging at some political opponent, in this case the target being New York Governor William Cosby and his allies, among them a prominent merchant, James DeLancey. A German-born printer, John Peter Zenger, was hired to edit and produce the paper. Zenger produced a logical case for the right of the people to be critical of their rulers, but on the back page were criticisms and thinly veiled attacks against the colonial governor. Governor Cosby shut down the paper, charged Zenger with seditious libel, and had him jailed for ten months, until his trial in August 1735. At this time, Hamilton was a Philadelphia attorney who had already established a stellar reputation as an attorney. At the time of the trial, popular belief held that a writer or publisher is guilty of libel if the published material was hurtful to an important citizen. Some stated the law current at the time as "the greater the truth, the greater the libel," and thus the only question would be one of authorship of such hurtful writings. At this time, the American colonies were still four decades away from revolution, and there was a great deal of respect for colonial governors, who were appointed by the Crown as authority and representatives of the mother country.

*Excerpt:* "The loss of liberty to a generous mind is worse than death....This is what every man that values freedom ought to consider; he should act by judgment and not by affection or self-interest; for where those prevail, no ties of either country or kindred are regarded; as, upon the other hand, the man who loves his country prefers its liberty to all other considerations, well knowing that without liberty life is a misery....Power may justly be compared to a great river; while kept within its bounds, it is both beautiful and useful, but when it overflows its banks, it is then too impetuous to be stemmed; it bears down all before it, and brings destruction and desolation where it comes. If, then, this be the nature of power, let us at least do our duty, and, like wise men who value freedom, use our utmost care to support liberty, the only bulwark against lawless power....The laws of our country have given us a right—the liberty of both exposing and opposing arbitrary power (in these parts of the world at least) by speaking and writing truth."

*Impact:* Andrew Hamilton admitted Zenger's authorship of the material that was offensive to Governor Cosby and his supporters, but he turned the tables on his adversaries by reversing the argument: Zenger's *Journal* could not be libelous *because* the published articles were truthful. He further argued, against the settled practice, that the jury and not the judge should decide the truth of the published statements. This was truly a bold legal maneuver, asking the jurors to ignore the law and instead consider the truthfulness of the statements Zenger printed. Although the judges ruled Hamilton's argument out of order, the jury was swayed by his logic and appeal. Hamilton convinced the jurors that the charges against the royal governor were true. His defense carried the day and John Peter Zenger was acquitted. This was a signal victory for freedom of the press in the British colonies. The *Zenger* decision established a precedent for truth being a defense against charges of libel. The trial also demonstrated a stiff resolve that the American colonists did not feel duty-bound by British civil law. The "not guilty" verdict led the liberal trend elsewhere by enacting a libel law admitting truth as a defense. Most important, the colonial American press was strengthened for its revolutionary role in the volatile 1770s.

*Contemporary Application:* An advocate who dares to be bold and advance a proper and progressive argument in a legal or political situation will be remembered by historians in highly favorable terms.

*Connection to Today:* The *Zenger* case was the first landmark in the tradition of a free press. Though it was a radical notion at the time—after all, the religious duties of Christian citizens included respect for royalty and saying only good things about rulers in power—freedoms of speech and press were later to become the law of the nation as the First Amendment in the Bill of Rights. While freedom of the press was not entirely secured by the *Zenger* decision, the case laid the foundation. Though our federal court system may wrestle with a number of issues related to its application, there is no doubt that our national First Amendment forms a huge part of the foundation of American democracy. One might argue that without the liberties assured in the First Amendment that the nation, even with majority rule and popular franchise, could not be a true democracy.

# 12. Patrick Henry, Address to the Second Virginia Convention, March 23, 1775

*Speaker:* Patrick Henry (1736–1799) had the temperament and appearance of a frontiersman, but he grew up on the outskirts of Richmond and was well educated enough to "hold his own" with some of Virginia's best known political leaders. Through influential friends, he was licensed to practice law and made a name for himself. He loved forensic dueling and could question and analyze the arguments he heard from others. As an attorney, he was a persuasive speaker at the bar. He had a reputation for being a radical and was known for his fiery orations. Once elected to the Virginia House of Burgesses in 1763, he became an outspoken advocate of the rights of the colonies. Henry first made his reputation as an orator in the courtroom in the Parson's Cause proceedings in 1763. One of his most famous quotes came in 1765, when Henry spoke in opposition to the British Stamp Act that imposed new taxation on the colonies: "Caesar had his Brutus, Charles the First his Cromwell, and George III…[interruptions with cries of 'Treason, Treason'…]…may profit from their example. If this be treason, make the most of it." Henry's persuasiveness as a speaker was not only rooted in his intelligence and quick thinking, but also in his fiery delivery. Henry was the first governor of the state of Virginia, and he served the state and the nation in many other public positions. Henry's contemporaries praised his rhetorical eloquence. He was lauded and held in high esteem by political leaders such as George Mason and John Adams. Thomas Jefferson called his eloquence sublime and viewed him as "the greatest orator that ever lived" and claimed that "as a popular orator…he appeared to me to speak as Homer wrote."

*Occasion:* Throughout the colonies there had been talk of revolution. Henry had already established himself as a decisive leader and an advocate for natural rights of humanity. As relations with the mother country were deteriorating rapidly in the mid-1770s, Henry began pushing the cause of independence. A revolutionary convention was called at Richmond, and on the third day of the meeting Henry offered a motion that the colony of Virginia "be immediately put into a posture of defense—in essence, prepare for war with the mother country." Several delegates rose to deliver impromptu speeches against Henry's resolution, basically denouncing it as premature.

*Excerpt:* "I have but one lamp by which my feet are guided, and that is the lamp of experience. I know of no way of judging of the future but by the past.... The war is inevitable. And let it come! I repeat it, sir; let it come!...The war is actually begun! The next gale that sweeps from the North will bring to our ears the clash of resounding arms! Our brethren are already in the field! Why stand we here idle? What is it that gentlemen wish? What would they have? Is life so dear, or peace so sweet, as to be purchased at the price of chains and slavery? Forbid it, Almighty God! I know not what course others may take, but as for me, give me liberty, or give me death."

*Impact:* Patrick Henry saw the whole issue that Virginia faced was a matter "nothing less than freedom or slavery." He thus considered his duty to seek and speak truth as crucially important. As a persuasive speaker, Henry answered the objections of other leading Virginians to his proposal. An eyewitness account spoke of the speaker's intensity and volume and how mesmerized everyone in the assembly became. The proposal Henry had offered was approved by a voice vote. The Revolution, at least in Virginia, was launched. As the patriot cause became more accepted, with the verdict of history being on the side of the patriots, then Patrick Henry's passion and eloquence have shone even brighter. The historian George Bancroft concluded, "This is the way the fire began: Virginia rang the alarm-bell for the continent" (Quoted in Oliver, *History of Public Speaking in America*, p. 59). Later, eight colonies adopted resolutions modeled on those Patrick Henry had introduced and advocated so eloquently. Some historians rank this speech as the second best known speech in American history, the first being the Gettysburg Address. One might justifiably rank this speech in the top ten orations of all American history. Indeed, Patrick Henry lives today in popular folklore as one of America's earliest and most eloquent advocates of political liberty and nationhood and the willingness to pay any price to win that liberty.

*Contemporary Application:* Genuine passion and the "rightness" of a cause, at least in the minds of listeners, combined with a strong and fiery delivery, will persuade almost any audience.

*Little Known Fact:* Though Patrick Henry was a fervent advocate of revolution, he was equally as passionate in his opposition to the proposed Constitution of the new nation. For almost a month in 1788, he led an intensive fight to defeat ratification of the new U. S. Constitution, speaking often and at great length in the Virginia convention. His great concern was the power of a strong national government, a concern shared by many of his countrymen. Attesting to his rhetorical effectiveness, Virginia was one of the two major states which at first delayed ratifying the new Constitution. Though as a young attorney and legislator he had been highly ambitious, between 1794 and 1799, he declined a number of opportunities to run for national offices or be appointed to important positions.

*Another Little Known Fact:* We do not have verbatim transcripts of Henry's speeches, and the text of this famous speech has come down to us through Henry first biographer, William Wirt, in his *Life and Character of Patrick Henry,* published in 1817. Wirt's reconstruction was based on accounts by witnesses to the speeches, but has been accepted as reasonably accurate in depicting Henry's actual words and rhetorical style.

# 13. James Otis, Against the Writs of Assistance, February 10, 1761

*Speaker:* James Otis (1725–1783) came from a distinguished Massachusetts family, and, after graduating from Harvard College in 1743, was trained as a lawyer. His gifts and talents took him in several directions. Otis was a respected Latin scholar, a popular Boston politician, and a forceful advocate for the rights of the colonists within the British Empire. He began his career as an attorney in Boston in 1750. Ten years later he served as the king's advocate general of the vice-admiralty court when the British government empowered customs officials to search any house for smuggled goods. Otis was well-read in the political philosophy of John Locke, as was Thomas Jefferson, and he also held strong religious beliefs. Some historians credit him with introducing the phrase "no taxation without representation." He was an eloquent writer, especially of essays and pamphlets, and, from all contemporary reports, a fiery orator. His reputation and prominence in the colonial 1760s was probably matched only by Patrick Henry. Along with Samuel Adams, Otis became one of the fieriest of the Boston radicals who agitated for revolution. In his speeches and writings he developed a powerful case for equality, years before Thomas Jefferson immortalized such a concept in the famous Declaration of Independence. Otis insisted that women and blacks enjoyed the same natural rights as white males, a most progressive position for his time.

*Occasion:* Otis resigned his position as the king's advocate general and, in February 1761, argued in court against these "writs of assistance." A writ of assistance was a kind of "John Doe" search warrant that gave any British authority a "free pass" anywhere, business or private home, to enter and search for smuggled goods. Such goods would have been smuggled presumably for the purpose of evasion of British taxes. The occasion marked a time of tension between British authorities and colonial Americans who were feeling their rights as British citizens were being jeopardized. According to eye witness reports, the courtroom at Boston Old State House was packed, and Otis poured forth a torrent of eloquence that extended over a period of four or five hours. No complete text seems to exist, but the essence is reconstructed by notes taken by Joseph Hawley, another Massachusetts Bay lawyer, and John Adams, and is reflected also in essays Otis wrote for publication.

*Excerpt:* "Now one of the most essential branches of English liberty is the freedom of one's house. A man's house is his castle; and whilst he is quiet, he is as well guarded as a prince in his castle....I will to my dying day oppose...all such instruments of slavery on the one hand and villainy on the other as this Writ of Assistance is...And as it is in opposition to a kind of power...which in former periods of English history cost one King of England his head and another his throne...No acts of parliament can establish such a writ; though it should be made in the very words of the petition, 'twould be void. An act against the constitution is void."

*Impact:* Otis argued with passion and eloquence as he represented the Massachusetts Bay merchants who were determined to oppose the granting of further writs. Interestingly, Otis was a second choice as attorney; Benjamin Pratt turned down the assignment in order to serve as chief justice of the Superior Court of New York. Since there were no legal grounds on which to oppose the Writs of Assistance, Otis fervently insisted that they trampled on the people's liberty. Otis was a brilliant attorney and he drew his ideology from the writing of Edward Coke, an authority on Common Law, the Magna Carta, and the Common Law which incorporated fundamental principles of right and justice. Hence, for Otis, there was a "supreme law" or "natural law." And any act of Parliament could be controlled (disobeyed) or voided if that act were in violation of supreme or natural law. Therefore, the Writs of Assistance were illegal because they violated a basic tenet of supreme or natural law—every man must be secure in his own home. The occasion has been reconstructed by John Adams, who was present in the courtroom. In his *Autobiography* Adams describes this speech, which to his dying day this listener considered as perhaps the most remarkable speech he had ever heard. "Otis was a flame of fire…Every man of an immense crowded audience appeared to me to go away, as I did, ready to take arms against the Writs of Assistance," wrote John Adams. "Then and there, was the first scene of the first act of opposition, to the arbitrary claims of Great Britain. Then and there, the child Independence was born." Adams was greatly moved and influenced by Otis' rhetoric, and one could not ask for a more qualified witness or rhetorical critic. "His passions blaze; he is liable to great inequities of temper," Adams recalled. Of course, as most know, John Adams was slated to become the second president of the United States.

*Contemporary Application:* When an orator combines high intelligence and cogent arguments with deep passionate expression, an audience will be swayed. And when the stakes are high and principles contain national interest, that orator can establish a lasting legacy.

*Little Known Fact:* Otis lost the case, but his attack on the Writs of Assistance helped lay the foundation for the breach between Great Britain and her continental colonies, and his "natural law" arguments were used by other colonial speakers in making a persuasive case against other acts of Parliament.

*Postscript:* Otis attended the Stamp Act Congress in 1765, though a blow to the head by a British officer left him insane. By 1771 his behavior became increasingly erratic. The random firing of pistols and breaking windows alerted his family to a mental illness, and he was given asylum on a country farm. Thus he missed active participation and appreciation for some of the more exciting and successful adventures of the American Revolution he helped to inspire.

# 14. George Washington, Charge to his Officers, March 15, 1783

*Speaker*: George Washington (1732–1799) has been the subject of more myths and tales than any other American, thus underscoring his heroic qualities and unquestioned leadership abilities. No one considered Washington a great public speaker, least of all Washington himself. He was a planter-surveyor, who became a home-grown American military hero. He was unanimously chosen commander of the Continental Army, and though he lost battles, he did inspire fierce loyalty among his officer corps—he thus spoke with credibility.

*Occasion:* The first form of American government was the Articles of Confederation, and the greatest challenge facing the Confederation was placing the new nation on sound financial footing. The war had cost a staggering $160 million, a sum well in excess of the taxes raised to pay for it. Public faith in government had declined immensely. The appointment of Robert Morris, a wealthy Philadelphia merchant, as Superintendent of Finance, became a divisive action when Morris proposed that the states collect a national import duty of five percent, though only one state (Rhode Island) rejected it. Morris and a New York congressman, Alexander Hamilton, engineered a strategy of secretly persuading some army officers, then encamped in Newburg, New York, to threaten a coup unless the national government was empowered to levy taxes needed to raise their pay. This was indeed a perilous moment in the life of the fledgling American republic. Indeed, the officers were angry over the failure of Congress to honor its promises to the army regarding salary, bounties and life pensions. Rumors circulated from Philadelphia that the new Confederation was going broke and that the officers might not be compensated at all. Anonymous letters were being circulated that addressed complaints and called for meetings. Washington was able to halt one meeting. Eventually, another letter was circulated that suggested Washington was sympathetic to the claims of irate officers. And so, on March 15, 1783, Washington's officers gathered in a church building in Newburgh, thus, due to power within a military force, effectively holding the fate of America in their hands. To the surprise of many, General Washington showed up. Though given a chilly reception by his men, he nevertheless personally addressed them.

*Excerpt:* "Let me entreat you, gentlemen, on your part, not to take any measures which, viewed in the calm light of reason, will lessen the dignity and sully the glory you have hitherto maintained; let me request you to rely on the plighted faith of your country, and place a full confidence in the purity of the intentions of Congress; that, previous to your dissolution as an army, they will cause all your accounts to be fairly liquidated, as directed in their resolutions, which were published to you two days ago, and that they will adopt the most effectual measures in their power to render ample justice to you, for your faithful and meritorious services. And let me conjure you, in the name of our common country, as you value your own sacred honor, as you respect the rights of humanity, and as you regard the military and national character of America, to express your utmost horror and detestation of the man who wishes, under any specious pretenses, to overturn the liberties of our country, and who wickedly attempts to open the floodgates of civil discord and deluge our rising empire in blood. By thus determining and thus acting, you will pursue the plain and direct road to the attainment of your wishes. You will defeat the insidious designs of our enemies, who are compelled to resort from open force to secret artifice. You will give one more distinguished proof of unexampled patriotism and patient virtue, rising superior to the pressure of the most complicated sufferings. And you will, by the dignity of your conduct, afford occasion for posterity to say, when speaking of the glorious example you have exhibited to mankind, '"Had this day been wanting, the world had never seen the last stage of perfection to which human nature is capable of attaining."'"

*Impact:* Though we have no record of George Washington's manner of delivery, we can only imagine the passion in his voice and physical manner. The General appealed to his officers' honor, reasoned with them about patriotism for the new nation, and urged patience and good will. As the story is told, the first response from the General's men was quite negative. Then, Washington pulled out a letter from a member of Congress that explained the dire financial straits of the new nation. Before he could begin reading, the General pulled out a pair of reading glasses. Few men even knew he needed glasses. This was a tender moment of vulnerability—the soldiers were touched by the speaker's passion and by remembering how much they had endured and risked together to arrive at that moment. After the letter was read, Washington laid it on the table and walked out of the room, fully aware of his men's sentiments. The officers cast a unanimous vote to adhere to the rule of Congress. The speech must be considered a success because the address effectively ended the plot. The experiment in American democracy was to be continued. Though Morris and Hamilton may not have intended for a coup to occur, their willingness to take such a risk demonstrated the new nation's perilously fragile financial situation and the vulnerability of its political institutions.

*Contemporary Application:* National military heroes possess a strong *ethos* before almost any kind of audience, especially an audience of subordinate officers who have respected the commanding officer's leadership.

*Connection to Today:* The Articles of Confederation, our nation's first constitution, contained a number of weaknesses, one of which was the requirement for unanimous agreement among all the states in matters of any national tax. Due to these weaknesses, a general consensus arose that a new constitution should be drafted. This draft was completed four years later in Philadelphia, and we still live under that U. S. Constitution.

# 15. George Washington, Farewell Address, September 17, 1796

*Speaker:* George Washington may well be the most familiar name in all American history, even if a majority of Americans know little more about him other than the fact he was our first president. He had a meager formal education and did not seem to possess a sharp or creative mind. He clearly had political ambitions, having served as a member of the Virginia House of Burgesses for sixteen years and attending two Continental Congresses and also later serving as president of the Constitutional Convention. Washington established his reputation first by surviving the French and Indian War and becoming something of a homegrown American military hero. He volunteered to serve as commander without pay. His reputation became unassailable by leading the Continental Army to victory, especially known for appeals and addresses that held his army together while it endured the horrors of a winter at Valley Forge, Pennsylvania, remaining there till June 1778; an estimated 2,500 soldiers out of 10,000 died during those six months. Washington was chosen without challenge as the first president of the new nation. He accepted a second term with some reluctance, but refused a third term, thus setting a precedent that would not be broken by American presidents until Franklin Roosevelt was elected to a third term while the nation was on the verge of entering a world war. In a world of nation-states ruled by kings with hereditary happenstance and by petty tyrants, Washington's humble willingness to relinquish power to an elected successor demonstrated that the American republican experiment was off to a good start. How difficult to imagine Washington as a great orator! His persuasiveness would reside in a personal *ethos* that inspired fierce loyalty, first among his officer corps when he was commander, then among his cabinet and the citizenry when he was president.

*Occasion:* How appropriate for an important leader to give parting counsel to those who would follow in leadership and to the nation as a whole! Other U. S. presidents have followed this example. While there were differences of opinion among Americans—strong differences, for sure—the major political party system we know today did not exist in Washington's time. This address was delivered to the cabinet, a group of men who would continue in leadership as Federalists after the President retired.

*Excerpt:* "Excessive partiality for one foreign nation and excessive dislike of another cause those whom that actuate to see danger only on one side, and serve to veil and even second the arts of influence on the other....The great rule of conduct for us in regard to foreign nations is, in extending our commercial relations to have with them as little political connection as possible....Our detached and distant situation invites and enables us to pursue a different course....Why, by interweaving our destiny with that of any part of Europe, entangle our peace and prosperity in the toils of European ambition, rivalship, interest, humor or caprice?"

*Impact:* Washington's audience was small, but his reputation was huge and his words were heeded with seriousness. This man had become the living symbol of the American Revolution and now, concluding his service as the first president, another important milestone had been reached. The President counseled, first, against the dangers of sectionalism; second, against the strife of political factions; third, to preserve religion and morality as the "great pillars of human happiness" and to promote "institutions for the general diffusion of knowledge"; and fourth, to maintain neutrality relations with other nations. Judged through the lens of history, each of these admonitions seems as urgent and relevant in twenty-first century America of over three hundred million people as in the early national period of three million.

*Little Known Facts:* As noted, George Washington was not a great speaker, lacking the delivery skills of some of his contemporaries such as Fisher Ames, Alexander Hamilton, Patrick Henry, or James Otis. He was anything but dynamic. Yet, he possessed a sterling reputation based on a life-time career as military general and statesman. And his public addresses came at pivotal moments in the young nation's history. No other man in America could have united the country behind the new government. He was considered in the new nation and also in Europe as the greatest man of his age. However, despite his charisma, Washington would never be regarded as one of the nation's great orators. He believed he should express himself more through actions than words. "He is a man of very few words," declared one of his contemporaries, Charles Wilson Peale, in 1775, "but when he speaks it is to the purpose." The reverence that has been given this speech may explain the consternation and disappointment that arose in the nineteenth century when the general public learned that Alexander Hamilton had been the principal author of the address as well as other addresses. In fact, Washington used a team of ghostwriters that included Hamilton, James Madison, Edmund Randolph, Timothy Pickering, and others. Yet Washington superintended the speechwriting process and the addresses clearly bore his stamp while eliminating his insecurity about writing prose.

*Contemporary Application:* Even though one might not be known as a powerful speaker, sometimes one's personal *ethos* is so high that even the briefest statement or observation is received and accepted as an utterance of great significance and high importance.

*Connection to Today:* With American political leaders attempting to use U. S. military and economic power to control what happens in the Middle East and other parts of the world, the first president's warnings about getting entangled in the affairs of foreign nations seem as relevant in our time as they did in 1796. Of course, American corporate power has interests all around the globe, and our citizens live and work in almost all nations in the world, thus we might ask if there is a danger in isolationism. Point being, the issue is omnipresent in our national life.

# 16. Daniel Webster, Against Nullification, January 26-27, 1830

*Speaker:* Daniel Webster (1782–1852) built the reputation of the foremost orator of his generation, a reputation rightfully earned. In fact, many students today seem unaware that Webster was one of the most dynamic and effective public speakers in all American history. This speaker had served in a variety of political positions, including secretary of state under two presidents; he ran for president in 1836 and 1840 on the Whig ticket. With Henry Clay and John Calhoun, he comprised the great triumvirate of the U. S. Senate, and in his home state he was sometimes called "the god-like Daniel." His sterling reputation as orator stemmed, in large part, from the diversity of excellence in speaking situations—political speaking, legislative debate, forensic speaking (as attorney), and *epideictic* speaking (ceremonial). He spoke persuasively before the Supreme Court in defense of the charter of Dartmouth College (*Dartmouth v. Woodard*, 1819; the court agreed with Webster that the charter had been violated) and he also argued in two other important cases: *McCullough v. Maryland*, 1819 (defending the constitutionality of the U. S. Bank), and *Gibbons v. Ogden*, 1824 (extending the power of the federal government); he spoke in the Knapp-White criminal murder case in Salem (1830) in which he won a conviction; he spoke ceremonially more than once at the Bunker Hill monument (1825 and 1843); and his best ceremonial speech was "Adams and Jefferson," delivered in Boston's famed Faneuil Hall, August 2, 1826. His last great ceremonial speech that was so highly acclaimed was "Addition to the Capitol," delivered in 1851. Little wonder that Adams exclaimed: "Mr. Burke is no longer entitled to the praise—the 'most consummate orator of modern times'….this oration will be read five hundred years hence with as much rapture as it was heard." And John Greenleaf Whittier poetically praised

Webster: "New England stateliest of man, in port and speech Olympian, When no one met, at first, but took a second awed and wondering look."

*Occasion:* This speech was the climax of a heated Senate debate between the senator from Massachusetts and Senator Robert Hayne of South Carolina in 1830. Hayne spoke for the states that would later become the Confederacy, which opposed the tariff. He also cited Vice President John C. Calhoun's theory of nullification, under which a state could "nullify" a federal law that it believed unconstitutional, and, if necessary, simply secede from the Union if necessary to protect its interests. Webster defended the authority of the national government and criticized the doctrine of states' rights. His famous second reply to Hayne (a rebuttal) ran 30,000 words in length. Washington excitement was running high. The chamber in the basement of the Capitol was filled. People knew history was being made by this debate. Webster maintained the Constitution was a product of "we the people" and that nullification would result in chaos or worse. Indeed, as Webster eloquently argued, liberty and union were not incompatible.

*Excerpt* [peroration]: "When my eyes shall be turned to behold for the last time the sun in heaven, may I not see him shining on the broken and dishonored fragments of a once glorious Union, on states dissevered, discordant, belligerent, on a land rent with civil feuds, or drenched, it may be, in fraternal blood! Let their last feeble and lingering glance rather behold the gorgeous ensign of the republic, now known and honored throughout the earth, still full high advanced, its arms and trophies streaming in their original luster, not a stripe erased or polluted, nor a single star obscured, bearing for its motto, no such miserable interrogatory as 'What is all this worth?' nor those other words of delusion and folly, 'Liberty first and Union afterwards,' but everywhere, spreads all over in characters of living light, blazing on all its ample folds, as they float over the sea and over the land, and in every wind under the whole heavens, that other sentiment, dear to every true American heart—Liberty and Union, now and forever, one and inseparable."

*Impact:* Historians contend that Webster clearly won the debate, if for no other reason than his arguments were sound and effective. No less of a personage than Abraham Lincoln was greatly influenced in his views on the Union by Webster. Some have argued that the rhetorical eloquence of Webster delayed the beginning of the Civil War by a generation. True enough, Webster's reputation as an orator had already been established, especially in his ceremonial speaking—speeches that were circulated widely and drawn upon in American education for study, declamation, and providing the young and old alike of the new nation what it needed (heroes, myths, shibboleths). Webster eventually argued before the Supreme Court 168 times and he offered many models of criminal prosecution. And Webster's ceremonial speeches meet standards of excellence for incorporating a discussion of so many pressing issues of the speaker's age, such as the shame of slavery and the value of Union. The Senator could prescribe a course for the future based on emerging American values and national expansion that would make for a better American society. Yet it is this speech, the Senate oration and reply to Hayne, which solidified Webster's great reputation as the greatest orator in his time as well as advanced a realistic nationalist ideology for the future.

*Contemporary Application:* One's reputation for genuine greatness in rhetorical practice must be based on factors in Webster's speaking career—intelligence, eloquence in style (language), skill in delivery, diversity of knowledge and speaking occasions. Yet another big factor looms large—having one's ideology of nationalism vindicated by history.

*Little Known Fact:* While John Adams and Thomas Jefferson possessed different personalities holding different political philosophies, they died on the same day: July 4, 1826, exactly fifty years after the signing of the Declaration of Independence. And almost a month later, Webster delivered his eulogy of these two leaders whose dual deaths on a national holiday captured national attention and added to the mystique.

# 17. Ralph Waldo Emerson, The American Scholar, August 31, 1837

*Speaker:* Ralph Waldo Emerson (1803-1882) was a preacher, essayist, poet, and popular lecturer who was active in the American Transcendentalist movement, composed of a small but highly creative group of thinkers, speakers, and writers. Transcendentalists are not easily described, but possessed passion for both religion and philosophy, were highly rational, loved nature, and placed emphasis on intuition and self-reliance. Emerson began his professional life as a preacher in the Unitarian Church in Boston which contained a disproportionate number of intellectuals and thinkers—feminists, reformers, ministers, essayists, poets, novelists, speakers, journalists, historians, and philosophers. There was a deep intellectual culture of the Unitarian Church in Boston that challenged ministers when standing before the assembled congregation. Emerson exemplified this new style of preaching before a liberal, intellectual, elite audience as well or better than any other speaker. His essays on himself seem to depict someone who felt that he had failed in his young life by indolence, apathy, and wasted opportunities. He secured his first pulpit at the Second Church in Boston. One custom in that era was the exchange of pulpits, and thus Emerson exchanged pulpits with other preachers, meaning that his repertoire of almost two hundred sermons got repeated several times. Yet his personal struggles with doubts, confusion, and uncertainty, combined with the tragic death of his first wife, led him to intellectual and emotional turmoil. Soon Emerson became embroiled in a minor dispute over the administration of the Lord's Supper (he refused to preside). He resigned from the pulpit in 1832, after only three years tenure. He did not resign membership from the church or from the ministry, however, and continued to accept speaking invitations. As a speaker, Emerson could be eloquent but was certainly not spellbinding in delivery. He read his sermons from full manuscript (not unusual for Unitarian preachers) at a slow pace (around a hundred words per minute); his rate was unvaried and sedate. Whatever impressive effect he achieved with a listening audience came from the content and language, not from the delivery. Emerson was more diverse than being a man simply preaching sermons. He was also both an essayist and lecturer, now a greater part of his enduring legacy than any sermons. One lecture entitled "Eloquence" showed Emerson's awareness of the importance of adapting to one's audience: "The audience is a constant meter of the orator." He continued to postulate there is something excellent in every audience, and the speaker should tap into that virtue. He had great respect for the power of "Eloquence" and even presented a lecture by that name. Emerson's definition of eloquence is simple: "The power to translate a truth into language perfectly intelligible to the person to whom you speak." Emerson also delivered lectures on Renaissance artists and literary figures, and he garnered fees for these lectures ranging anywhere from five or ten dollars up to over three hundred dollars for a series of eight lectures. The lyceum was an ideal forum, and for more than thirty years Emerson brought his lectures to many towns and cities, often undergoing travel hardships to meet appointments, often winning more readers than listeners. He delivered only a few political addresses, yet for all his varied topics in speaking and writing, Emerson was ahead of his time.

*Occasion:* This speaking occasion was an early afternoon meeting at the First Parrish Church, Cambridge, Massachusetts. The audience consisted of many distinguished intellectuals: The Phi Beta Kappa Society and their guests, university officials, leading scholars and educators, and others with literary interests. At thirty-four years of age, Emerson was unestablished as a professional and yet not unknown. In this address, the speaker considered the scholar from a contemporary perspective and regarded the scholar as the cultivated intellect influenced by books, nature, and action.

*Excerpt:* "The scholar is the delegated intellect. In the right state he is *Man Thinking*. In the degenerate state, when the victim of society, he tends to become a mere thinker, or still worse, the parrot of other men's thinking."

*Impact:* Emerson was the kind of speaker who only elicited quiet appreciation and deep respect from the listeners willing to engage in reflection and critical thinking. Listeners rarely displayed intense visible emotion. Few popular speakers in American history held an audience so select and focused in its interest. This speech advanced Emerson's reputation for "literary orations" delivered before college gatherings, and it became his best address and his best known in that category. Each generation of thinkers continues to discover Emerson for itself, and his philosophy seems to be at the core of much contemporary "New Age" doctrine.

*Interesting Facts:* Emerson's themes for essays and speeches were essentially the same. The best known essay was entitled simply "Self-Reliance," and it appeals to the inner self, to intuition, and to nature as guides to life and reality. The essay contains a famous quote: "A foolish consistency is the hobgoblin of little minds, adored by little statesmen and philosophers and divines....To be great is to be misunderstood." The "Concord Hymn" was the poem for which he was best known; it was a favorite entry in American schoolbooks until the 1930s. And the speech for which Emerson is best known is the Harvard Divinity School Address, delivered July 15, 1838, with mixed reactions. For some contemporary students, understanding the speech's insight and profundity might be as challenging today as for listeners in 1838. The speaker contended that the search for divinity was internal—divinity is within each human soul, the only god is within (a kind of divine immanence). Emerson urged ministers to reject external authority in religion and speak from their own experience and insights.

*Contemporary Application:* One may be a great thinker and an excellent scholar, but this does not automatically translate into being a popular, spell-binding orator. Often the written essays will become a greater part of one's legacies than the speeches delivered on the same topics.

# 18. Wendell Phillips, Murder of Lovejoy, December 8, 1837

*Speaker:* Wendell Phillips (1811–1884) was born into an aristocratic political family (his father was a Boston mayor) and educated at Harvard College and Law School. As a young man he was trained to be an effective speaker and enjoyed using his giftedness as an orator. Phillips became the most famous of all the antislavery orators, but also became a reform speaker for other causes such as women's rights, labor, temperance, fair treatment for Native Americans and Chinese immigrants, prison reform, abolition of capital punishment, and education. Though often in opposition to organized religion, he was a man of conviction. Over his lifetime, he probably delivered thousands of speeches for liberal causes and accepted invitations to speak in a wide variety of venues and forums. He became one of the best known and most popular speakers in the lyceum movement. Ironically, Phillips never held political office, though his credibility and influence were surely greater than a vast majority of office-holders, at least among antislavery folk. In fairness, Phillips was not respected by everyone as he developed a reputation for being a radical agitator from those who opposed his moral positions. Furthermore, he moved to the extreme position of the Garrisonians, who placed their curse upon the U. S. Constitution and advocated abolitionists should neither vote nor hold office under that Constitution because it supported slavery. In 1838 he presented a genteel lecture on "The Lost Arts" which he presented more than two thousand times over the next forty-five years, becoming his most popular lecture. In June 1840 he and his wife traveled to London to address the World Antislavery Convention. When the few distinguished American women who attended the convention were questioned for credentials and shuttled to the gallery as spectators rather than participants, Phillips promptly added the women's rights movement to his program of reform. Meantime, Phillips traveled the Northern states to address abolitionist societies and mass general public meetings. As a speaker he always dressed and spoke in a dignified and respectful manner. His own expressed ideal of oratory was "animated conversation." As a master of extemporaneous and impromptu speaking, he shunned manuscript and notes; his compelling power was the force of his ideas. On January 20, 1861, he took the pulpit of Theodore Parker's Unitarian church to preach a sermon praising disunion. After the Emancipation Proclamation, this reformer continued to publicly advocate the rights of the freedmen. The lyceum lecture platform provided ready audiences for Phillips' lectures, earning him from $10,000 to $15,000 a year, although he always gave his reform speeches free.

*Occasion:* A meeting had been called for public discussion of the significance of an ugly and tragic incident—a lawless mob from Missouri had shot to death the Rev. Elijah P. Lovejoy at Alton, Illinois. The famous Boston Unitarian preacher William Ellery Channing presided. Lovejoy was owner and publisher of a press, a courageous writer who had penned a strong editorial condemning a mob for burning alive a black man. The minister was simply attempting to protect his printing press from destruction by proslavery vigilantes who did not even live in his state. This important meeting was being conducted at the Boston's prestigious Faneuil Hall with five thousand in attendance. Resolutions condemning mob action as well as defense of First Amendment rights had been proposed. Perhaps to Phillips' and other abolitionists' surprise, James T. Austin, attorney general of Massachusetts, presented a bitter speech of opposition to the resolutions. Austin justified the mob's cruel action, comparing it with the Boston Tea Party prior to the Revolution. There is some controversy as to whether Phillips had planned to speak; though his speech may have been impromptu, his ideas were well digested and powerful. Phillips, only twenty-six years old at the time and relatively unknown, rose and pushed his way to the podium, and, given clearance to speak, began to express eloquently his position and his passion. His main argument was simple: Slavery is a moral evil and at least Lovejoy should have been granted protection of his constitutional right of freedom of the press. To Phillips, there was no comparison between the mob from Missouri and the mob at the Boston Tea Party, as the latter was protesting unconstitutional and illegal acts of the Parliament in the mother country.

*Excerpt:* "A comparison has been drawn between the events of the Revolution and the tragedy at Alton. We have heard it asserted here in Faneuil Hall, that Great Britain had a right to tax the Colonies, and we have heard the mob at Alton, the drunken murderers of Lovejoy, compared to those patriot fathers who threw the tea overboard!....Sir, when I heard the gentleman lay down principles which place the murderers of Alton side by side with Otis and Hancock, with Quincy and Adams, I thought those pictured lips [pointing to the portraits on the walls] would have broken into voice to rebuke the recreant American—the slanderer of the dead!"

*Impact:* This truly was an address to a polarized audience, or at least there was a strong and vociferous minority determined to interrupt the speech and discourage the young speaker. Cries and shouts from both sides were disruptive, yet Phillips was determined to speak his mind and soul. The eloquence of the speaker dominated the action of the assembly. According to George William Curtis, an outstanding orator himself, this speech was one of the three greatest rhetorical triumphs in American history to this point, alongside Patrick Henry's eloquent appeal for liberty at Williamsburg and Abraham Lincoln's Gettysburg Address: "Three and there is no fourth." Many in the audience held strong humanitarian ideals and were introduced to Phillips for the first time. His career as a public reform speaker began as a result of his eloquence. Hundreds of Phillips' orations and lectures followed.

*Contemporary Application:* A speaker who passionately discusses a major moral issue and clearly and courageously stands up for truth will be honored for advancing justice and reform.

# 19. Angelina Grimke, Bearing Witness Against Slavery, May 16, 1838

*Speaker:* Angelina Grimke (1805–1879) was a most unlikely reformer who became the most prominent woman orator of the 1830s. She, along with her sister Sarah and twelve other siblings, was born into a wealthy slaveholding family in Charleston, South Carolina, and was given every possible advantage a young girl of that generation could receive, including private tutors. Raised as an Episcopalian, both she and sister Sarah observed slavery first-hand and came to detest the practice. The sisters created an underground school for teaching reading and writing skills to slaves in violation of state laws. In her diary, Angelina wrote about the strategy for clandestine teaching of slaves and her feeling of personal gratification for this act of civil disobedience. The two moved to Philadelphia where they became Quakers, an affiliation which drove their activism within the abolitionist movement. In 1836 Grimke wrote "An Appeal to the Christian Women of the South," urging her reading audience to join the fight against slavery. The pamphlets were burned in South Carolina and the sisters were threatened with arrest if they should return to their home state. Meantime, the sisters drew sizable audiences of women in the North as they spoke, first in parlor meetings, and then to larger audiences in churches and halls. Their big appeal was their Southern heritage and first-hand experiences with slavery. Men, usually husbands of women attending, were drawn to these meetings, perhaps out of curiosity over a female orator but also interest in the reality of slavery. Recognition of Angelina's eloquence grew as her fame spread. Her fame spread throughout New England in the late 1830s, and she drew audiences of three or four thousand in Boston with listeners sitting spellbound for two hours or more to her discourses. Angelina's *ethos* was based on courage and humility. She engaged in debates on slavery and was the first woman in American history to publicly debate a man. In her speeches she explained that she and her family had been a part of the terrible system of slavery—a penitent part—but she had now come to plead for the slaves. Courageously she argued that the North, too, was a vital supporter of slavery, and that there was as much racial prejudice in the North as in the South.

*Occasion:* Two days after her marriage to Theodore Weld, a fellow abolition activist, Grimke accepted an invitation to speak at the National Antislavery Convention in Pennsylvania Hall, a new and impressive venue with the motto "Virtue, Liberty, Independence" carved in gold letters over the stage. Before the meeting, notices had been posted warning that this new hall would be destroyed by fire by the opponents of abolition. While Grimke spoke, an unruly crowd outside maintained a constant uproar, and then pelted stones against the window.

*Excerpt:* "Do you ask, then, 'What has the North to do?' I answer, cast out first the spirit of slavery from your own hearts, and then lend your aid to convert the South. Each one present has a work to do, be his or her situation what it may, however limited their means, or insignificant their supposed influence. The great men of this country will not do this work; the church will never do it. A desire to please the world, to keep the favor of all parties and of all conditions, makes them dumb on this and every other unpopular subject. They have become worldly-wise, and therefore God, in his wisdom, employs them not to carry on his plans of reformation and salvation. He hath chosen the foolish things of the world to confound the wise, and the weak to overcome the mighty....We may talk of occupying neutral ground, but on this subject, in its present attitude, there is no such thing as neutral ground....If you are on what you suppose to be neutral ground, the South looks upon you as on the side of the oppressor. And is there one who loves his country willing to give his influence, even indirectly, in favor of slavery—that curse of nations? God swept Egypt with the besom of destruction, and punished Judea also with a sore punishment, because of slavery. And have we any reason to believe that he is less just now?—or that he will be more favorable to us than to his own 'peculiar people?'"

*Impact:* This was truly a courageous speech in a most hostile environment. Grimke began by adapting words from John the Baptist to his critics, "Men, brethren, and fathers—mothers, daughters, and sisters, what came ye out for to see? A reed shaken with the wind? Is it curiosity merely, or a deep sympathy with the perishing slave, that has brought this large audience together?" Stones began to pelt the building. "As the tumult from without increased, and the brickbats fell thick and fast," recalled William Lloyd Garrison, "[Grimké's] eloquence kindled, her eyes flashed, and her cheeks glowed." Grimké, a daughter of slaveholders, seemed to thrive in situations that underscored her vulnerability. She rose to the challenge and spoke for an hour, all the while knowing the building could be set on fire at any moment. "What would the levelling of this hall be? Any evidence that we are wrong or that slavery is a good and wholesome institution? What if the mob should now burst in upon us, break up our meeting, and commit violence upon our persons, would that be anything compared with what the slaves endure?" At the end of the evening, the mob burned the new hall to the ground. This was the climax of Grimke's abolition crusade, and as a newly married woman she retired to private life filled with reform activities.

*Contemporary Application:* History will be kind to those who speak eloquently with undaunted courage in the most hostile and dangerous environment.

*Connection to Today:* Women such as Angelina Grimke were among courageous pioneers in both women's rights and social justice.

# 20. Frederick Douglass, The Church and Prejudice, November 4, 1841

*Speaker:* Frederick Douglass (1817–1895) was a brilliant speaker, writer, journalist, political activist, reformer, and humanitarian. He was a towering figure in the movement to abolish slavery. Douglass was born in Maryland in 1817 or 1818, and in what month or day he never knew, and to a slave woman he seldom saw and a white father he never knew. His mother died when he was seven, and he was raised by his grandmother on a plantation in Maryland, then sent to be a house slave in Baltimore at age eight. He simply chose to celebrate his birthday on February 14. When he was twenty, with fake uniform and papers identifying him as a sailor, he boarded a train for New York and left behind the wretched, abusive life of slavery. Yet he could never leave behind the life of being an object of prejudice and discrimination, and some of his most eloquent addresses were presented as a runaway fugitive. Always attempting to improve his education, Douglass joined a number of organizations that promoted reform. As for his training as a speaker, he drew from several traditions and sources: wide reading; attending public lectures; practicing the secular art of storytelling; observing the religious art of black preaching; and actual practice and experience. He was especially moved by the speaking and writing of abolitionist William Lloyd Garrison, and Garrison, upon hearing Douglass speak, returned mutual respect. In the 1840s, Douglass espoused the radical, uncompromising principles of Garrison and his company of supporters, denouncing the ties to slavery maintained by both business and religious institutions. In their speeches, they argued that the Constitution was a proslavery document and, as such, it was neither moral nor viable. With other Garrisonians, Douglass believed the strategy of moral persuasion constituted the best means of ending slavery in the nation. This reform orator possessed several gifts as a persuasive speaker: brilliant mind; life experience as a former slave; excellent delivery skills; strong *ethos* (ethical character); and skilled strategy in use of supporting materials to build his arguments (first-hand experience; illustrations; instances; anecdotes; humor; even sarcasm and ridicule). As a skilled wordsmith, he had an impressive career as a journalist and newspaper editor. Later, he became involved in political speechmaking, especially as a post-Civil War black Republican.

*Occasion:* With his reputation as abolitionist orator, with such high *ethos* based on personal slavery experience, Douglas was invited to speak to an anti-slavery conference in Nantucket in 1841. Clearly, as a Christian who had been taught the Bible, Douglass understood and applied Scripture. Inspired by a sense of divine justice, several black Christians began to raise their voices against the heinous system of slavery and to the white evangelical faith that so often condoned and practiced it. Douglass was the most powerful black voice among reformers. Only twenty-three years old at the time, he trembled with nervousness as he stood at the podium. Before him sat abolitionists who had travelled to Nantucket to hear him and others speak on this vital topic. Filled with passion, Douglass soon overcame his nervousness and delivered a stirring, eloquent speech about his life as a slave.

*Excerpt:* "All this prejudice sinks into insignificance in my mind, when compared with the enormous iniquity of the system which is its cause—the system that sold my four sisters and my brothers into bondage—and which calls in its priests to defend it even from the Bible!...I used to attend a Methodist church, in which my master was a class leader; he would talk most sanctimoniously about the dear Redeemer, who was sent 'to preach deliverance to the captives, and set at liberty them that are bruised'—he could pray at morning, pray at noon, and pray at night; yet he could lash up my poor cousin by his two thumbs, and inflict stripes and blows upon his bare back, till the blood streamed to the ground! All the time quoting scripture, for his authority, and appealing to that passage of the Holy Bible which says, 'He that knoweth his master's will, and doeth it not, shall be beaten with many stripes!' Such was the amount of this good Methodist's piety."

*Impact:* Douglass used the occasion for a courageous explanation of how white Christians retained prejudice against black people and even self-servingly used their religious teaching to sustain such racist attitudes and practice. The young reformer spoke with such eloquence that he was then engaged as an agent for the Massachusetts Anti-Slavery Society. He became a leading abolitionist speaker, yet critics doubted the authenticity of his stories; in response, he wrote his autobiography—*Narrative of the Life of Frederick Douglass*—in 1845. After spending two years abroad on a lecture tour, Douglass returned with enough money to purchase his freedom and launch his own abolitionist paper, the *North Star*, in Rochester, New York, in 1847. Not simply because Frederick Douglass addressed the moral dimensions of equality and justice that we list him among the best American moral reform and religious speakers, but also because he had prophetic words for Christian leaders and the church in general. His words encouraged other black reform speakers and preachers, both of his generation and subsequent ones. Douglass summarized his concern in a declaration that has haunted Christians since: "Between the Christianity of this land and the Christianity of Christ, I recognize the widest possible difference."

*Contemporary Application:* A speaker who addresses a major reform issue with passion and courage, and whose position is on the "right side of history," will establish an enduring legacy for one's life work regardless of the speaker's immediate success.

*Connection to Today:* The theme of "church and race" as discussed by Frederick Douglass is a theme picked up by other black reform speakers who followed him in subsequent generations, especially Martin Luther King, Jr. We may conclude that King was the greatest civil rights preacher and reform leader of the twentieth century, just as Douglass was the greatest civil rights speaker of the nineteenth century.

# 21. Elizabeth Cady Stanton, Declaration of Sentiments, July 19, 1848

*Speaker:* Elizabeth Cady Stanton (1815–1902) was the best known of a small group of females who advocated eloquently and persistently for equal rights for all American women. She began a reformist speaking career at age twenty-five and it continued vigorously for over sixty years. Both the press and her peers considered her "the first U. S. feminist" and "the foremost American woman intellectual of her generation." And while women's equal rights was her primary cause and commitment, she also crusaded for other reformist causes, including antislavery, temperance, and labor reform. Her speaking and writing career was prolific, traveling to many U. S. cities and facing a wide variety of audiences. From 1869 to 1881 Stanton lectured for the New York Lyceum Bureau.

*Occasion:* In 1840 Cady Stanton and Lucretia Mott had attended the first World's Antislavery Convention in London, where they had been refused seats as delegates on account of their gender. Their sense of injustice over the treatment of all women, especially in their home country, continued to grow; that emotional energy was channeled into fiery oratory and strategy planning. Stanton and Mott spoke of their "long-accumulating discontent" and made a public call for a Woman's Rights Convention to discuss the "social, civil, and religious rights of women." Thus, the first women's rights convention in the USA was conducted in the Wesleyan Chapel in Seneca Falls, New York, in July 1848. The church was quickly filled and the opening meeting drew some three hundred participants. The audience included forty men, and no woman dared open the meeting (Lucretia's husband, James Mott, called the meeting to order), but soon Stanton took control and delivered a series of charges and comments. The most important presentation was Stanton's reading aloud the draft of her Declaration of Sentiments, which called for rights of women, especially voting rights. The form and language deliberately imitated that of the Declaration of Independence and drew inspiration from the basic idea that government without representation is both morally and politically wrong.

*Excerpt:* "When, in the course of human events, it becomes necessary for one portion of the family of man to assume among the people of the earth a position different from that which they have hitherto occupied, but one to which the laws of nature and of nature's God entitle them, a decent respect to the opinions of mankind requires that they should declare the causes that impel them to such a course….The history of mankind is a history of repeated injuries and usurpations on the part of man toward woman, having in direct object the establishment of an absolute tyranny over her. To prove this, let facts be submitted to a candid world….Now, in view of this entire disfranchisement of one-half the people of this country, their social and religious degradation—in view of the unjust laws above mentioned, and because women do feel themselves aggrieved, oppressed, and fraudulently deprived of their most sacred rights, we insist that they have immediate admission to all the rights and privileges which belong to them as citizens of these United States….In entering upon the great work before us, we anticipate no small amount of misconception, misrepresentation, and ridicule; but we shall use every instrumentality within our power to effect our object. We shall employ agents, circulate tracts, petition the State and national Legislatures, and endeavor to enlist the pulpit and the press in our behalf. We hope this Convention will be followed by a series of Conventions, embracing every part of the country….Firmly relying upon the final triumph of the Right and the True, we do this day affix our signatures to this declaration."

*Impact:* This address was published extensively, though, not surprisingly, it was ridiculed in the press and denounced in the pulpit. Even some who signed withdrew their names after the storm of ridicule began to break. Nevertheless, this address must truly be appraised as a success, and the actual Declaration is one of the great documents in American history. The effectiveness is rooted in several factors, one being the creativity of Stanton in drawing both inspiration and ethical appeal in adducing both the logical argument and the actual language of Thomas Jefferson in the Declaration of Independence. In fact, some of Jefferson's words—beginning with "We hold these truths to be self-evident"—are quoted directly. Just as Jefferson built his case against the king of England by citing a litany of injustices against the colonists, Stanton uses the same strategy in citing a litany of injustices perpetrated by men against women ("all men" was substituted for "King George"). In each Declaration, of course, the long listing of injustices and abuses seems overwhelming. After debate, the Declaration was adopted and signed by sixty-eight women and thirty-two men. The call for votes for women was controversial in 1848, even among members of the infant women's movement, as many thought it would hold back progress on other movements. This Declaration, and the speaking of Stanton to present and defend it publicly, generally marks the beginning of the American women's rights movement. Cady Stanton, along with those who collaborated on the draft (Lucretia Mott, Martha C. Wright, and Mary Ann McClintock) had courageously touched a responsive chord in the hearts of progressive and brave women throughout the nation. Cady Stanton became the movement's chief public advocate.

*Little Known Fact:* Frederick Douglass attended the convention and his support of the Declaration helped pass the resolutions. He praised the document as the "grand movement for attaining the civil, social, political, and religious rights of women."

*Contemporary Application:* When a speaker can link one's cause and argument with a well-known document, such as the Declaration of Independence, then one dramatically gains attention and renders a powerful argument—especially when the logic is sound and the cause is right and just.

*Connection to Today:* The women's rights movement has enjoyed many deserved successes, even if many landmark successes were delayed, yet gender equality and equal justice remain issues in the American society.

# 22. Henry Clay, The Compromise of 1850, February 6 and 7, 1850

*Speaker*: Henry Clay (1777–1852) was a strong unionist, a trained and practicing attorney from Lexington, Kentucky, a member and speaker of the House of Representatives for eleven years, a leader of the "war hawks" (advocating the War of 1812), a U. S. senator (from 1831-42; and 1849-1852), a secretary of state under John Q. Adams, and a candidate for president at least three times, though never elected. Clay was an impassioned political orator with a magnificent voice and author of hundreds of speeches that stirred popular audiences throughout the young nation. Born in Virginia, Clay had natural gifts of eloquence though only three years of formal education; as a speaker he was probably influenced most by Patrick Henry's eloquence and the stories about the Virginian. He was brilliant, if not polished. He spoke directly in plain English, reflecting the values and tastes of his western audiences. As a nineteenth century "playboy," he was often criticized for his "moral delinquency." More damaging was a general public suspicion that Clay harbored strong personal ambitions that guided his political course. He never achieved that highest office he sought, with one critic suggesting he could get more men to listen to him and fewer to vote for him than anyone in America. Clay's fame was achieved in political address and debate, though he disliked lecturing and ceremonial speaking. He could cast a spell of fascination upon his audience and draw large crowds to his personal appearances in various states. Two constant references in his speeches were "the Founding Fathers" and "the Union." Late in life he wrote: "If anyone desires to know the leading and paramount object of my public life, the preservation of this Union will furnish him the key." Clay disliked slavery, but felt it had to be endured, and he detested the abolitionists for risking the Union to serve their purposes. He was considered, along with Webster and Calhoun, one of the "Great Triumvirate" or the "Immortal Trio" of great U. S. senators and national leaders of his generation.

*Occasion*: A speech from Henry Clay was deemed of national importance. Of the hundreds he presented, this "Compromise Speech" was his most significant. At seventy-three years of age, Clay came from a retreat at Ashland, Kentucky, to address the Congress in an effort to allay bad feelings and to "save the Union." The audience, like that for Webster's argument a month earlier, overflowed the Senate galleries, packed the hallways, and congested the rotunda. His entire purpose was to develop the eight resolutions for dealing with slavery in the Mexican territorial acquisitions, including his conviction that California should be admitted as a state without reference to slavery; the U.S. should assume indebtedness Texas had incurred prior to statehood; and Congress had no power to interfere with slave trade between slaveholding states. Those were his convictions.

*Excerpt*: "Mr. President, I am directly opposed to any purpose of secession, of separation. I am for staying within the Union, and defying any portion of this Union to expel me or drive me out of the Union…[after assuring the South could better vindicate their rights by remaining within the Union than by being expelled without ceremony and authority, the speaker predicted the dissolution of the Union would be followed by war]…Such a war, too, as that would be, following the dissolution of the Union! Sir, we may search the pages of history, and none so furious, so bloody, so implacable, so exterminating… none of them urged with such violence….as well that war which shall follow that disastrous event—if that event happens—of dissolution. After war, some Philip of Alexander, some Caesar or Napoleon, would rise…and crush the liberties of both the dissevered portions of this Union. [Clay asked his audience to visualize…"the extinction of this last and glorious light which is leading all mankind"]…And, finally, Mr. President, I implore, as the best blessing which Heaven can bestow upon earth, that if the direful and sad event of dissolution of the Union shall happen, I may not survive to behold the sad and heart-rending spectacle."

*Impact:* Clay delivered one of the longest of the important speeches in the American Congress—he spoke for two and a half hours during the first day and at least that long the following day. When the exhausted speaker completed his two-day address, both men and women rushed to congratulate him and demonstrate personal affection. Printed copies were demanded, and some 100,000 copies were quickly printed and distributed by the *Daily Globe*. Public response to the speech was overwhelmingly affirmative. The orations of both Webster and Clay most surely delayed the great conflict by at least a decade. Congress passed the essentials of Clay's proposals, and sectional animosity and distrust subsided for the time. The Union he loved had been preserved— for the time being. So this speech must be judged a success, even though a military campaign was eventually required for settlement of the struggle. Clay established his reputation as the "Great Pacificator" or "Great Compromiser," and he solidified that reputation with this speech for legislation now called the "Clay Compromise of 1850." His prominence in public life and effective advocacy of national interests cannot be understood or explained apart from his exceptional ability in public speaking.

*Interesting Fact:* Clay prophesied the coming of terrible war if sectional differences were not resolved, and he was so correct about a terrible war. He also received the wish he expressed in many speeches—that, if this terrible war came that threatened the Union, he would not be alive to witness the skirmish and feel the wounds of conflict.

*Contemporary Application:* The word "compromise" may have a negative connotation to some, but a genuine compromise may well be the only strategy for preserving values that all cherish within an organization or community. Effective advocacy of compromise is typically a prerequisite for successful acceptance and implementation of a reasonable and workable plan that gives all parties in a conflict situation something of value.

# 23. John C. Calhoun, On the Compromise of 1850, March 4, 1850

*Speaker:* John C. Calhoun (1782–1850) served in many roles after his graduation from Yale in 1804. He served as an attorney who practiced law in both Connecticut and South Carolina; he was a member of the South Carolina legislature; member of Congress; secretary of war under President Monroe; vice president of the United States under Presidents John Quincy Adams and Andrew Jackson; secretary of state under President Tyler; senator from South Carolina. Calhoun was a man of intelligence and principle. He was not a powerful orator, and his speeches were largely dry expositions of his political ideology. Few, if any, speeches achieved fame, and the orations have been described as "dry intellectuality," as perhaps befitting the stereotype of a philosopher. Yet, Calhoun's importance lies in his intellectual explanation and defense of the Southern position on states' rights and slavery. For this rhetorical defense, Calhoun became known both as the "cast iron man" and the "great nullificator." He had begun his political career as a strong nationalist, championing the causes of national government and broad constructionism, arguing for the national bank and the tariff. Later, Calhoun considered the "Tariff of Abominations" to be protecting only the North. He advanced the theory that a state could determine whether an act of Congress was constitutional, and, if not, could declare the act "null and void." Gradually, it was realized it would take disunion and secession to enforce such acts. Along with Clay and Webster, Calhoun was considered a member of the "Great Triumvirate" or "Immortal Trio" of national political leaders of his generation.

*Occasion:* The doctrine of nullification was given national publicity in January 1830 with the famous Webster-Hayne debate in the Senate. Calhoun had both spoken and written (sometimes anonymously): That sovereignty was absolute and indivisible; that ultimate power resided with the states and not with centralized government; that the U. S. Constitution was not a supreme law but a compact or mere agreement between sovereign states; that a state could nullify a federal law and refuse to enforce it if the law were against the best interests of the state. This speech was delivered before the Senate at a time when Calhoun was ailing, and it was his last and perhaps greatest speech. In fact, the Senator's health was so poor that it was read to the Senate by Senator Mason of Virginia. Calhoun approved the purpose of the Compromise Bill of 1850, but criticized it for failure to provide the South with adequate guarantees.

*Excerpt:* "It is time, senators, that there should be an open and manly avowal on all sides as to what is intended....If the question is not now settled, it is uncertain whether it ever can hereafter be; and we, as the representatives of the States of this Union regarded as governments, should come to a distinct understanding as to our respective views, in order to ascertain whether the great questions at issue can be settled or not. If you who represent the stronger portion, cannot agree to settle them on the broad principle of justice and duty, say so; and let the States we both represent agree to separate and part in peace. If you are unwilling we should part in peace, tell us so; and we shall know what to do when you reduce the question to submission or resistance. If you remain silent, you will compel us to infer by your acts what you intend....I have now, senators, done my duty in expressing my opinions fully, freely, and candidly on this solemn occasion. In doing so I have been governed by the motives which have governed me in all the stages of the agitation of the slavery question since its commencement. I have exerted myself during the whole period to arrest it, with the intention of saving the Union if it could be done; and if it could not, to save the section where it has pleased providence to cast my lot, and which I sincerely believe has justice and the Constitution on its side. Having faithfully done my duty to the best of my ability, both to the Union and my section, throughout this agitation, I shall have the consolation, let what will come, that I am free from all responsibility."

*Impact:* This speech was the apex of Calhoun's political career. The speaker's function was to keep alive a minority viewpoint and make the strongest case possible for that viewpoint, thus rendering it intellectually defensible. Calhoun merited respect for his passion, intellect, and devotion to the South, but he did not convince Northerners and Unionists that his position was tenable. Clearly, it was not simply state sovereignty that Calhoun sought to protect, but the South's economic interests. On Sunday morning, March 31, Calhoun died, making one final effort to speak. Both Clay and Webster joined the many senators who presented eulogies on Calhoun. The principle he stood for, that is, his central doctrine of states' rights, could not be laid to rest for many decades to come, even if advocates such as Alabama Governor George Wallace and many other Southerners would not take it to the extreme of secession.

*Interesting Fact:* Not beyond using sarcasm in referencing Webster's own eloquent speech, Senator Calhoun exclaimed about the Union: "It cannot, then, be saved by eulogies on the Union, however splendid or numerous. The cry of 'Union, Union—the glorious Union!' can no more prevent disunion than the cry of 'Health, health!' on the part of a physician can save a patient lying dangerously ill."

*Contemporary Application:* Dry intellectuality and cold, dispassionate logic may display a brilliant mind, but will do little to enhance one's legacy if the speeches support a losing, untenable political cause. Calhoun may be remembered for his intellect, courage, and loyalty, but not for his untenable political ideology. The defense of slavery, even in the nineteenth century, is not a theme on which to construct greatness.

# 24. Charles Sumner, Crime Against Kansas, May 19 and 20, 1856

*Speaker*: Charles Sumner (1811–1874) delivered hundreds of speeches during his political career and, in 1869, wrote: "These speeches are my life." As a senator from Massachusetts, having been trained in law, he devoted his immense energy and powerful oratory to two great causes: The eradication of war (being naïve enough to believe that could be accomplished soon) and the eradication of slavery. Sumner was not a total pacifist, but he was a radical abolitionist who worked to destroy the Confederacy, maintain good relations with European nations, restrict the political power of former Confederates during Reconstruction, and to increase the rights and liberties of the freedmen. He became an uncompromising and impatient radical abolitionist even when abolitionism was not a popular cause in his home state. Among those who favored abolition, Sumner possessed great *ethos*, especially after the attack by Preston Brooks; indeed, he had become a great martyr for abolition. For all others, Sumner lacked skills of friendship and diplomacy, thus he did not always win over his immediate audience. He could be blunt, calling the proverbial spade a spade, thus inducing anger in some listeners. His presence was commanding; he understood the power of emotional appeal, though his delivery was neither conversational nor direct. His platform presence was imposing. Standing six feet and four inches, with a massive frame, his deep, sonorous voice was clear and powerful. His gestures were unconventional rather than graceful, yet vigorous and impressive. His literary style was florid, with much detail, allusion, and quotation, often from the Bible as well as from the Greeks and Romans. As the Massachusetts senator continued to arouse controversy, he began to draw large audiences. A trip to Europe was a big factor in his thinking, and he was influenced by the preaching of William

Ellery Channing. After the Civil War, Sumner was known as one of a handful of Radical Republicans who sought major changes in Southern states.

*Occasion:* When Seward introduced a bill for the admission of Kansas territory as a state, the Senate began a vigorous debate. After all, Kansas had been a territory where slavery and antislavery interests had bloody clashes. Sumner spoke over the course of two days, his principal argument being that slavery interests had committed crimes against the people in Kansas that were in violation of the Constitution (especially the Bill of Rights), against nature itself, and against the Missouri Compromise, which was supposed to guarantee freedom in the remaining Louisiana Territory north of 36' 30'. He saw the South as attempting to impose slavery upon the entire nation, and that the solution was immediate admission of Kansas to the Union as a free state. The speech was prepared for the U. S. Senate in written manuscript, but delivered both from memory and at times extemporaneously.

*Excerpt:* "Not in any common lust for power did this uncommon tragedy have its origin. It is the rape of a virgin Territory, compelling it to the hateful embrace of slavery; and it may be clearly traced to a depraved desire for a new Slave State, hideous offspring of such a crime, in the hope of adding to the power of slavery in the National Government…. The senator from South Carolina [Andrew Butler, co-author, along with Stephen Douglas, of the Kansas-Nebraska Act] has read many books of chivalry, and believes himself a chivalrous knight with sentiments of honor and courage. Of course he has chosen a mistress to whom he has made his vows, and who, though ugly to others, is always lovely to him; though polluted in the sight of the world, is chaste in his sight -- I mean the harlot, slavery. For her his tongue is always profuse in words."

*Impact:* Sumner began the speech at one o'clock on May 19. From the introduction in which the Senator pledged to display the proslavery crime against Kansas "without a single rag, or fig-leaf, to cover its vileness," until he finished three hours later, the crowded chamber was hushed. The following day Sumner resumed his long speech, this time launching a carefully rehearsed attack against Senators Douglas, Butler, and Mason. The speech has few equals in terms of acerbic, personal denunciation. His language was inflammatory. Preston Brooks (Rep., South Carolina), Senator Butler's cousin, felt intense anger stirred by the oration, and at first considered challenging Sumner to a duel. Two days later, on the afternoon of May 22, Brooks confronted Sumner as he sat writing at his desk in the almost empty Senate chamber: "Mr. Sumner, I have read your speech twice over carefully. It is a libel on South Carolina, and Mr. Butler, who is a relative of mine." As Sumner began to stand up, Brooks beat Sumner severely on the head before he could reach his feet, using a thick cane with a gold head. Sumner was knocked down, but Brooks continued to strike Sumner senselessly. Blinded by his own blood, Sumner staggered up the aisle and collapsed, lapsing into unconsciousness. Brooks continued to beat the motionless Sumner until his cane broke, at which point he left the chamber. This qualifies as one of the most negative reactions to a speech ever delivered. Southern newspapers denounced the speech. Northerners were outraged, claiming the South could no longer tolerate free speech. Conversely, Southern newspapers hailed Brooks as a hero, and hundreds of Southerners sent him a new cane. The entire episode demonstrated the intensity of feeling and the polarization of the young nation over the slavery issue. This is the one speech for which Sumner is best known.

*Contemporary Application:* Dealing with a hot-button issue by using denunciation of opponents, name-calling, and emotional language not only deepens polarization, but may be considered "fighting words" that could bring out the worst in audience members. Obviously rhetoric can be used as a weapon in clash and advocacy of ideas.

*Irony:* Senator Sumner was passionately devoted to two great causes—anti-war and anti-slavery—yet his idealism for one had to be compromised to justify his support for the other.

# 25. Sojourner Truth, "Ain't I Woman?" May 29, 1851

*Speaker:* Sojourner Truth (circa. 1797–1883) was born as Isabella Van Wagenen and was one of thirteen slave children in a slave family in Hurley, New York, a few miles above New York City. The slaves worked in a Dutch household, thus young Isabella learned and spoke Dutch for the first years of her life. She escaped from slavery with her daughter in 1826, became a Christian during this period of her life, and in 1843 she changed her name from Isabella to Sojourner Truth. She joined the Methodist Church and soon became a lay preacher, traveling around the region preaching the gospel and applying it to issues of social justice. "The Spirit calls and I must go," she told friends. She spoke at church houses, revivals, camp meetings, town squares, and even at conventions and more formal meetings—anywhere there was a willing audience. Not everyone liked Sojourner Truth, of course, but many large audiences did thrill to her speaking. Like Frederick Douglass, she had a compelling story to tell. She met and impressed other notable reformers, including William Lloyd Garrison, who published her autobiography, Frances Gage, Frederick Douglass, David Ruggles, Lucretia Mott, Susan Anthony, and Harriet Beecher Stowe—all willing to give Truth their staunch support. In her career Sojourner Truth spoke to hundreds, if not thousands, of audiences. She was a woman of remarkable intelligence, despite her illiteracy. Truth both preached and lectured on several key issues of her time: Abolition, women's rights, and prison reform. Standing at a height of almost six feet, she made an imposing presence before an audience. Her platform style was unique and unforgettable. Some observers stated her low-pitched voice almost sounded masculine. Truth was a fiery, passionate abolitionist and strong advocate of women's rights. She typically made logical arguments based on basic principles of equality and fairness: "Men has got their rights, and women has not got their rights. That is the trouble." The logical appeal was strong, even if many males in the audience did not agree, yet she could charm audiences with her wit and originality. "If the first woman God ever made was strong enough to turn the world upside down all alone," she often declared, "these women together ought to be able to turn it back and get it right side up again. And now that they are asking to do it, the men better let them."

*Occasion:* The speech for which Truth is best known was not about abolition, but women's rights. The oration was delivered in 1851 at an Ohio Women's Convention in Akron, and the address leveled a classic attack against gender inequalities in America. According to one historian, Alice Felt Tyler (in *Freedom's Ferment*), not all conference members welcomed Truth's appearance as a speaker; after all, her main cause had been abolition and not women's suffrage. There had been a number of "reverend gentlemen" that had already spoken for several hours, but, then "the old colored woman rose slowly from her seat on the pulpit steps and spoke in deep tones to a suddenly hushed audience." Truth stood as a tall and gaunt speaker, wearing her plain gray dress and white turban, but her mind was clear, her heart was sincere, and her rhetorical questions were piercing.

*Excerpt:* "Ain't I a woman? Look at my arm! I have ploughed and planted and gathered into barns, and no man could head [sic] me! Ain't I a woman? I could work as much and eat as much as a man—when I could get it—and bear the lash as well! Ain't I a woman? I have borned thirteen chilern, and seen 'em mos' all sold off to slavery and when I cried out with my mothers' grief, none but Jesus heard me! And ain't I a woman?….Den dat little little [sic] man in black dar [sic], he say women can't have as much rights as men, cause Christ wasn't a woman! What did Christ come from? Whar did your Christ come from? From a woman! Man had nothin' to do wid Him!"

*Impact:* This speech has earned its place as a powerful statement in the folklore of American cultural history. Sojourner Truth chose a name for herself that would not be forgotten and embraced causes that put her on the right side of history. She knew she would be traveling for the Lord, thus she chose "Sojourner," and that she must speaking realities, thus "Truth" as a last name. Her reform career began as a curiosity and ended as a legend. She became a symbol for a strong black woman, in essence, a member of two minority groups. The strength of her rhetoric was not so much in her *logos* (logic), but in her *pathos* (emotion) and especially in her *ethos* (source credibility)—as a slave who became a preacher and reformer who had lived the existential truth of her message. From a slave to a legend—this could describe Frederick Douglass, of course, but it also describes Truth. Along with Harriett Tubman, Truth has been honored as one of the two outstanding African-American women of the nineteenth century.

*Little-Known Fact:* Two texts of the speech were compiled, one by a newspaper editor within a month or so after the speech was presented and another text reconstructed by Frances Gage twelve years later in 1863. The Gage reconstruction is the only one that has the battle cry "Ain't I Woman?" and some rhetorical critics have suggested that Truth, with her Dutch and New York background, would not have spoken with the Southern slang and pronunciation (preserved in our excerpt above) that saturates the Gage text. Regardless, the theme is clear and the speaker inspired audiences and empowered women, especially black women, wherever she graced the platform.

*Contemporary Application:* Audiences are most swayed by a deeply honest and passionate expression of the speaker's heart and personal experience, and will not miss the eloquence despite the speaker's peculiarities of grammar or dialect.

## 26. Frederick Douglass, "What to the Slave is the Fourth of July?" July 5, 1852

*Speaker:* Frederick Douglass was a brilliant speaker, writer, political activist, and humanitarian. He was a towering figure in the movement to abolish slavery. Who might have been the most credible, the most effective, and the most inspiring of the reformers who spoke out against slavery? The answer, most likely, would be a man who was actually born into slavery, toiled and sweated as a slave, and who, with assistance from a mistress, taught himself how to read and then pursued a variety of subjects of learning, escaped slavery, practiced his oratory to become eloquent, and risked his life at times on the speaking circuit to address the most vital moral issues of his generation—this describes Frederick Douglass! An effective black orator before the Civil War was an anomaly indeed, and given social and cultural attitudes toward African-Americans in that time, the black speaker was seldom thought of as a leader, if even to be taken seriously. Not simply because Frederick Douglass addressed the moral dimensions of equality and justice that we list him among the most important American moral reform and even religious speakers, but also because he had prophetic words for Christian leaders and the church in general. Yet he could never leave behind the life of being an object of prejudice and discrimination, and some of his most eloquent addresses were presented as a runaway fugitive. Having been a slave, he could speak with strong *ethos*, having existentially lived the truth of his message of pain and injustice. His professional lifetime was filled with many powerful rhetorical moments. His skills as public persuader were undeniable.

*Occasion:* Invited to speak to an anti-slavery gathering in Nantucket in 1841, Douglass spoke with such eloquence that he was engaged as an agent and lecturer for the Massachusetts Anti-Slavery Society. He honed his speaking skills by speaking abroad for two years on a lecture tour, and then returned to Rochester, New York, in 1847 to launch his own abolitionist paper. In 1852 he was invited to speak in Rochester on the occasion of Independence Day. A Fourth of July oration is designed to venerate the nation, its heroes, its heritage; the address is intended and expected to be uplifting, patriotic, and inspiring. Yet Douglass was both willing and courageous enough to violate these traditions and expectations and speak prophetically. The irony of American mythology and sacred rites and the coexistence of human chattel slavery was never lost on this reformer—and he could only speak out! In many speeches and lectures, Douglass attacked the hypocrisy of the United States in general and the Christian church specifically.

*Excerpt:* "I am not included within the pale of this glorious anniversary! Your high independence only reveals the immeasurable distance between us. The blessings in which you, this day, rejoice are not enjoyed in common...This Fourth of July is yours, not mine. You may rejoice. I must mourn....What to the Slave is the Fourth of July? I answer: a day that reveals to him, more than all other days in the year, the gross injustice and cruelty to which is the constant victim....You boast of your love of liberty, your superior civilization and your pure Christianity, while the whole political power of the nation.... solemnly pledge to support and perpetuate the enslavement of three millions of your countrymen!" ....'Of one blood God made all nations of men to dwell on the face of the earth' (Acts 17: 26), yet you notoriously hate (and glory in your hatred) all men whose skins are not colored like your own....The existence of slavery in this country brands your republicanism as a sham, your humanity as a false premise, and your Christianity as a lie."

*Impact:* The largely white audience was more than simply surprised—many listeners were stunned! Douglass had begun his address with conventional praise for the well-known accomplishments of the Founding Fathers. And then he turned the tables. An old definition of a prophet comes to mind—one who "comforts the afflicted and afflicts the comfortable." Douglass was often the prophet, never more so than in this speech that received a larger audience through published excerpts that were circulated in abolitionist circles. Douglass' reputation was well established by the beginning of the Civil War. Large audiences gathered at every venue in which he spoke. He believed that black men should fight for their freedom and/or the freedom of other black men and women. In 1863 Douglass conferred with Abraham Lincoln on the treatment of black soldiers in the Union army, and after the war he conferred with Andrew Johnson on the topic of suffrage for freedmen. After the war, and during Reconstruction, Douglass continued to speak for human rights, especially for women's suffrage, and he attacked the racism and other discrimination he witnessed in various organizations. On February 20, 1875, after having been given a standing ovation by the National Council of Women convention earlier in the day, he died of a massive stroke or heart attack.

*Contemporary Application:* There is an old over-simplification about there being only two kinds of speakers—those who have something to say and those who have to say something. Too many ceremonial occasions tap the talents of speakers who "have to say something" befitting the occasion. Douglass truly "had something to say" from his heart, emanating from a lifetime of experience. A speaker who speaks one's passion and delivers it courageously before an audience that may or may not agree will truly impact the course of history in some way, great or small.

*Connection to Today:* One easily sees that Frederick Douglass pioneered in a tradition of African-American orators that courageously and prophetically confronted white Americans on the issue of racial justice and equal rights, a pantheon that certainly includes Martin Luther King, Jr. With courage and forthrightness, Douglass played a vital role in the eventual arrival of social justice for African-Americans, though clearly racial issues and tension abide.

## 27. William Lloyd Garrison, No Compromise With Slavery, February 14, 1854

*Speaker:* William Lloyd Garrison (1805–1879), born in Massachusetts and brought up in a broken home and poverty, matured in his thinking about reform issues, and then learned every possible skill of the rhetorician—the fiery public speech; the published editorial; speaking and writing campaigns; and dramatic nonverbal demonstration. He championed a number of reformist causes (including women's suffrage, pacifism, and prohibition), yet abolitionism was the one for which he became best known. In 1829, after two early ventures in publishing and editing reform-minded papers, he joined a Quaker friend, Benjamin Lundy, in issuing the *Genius of Universal Emancipation*, an abolitionist paper in Baltimore. In 1830 he spent seven weeks in jail for libel after writing an editorial denouncing a Newburyport merchant engaged in the slave trade. In 1832 he founded the New England Anti-slavery Society and, one year later, the American Anti-Slavery Society. Garrison had truly developed a strong passion for abolishing American slavery, thus he not only conducted speaking tours before audiences willing to listen to his moral and practical arguments, but he also began publishing *The Liberator*. His philosophy was succinctly stated on the first page of the first issue: "I do not wish to think or speak or write with moderation….I am in earnest—I will not equivocate—I will not excuse—I will not retreat a single inch—AND I WILL BE HEARD." Clearly, Garrison minced no words in his denunciation of slavery. The speaker was balding, sober in appearance with a professorial air, and dressed in black apparel, yet obviously passionate. His rhetoric was a harsh and unrelenting attack on the defenders of slavery. Little wonder that Garrison was almost always in a storm of controversy, often booed, jeered, even stoned and mobbed at times by angry Southern sympathizers—the plight of many other abolitionist speakers.

*Occasion:* The crusade against slavery began around 1830. The first significant speech of the reform-minded Garrison delivered on the evil of slavery was an oration presented July 4, 1829, at the Park Street Church in Boston. There, he asserted "the right of the free States to demand a gradual abolition of slavery, because, by its continuance, they participate in the guilt thereof." From this speech and in the following few months, Garrison moved from "gradualism" to "immediatism" in abolition. In the 1830s he began making speeches attended by prominent citizens, especially area ministers, and he certainly influenced other abolitionists, such as Wendell Phillips and Parker Pillsbury. This speech was presented at the Broadway Tabernacle in New York, and the speaker's "no compromise" position was stoutly defended as "the highest expediency, the soundest philosophy, the noblest patriotism, the broadest philanthropy, and the best religion extant."

*Excerpt:* "The abolitionism which I advocate is as absolute as the law of God, and as unyielding as his throne. It admits of no compromise. Every slave is a stolen man; every slaveholder is a man stealer. By no precedent, no example, no law, no compact, no purchase, no bequest, no inheritance, no combination of circumstances, is slaveholding right or justifiable. While a slave remains in his fetters, the land must have no rest. Whatever sanctions his doom must be pronounced accursed. The law that makes him a chattel is to be trampled underfoot; the compact that is formed at his expense, and cemented with his blood, is null and void; the church that consents to his enslavement is horribly atheistical; the religion that receives to its communion the enslaver is the embodiment of all criminality. Such, at least, is the verdict of my own soul, on the supposition that I am to be the slave; that my wife is to be sold from me for the vilest purposes; that my children are to be torn from my arms, and disposed of to the highest bidder, like sheep in the market. And who am I but a man? What right have I to be free, that another man cannot prove himself to possess by nature? Who or what are my wife and children, that they should not be herded with four-footed beasts, as well as others thus sacredly related?"

*Impact:* Though disdained and persecuted by those who disagreed, Garrison's searing rhetorical efforts ushered a new era in American thinking—that gradualism and irresponsibility were no longer appropriate in abolitionist thinking; that slavery must be denounced as an evil; those who were not against slavery were in favor of it; and that slavery must be fought immediately by any and every means available. Garrison argued three assumptions in this persuasive speech: (1) All men are created equal and whatever turns a man into a "thing" is the worst form of oppression; (2) Despite our national heritage of freedom, the wealth, enterprise, literature, politics, and religion of the nation all support slave interests that eventually will destroy the nation; and (3) There can be no compromise with the evil of slavery, even for the purpose of preserving the Union. The speaker could use both constitutional and religious arguments. With this speech, Garrison further solidified his position as a radical. Not only in this speech but in all other reform addresses, Garrison could prick the conscience of his listeners and rouse moral indignation, thus making increasing numbers of Americans realize that slavery was neither right nor natural, thus it was indefensible.

*Little Known Fact:* On July 4, 1850, at a meeting in Framingham, Massachusetts, Garrison performed the ultimate act of defiance against those who wanted to preserve the Union first and abolish slavery second—he set fire to a copy of the U. S. Constitution, exclaiming: "So perish all compromises with tyranny!" Because the Constitution acknowledged slavery, Garrison often called that document "a covenant with death, an agreement with hell" (adducing Old Testament prophetic language).

*Contemporary Application:* If one chooses an uncompromising, "in your face," agitating rhetorical style, similar to that of the Old Testament prophets, then one should prepare to be stoned, figuratively or literally.

# 28. Abraham Lincoln, "House Divided" Address, June 16, 1858

*Speaker:* Abraham Lincoln was born in 1809 near Hodgenville, Kentucky, though almost always associated with the state of Illinois. The progression from a humble birth to becoming one of the greatest U. S. presidents was marked both by various occupations as well as setbacks and political defeats. Lincoln was self-educated, but became one of the most reputable lawyers in Illinois. He tried his hand at a variety of occupations—flatboatman, storekeeper, postmaster, surveyor, blacksmith—before studying law and then eventually entering politics. One might say that Lincoln was striking in physical appearance—true enough, though not striking in a positive way. He seemed lacking in "outward natural graces," and thus not naturally at ease in public speaking situations. Yet he had true intellectual curiosity and a retentive mind. In the frontier West of the early nineteenth century, there were opportunities for Lincoln to have an audience at outdoor gatherings and then in the courtroom where crowds attended sessions to see the judges and to hear the lawyers contend with both argument and wit for victory and fame. Lincoln was fully aware of the power of the spoken word, and a career in politics seemed the most interesting way to escape any occupation that required intense physical labor. The countryside was Lincoln's auditorium, and the young Abe was willing to practice an oration whenever only a handful of eager friends were willing to sit and listen. He found small audiences at home, in neighborhood social meetings, in shops, and in the country store. In these impromptu speeches, he shared his wisdom, insight, stories, and humor. His first political speech seems to have been made on a stump in an impromptu refutation of a backwoods orator ranting against the "old-line Whigs" (Lincoln had strong sympathies for the Whigs). When he announced his candidacy for the state legislature in 1832, the stump speaking art became even more important to him as he was relatively unknown at that time. (More on Lincoln as a speaker in discussion of other Lincoln speeches.)

*Occasion*: By the 1850s Lincoln had already established a reputation for himself as an up-and-coming political figure in the Whig Party. One important speech by Lincoln as a member of the House of Representatives was delivered in the House chamber on January 12, 1848—a speech of dissent to President Polk's Mexican War policy. Lincoln waged an argument that, point by point, sought to refute every contention the President had advanced in justifying the war. From the perspective of history, Lincoln seems morally and politically wise on the Mexican War issue, though at the time the young representative was labeled unpatriotic, and even some of his constituents branded him as a "Benedict Arnold." Such discouraging reception to the speech appears to have contributed to Lincoln's voluntary withdrawal from politics in 1849. In the 1850s slavery continued to be the volatile issue that could not be swept under the rug. In 1854, in his forty-fifth year, the passage of the Kansas-Nebraska Act stirred him as nothing previously. In August he began a new series of speeches, which culminated in his famous exposition at Springfield on October 4; herein, he explained his certainty that slavery's "ultimate extinction" would occur because slavery was morally wrong, and abolition could be accomplished under the Constitution by simply preventing its extension into any new territories. Just as the Whig Party was dying, the notoriety of Lincoln was rising along with a new political party known as Republican. In June 1858 in Springfield, the new Republican Party agreed to nominate Lincoln as a candidate to the U. S. Senate. The nominee then turned to careful preparation of an acceptance speech that would state clearly his position on slavery, his accusation against the Democrats for abetting the expansion of slavery, his analysis of recent, critical events, and his prediction about the future of the nation.

*Excerpt*: "'A house divided against itself cannot stand.' I believe this Government cannot endure permanently half slave and half free. I do not expect the Union to be dissolved—I do not expect the house to fall—but I do expect it will cease to be divided. It will become all one thing, or all the other."

*Impact:* This speech turned out to be pivotal in Lincoln's political career, not only garnering national publicity, but laying a foundation for which the nominee would, two years later, run for the nomination to the nation's highest office. Lincoln drew from his knowledge of the New Testament to advance a figurative analogy, borrowing words of simple wisdom from Jesus: "A house divided against itself cannot stand." The brief phrase was so poignant that it provided the informal name for the speech. Surely everyone in the Bible-believing, churchgoing audience had heard Jesus' proverb from sermons or Bible study. Lincoln used the speech to accuse the Democratic Party of abetting the expansion of slavery and to analyze three recent, critical events: (1) the Kansas-Nebraska Act, which allowed voters in western territories to decide if they wanted slavery; (2) the Supreme Court's *Dred Scott* decision of 1857, which held that blacks were not [and could not be] citizens of the U. S.; and (3) the bitter controversy over the legitimacy of the Lecompton Constitution, a document written by pro-slavery settlers attempting to avoid a popular referendum (when submitted to voters it was overwhelmingly rejected). The highly partisan audience seemed to enjoy Lincoln describing these events as "a piece of machinery" constructed by "Stephen, Franklin, Roger, and James"— Senator Douglas, ex-President Franklin Pierce, Chief Justice Roger Taney, and President James Buchanan—all Democrats. This speech sounded radical to a national audience, yet served as Lincoln's dress rehearsal for his seven debates with Stephen Douglas, the Democratic nominee for the Senate.

*Contemporary Application:* A proverb or a figurative analogy does not prove anything, especially for an audience that tends not to concur with the speaker, but it can indeed make a speech memorable to a highly friendly, partisan gathering.

# 29. Abraham Lincoln, Cooper Union Address, February 27, 1860

*Speaker:* Lincoln was not a born orator who possessed a terrific voice and confidence that commanded immediate attention. His voice was higher pitched than most male public speakers and at times he wrestled with stage fright. Yet Lincoln did have an inquiring and retentive mind, was an avid reader, and enjoyed telling stories. He practiced his speaking by doing oral reading, later learned to enjoy debating (which he put to good use when running for the Senate against Stephen Douglas in 1858), and was willing to mount a stump and present a speech whenever there were listeners gathered to listen. His great dislike for manual labor may have led him to seek a career in law and then politics. Lincoln typically displayed courage in his oratory. In 1848 he spoke out strongly against the Mexican War and was strongly rebuffed. His political career rose in the 1850s, a decade of crisis, and on June 16, 1858, he delivered his famous "House Divided" speech in Springfield, Illinois, that brought nomination for U. S. Senator, and this led to a series of seven nationally publicized debates for the Senate seat with Democratic candidate Stephen A. Douglas. In these speeches and debates, the candidate persistently used argument, history, homely illustrations, and rhetorical questions to wage arguments against Douglas' doctrine of "popular sovereignty." His rhetorical strategy kept Douglas always on the defensive. (For more discussion on the debates, see the chapter "Town Meeting of the Mind.")

*Occasion:* Lincoln's debate performance with Douglas attracted the attention of many eastern Republicans, so he received an invitation in the fall of 1859 to speak in a lecture series sponsored by Henry Ward Beecher's Plymouth Church in Brooklyn. After consultation, the event was transferred to New York City and sponsored by the "Young Men's Central Republican Union," otherwise known as Cooper Union, a forum for progressive causes. The venue was a well-known lecture hall fitted with two thousand revolving chairs upholstered in red leather, though a number of pillars obstructed the view between speakers and audiences. The meeting was well-publicized and the hall was almost filled, even if Lincoln was not considered a leading candidate for presidential nomination at that time. William Cullen Bryant was chosen as chairman, and he gave Lincoln a brief, yet gracious, introduction. Lincoln never worked as hard in preparing any previous speech as he did this one. The stakes were high. The issue was crucially important: Did the Founding Fathers believe, with Lincoln, that the control of slavery in the territories rested with Congress, or did they believe, with Douglas, that this authority rested with the territories? Lincoln no longer dealt with probabilities, but with direct evidence the Founders intended to leave slavery where it existed, an evil to be tolerated but not extended. The speaker also wanted to convince his audience that the political philosophy of his main opponent, Stephen Douglas, would lead to the nationalization of slavery. Standing to speak, Lincoln at first did not seem so confident or impressive; some listeners noted the uneven pant-leg length on the speaker.

*Excerpt:* "If our sense of duty forbids this [extension of slavery], then let us stand by our duty fearlessly and effectively....Neither let us be slandered from our duty by false accusations against us, nor frightened from it by menaces of destruction to the government, nor of dungeons to ourselves. Let us have faith that right makes might, and in that faith let us to the end dare to do our duty as we understand it."

*Impact:* This has been called Lincoln's "President-making Address." Before the speech, the speaker was a "dark horse" candidate at best, known only for debating Douglas in an unsuccessful campaign for the Senate. Lincoln drew a large audience for the speech, and he drew an enthusiastic response—often they jumped to their feet in loud applause and cheers. Influential citizens attended the event, publicized the message, which was also widely distributed in the press and read all over the nation. Horace Greeley rushed Lincoln over to the *Tribune* office to read proof on the speech, so that it could appear in the next edition. Invitations to speak came pouring in; hence, the rising politician followed this triumphant reception in New York with a speaking tour of New England that brought careful attention of important delegates in the Northeast. Lincoln considered this speech the culmination of his thinking on the national slavery issue. He refused to speak during the presidential campaign because he believed he could add nothing to his clearly reasoned position. This was manifestly a rhetorical triumph for Lincoln, a combination of political skill with noble ideals and a practical purpose—qualities always needed in a democratic society. Two months and twenty-three days after this successful oration, Abraham Lincoln was nominated for the presidency by his party.

*Contemporary Application:* The Cooper Union Address shows that a person seeking candidacy to high office must appeal to logical argument that is buttressed with strong evidence if one desires to win the confidence and vote of intelligent citizens. The speech appealed to the intelligence and moral convictions of the immediate audience. The speaker avoided demagoguery and fallacious reasoning. Admittedly, he enjoyed a warm and supportive audience that appreciated the courage of his convictions.

*Connection to Today:* Students in history and political science continue to debate whether the framers of the Constitution intended to end slavery. They also enjoy rating the best and the worst U. S. presidents. Many historians, if not most, would rank Lincoln in first place. How interesting to trace the growth in stature of Lincoln through his public speeches: As a young man, he spoke first for himself; then for a new political party; then for a faction within that new party; then for a nation threatened by division and disunion; then for a nation torn asunder by fratricidal war. Then, finally, he learned to speak as philosopher, "theologian," and compassionate father for humankind—thus, provincial, partisan, nationalist, and humanist.

# 30. Abraham Lincoln, First Inaugural Address, March 4, 1861

*Speaker:* Abraham Lincoln, whose election months earlier seemed like the proverbial "last straw" for most Southerners, was facing a divided nation. Although Lincoln had been elected, in part, because of his reputation as a moderate, Southerners viewed his election as a rejection of slavery and the political power of slave owners. The speaker was crippled by partisan, slanted, and, in some cases, downright erroneous views that were circulated about him. To a majority of Southerners, Lincoln was a "radical abolitionist," "a traitor to his country," and, even worse, "an Illinois ape." Clearly, Lincoln's *ethos* had not been established with either side. He sought to get across clearly that he wanted neither war nor disunion. Yet, through it all, Lincoln's commitment to maintaining the Union was absolute. Contemporaries never thought of Lincoln as a great speaker in the traditional sense.

*Occasion:* Between 25,000 and 50,000 citizens had gathered for the ceremony near the Capitol steps, many seeing Lincoln for the first time, where the President-elect took his oath of office. Seven Southern states had already rescinded and abrogated their membership in the Union by adopting secessionist ordinances and more were expected to follow. The Confederate States of America had been formed in Montgomery, Alabama, a month earlier. Jefferson Davis had already been named president of the Confederacy. Thus, Lincoln addressed a nation on the verge of dissolution and civil war. His goal was to hold the nation together, or at least to avert a civil war. The President gave much advance thought and preparation to this speech, the most important one that he could deliver at that point in his career. He had copies of speeches on the Union and national unity as delivered by Henry Clay, Daniel Webster, and others as "food for thought" in his own preparation for this address. The address went through several drafts after consultation with various Republican leaders, especially William Seward, who greatly influenced the ending of the speech.

*Excerpt* [Peroration in which Lincoln becomes no longer the advocate, but a compassionate father, the benevolent and hopeful counselor]: "In your hands, my dissatisfied fellow countrymen, and not in mine, is the momentous issue of civil war. The Government will not assail you. You can have no conflict without being yourselves the aggressors. You have no oath registered in heaven to destroy the Government, while I shall have the most solemn one to preserve, protect, and defend it....We are not enemies, but friends. We must not be enemies. Though passion may have strained, it must break our bonds of affection. The mystic chords of memory, stretching from every battlefield and patriot grave to the very living heart and hearthstone all over this broad land, will yet swell the chorus of the Union, when again touched, as surely they will be, by the better angels of our nature."

*Impact:* Most likely, no presidential Inaugural Address went through as careful period of preparation, consultancy, changes, and reflection as this speech. The address was a last ditch effort to avert a terrible war and preserve the Union. That goal failed. Reaction to the address was largely predictable. Lincoln also needed to make clear that the Union would defend itself, that violence against the federal government would be considered rebellion, and that secession from the Union was not lawful. The speaker did communicate those ideas, at least for those who were listening. In the South, Lincoln's heart-felt plea fell on deaf ears; listeners in the new Confederacy interpreted the address to mean that war was inevitable. And perhaps it was—the terrible War began on April 12, 1861, when Confederate forces bombarded Fort Sumter at Charleston, South Carolina. Following the fall of Fort Sumter, then Virginia, Arkansas, North Carolina, and Tennessee joined the Confederacy.

*Interesting Facts/Irony:* When the President-elect rose to speak, he was visibly troubled by what to do with his tall stovepipe hat. Noting his perplexity, his

long-time political opponent Douglas offered, "Permit me, Sir," and took the
hat and held it during the ceremony. Reports vary on how strong Lincoln's
voice was during the speech, but "acres of people" were present and supposedly
everyone was able to hear the words. When the speech was completed, the
frail, eighty-four-year-old Chief Justice Taney, whose untenable and foolish
decision in *Dred Scott* had fostered Lincoln's political career, tottered forward
to administer the oath of office to the sixteenth president of the United States.

*Contemporary Application:* How do rhetorical critics rate this speech? Lincoln's
task was herculean—to be conciliatory, but firm. Clearly, had the address
convinced the Confederate states to shun war and re-unite with the Union, we
would rate the address a rousing success and list it among our top ten public
addresses. How unfortunate that Lincoln was not better known, North and
South, at the time of this Inauguration! Had citizens in all states understood
his peaceful intent, his pondering on the role of government, his effort to
understand the plight of citizens (even slaveholders) on both sides, and his
complete lack of emotional bitterness, then so much of the tragedy might
have been avoided. This shows that when issues are complex and there are
various stakeholders in a conflict who hold their position with a sense of moral
certainty, effective communication is extremely difficult to achieve. Republicans
were generally content with the speech's "moderation" and "firmness," while
Confederates and their sympathizers branded it a declaration of war. Yet, still,
though war followed, let us not judge the speech a failure. What newly elected
president from the Republican Party could have prevented the outbreak of
Civil War? To use an analogy, we must not assume that a jumper who clears
the bar set at three feet high is necessarily a more skilled athlete and better
jumper than one who barely misses clearing a bar at seven and a half feet.

*Connection to Today:* In almost every generation of Americans, seemingly, there
is a president who must deliver a speech that calls for peace or explains and
justifies the reasons for war.

# 31. Henry Ward Beecher, Liverpool Address, October 16, 1863

*Speaker:* Henry Ward Beecher (1813–1887) seemed to specialize in the grace and love of the Lord. He was a celebrated clergyman-abolitionist and the nation's best-known preacher. He was the second or third best-known man in the North, after Lincoln and possibly Grant, and he ushered in a new style of religious oratory with his terrific voice and captivating delivery. Beecher is still rated as one of the greatest preachers in American history and has also been dubbed "the Shakespeare of the Pulpit." Henry Ward was the son in the famous family of his father Lyman Beecher (1775–1863), himself a noted Calvinist preacher and educator, and he was the brother of two sisters, Catharine and Harriett, who made significant contributions in reform (Harriett was the author of *Uncle Tom's Cabin*). Beecher was alleged to have suffered a stammering problem in his speaking, but learned to overcome it and pursued higher education. Beecher polished his skills as an orator on the lecture circuit where he commanded handsome fees as a speaker. His oratorical style was renowned for humor, dialect, and even slang. In 1847 he was called to become the first pastor for the Plymouth Church in Brooklyn, the pulpit from which he built his fame. Beecher stood more on a stage that was thrust into the midst of his hearers than behind a pulpit (a simple table made of olive wood from Jerusalem). Rejecting the stern Calvinism of his father's theology, Beecher included themes of social justice in his preaching, for indeed he was more interested in moral reform and social justice than in orthodox doctrine. In the New York area, people came by trolley, horseback, on foot, and by boat ("Beecher's boats") to hear the popular religious orator speak to the rising middle class in his 3,200-seat church every Sunday. He possessed confidence, rhetorical skill, a dramatic imagination, and a flair for theatricality. Obviously not at all reluctant to embrace controversial causes, Beecher for twenty years decried slavery from his pulpit. He also funded causes that purchased the freedom of slaves as well as rifles to be sent to abolitionist forces in Kansas territory. The rifles sent to abolitionist fighters were called "Beecher Bibles." On the church's semi-circular stage he conducted a mock slavery auction that had a dramatic impact on everyone assembled. Some thought of him as "the P. T. Barnum of the pulpit." Beecher was an outspoken defender of Abraham Lincoln and the Union cause during the Civil War, though he did not shy away from leveling criticism on the President for not making the abolition of slavery a chief cause for conduct of the war.

*Occasion*: As the Civil War continued, there was increased Northern concern about growing British sympathy toward the South. At either the suggestion or request of Lincoln, Beecher traveled to England and Scotland in 1863 and delivered powerful orations to English-speaking audiences that were troubled by the loss of Southern cotton during the War. Before estimated audiences of five to six thousand people, mainly labor audiences, Beecher delivered speeches in Manchester, Glasgow, Edinburgh, Liverpool, and London. At Liverpool in Philharmonic Hall, October 16, 1863, he encountered his most hostile audience. One placard was raised that said, "Let Englishmen see that he gets the welcome he deserves." Beecher later reported about this occasion: "I sometimes felt like a shipmaster, attempting to preach on board a ship through a speaking trumpet, with a tornado on the sea and a mutiny among men."

*Excerpt*: "Great Britain…aside from moral considerations, has a direct commercial and pecuniary interest in the liberty, civilization, and wealth of every people and every nation on the globe. You have also an interest in this because you are a moral and religious people. You desire it from the highest motives; and godliness is profitable in all things….But if there were no hereafter, and if man had no progress in this life, and if there were no question of moral growth at all, it would be worth your while to protect civilization and liberty, merely as a commercial speculation."

*Impact:* Beecher's addresses at Liverpool and Manchester are still considered models of strategy for dealing with intensely hostile audiences that interrupt speakers with taunts, jeers, and booing. In Liverpool, the speaker was able to establish identification with his audience and appeal to their higher instincts of open-mindedness and fair play. As the oration continued, Beecher began to win over his audience. Employing an economic and national self-interest argument, he reasoned that support for the Confederacy and a Confederate victory would mean English complicity in a "slave empire from ocean to ocean that should have fewest customers and the largest non-buying population." This speech and others in the speaking tour helped turn European popular sentiment against the Confederate cause and was a major factor in preventing European recognition of the Confederacy as a separate nation.

*Contemporary Application:* The persuasive speaker facing a hostile audience must first establish identification or rapport with one's audience, attempt to be a fair and reasonable source of information and reasoning, and then link one's thesis with the deepest interests and needs of that audience.

*Little Known Facts:* When a keynote speaker was being considered for the raising of the national flag at Fort Sumter, where the Civil War began, the story is told that Lincoln selected Beecher to deliver the oration. "We had better send Beecher down there to deliver the address on the occasion of raising the flag," the beleaguered President stated, "because if it had not been for Beecher, there would never have been a flag to raise." After the war, Beecher urged a generous treatment of the South and spoke words of kindness about Robert E. Lee. He also supported other reform movements such as women's suffrage and temperance, and he argued for the right of Chinese to immigrate and become citizens in the United States. One sermon series used logical reasoning to reconcile Christianity and evolution.

# 32. William M. Evarts, Defense of President Andrew Johnson, May 7, 1868

*Speaker:* William M. Evarts (1818–1901) was a man of many interests and causes to which he could devote his intellect. Yet nothing summoned a devotion quite as powerfully as did clear devotion and passion for the study and practice of law. Evarts attended Yale College where he studied rhetoric and public address, practiced his oratorical skills, and engaged in collegiate debate with distinction. Early in life he entertained legal and political aspirations. Evarts' speech at a mass meeting in New York's Castle Garden was significant as his first recorded address, delivered October 30, 1850. The speech was an effective argument in refuting many of the objections that had been leveled against the Fugitive Slave Law; Evarts argued the law was valid, thus some took the speech to mean he favored slavery. Early in his legal career, he opened his own law firm and then held important positions as a U. S. attorney. He was chairman of the New York delegation at the Republican convention that nominated Lincoln for the presidency, and he was a candidate for the U. S. Senate in 1861. However, Evarts was best known for his service as lead defense counsel in the Johnson impeachment trial before the U. S. Senate. He was active in Republican Party politics, eventually serving as U. S. secretary of state, 1877-1881, and U. S. senator, 1885 to 1891. As a public speaker, Evarts admired the model of Cicero, giving the ancient Roman credit for being the "greatest lawyer among orators and the greatest orator among lawyers." In his defense of both Johnson and Beecher, he referenced Cicero as his model. The Johnson and Beecher trials were two of the most important cases in this period of American history.

*Occasion:* Andrew Johnson was the first president to take high office after an assassination and he was slated to experience another "first"—the first president to be impeached. In light of the radical measures taken by Republicans in Congress, the new president did everything he could to block Reconstruction. His purpose was to slow the process until 1868 in the hope that Northern voters would repudiate Reconstruction in the election that year. When Johnson removed Secretary of War Edwin Stanton, this appeared to violate the Tenure of Office Act, so the House impeached Johnson on February 24, 1868. Impeachment by the House does not remove an official from office. Impeachment is more like a grand jury indictment that must be tried by a petit jury, in this case the U. S. Senate, which sat as a court presided over by the chief justice; two-thirds of the Senate must vote in favor of conviction to remove a president from office. The cards were stacked against President Johnson, and the choice of the defense attorney was crucially important as the Republican-controlled Senate would be a huge challenge to convince for acquittal. Johnson chose Evarts as a member of his defense team during the President's removal trial in the Senate. The lawyer had been suggested by Secretary of State William Seward, a fellow-Republican and friend from New York. In mid-April, the President privately expressed his dissatisfaction with Evarts, whom he thought had let House prosecutor Benjamin Butler engage in unchecked character assassination. By early May, however, an emotionally rejuvenated Johnson concluded that he was "greatly pleased with Evarts' efforts." Though a talented orator, finding a single passage in such a lengthy appeal with long and winding sentences is itself a big challenge.

*Excerpt:* "Truth is to the moral world what gravitation is to the material."

*Impact:* On May 16, 1868, the Senate voted 35-19 in favor of conviction, but that fell one vote short of the two-thirds needed for removal of the President. Evarts' rhetoric proved pivotal in obtaining an acquittal after a long and complicated trial. The speaker's exposition and argument extended over four days and included a wide scope of material almost encyclopedic in nature. Evarts' appeal was essentially intellectual. Two features stand out: literary allusions from the classics in the speech content and the utter length of the summary exposition and plea, covering a period of four days (fourteen hours altogether). One contemporary called Evarts "the long sentence champion." The speech may be criticized for its length, as the speaker began to lose attention when the end seemed never to be sight. On the other hand, the speech can be judged successful in that it was instrumental in preventing Congress from using impeachment and conviction as political weapons. Johnson rewarded Evarts by appointing him attorney general. Evarts served in that position until the end of the Johnson administration in March 1869. Evarts' reputation as an orator grew, especially as a ceremonial speaker. Perhaps his most important ceremonial speech was the "Centennial Oration" in Philadelphia, on July 4, 1876; to be chosen as the keynote orator indicated the esteem in which Evarts was held. His speech was entitled "What the Age Owes to America" and was stylistically eloquent, as may be expected in ceremonial speaking.

*Contemporary Application:* One's speaking may impact the course of history; however, if the speaker is excessively lengthy and tiresome, the audience will never forget such long-windedness and may not forgive it.

*Little Known Fact:* Evarts was selected to defend America's most popular and best-known preacher, Henry Ward Beecher, against the charge of adultery with the wife of Theodore Tilton. Evarts spoke for eight days in this trial. He argued that the husband who brought the charge was disreputable and Beecher, the accused preacher, was a man of honor and nobility. The trial ended in a hung jury, thus acquitting Beecher.

*Connection to Today:* Threats of impeachment are frequent; actual impeachment is rare. Much of the nation's political life and media focus during 1998 and 1999 revolved around charges about President Bill Clinton's personal behavior in the White House. Again, it was Republicans that pushed successfully for impeachment of the President on two articles (one for perjury and one for obstruction of justice). The trial ended on February 12, 1999, with acquittal on both charges.

# 33. Henry Grady, The New South, December 21, 1886

*Speaker:* Henry W. Grady (1850-1889) was foremost a journalist and editor and secondly a speaker, but his main calling was representing the South and its post-war challenges and problems. Grady was a writer with a keen intellect, an editor with an understanding of post-Civil War America, and part owner of the *Atlanta Constitution.* His life was devoted to the study and practice of oratory. Unfortunately, he died as a young man of pneumonia, and it was not until he was thirty-six, three years before his death, that he delivered a speech that attracted more than local attention. Yet so successful was this speech, which became known as "The New South," that immediately Grady became known as an outstanding orator and spokesman linked with that movement called "The New South." Other speakers, of course, had pled for harmony between the two sections (North and South), but Grady's rhetorical themes of harmony and unity were more effective and more publicized than the pronouncements of other speakers. He had returned to Boston in 1889 to present speeches on "The Race Problem," but there, in the city of Garrison, Phillips, and Sumner, he became ill and died only two days before Christmas 1889.

*Occasion:* Southern whites had already experienced two decades to rebuild their culture, and yet some refused to relinquish the legacy of the defeated plantation-South. Prominent businessmen of the North were fully aware that many in the South had celebrated the "Lost Cause" by organizing fraternal and sororal organizations such as the United Daughters of the Confederacy (UDC), open only to whites who could prove their relation to the "first families" of the South. Its members honored Confederate heroes in various ways, from statues to grave decoration. And yet not all Southerners revered the "Lost Cause." There was Northern concern about the wisdom and security of sending capital into the South and about the trust that could be placed in the hands of Southern politicians. There was a deeper question about whether the Southern people, despite the end of the war, could meaningfully integrate socially, politically, and economically with the rest of the nation. What kind of remaining adjustments, socially and psychologically, needed to be made? In this context, the ultra-conservative New England Society invited Grady to become one of a half-dozen speakers for the annual banquet they would hold near the end of the calendar year. It was not an election year, and Grover Cleveland had just started his first term as the first post-war Democratic president. There were some three hundred influential financiers and business leaders who composed the audience. Many prominent Northern leaders, both political and business, earnestly sought reconciliation between the North and the South. All present for this speech seemed open to the idea of reconciliation with the Southern post-war generation. And in its eighty-one year history, no Southerner had been asked to address the financiers, businessmen, financiers, editors, and clergymen who constituted this prestigious New England Society, meeting this time at Delmonico's in New York City. Interestingly, distinguished clergyman DeWitt Talmadge and General William Sherman were in the audience for brief public remarks, the latter making disparaging anecdotes that belittled the Southern people. When Grady arose to speak, he experienced a severe rush of adrenaline and stage fright, by his own admission.

*Excerpt:* "There was a South of slavery and secession—that South is dead. There is a South of union and freedom—that South, thank God, is living, breathing, growing every hour....We have planted the schoolhouse on the hilltop and made it free to white and black. We have sown towns and cities in the place of theories, and put business above politics....We have established thrift in city and country. We have fallen in love with work."

*Impact:* This address must be rated as the best speech by a Southerner to a Northern audience since the end of the Civil War. Grady spoke about the

New South in a way which brought identification of both sections together and simultaneous attraction for Southern as well as Northern adherents. In a sense, this could almost be described as a speech before a hostile audience. Grady spoke with unabashed pride about the New South, speaking of the region as "prostrate and bleeding South, misguided perhaps, but beautiful in her suffering, and honest, brave and generous always." Yet the audience was won over. Listeners responded with prolonged applause, as though there was some surprise in the kindness, insights, and reconciliatory tone of the speaker. The end result was that Grady's remarks were circulated to a wider reading audience, additional speaking opportunities were afforded, and Grady received national recognition as a prominent speaker with a noble cause. Grady's tactics included a surprising use of humor, taking a bold plunge to make a comment about General Sherman, "who is considered an able man in our hearts, though some people think he is a kind of careless man about fire"….[then a pause]….."from the ashes he left us…somehow or other we have caught the sunshine in the bricks and mortar of our homes…and have builded therein not one ignoble prejudice or memory." This was a two-fold successful rhetorical strategy—it acknowledged the famous Union general, so loved in the North that many had urged him to run for president, and, it had defused the tension with a Southern public speaker addressing a Northern audience that included the general who had set fire to Atlanta. The lines constituted a masterpiece of humorous identification. And then, Grady dared to deal with the race issue in the South, and in a tactful way stated that Northern people should leave that issue "to those with whom his lot is cast." The address brought national prominence to Grady.

*Contemporary Application:* When addressing a hostile audience, begin by using humor to defuse the tension, then move to being as progressive in your thinking as possible, always looking toward the good of the future.

# 34. Susan Anthony, Women's Right to Vote, June, 1873

*Speaker:* Susan Brownell Anthony (1820–1906), raised in a liberal Quaker family in Massachusetts, emerged from school teaching to become a prominent, independent, and well-educated American civil rights leader and reformer. Though not acclaimed for her oratory, as an unmarried woman she traveled thousands of miles and spoke frequently on behalf of several causes, especially women's suffrage, for some forty-five years. She worked actively in the temperance and abolition movements in New York. In 1851 she met Elizabeth Cady Stanton, who was then raising a large number of children. A deeply religious woman, a Quaker turned liberal, Anthony was able to travel, organize, and speak during the period when Stanton needed to remain home. Both Anthony and Stanton joined the lecture circuit about 1870, occasionally traveling together, usually from mid-autumn to spring. The timing was right because the nation was beginning to discuss women's suffrage as a serious matter. Lecture bureaus scheduled their tours and handled the travel arrangements, which generally involved traveling during the day and speaking at night, sometimes for weeks at a time, including weekends. Their lectures brought new recruits into the movement who strengthened suffrage organizations at the local, state, and national levels. Anthony was superb as organizer, though not riveting as a speaker. Their journeys during that decade covered a distance that was unmatched by any other reformer or politician. When she first began campaigning for women's rights, Anthony was harshly ridiculed and accused of trying to destroy the institution of marriage. Yet her audiences were often large, at times numbering up to three thousand. Public perception changed radically during her lifetime, however. Anthony traveled west, and her lectures in Washington and four other states led directly to invitations for her to address the state legislatures there.

*Occasion:* In the 1872 presidential election, Anthony led a group of women in Rochester, New York, to the polls to vote. Since women's suffrage was illegal, she was arrested and indicted in the case of *United States v. Susan B. Anthony.* Before her trial in June 1873, Anthony traveled widely in upstate New York, giving this speech about the injustice of denying women the right to vote. She pleaded not guilty, and in this famous speech she asserts that voting is her legal right as a United States citizen under the Constitution which promises all people the blessings of liberty.

*Excerpt:* "It was we, the people; not we, the white male citizens; nor yet we, the male citizens; but we, the whole people, who formed the Union. And we formed it, not to give the blessings of liberty, but to secure them; not to the half of ourselves and the half of our posterity, but to the whole people--women as well as men. And it is a downright mockery to talk to women of their enjoyment of the blessings of liberty while they are denied the use of the only means of securing them provided by this democratic-republican government--the ballot....For any state to make sex a qualification that must ever result in the disfranchisement of one entire half of the people is to pass a bill of attainder, or an ex post facto law, and is therefore a violation of the supreme law of the land. By it the blessings of liberty are forever withheld from women and their female posterity. To them this government has no just powers derived from the consent of the governed. To them this government is not a democracy. It is not a republic. It is an odious aristocracy; a hateful oligarchy of sex; the most hateful aristocracy ever established on the face of the globe; an oligarchy of wealth, where the right govern the poor. An oligarchy of learning, where the educated govern the ignorant, or even an oligarchy of race, where the Saxon rules the African, might be endured; but this oligarchy of sex, which makes father, brothers, husband, sons, the oligarchs over the mother and sisters, the wife and daughters of every household--which ordains all men sovereigns, all women subjects, carries dissension, discord and rebellion into every home of the nation."

*Impact:* This speech, delivered about forty times to various audiences before her trial and then recited before the court in 1873, constitutes one of the greatest statements ever uttered on behalf of women's suffrage. Anthony argued no Constitutional amendment was needed to "give" women the vote, because the Fourteenth Amendment, passed in 1868, declared that "all persons born or naturalized in the United States" were citizens and entitled to the rights of citizenship. Her logic was cogent. Since women were persons and citizens, she insisted they were already fully entitled to vote. Though ultimately convicted and fined, she refused to pay the fine. No attempt was made to collect.

*Connection to Today:* Anthony did not live to see the achievement of women's suffrage at the national level, but she was proud that her voice was being heard and that progress in the women's movement had been made. At the time of her death, women had achieved suffrage in Wyoming, Utah, Colorado and Idaho, and several larger states followed soon after. Legal rights for married women had been established in most states, and most professions had at least a few women members and thousands of women were attending colleges and universities, up from zero a few decades earlier. While she did not consider herself a skilled orator, her passion and indefatigable service to the social and economic rights and betterment of women made her the most outstanding feminist leader of the nineteenth century. She became the first non-fictitious woman to be depicted on U.S. currency when her portrait appeared on the silver dollar. She has also been depicted in a humorous 2017 skit on *Saturday Night Live.*

*Contemporary Application:* A younger generation may not fully recognize how challenging it has been to achieve basic human rights often taken for granted and how much debt is owed to reform leaders who devote lives of sacrifice and endeavor to advance a just cause.

# 35. Young Joseph, "Chief Joseph," Speech of Surrender, October 5, 1877

*Speaker:* The story of Chief Joseph (1841–1904) could be traced as far back as the Lewis and Clark expedition that reached the Columbia River in the fall of 1805, where the two explorers met the Nee-me-poo Indians, whom the French called Nez Perces (pierced noses). The Indians could have killed the exhausted and hungry explorers, but instead they welcomed and fed them and assisted them on their journey. Indeed, the Indians were extending traditional hospitality to strangers. The Nez Perces were intelligent people who built huge herds and gained a reputation as skilled riders and breeders, and they pursued peaceful relations with incoming European-Americans, even establishing trade agreements. Presbyterian missionary Henry Spalding and his wife went to live and work among the tribe and other missionaries followed. A number of treaties were signed with the Nez Perces that granted land reservation for the tribe. However, more and more immigrants and miners overran the Indian Territory. A new treaty offering reduced land reservation was offered the tribe, but Old Joseph refused to sign the treaty. His people lived in the Wallowa valley in Oregon, and just before he died in 1871 old Joseph made his son promise never to sell his homeland. Young Joseph came under terrific pressure to break that promise. Settlers began to encroach into the valley belonging to the Indians, who were then told to sign a new treaty or vacate all territory.

*Occasion:* Young Joseph persuaded his people to move rather than go to war with white Americans. There was sporadic gunfire along the Salmon River. Three U. S. warriors were killed, and then the U. S. army attacked the Nez Perces, but the Indians routed the military. The military retreated, then counter-attacked, killing men, women, and children. The Nez Perces retreated in the direction of Canada, but encountered more resistance along the route. Often they fended off pursuing troops. Gunfights with the military continued. The Indians lost many of their horses, and their children were hungry and cold in the snow. While about three hundred made it to Canada, Joseph finally accepted General Nelson Miles' entreaty to surrender. We can only imagine an outdoor setting for this speech with the Chief, surely with crestfallen countenance and sad voice, speaking for his people amidst U. S. military officials. The surrender speech, as reported by Lieutenant Charles Erskin Wood, has become famous.

*Excerpt:* "Tell General Howard I know his heart. What he told me before, I have it in my heart. I am tired of fighting. Our Chiefs are killed; Looking Glass is dead, Ta Hool Hool Shute is dead. The old men are all dead. It is the young men who say yes or no. He who led on the young men is dead. It is cold, and we have no blankets; the little children are freezing to death. My people, some of them, have run away to the hills, and have no blankets, no food. No one knows where they are - perhaps freezing to death. I want to have time to look for my children, and see how many of them I can find. Maybe I shall find them among the dead. Hear me, my Chiefs! I am tired; my heart is sick and sad. From where the sun now stands I will fight no more forever."

*Impact:* The noble and courageous trek of the Nez Perces tribe, Chief Joseph's dignified conduct, and his tragic eloquence that expressed the pain and futility of fighting and killing, all captured public attention. Despite sympathy for the Nez Perces and admiration of their courage, Washington policymakers did not allow them to return to their traditional home place, and over four hundred Native Americans were dispatched to Ft. Leavenworth in November 1877. In the summer of 1878 the Nez Perces were moved to the northeastern corner of present-day Oklahoma where they huddled in refugee camps and endured hunger, misery, and malaria. Soon, more than a fourth of them died.

*Interesting Fact:* Chief Joseph traveled to Washington in January 1879, met with the President, and made an eloquent two-hour speech to a gathering of President Hayes' cabinet members, congressmen, and others in Lincoln Hall, where the speaker received a standing ovation. Joseph began his speech with words of sadness: "When I think of our condition, my heart is heavy. I see men of my own race treated as outlaws and driven from country to country, or shot down like animals." Then Joseph rhapsodized of a time when all peoples could become one, "brothers of one father and mother," living under the same sky and enjoying the same government. He closed earnestly: "For this time the Indian race is waiting and praying. I hope no more groans of wounded men and women will ever go to the ear of the Great Spirit Chief above, and that all people may be one people." Despite his eloquence, Chief Joseph died at age sixty-four without ever making it back to the land he promised his father he would never relinquish.

*Contemporary Application:* A poignant appeal by a spokesperson for a maligned and wounded people sometimes fails to elicit a sympathetic response, but those words, if kept alive by history, may become classic for their eloquent expression of the longing of the human spirit.

*Connection to Today:* There have been a number of notable speeches by Native Americans, the most powerful being addresses in which speakers spoke eloquently for freedom, property, and other rights. Native life revolved around the spoken word, as Indian culture was an oral culture. The white person's stereotype of Indian communication holds Indians as virtual mutes—one syllable, grunting communicators responding to others in the most rudimentary way, and that Tonto would be a good role model in communication. Indeed, an objective study of Indian oratory over nearly five centuries of Native American history would reveal individual eloquent expressions of resistance, outrage, sadness (even lament), reflection, meditation, appeal, and persuasion.

# 36. Robert Ingersoll, Eulogy at his Brother's Grave, June 2, 1879

*Speaker:* For more than twenty years, Robert G. Ingersoll (1833–1899) was a top ranked attorney, political campaigner, lecturer, and orator on special occasions. His father was a Congregational minister, and he did much reading in his father's theological and literary library. Ingersoll attended law school, later establishing a law partnership with his brother in the 1850s. He fought in the Civil War and was captured in Tennessee, then paroled to return to his law practice. Few American speakers have addressed themselves to as many varied audiences and won as much strong praise from their peers. Ingersoll was one of the warmest and most congenial personalities of any public speaker of his day. He was intellectually honest, sincere, earnest, and forthright, even if those admirable traits stirred the ire of many in his audience, especially fundamentalist Christian listeners. He was known as "the Great Agnostic" by inflamed orthodox clergy and laity because of his attacks on religion and the Bible. Ingersoll could vary his method of delivery, depending on the occasion, however he almost always communicated directly with his audience through genuineness, naturalness, congeniality, and, often, used humor and colloquial expressions. Many contemporaries, including Henry Ward Beecher, praised his brilliance and eloquence as a speaker. Though he delivered campaign speeches, he is best remembered for eulogies and other special occasion addresses. As one of the most popular lecturers in James Redpath's Lyceum Bureau, he made his living from the platform. Few have exceeded his persuasive power over an audience.

*Occasion:* Ingersoll was more of a skeptic and agnostic than an infidel. He felt a literal reading of the Bible's narratives rendered any claims to inerrancy to be ridiculous, thus he had a "running feud" with many prominent ministers.

Robert and his brother Ebon, the latter a prominent Illinois political and legal figure, had been intimately united in opposition to organized, orthodox religion, thus they opposed orthodox funeral services. The two brothers agreed that the surviving one should speak at the other's last rites. Several prominent national figures—including the Vice President Adlai Ewing Stevenson and the future President James A. Garfield—served as pallbearers. The ceremony itself was limited to Ingersoll's brief remarks.

*Excerpt:* "My friends, I am going to do that which the dead oft promised he would do for me. The loved and loving brother, husband, father, friend, died where manhood's morning almost touches noon, and while the shadows still were falling toward the west. He had not passed on life's highway the stone that marks the highest point, but, being weary for a moment, lay down by the wayside, and using his burden for a pillow, fell into that dreamless sleep that kisses down his eyelids still. While yet in love with life and raptured with the world, he passed to silence and pathetic dust....Life is a narrow vale between the cold and barren peaks of two eternities. We strive in vain to look beyond the heights. We cry aloud, and the only answer is the echo of our walling cry. From the voiceless lips of the unreplying dead there comes no word; but in the night of death, hope sees a star and listening love can hear the rustle of a wing. He who sleeps here, when dying, mistaking the approach of death for the return to health, whispered with his last breath: 'I am better now.' Let us believe, in spite of doubts and dogmas, and tears and fears, that these words are true of all the countless dead. And now to you who have chosen, from among the many men he loved, to do the last sad office for the dead, we give his sacred dust. Speech cannot contain our love. There was, there is, no greater stronger, manlier man."

*Impact:* Ingersoll's eulogy is acknowledged as one of the most eloquent of all American orations and has been published in many anthologies. Like Lincoln's Gettysburg Address, the speech is brief yet made memorable by picturesque language and abundant stylistic devices such as alliteration and rhyme. The peroration of this speech has been oft-quoted by clergy at funeral services. Thus, the address has lived on as great American literature. His expression, "Hope sees a star and listening love can hear the rustle of a wing," gave insight into his own religious thinking. Many clergy who noted his opposition to organized religion cite this statement as evidence that deep inside his mind and heart Ingersoll was actually a believer in God and immortality or that he earnestly wanted to believe. More than Beecher and other "liberals," Ingersoll was greatly influenced by European rationalism as espoused by Voltaire, Paine, and then Darwin, and Huxley. With a reputation for excellence in eulogies, Ingersoll also delivered public tributes at the gravesites of a child (January 8, 1882), and for Roscoe Conkling, Walt Whitman, Thomas Corwin, and Henry Ward Beecher. Ingersoll is something of a folk hero for contemporary free thinkers.

*Contemporary Application:* A speaker who is intelligent, well-prepared, and eloquent in expression, will gain the respect of the majority in the audience and be highly regarded by future generations.

*Interesting Fact:* Ingersoll gave numerous speeches as a popular lecturer, speaking in nearly every city of any size in the Midwest. His most provocative lecture, entitled "The Mistakes of Moses," makes a running tour of the first five books of the Bible and points out what, to him, exist such incredible and unlikely details that those Old Testament stories could not be taken either as inerrant or literal history. Ingersoll had many in his audience heartily laughing when he discussed religion, all the while stirring both anger and frustration among orthodox believers who were present. Not surprisingly, his religious ridicule provided fodder for preachers to load up in personal attacks against him, and some preachers publicly denounced him as "the Great Blasphemer"— not that Ingersoll cared or could be slowed down! His popular lectures have been published in book form.

# 37. Samuel Gompers, "What Does the Working Man Want?" May 1, 1890

*Speaker:* In the late nineteenth century, the growing power of industrial corporations and the declining power of workers gave rise to social tensions reminiscent of the sectional crisis that triggered the Civil War. The labor movement became embroiled in controversy stirred by a number of fiery, eloquent speakers, none more fervent than Samuel Gompers (1850–1924). Born in London, he immigrated to New York as a young boy and eventually followed his father's trade as a cigar maker. He pursued studies at Cooper Union Institute and studied law and politics on his own; he was active in a social and debating club. Most of all, he learned through the real life experience of observing working conditions in the sweat shops of the Lower East Side of New York which became his base. Gompers was not interested in utopian dreams of an ideal society, nor was he interested in organizing labor for the purpose of political ends. He stuck to basic employee issues such as hours, wages, and safety. He did work in the mayoral campaign of Henry George in 1886, but labor—not politics—was his primary passion. On December 7, 1886, Gompers delivered an eloquent address to the Federation of Organized Trades and Labor Unions, extoling the benefits of trade unionism, explaining his understanding of the psychology of employees, and declaring that labor leaders were "against riot, tumult, and anarchy" and assuring that society was safe with trade unionism. The speech evoked such a favorable response that the American Federation of Labor was formed, and Gompers was elected president. He held that position, except for one year, until his death. His adult life was almost a continuous public speaking career before labor groups, business, political, and educational groups in the United States and Europe. As a speaker, Gompers posed a striking appearance. Though short in stature, about five feet and three inches, he had broad shoulders, massive chest, and a large head supported by a thick neck, with his torso on short, stubby legs. He spoke almost exclusively in an extemporaneous style, usually without notes as he knew passionately what he wanted to communicate. There were few if any references to anything scholarly in his messages, but the personal pronoun "I" is used frequently due to the speaker's sharing personal experiences in the labor force. All of this rendered a spontaneity and sincerity to his style.

*Occasion:* The decades after the Civil War were times of tension in the American labor force. Corporations and other capitalists seemed chiefly concerned with high business profits and personal wealth. There were wild swings in the business cycle. Two prolonged depressions, one beginning in 1873 and the other in 1893, threw as many as two million laborers out of work. Skilled workers were hit hard: unhealthy working environments; excessive hours of labor; continued wage reductions; and exploitation of women and children. Employers bitterly opposed and resented labor unions and sought court injunctions to break boycotts and strikes. In this context, there was both despair as well as a growing spirit of revolt among workers. In general, the public was hostile to the labor movement and suspicious of radicalism. In this and other addresses, Gompers sought to remove the radical image that business leaders and employers tried to pin on labor and to demonstrate that workers wanted what everyone else wanted: a better life, fair wages, decent and safe working conditions, and time for cultural enrichment. This speech was delivered in Louisville, Kentucky, when Gompers was campaigning to establish the eight-hour workday.

*Excerpt:* "We want time...time with which our lives begin; time with which our lives close; time to cultivate the better nature within us; time to brighten our homes. Time which brings us from the lowest condition up to the highest civilization; time so we can raise men to a higher plane....We want eight hours and nothing less. We have been accused of being selfish, and it has been said that we will want more...We do want more."

*Impact:* This speech had a receptive audience that frequently cheered Gompers' declarations and comments. While clearly no scholar or precise thinker, Gompers conveyed understanding of the plight of the worker. With this speech and hundreds of similar addresses, he made a successful career speaking to labor and for labor. Gompers increased his credibility with this address and proved that he could speak persuasively for skilled laborers. The American Federation of Labor (AFL) became a collection of skilled craft unions. Gompers' oratory, as well as dedication from other labor leaders, led the AFL's effectiveness in working for laborers' specific interests rather than broad social changes sought by Socialists and anarchists. This is reflected in its growth—with approximately 150,000 members in 1886, the federation passed the million mark in 1901. The emerging labor movement, for better or worse, bore the unmistakable image of the character of Gompers' philosophy and policies, and it survived despite adversity and internal dissension.

*Contemporary Application:* The ability to identify with one's listeners, as one of them in real life experience, will facilitate a leader's persuasive skills and effectiveness, even when that speaker lacks high intellectual or educational achievements.

*Interesting Fact:* There is no labor party in the U. S., unlike the political structure of some other nations. One reason for this fact is the thinking and speaking of Samuel Gompers. On December 19, 1918, Gompers presented an address at the Continental Hotel, New York City, in which he argued against a proposal to form a new political party—a labor party. Almost ten days after the speech, the executive council of the AFL unanimously endorsed Article II, Section 8, of the AFL constitution: "Party politics, whether they be Democratic, Republican, Socialist, Populistic, Prohibition, or other, shall have no place in the Conventions of the American Federation of Labor." Since the era of Franklin Roosevelt, the Democratic Party has largely represented the interests of the American labor force and unionism.

# 38. Elizabeth Cady Stanton, The Solitude of Self, January 20, 1892

*Speaker:* Elizabeth Cady Stanton lived a remarkable life, full of achievement and recognition as America's leading feminist. She enjoyed a prolific career as a reformer, and, while best known as an orator for over six decades, she was also a writer and editor. The subject area of her writing and editing, of course, was women's rights. She also edited and wrote parts of the controversial *The Woman's Bible* (1895, 1898). Stanton delivered speeches as a lecturer within the New York Lyceum Bureau from 1869 to 1881, traveling to at least thirty cities and delivering speeches to various audiences. Her fees of $3,000 a year were sufficient to provide a higher education for her seven children. She was a founder of the American Equal Rights Association, the National Woman's Loyalty League, and the National Woman Suffrage Association. Additionally, she was the first woman to run for the United States Congress. Stanton was an excellent orator, often addressing mixed audiences in an age when a large percentage of the American public felt it inappropriate, even shameful and sinful, for a woman to speak publicly and exercise leadership skills. Little wonder, then, she had more than her share of opponents and detractors. Stanton is best known for her role in drafting and then delivering the Declaration of Sentiments to the Seneca Falls Convention in 1848, a conference and address that historians consider the launching of the women's movement within the USA. Long before the speech cited here was presented, Stanton had established her place as the outstanding U. S. feminist reformer of the nineteenth century.

*Occasion:* Stanton delivered "The Solitude of Self' three times over a three-day period: first to the House Committee on the Judiciary on January 18, then before the NAWSA convention on January 20, and finally to the Senate committee on suffrage later that day. The immediate audience for this speech was overwhelmingly male, providing another opportunity to inform and exhort legislators in what women need and deserve most. The speech was reprinted in the *Congressional Record* and the *Woman's Journal*.

*Excerpt:* "The strongest reason why we ask for woman a voice in the government under which she lives; in the religion she is asked to believe; equality in social life, where she is the chief factor; a place in the trades and professions, where she may earn her bread, is because of her birthright to self-sovereignty; because, as an individual, she must rely on herself. No matter how much women prefer to lean, to be protected and supported, nor how much men desire to have them do so, they must make the voyage of life alone, and for safety in an emergency they must know something of the laws of navigation. To guide our own craft, we must be captain, pilot, engineer; with chart and compass to stand at the wheel; to match the wind and waves and know when to take in the sail, and to read the signs in the firmament over all. It matters not whether the solitary voyager is man or woman….And yet, there is a solitude, which each and every one of us has always carried with him, more inaccessible than the ice-cold mountains, more profound than the midnight sea; the solitude of self. Our inner being, which we call our self, no eye nor touch of man or angel has ever pierced. It is more hidden than the caves of the gnome; the sacred adytum of the oracle; the hidden chamber of Eleusinian mystery, for to it only omniscience is permitted to enter. Such is individual life. Who, I ask you, can take, dare take, on himself the rights, the duties, the responsibilities of another human soul?"

*Impact:* Stanton delivered this speech when she was seventy-six years old, at the end of a career dedicated to reform. The speech is considered to be the finest statement of her feminist ideology, the sharing of her personal philosophy. The speaker argues forcefully and directly, yet harbors no sense of animosity, condemnation, self-congratulation, or complacency. As always in arguing the feminist cause, Stanton draws from natural rights philosophy. Clearly, she had not backed away from her lifelong passion for the feminist cause. She was unrelenting in her demand for "self-sovereignty" in all areas of women's lives—in government, the trades and the professions. Her contention: Until there is equality, women remain "ostracized," and "to refuse political equality is to rob the ostracized of all self-respect; of credit in the marketplace; of recompense in the world of work; of a voice in choosing those who make and administer law....Robbed of her natural rights, handicapped by law and custom at every turn, yet compelled to fight her own battles, and in the emergencies of life to fall back on herself for protection." According to Stanton, only women fully understand their plight: "Whatever the theories may be of women's dependence on man...he cannot bear her burdens." Frederick Douglass was struck in awe of the speech ("After her—silence," he reported), and Susan B. Anthony called this address "the strongest and most unanswerable argument and appeal made by the pen or tongue for the full freedom and franchise of women" (Quoted in Campbell and Huxman's *The Rhetorical Act*, 4th edition, p. 222).

*Contemporary Application:* This speech was the climax of a long career of reform advocacy. Stanton considered it to be "the best thing I have ever written." The most effective speakers develop a passion for an honorable cause and devote their lives to advancing that cause. When a lifetime is spent in such relentless and sacrificial advocacy, that person has earned the right to reflect on the past and share what remains to be accomplished by a future generation.

*Connection to Today:* Some one hundred and twenty-five years after this speech was presented, feminists and political leaders are still speaking about the need to close the gender gap in terms of certain rights, especially equal pay for equal work.

# 39. Booker T. Washington, Atlanta Exposition Address, September 18, 1895

*Speaker:* Booker T. Washington (1856–1915) was born a slave in Franklin County, Virginia, worked in a salt furnace and a coal mine until he was able to enter Hampton Institute, then becoming a school teacher; he later entered Wayland Seminary, then returned to teaching. Washington came to prominence during the emergence of the "New South." He was chosen principal of Tuskegee Normal and Industrial Institute in Alabama, serving from 1881 to 1915. During these thirty-four years, Washington built Tuskegee from an impoverished, struggling school into a major institution with 1,500 students. He once declared in his autobiography, *Up From Slavery,* that he never planned to devote much of his life to public speaking, yet during his career he delivered from two to four thousand speeches. Though he preferred to produce achievements rather than talk about them, Washington probably never made a speech that did not advance his cause and his program; thus his speeches were persuasive presentations. That program was "Negro advancement" and racial harmony in America. Washington believed the path to advancement for blacks was through industrial education, small scale entrepreneurship, and hard work. The black man could thereby make himself useful, even indispensable, to his own community. The desirable character traits for African-Americans would be industry, dependability, honesty, pride, patience, temperance, and moral goodness—and industriousness was second to none. In promoting this program, Washington spoke to all kinds of audiences: Northern groups, Southern groups, educated groups, and uneducated audiences. He spoke on numerous special occasions. More than any other black orator, Washington's own character and personality provided the greatest source of his persuasiveness. That *ethos* was enhanced by the speaker's modesty and humility. In no speech does Washington speak of what "I did" in developing

Tuskegee. He often gives credit to others and his speeches are sprinkled with "I believe" and "it seems to me." He always exhibited courtesy and tact, never playing the North and South against each other. His speeches were delivered in a lively, direct conversational mode.

*Occasion:* The South in the late nineteenth century seemed as fully segregated as in the days of slavery. Minority rights in the South had been imperiled by the passage of Jim Crow laws. The idea of any black leader even discussing and attempting advancement of racial desegregation and racial integration in social contexts seemed so unrealistic and unlikely. The audience of the Cotton States and International Exposition in Atlanta was largely a white gathering, and the very fact that Washington was invited to speak was considered newsworthy. There were some blacks in attendance, also, and once again Washington was challenged by the need for audience adaptation. In his speech the speaker asked whites to take note of "our humble effort at an exhibition of progress," and he counseled fellow African-Americans to cultivate "the common occupations of life," to develop friendly relations with their white neighbors, and to begin "at the bottom" and not the top.

*Excerpt:* "In all things that are purely social we can be separate as the fingers, yet one as the hand in all things essential to mutual progress."

*Impact:* This address reinforced Booker T. Washington's reputation as an orator, and it became the most notable speech he ever delivered. The speech demonstrates the speaker's skill in choosing simple illustrations and stylistic devices to support his main points. The figurative analogy in the above excerpt illustrates how analogies and similes can clarify and enliven the basic theme. Washington began his oration with a simple story of a ship lost at sea for many days and the captain finally sighted another vessel, then sent out a signal: "Water, water, we die of thirst." And the answer came back at once: "Cast down your bucket where you are," and after several similar exchanges the captain who was lost then realized they were sailing in the fresh water of the mouth of the Amazon River. The application: "To those of my race, I would say [rather than waiting or complaining] 'Cast down your bucket where you are.'" The immediate response to Washington was positive from white listeners. They cheered his speech, and he was highly acclaimed and respected by white Southerners and Northerners. Little wonder over the enthusiastic reception by white listeners after all—The speaker had contended that "the wisest among my race understand that agitation of questions of social equality is the extremist folly, and that progress in the enjoyment of all privileges that will come to us must be the result of severe and constant struggle rather than of artificial forces." In 1901 Washington was invited by President Theodore Roosevelt to visit the White House. And from the time of this address until his death, Washington was considered the most powerful black American of his day. On the other hand, black leaders such as W. E. B. Du Bois rejected his counsel for moderation and patience and called this speech the "Atlanta Compromise." These leaders also rejected Washington's emphasis on industrial education at the expense of academic education and the opportunity to rise in professional careers.

*Contemporary Application:* Washington demonstrated that a person can face stage fright head on and become a renowned speaker. In *Up From Slavery*, he confessed: "I always suffer intensely from nervousness before speaking. More than once, just before I was to make an important address, this nervous strain has been so great that I have resolved never again to speak in public." Nonetheless, he established a strong reputation as an orator.

*Connection to Today:* Washington would seem an "accomodationist" on race relations by today's standards. Today, some might consider him the quintessence of an "Uncle Tom," a black leader committed to accepting and rationalizing second-class status of his own people. Yet Washington must be understood in terms of the historical context in which he lived, taught, and spoke, and thus deserves recognition for advancing educational causes among African-Americans in the nineteenth century. The same could be said for educational leaders of other historic black colleges and institutes of the later national period.

# 40. William Jennings Bryan, "Cross of Gold" Convention Address, July 9, 1896

*Speaker:* William Jennings Bryan (1850–1925) was undoubtedly the voice of the "common people" of America for a full generation. For more than thirty-seven years, he spoke for his party, dominating every Democratic national convention, voicing his belief in the inherent dignity of the ordinary citizen. "The Great Commoner" was a politician, for sure, becoming a national figure at thirty-six, but he is best remembered as a dynamic public speaker, one of the most effective orators in the nation's history. He was an attorney, Chautauqua lecturer, member of Congress, newspaper editor, Democratic leader, and vigorous campaigner. There is no way to know exactly how many speeches he delivered in a lifetime, numbering in the thousands on a range of topics in the fields of religion and politics. Bryan was nominated three times for the office of president and experienced defeat each time, yet he probably saw more clearly the danger in more aspects of public policy than any public figure of his day—His ideas on gold, taxation, and imperialism have been vindicated by history. Bryan was called a "silver-tongued orator," an old and vague cliché, for sure, but the label was rooted in a total public consensus—Bryan's speaking skills constituted the most dynamic and compelling strategy in a long and honorable political career. Friends and enemies attested to his effectiveness as an orator. Only after he turned to espouse fundamentalist Christian causes and delivering numerous lectures and sermons on the Christian faith was his reputation sullied in the minds of some Americans, especially academics and other professionals.

*Occasion:* One of the most divisive issues of the late nineteenth century was whether the federal government should increase the circulation of money, a policy which would alleviate the squeeze on very poor workers and family farmers by coining silver instead of relying on the gold supply. Enthusiasm for a third party was strong in the mountain states and plains, and the People's Party was organized with a platform that called for unlimited coinage of silver and other progressive federal action to benefit income-strapped farmers and workers. The Populists did not win an election, but Democratic dissidents took over their party and adopted free silver as the centerpiece of their program. Enter William Jennings Bryan, the new and charismatic "silver-tongued orator," a one-term congressman from Nebraska, who had taken up the cause of free silver. He came to this Democratic convention as a young delegate, only thirty-six years old, but was given the opportunity to make the closing speech in the debate on the silver plank of the party's platform. Consider that the convention and its oratory occurred in the age before radio and television.

*Excerpt:* "If the gold standard advocates win, this country will be dominated by the financial harpies of Wall Street. I am trying to save the American people from that disaster—which will mean the enslavement of the farmers, merchants, manufacturers, and laboring classes to the most merciless and unscrupulous gang of speculators on earth—the money power....We defy them....If they dare to come out in the open...we will fight them to the utter-most. Having behind us the producing masses of this nation and the world, supported by the commercial interests, the laboring interest, and the toilers everywhere, we will answer their demand for a gold standard by saying to them: You shall not press down upon the brow of labor this crown of thorns, you shall not crucify mankind upon a cross of gold."

*Impact:* The convention speech was wildly effective—it catapulted Bryan to the presidential nomination. After repeated applause, the peroration (closing) of the speech brought the house to its feet in a frenzy of thunderous cheering. Throughout a long and vigorous career of public speaking, this speech always remained his best and most effective effort, especially in terms of the immediate response. The speech led delegates to insist Bryan be placed at the top of the

Democratic ticket, thus making him the youngest presidential candidate in American history, only a year older than the minimum age stipulated by the Constitution. In the '96 campaign, Bryan toured the country in a whistle-stop campaign, traveling 18,000 miles in twenty-one states and speaking to five million (fifteen to thirty speeches a day), and the Republicans, realizing his speaking influence, spent an overwhelming amount of funds to defeat him. In this pre-electronic age, Bryan's speech became the standard by which to measure political oratory, with plain and simple language understandable to readers of cold print as well as to 20,000 listeners in a hot convention hall. The 1896 election was the most impassioned and exciting in a generation as many citizens believed the fate of the nation hinged on the outcome. Republican rhetoric aroused fear about the Democrats, and William McKinley rode to victory by carrying every state in the northeast quadrant of the country while Bryan carried most of the South and West.

*Contemporary Application:* While the style of delivery has now changed from the old-fashioned one that relied on a loud and dramatic voice and almost exaggerated gesturing in contrast to the lively conversational style, there is one factor that has not changed—the role of emotion in stirring the passions which lead to action. We may also consider the role of "social facilitation," wherein the response of most listeners gathered for a speech will influence the emotional response of most others in the audience. Another application: It takes more than a rousing speech to win a general election.

*Connection to Today:* In many ways, Bryan's dynamic effectiveness as a public speaker in the late nineteenth and early twentieth centuries is similar to Ronald Reagan's effectiveness as a public speaker in the 1970s and 80s. The chief difference, of course, is that Reagan was nominated twice and elected twice as president and Bryan was nominated three times and not elected once. Yet both were great speakers, and the latter had the advantage of electronic communication.

# 41. Albert J. Beveridge, March of the Flag, September 17, 1898

*Speaker:* Albert Jeremiah Beveridge (1862–1927), a student of rhetoric and public speaking, established a reputation as one of the most eloquent Congressional speakers of his generation. He was an ardent nationalist and jingoist, employing public speaking to advance his ideology. Born in Ohio, Beveridge was trained in speaking and debate at various schools, then entered the law profession in Indianapolis in 1886. He campaigned for the Republican tickets in the 1880s and 90s, practiced law for a decade, and was elected to the U. S. Senate in 1899. He was re-elected to the Senate in 1905, and was a highly popular campaign speaker in 1896, 1900, 1904, and 1908. Beveridge delivered the keynote address at the national convention of the Progressive Party at Chicago, 1912, and he took to the stump for Roosevelt in that campaign. He campaigned for Hughes in the election of 1916, and was an unsuccessful candidate for the Senate in 1922. While known for his imperialism, Beveridge was indeed a Progressive, thus he became an advocate of child-labor reform and tariff reform. His ideology reflected economic conservatism, political nationalism, and social liberalism—definitely reflecting the prevailing American attitude of the Progressive period. Beveridge was known chiefly as a formal orator, the keynoter for many political campaigns as well as a stump speaker, yet he was also highly skilled as an extemporaneous speaker. In 1908 alone he delivered more than four hundred fifty political speeches.

*Occasion:* Beveridge was one of a group of politicians, intellectuals, and military strategists who viewed national expansion as a key ingredient to the pursuit of world power. These imperialists wanted the United States to take its place alongside Britain, Russia, Germany, and France as a great imperial nation. They believed the U.S. should build a strong navy, fortify its position in the Caribbean, and then extend its influence and markets into Asia. Many imperialists were Social Darwinists, believing that the U. S. destiny required it prove itself the military equal of the strongest European nations and the master of "lesser" peoples of the world. Imperialist sentiment in Congress and throughout the nation gained strength, fueled by "jingoism." Jingoists were nationalists who thought that a swaggering foreign policy and a willingness to go to war would enhance their nation's glory; they were constantly on alert for insults to their nation's honor and swift to call for military retaliation. Jingoism was a predatory brand of nationalism. On this occasion Beveridge addressed a packed and wildly enthusiastic audience in Indianapolis. His rhetoric was an eloquent defense of American imperialism rooted in the assumption that might makes right and that America should seize the occasion to extend its rule across the globe.

*Excerpt:* "It is a noble land that God has given us; a land that can feed and clothe the world; a land whose coastlines would enclose half the countries of Europe; a land set like a sentinel between the two imperial oceans of the globe, a greater England with a nobler destiny...It is a glorious history our God has bestowed upon His chosen people; a history heroic with faith in our mission and our future....In this campaign, the question is larger than a party question. It is a world question. Shall the American people continue their march toward the commercial supremacy of the world?...Hawaii is ours; Puerto Rico is ours; at the prayer of her people Cuba finally will be ours; in the islands of the East, even to the gates of Asia, the flag of a liberal government is to float over the Philippines, and may it be the banner that Taylor unfurled in Texas and Fremont carried to the coast....The march of the flag! In 1789 the flag of the Republic waved over 4,000,000 souls in thirteen states, and their savage territory which stretched to the Mississippi, to Canada, to the Floridas...the infidels to the gospel of liberty raved, but the flag swept on!.... And the question you will answer at the polls is whether you will stand with this quartet of disbelief in the American people, or whether you are marching onward with the flag."

*Impact:* This oration was carefully prepared, sweeping in tone, and delivered with power. It should be considered as one of Beveridge's greatest speeches. The address committed the Indiana Republicans to imperialism and became a widely distributed and effective campaign document. Thousands of copies were printed for distribution throughout the nation. From Beveridge's point of view, the speech was an important factor in his subsequent election to the U. S. Senate. On December 4, 1899, Beveridge was sworn in as a member of the Senate. Having already sailed to the Philippines and spending three months observing and chronicling every phase of life there, the young senator had established a reputation as a specialist on the Philippines. He then began making a number of speeches on the Philippines and American expansion in general. One of his most famous addresses was "The Philippine Question," delivered January 9, 1900. Beveridge's speeches drew large audiences and were widely publicized; his utterances were quoted by newspapers all over the country.

*Contemporary Application:* Sometimes a great orator can produce a legacy of mixed reviews—to be praised for eloquence in one field of endeavor and criticized in another. Beveridge is praised for his eloquence in demanding an end to the exploitation of child labor in this nation and, yet, at best, forgiven for his fervent rhetoric that advanced imperialist goals and ideals that deepened the government's involvement in the affairs of distant lands—an ideology rooted in racism and ethnocentrism.

*Little Known Fact:* Near the end of his life, Beveridge turned to writing a variety of books and magazine articles; he enjoyed writing about popular American political figures such as Marshall and Lincoln. Yet the retired senator had always considered himself to be an orator, and one of the books he wrote was entitled *The Art of Public Speaking,* published in 1924.

# 42. William Jennings Bryan, Imperialism, August 8, 1900

*Speaker:* Having established his popularity with his famous "Cross of Gold" speech, and the ensuing political campaign, William Jennings Bryan was never out of the national limelight. This politician-orator, the center of so much adulation among the common people, certainly had his enemies and detractors. Some political enemies stereotyped him as a wild-eyed radical, imbued with foreign ideologies and professing class conflict as his creed. Instead, he was most stirred by the ideas of Thomas Jefferson and Jacksonian democracy, not socialism or anarchism. Born in Salem, Illinois, in 1860, with a father who served in the state senate and was twice elected a judge, young Bryan's first ambition was to become a Baptist minister, then maybe a farmer. Soon, however, the excitement of political campaigns captured his interest. Bryan was not a great thinker, but he was a great popularizer. He did not have an inventive mind, but courageously championed ideas he felt were paramount issues because they expressed the feelings of the masses. He was more of an evangelist than a scholarly political scientist. He certainly was not a demagogue, but he spoke on the issues that concerned ordinary people. The sources of Bryan's greatness as a public speaker: (1) His strong *ethos*, or source credibility; he was a gentleman, earnest and sincere and perceived as a man of noble character and good will, even before eastern audiences. (2) His superb and impassioned delivery; he had an impressive, thunderous manner, perhaps unequalled in his generation (carrying quality with perfect articulation) with the confidence to use it to maximum effectiveness before the largest of audiences. (3) His ability to clarify and simplify an issue where unsophisticated people could understand it, using simple words and analogies, and drawing illustrations from the Bible, nature, and history. Little wonder he was known as "the Great Commoner." Bryan believed that persuasion was not from mind to mind, but from heart to heart. In the last days of a long career, he was a self-appointed spokesman for Bible literalism and Christian fundamentalism—a cause that took him to Dayton, Tennessee, for a trial that became one of the great cultural events in American history.

*Occasion:* During his campaign for his candidacy for the presidency in the general election of 1900, Bryan ran under the banner of anti-imperialism for the Democratic Party. He had given a number of speeches that warned against the harms of American imperialism. The cessation of Spanish-American hostilities in 1898 found the U. S. in possession of a small empire that could grow in the likeness of European nation empires. Imperialist orators and a jingoistic press called for permanent dominion over Cuba, the Philippines, Puerto Rico, and Guam. Economic, political, religious, and emotional factors influenced the attractiveness of territorial expansion. The Democratic Party and Bryan posed anti-imperialism as the central issue of the campaign. The Republican Party defended annexing the Philippines as a form of expansionism that would make the U. S. more powerful. Among the many speeches on the topic, this speech was the one that drew the most commentary. Candidate Bryan was passionate in his belief that imperialism was wrong politically and religiously, and a violation of basic human rights.

*Excerpt:* "Someone has said that a truth once spoken, can never be recalled. It goes on and on, and no one can set a limit to its ever-widening influence. But if it were possible to obliterate every word written or spoken in defense of the principles set forth in the Declaration of Independence, a war of conquest would still leave its legacy of perpetual hatred, for it was God himself who placed in every human heart the love of liberty. He never made a race of people so low in the scale of civilization or intelligence that it would welcome a foreign master....We cannot repudiate the principle of self-government in the Philippines without weakening that principle here....Lincoln said that the safety of this nation was not in its fleets, its armies, or its forts, but in the spirit which prizes liberty as the heritage of all men, in all lands, everywhere, and he warned his countrymen that they could not destroy this spirit without planting the seeds of despotism at their own doors....Love, not force, was the weapon of the Nazarene; sacrifice for others, not the exploitation of them, was His method of reaching the human heart."

*Impact:* The rhetorical critic makes a distinction between an immediate impact and a long-range effect. Bryan's speeches on imperialism were well received before his many friendly audiences; yet among the larger voting public, the speaker did not convince enough voters to defeat McKinley in the general election. As for long-range judgment, Bryan's major ideas and arguments have been judged to be valid and realistic. Being diverse in his argumentation, Bryan properly focused on how imperialism was a moral issue for the American people. He also argued that sustaining an imperialist policy would necessitate maintaining a large standing army, cultivating a culture of militarism. His *pathos*, or emotional appeals, were made to values inherent in American democracy, and he urged that America should follow the words of its past presidents, specifically Jefferson and Lincoln. Bryan argued that accepting an imperialist policy would abandon the heritage of American democracy that made the United States the world power it was at that time.

*Contemporary Application:* We admire speakers who take a forthright stand on a highly controversial topic, whether or not we agree with the position.

*Connection to Today:* The Philippines were granted independence in 1946, but the issue of American foreign policy in smaller nations is omnipresent.

*Interesting Fact:* Bryan, "The Great Commoner," was a speaker without rival on the Chautauqua circuits, and did not lecture on politics in this setting. Of his Chautauqua addresses, the one most demanded was "The Prince of Peace," given in three thousand circuit tents over a period of two decades prior to his death. In outdoor speaking, Bryan seemed oblivious to heat or fatigue.

# 43. Theodore Roosevelt, Man With the Muckrake, April 14, 1906

*Speaker:* Fair to say, with some pun intended, Theodore Roosevelt (1858–1919) wore several hats: rancher, naturalist, outdoorsman, soldier, author, public servant, governor of New York, vice president, and then, upon the assassination of William McKinley (September 14, 1901), at age forty-two, he became the youngest chief executive in our nation's history. And through it all, he was a most active public speaker, bringing enthusiasm and energy to his thousands of orations. He devoted much of his public life to social reform, demonstrating concern for public welfare and compassion for the oppressed. His career in public speaking spanned a lifetime—he campaigned for governor and president, toured the country in making speeches, delivered commencement addresses and dedicatory remarks for public occasions, gave speeches of inspiration to patriotic and religious groups, and addressed audiences on four continents in pre-aviation days. Born into an aristocratic family in New York City, Roosevelt nevertheless developed great affection for "the people." Though sickly, asthmatic, and nearsighted as a boy, he reinvented himself as a vigorous outdoorsman in love with nature with an insatiable appetite for high-risk adventure—everything from "dude ranching" in the Dakota Territory, big game hunting in Africa, to wartime combat. Roosevelt did more than any previous president to extend federal control over the nation's physical environment, viewing the wilderness as a place to live strenuously, to test oneself against the rough outdoors, and to match wits against strong and clever game. He was a voracious reader as well as accomplished writer. Such was the *ethos* of the man who graced many a podium with an assertive, confident, and swaggering manner. He was a believer in the superiority of the English-speaking people, yet appointed members of "inferior" races to important posts in his administration. With the masses, he was immensely popular—rarely has a president's personality so enthralled the American public! Theodore Roosevelt is the only twentieth-century president immortalized on Mount Rushmore.

*Occasion:* As Roosevelt took office, he soon launched an aggressive anti-corruption campaign, especially against the nation's most powerful industries and corporate monopolies, earning him a nickname of "trust-buster." This "house cleaning" crusade exposed a seemingly non-stop parade of unscrupulous officials in both the governmental and private sectors. The unintended consequence, however, was that the zeal that rooted out dishonest operators washed over into many honest men who were publicly smeared by rumors and unfounded charges. Muck-raking had turned into "yellow journalism," and the general public was confused. This, according to the President, made it difficult to arouse the public "either to wrath against wrongdoing or to enthusiasm for what is right." Roosevelt, therefore, sought to return accuracy and honesty to the reform movement when he seized a speaking occasion at the laying of the cornerstone of the Congressional Office Building in Washington, urging restraint on the exposure campaigners. In the audience were senators and representatives, Supreme Court justices, members of the diplomatic corps and interested spectators and citizens—all gathered to listen to their chief executive appeal to "The Man with the Muckrake" to exercise restraint and let the pursuit of truth guide the strategy of reforms.

*Excerpt:* "My plea is not for immunity to, but for the most unsparing exposure of, the politician who betrays his trust, of the big businessman who makes or spends his fortune in illegitimate or corrupt ways. There should be a resolute effort to hunt every such man out of the position he has disgraced. Expose the crime and hunt down the criminal, but remember that even in the case of crime, if it is attacked in sensational, lurid, and untruthful fashion, the attack may do more damage to the public mind than the crime itself....We must strive to secure a broader economic opportunity for all men, so that each shall have a better chance to show the stuff of which he is made."

*Impact:* Consistent with his oral style, Theodore Roosevelt delivered this speech with impassioned delivery. He began by adducing a story from a classic in English literature (Bunyan's *Pilgrim's Progress*), then reiterated his desire to combat fraud. The speaker also inveighed against those who fabricated stories and dug up dirt—"muckrakers," as he called them—merely to sell newspapers or ruin enemies. The speech was wildly effective with the majority of citizens. Here was their president taking on a giant and taking it to task. "The Man with the Muckrake" became TR's best known metaphor, as this speech was presented almost verbatim many times after the original presentation. The speaker enhanced his reputation for courage. In this speech, Roosevelt is the exhorter, the preacher, and he is the president who spoke of his high office as being "the bully pulpit." An unintended effect, perhaps, was the label "muckrakers" became a badge of honor among journalists who were committed to exposing the unethical and repugnant aspects of American life. During the first decade of the century, "muckrakers" presented the public with a number of startling revelations about life in inner cities, corruption in state and local government, appalling work conditions in factors, to cite a few examples—all laying the ground work for progressive reform.

*Contemporary Application:* A speaker with high credibility, widespread popularity, and manifest passion will sway audiences easily and establish a great legacy.

*Connection to Today:* Investigative reporting, despite abuses that would still offend Teddie Roosevelt, is an important part of the contemporary media and serves a vital public interest. There will remain a legitimate question as to whether or not investigative reporting goes beyond bounds of decency and privacy in reporting on the private lives of public figures.

# 44. Theodore Roosevelt, "What Is a Bull Moose?" October 14, 1912

*Speaker:* Teddie Roosevelt, or TR, as many Americans called him, was truly one of the most popular presidents in our history. Among his audiences were many who did not care so much about his topic or content but they came to see and hear him. Theodore Roosevelt was a man of diverse interests and many talents, and it is unlikely he ever faced an audience in which he did not have much in common to discuss. He always associated himself with good causes, though humility was not one of his virtues. The enthusiasm he exhibited for various causes led many of his friends to describe him as a perpetual boy. For example, at the end of his presidency, he set off for Africa to face wild animals with his left eye useless from a blow received in boxing at the White House, his right eye never strong, and nine pairs of eyeglasses. The "Square Deal" represented the essence of TR's philosophy of economic reform, and by 1912 he was becoming more progressive in advocacy of progressive legislation that would advance social justice for workers, children, the poor, and minorities. Historians have not considered Roosevelt a great thinker, but acknowledge the simplicity and popularity of his ideas. Nor was he trained or sophisticated as an orator; he demonstrated little artistry, consistent with his "rough and ready" vigor of personality. His favorite saying, used often in public and in private, was an old African proverb: "Speak softly and carry a big stick; you will go far."

*Occasion:* An African safari could not keep TR satisfied, so he returned to the U. S., sought the Republican nomination from his hand-picked successor, William Howard Taft, then led a group of dissatisfied liberal Republicans out of the fold and into the Progressive Party. Claiming at one point that he was "as strong as a bull moose," Roosevelt gave the party its popular name. The candidate was a vigorous campaigner. In Milwaukee, Wisconsin, on

October 14, 1912, a saloonkeeper named John Schrank shot him, but the bullet lodged in his chest only after penetrating his steel eyeglass case and passing through a thick (fifty pages), single-folded copy of the speech he was carrying in his jacket. Roosevelt correctly concluded that since he was not coughing blood, the bullet had not completely penetrated the chest wall to his lung. He therefore declined admonitions to be taken to the hospital immediately. Instead, he delivered his scheduled speech with blood seeping into his shirt, speaking for ninety minutes. Later ex-rays showed that the bullet had lodged in Roosevelt's chest muscle but did not require extraction, and he carried it with him for the rest of his life.

*Excerpt:* "Friends, I shall ask you to be as quiet as possible. I don't know whether you fully understand that I have just been shot; but it takes more than that to kill a Bull Moose. But fortunately I had my manuscript, so you see I was going to make a long speech, and there is a bullet—there is where the bullet went through—and it probably saved me from it going into my heart. The bullet is in me now, so that I cannot make a very long speech, but I will try my best….I can tell you with absolute truthfulness that I am very much uninterested in whether I am shot or not….I am in this cause with my whole heart and soul. I believe that the Progressive movement is making life a little easier for all our people; a movement to try to take the burdens off the men and especially the women and children of this country. I am absorbed in the success of that movement."

*Impact:* The audience gasped when Roosevelt announced he had been shot, and then showed them the blood-stained shirt and fifty-page manuscript with both blood stains and a bullet hole. The speaker made several references to the assassination attempt and at times was interrupted by listeners urging him to seek medical assistance. Because of the bullet wound, Roosevelt was taken off the campaign trail in the final weeks of the race, yet in the minds of many voters this simply added evidence of TR's mythical invincibility. The story was an amazing one, not simply for the immediate audience but for the nation as a whole. Though the other two campaigners (Taft and Wilson) stopped their own campaigns in the week Roosevelt was in the hospital, they resumed it once he was released. For several reasons, Roosevelt failed to move enough Republicans in his direction, though winning 4.1 million votes (27%), compared to Taft's 3.5 million (23%). Wilson's 6.3 million votes (42%) were enough to garner 435 electoral votes. TR was certainly not the greatest speaker of his era, lacking Bryan's vocal skill, the dramatic artistry of LaFollette, or the intellectual dimension of Wilson. Yet his ideas of virtue in government and private and corporate life, his long and diverse speaking career, his support of good causes, and much more, would surely place Theodore Roosevelt among the top ten to fifteen American political speakers.

*Little Known Fact:* Perhaps the most radical speech Roosevelt presented was in the midst of a speaking tour in western states on August 31, 1910, at Osawatomie, Kansas. There he presented his New Nationalism, an ambitious welfare program that called for the federal government to stabilize the economy, foster social harmony, and protect the weak. In essence, human rights were extolled above property rights, yet his cousin Franklin D. Roosevelt generally receives credit for this ideology.

*Contemporary Application:* A speaker who has been struck by a bullet but insists on delivering one's speech will be judged either courageous or foolhardy by the audience. Best advice, even if not rattled by a pointed gun: Seek medical assistance.

*Connection to Today:* Americans remain impacted by the political ideology and subsequent public policy advocated by both Roosevelts, one a Republican and the other a Democrat.

# 45. Helen Keller, Strike Against War, January 5, 1916

*Speaker:* Few if any Americans in any era have provided the kind of personal, moral example and sheer inspiration than that provided by Helen Keller (1880–1968). Born in Tuscumbia, Alabama, she became sick at nineteen months, and, sadly, lost both her hearing and vision. Her parents sought a special teacher for Helen and the director for an institute for the blind recommended a young woman named Anne Sullivan. Sullivan set about the daunting task of teaching young Helen how to read and speak The relationship was a close one as the young teacher moved into the Keller household to be with Helen at all times. In 1890 Keller's family sent her to the Perkins Institute to learn how to better communicate. At nineteen years old, Helen went to Radcliffe College in Massachusetts, graduating in 1904. She was the first deaf and blind person to earn a Bachelor of Arts degree. Keller's career sought to improve the plight of poor and other blind people during her lifetime. She traveled to over thirty-nine countries with Anne to talk about her life and experiences. Perhaps it is in her capacity as a public speaker that Keller really established her reputation. Throughout her life, she had numerous speaking tours, drawing attention to causes often overlooked, and raising funds for charitable foundations. Though her voice was neither strong nor clear (Sullivan often stood by her side to repeat sentences, if necessary), she spoke on a wide variety of topics. Keller possessed terrific credibility as a speaker on issues related to disabilities, and she often made the point that her disabilities did not preclude the right to study the issues and express her views before audiences. In the mid-1920s, Keller and Sullivan embarked on a speaking campaign to raise two million dollars for the American Foundation for the Blind; in three years they addressed 250,000 people at 249 meetings in 123 cities. Few today are aware that Helen Keller became a socialist, and once she found her voice, she used it for the downtrodden. She campaigned against war and for women's votes and the working class, along with many other radical causes—and decried those who only pointed out her disability when they disliked her views!

*Occasion:* This speech was delivered in Carnegie Hall under the auspices of the Women's Peace Party and the Labor Forum. The conflict in Europe in the early twentieth century soon became so widespread on that continent that it would earn the name "The Great War." Yet, though that war seemed a full ocean away, President Wilson and others were calling for military support of the Allied powers. There arose strong anti-war sentiment, and Helen Keller, though not considered a political philosopher or activist, lifted her voice in opposition to military involvement in a foreign war.

*Excerpt:* "Some people are grieved because they imagine I am in the hands of unscrupulous persons who lead me astray and persuade me to espouse unpopular causes and make me the mouthpiece of their propaganda…My sources of information are as good and reliable as anybody else's. I have papers and magazines from England, France, Germany and Austria that I can read myself. Not all the editors I have met can do that. Quite a number of them have to take their French and German second hand. No, I will not disparage the editors. They are an overworked, misunderstood class. Let them remember, though, that if I cannot see the fire at the end of their cigarettes, neither can they thread a needle in the dark. All I ask, gentlemen, is a fair field and no favor. I have entered the fight against preparedness and against the economic system under which we live…. All you need to do to bring about this stupendous revolution is to straighten up and fold your arms. At a time when America was pressed to join what was then called 'The Great War'….we have no enemies foolhardy enough to attempt to invade the United States. The talk about attack from Germany and Japan is absurd. Germany has its hands full and will be busy with its own affairs for some generations after the European war is over…Strike against all ordinances and laws and institutions that continue the slaughter of peace and the butcheries of war. Strike against war, for without you no battles can be fought. Strike against manufacturing shrapnel and gas bombs and all other tools of murder. Strike against preparedness that means death and misery to millions of human beings."

*Impact:* The speech still impresses readers today just as it did a century ago with those who first heard it. Keller spoke courageously and never minced words. The fact remains that, not only was the speaker female, but also a female with severe disabilities, who gained attention and respect. The speaker desires no pity and, in fact, notes something she can do (thread a needle in the dark) that her editorial critics could not do. Her cause was an unpopular one, yet historians today are more likely to validate the isolationists' arguments against engagement in the Great War.

*Practical Application:* An intelligent, prepared speaker can have great *ethos* and effectiveness even if that speaker has severe disabilities.

*Connection to Today:* Helen Keller's stellar example of intelligence, perseverance, patience, and courage in spite of adversity still inspire and encourage all ages of people in every generation, especially people with disabilities. A biography of Keller as a speaker by Lois J. Einhorn captures the irony in its subtitle: "Sightless but Seen, Deaf but Heard."

*Little Known Facts:* Keller wrote an autobiography entitled *My Life.* The highly acclaimed play *Miracle Worker* is a drama based on Anne Sullivan and the challenges she faced in teaching young Helen. When Keller was in Japan, she met Hachiko, a famous Akita dog. She decided to adopt an Akita, and was the first person to bring an Akita to America.

# 46. Carrie Chapman Catt, Plea for Last, Hard Fight for Suffrage, November 4, 1917

*Speaker:* One of the most important and persuasive speakers in the American women's suffrage movement was a former journalist who became president of the National American Women's Suffrage Association (NAWSA). Carrie Chapman Catt (1859–1947) became one of the best known women in the U. S. in the first half of the twentieth century and has been on nearly all lists of famous American women. Her activism for the feminist cause can be easily traced to her college years at what is now Iowa State University. As a student, Catt defied rules and spoke during male debate contests and seldom missed an opportunity to speak up for women's rights. She graduated with a Bachelor of Science, was the valedictorian, and became the only female in her graduating class. After graduation she pursued a number of positions wherein she was typically the only female in the organization or office. She combined rhetorical skills with strategic organizational skills, both demonstrated by her ability to mobilize large numbers of advocates for women's rights. The NAWSA became by far the largest organization working for women's suffrage in the United States, and in her career she made hundreds of speeches for this important cause.

*Occasion:* Although Jeanette Rankin of Montana was elected to the U. S. House of Representatives in 1916 and fifteen states had granted women the right to vote by 1918, women in the suffrage movement discovered Congress was intransigent in extending voting rights to women at the national level. Indeed, the women's rights movement that began at the Seneca Falls convention had floundered in the 1870s and 1880s. In 1890 suffragists came together in a new organization, the aforementioned NAWSA as led by Stanton and

Anthony. Women's rights that were honored in sparsely populated western states reflected not so much egalitarianism but rather the conviction that women's supposedly gentler and nurturing nature would be employed to tame and civilize the men who had moved to the frontier. While five states followed the lead of other western states by enfranchising women in the years from 1910 to 1912, there was a series of setbacks in Eastern and Midwestern states. The movement regained momentum under Carrie Chapman's leadership and powerful rhetorical skills. Her leadership was acknowledged by an invitation to address the U. S. Congress, that along with other influential women (as well as political leaders such as Robert LaFollette, William Jennings Bryan, and George Norris), actively opposed participation in the war in Europe. During this period, it was both a rare occasion and an honor when a female was invited to address the U. S. Congress.

*Excerpt:* "Do you realize that women in increasing numbers indignantly resent the long delay in their enfranchisement? Your party platforms have pledged women suffrage. Then why not be honest, frank friends of our cause, adopt it in reality as your own, make it a party program, and "fight with us"? As a party measure -- a measure of all parties -- why not put the amendment through Congress and the legislatures? We shall all be better friends, we shall have a happier nation, we women will be free to support loyally the party of our choice, and we shall be far prouder of our history. There is one thing mightier than kings and armies-- aye, than Congresses and political parties – 'the power of an idea when its time has come to move.' The time for woman suffrage has come. The woman's hour has struck. If parties prefer to postpone action longer and thus do battle with this idea, they challenge the inevitable. The idea will not perish; the party which opposes it may. Every delay, every trick, every political dishonesty from now on will antagonize the women of the land more and more, and when the party or parties which have so delayed woman suffrage finally let it come, their sincerity will be doubted and their appeal to the new voters will be met with suspicion. This is the psychology of the situation. Can you afford the risk? Think it over….Women's suffrage is coming—you know it.

Will you, honorable senators and members of the House of Representatives, help or hinder it?"

*Impact:* Catt's speech was eloquent and persuasive. The address called for action at the national level and the Congress soon made the giant leap forward. There were other activists, of course, but this speech has rightly been ranked as one of the one hundred most significant speeches of the twentieth century. The suffragists achieved their goal of universal woman suffrage when the Nineteenth Amendment to the Constitution, guaranteeing women the right to vote, was ratified on August 26, 1920. The long wait was finally over. And while voter participation continued to decline after 1920, even still, the extension of the vote to women, 144 years after the founding of the nation, was a major political achievement.

*Contemporary Application:* There is great power in an idea whose time has come, and the idea is accepted and implemented even more rapidly when it is advocated with eloquence by someone who stands as a victim to injustice that must no longer be tolerated.

# 47. Woodrow Wilson, War Message to Congress, April 2, 1917

*Speaker:* Woodrow Wilson (1856–1924) brought a diverse background of experiences when he entered the White House in 1913. Born into a stern Presbyterian family in the Old South, he became one of the best educated presidents to serve the nation. He attended Davidson College, Princeton University, the University of Virginia Law School, then pursued a Ph.D. at Johns Hopkins. Wilson was a lawyer, professor of jurisprudence and economics, president of Princeton University, and governor of New York before serving as president of the United States. He always believed that his success as a political leader would be tied to his success as an orator. His father encouraged development of his skills in speaking and writing; he participated in literary and debate societies at the collegiate level, and he admired and studied the careers and eloquence of great British orators (especially Edmund Burke)—all contributing to his skill as an orator. As a professor, he organized and encouraged student debates. Wilson's personality has long been the subject of academic study and speculation. We do know he was reticent, almost anti-social, and that he continually fought bad health. Leading up to the election of 1912, both Republicans and Democrats pushed Progressive reform that was needed by the nation. While Theodore Roosevelt, William Jennings Bryan, and Robert LaFollette were well known national figures, Wilson emerged as a prominent representative of conservative causes and middle class respectability. Circumstances dividing the Progressive movement made it possible for Wilson to defeat Theodore Roosevelt (Progressive), Taft (Republican), and Debs (Socialist), even though he won only forty-two percent of the popular vote. Once in office, Wilson had the opportunity to work with a Democratic Congress to enact his New Freedom program. In general, Wilson mediated differing views of Progressivism in forging a strong reform program, and he enlarged the power of the executive branch, making the White House (more than the Congress) the center of national politics. Looming ahead, however, was a far greater, unavoidable international crisis.

*Occasion:* Most Americans had not anticipated the Great War that erupted in Europe in August 1914, and fewer still could have imagined that their nation would seriously consider getting involved. European nations drew up alliances on one side or the other—expansionist Germany of Kaiser Wilhelm II allied itself with the multinational Austro-Hungarian Empire, and, on the other side, Great Britain and France entered into alliances with tsarist Russia. Thus, squaring off in Europe were the Allied powers against the Central Powers. Most believed that the U. S. had no vital interest in the war and would not become involved, all the while their sympathies lay with Britain and the other allies. The "great rule" of Washington and Jefferson, reinforced by the Monroe Doctrine, was that the nation should remain aloof from international conflict and issues. Yet, neutrality seemed less and less possible, and public outrage erupted when a German submarine sank the British liner *Lusitania*, with a loss of nearly 1,200 lives, including 128 Americans. Wilson ran successfully for re-election in 1916 on the slogan, "He kept us out of war." The President attempted a number of sincere strategies to bring the warring sides together. In January 1917 he addressed Congress and spoke of his efforts to produce a formula for "peace without victory," a settlement without winners and losers. With prophetic irony, the President warned that a vindictive peace would sow the seeds of yet another European conflict. Germany pledged not to attack unarmed ships without warning, but in early 1917 resumed submarine warfare and sank several American merchant vessels. Wilson's tolerance and patience, as well as that of many Americans, had been exhausted. Thus, on April 2, Wilson asked Congress for a declaration of war.

*Excerpt:* "The world must be made safe for democracy. Its peace must be planted upon the tested foundations of political liberty....It is a fearful thing to lead this great peaceful people into war, into the most terrible and disastrous of all wars, civilization itself seeming to be in the balance. But the right is more precious than peace, and we shall fight for the things which we have always carried nearest our hearts—for democracy, for the rights of those who submit to authority to have a voice in their own Governments, for the rights and liberties of small nations…and make the world at last free. To such a task we can dedicate our lives and our fortunes."

*Impact:* This was a thirty-two minute address delivered in the evening to members of both Houses, the Cabinet, the Supreme Court, and the diplomatic corps. Wilson stated unequivocally: "We have no quarrel with the German people. We have no feeling toward them but one of sympathy and friendship," noting it was the German government that had "acted in entering this war." He explained in clear language the reasons justifying American intervention and described the German intentions as "a war against all nations" and "a challenge to all mankind." The audience exploded in cheers of sober support for the President's call to end neutrality and "make the world safe for democracy." After vigorous debate, the Senate passed the war resolution eighty-two to six, and the House 373 to 50. On April 6, 1917, the U. S. officially entered the Great War. This war message committed more than one million U. S. troops to one of the costliest and bloodiest conflicts in world history, and it transformed a rivalry among European powers into a movement for a free and democratic world order.

*Connection to Today:* The Great War re-drew the borders of nations in Europe and the Middle East and planted the seeds for the Second World War as well as provided a backdrop for the fighting and terrorism in the Middle East today.

*Contemporary Application:* A national leader with strong *ethos*, especially one of both eloquence and a reputation as a student of history, is capable of leading a large nation into a controversial war.

# 48. George Norris, Against Entry into the War, April 4, 1917

*Speaker:* George Norris (1861–1944) was a progressive Republican born in Ohio and practiced law in Nebraska, where he was elected to Congress in 1902. Ten years later he was elected to the U. S. Senate where he established himself as both a maverick and reformer for the next thirty years. Norris opposed both the entry into the Great War and the Treaty of Versailles, thus rightly gaining the reputation of a firm isolationist. His legacy also includes initiating the Twentieth Amendment to the Constitution, advancing the president's inauguration from March to January, thus greatly reducing the lame duck session of Congress. As a progressive he led the fight for presidential primaries and direct election of U. S. Senators. As an advocate of public ownership of hydroelectric power, he introduced the bill creating the Tennessee Valley Authority. After the war, Norris generally supported the policies of the New Deal legislation. He believed in the wisdom of the common people and in the progress of civilization.

*Occasion:* In April 1917 the U. S. faced a difficult decision: Remain neutral in the Great War or join the Allies in their fight against the Central Powers? Official neutrality during the nearly three years of bloody conflict seemed near impossible, and actions on both sides of the Atlantic had been edging the country closer to the brink of war. Despite their acceptance of a British mine blockade of the North Sea, many Americans were outraged when the German government announced a submarine blockade of Great Britain in February 1915, yet the Germans had stopped viewing the United States as neutral. The sale of munitions by the United States to the Allied powers was a clear indication of the U. S.'s partiality, and the Germans sought to halt U.S. shipments of supplies to the Allies. Another challenge led many Americans

148

to demand action: On May 7, 1915, the British passenger liner *Lusitania* was torpedoed and sunk by a German submarine, killing nearly 1,200 people, 128 of whom were Americans. Again, President Wilson maintained neutrality was the best possible course of action. The Germans backed away from unrestricted submarine warfare, allowing the Americans to remain at peace for two years. On February 25, 1917, the discovery and release of the Zimmermann telegram, from a high official in the German government to the German ambassador to Mexico, revealed that Germany intended to resume unrestricted submarine warfare and proposed an alliance with Mexico should the United States enter the war. Wilson was now convinced war was inevitable, thus he asked Congress for a declaration of war on April 2, 1917. The applause was deafening; however, not everyone in the chamber supported U.S. entry into the war. Senator George Norris stood before the Senate just two days after Wilson's request in order to advocate strong opposition to joining the war. In Norris' view, the United States had not been totally innocent in the escalation of hostilities with Germany. He asserted that the true motivating factors for U.S. entry into the war were financial in nature—the guarantee of repayment of loans to the Allies and the proceeds from continued munitions sales.

*Excerpt:* "There are a great many American citizens who feel that we owe it as a duty to humanity to take part in the war. Many instances of cruelty and inhumanity can be found on both sides. Men are often biased in their judgment on account of their sympathy and their interests....While many such people are moved by selfish motives and hopes of gain, I have no doubt that in a great many instances, through what I believe to be a misunderstanding of the real condition, there are many honest, patriotic citizens who think we ought to engage in this war and who are behind the President in his demand that we should declare war against Germany. I think such people err in judgment and to a great extent have been misled as to the real history and the true facts by the almost unanimous demand of the great combination of wealth that has a direct financial interest in our participation in the war.... It is now demanded that the American citizens shall be used as insurance policies to guarantee the safe delivery of munitions of war to belligerent nations. The enormous profits of munition manufacturers, stockbrokers, and bond dealers must be still further increased by our entrance into the war. This has brought us to the present moment, when Congress urged by the President and backed by the artificial sentiment, is about to declare war and engulf our country in the greatest holocaust that the world has ever known."

*Impact:* One might say the speech was not an immediate success, because it did not dissuade the Congress from denying the President the declaration of war he sought. On the other hand, Senator Norris established himself clearly as the strong and courageous leader among "the irreconcilables"—the group of senators who persistently refused to sanction or support in any way U. S. involvement in the Great War and the Treaty of Versailles. And Norris placed himself in good company with other courageous isolationists: feminist Carrie Chapman Catt, western progressives Robert LaFollette and William Jennings Bryan, and socialist Eugene V. Debs. Anti-war sentiment was unpopular in the nation, but Norris was regularly re-elected by his constituents until 1942.

*Contemporary Application:* History will always be kind to speakers who courageously advocate a minority position that not only deserved to be heard, but, from the perspective of time, may well have been the correct position.

*Little Known Fact:* Norris was one of eight senators eulogized in John F. Kennedy's study, *Profiles in Courage,* included for opposing Speaker Cannon's autocratic power in the House, for speaking out against arming U.S. merchant ships during the neutral period in World War I, and for supporting the presidential campaign of Democrat Al Smith, the candidate who was controversial due to his Roman Catholic faith and position against the Prohibition amendment.

# 49. Woodrow Wilson, For the League of Nations, September 6, 1919

*Speaker:* Woodrow Wilson rose to power in the Democratic Party in large part because of his public speaking career, traveling around the nation and speaking out on a number of issues, especially for progressive reform. His religious faith was strong, and he even delivered a lecture on the influence of the Bible in modern society entitled "The Bible and Progress," delivered in Denver on May 7, 1911, and widely circulated. Trained and adept as a public speaker, he often spoke impromptu and felt free to wander from a prepared text. His credibility was strong, being the best educated president to enter the White House at that time. His voice was clear and deliberate and his physical manner was free of wide-sweeping gestures, retaining something of the delivery of a college professor, which, of course, he had been. Despite all these assets, Wilson became something of a tragic figure in American political history, and the story of his fight for the League of Nations is at the center of this tragedy. This was the climactic fight of his career, the one cause and expected triumph on which this president hoped to create his legacy.

*Occasion:* After setting forth America's war objectives on January 8, 1918, in a speech that became known as the "Fourteen Points," President Wilson attempted to explain in more detail how to achieve a more democratic world system. The Allies never explicitly accepted the Fourteen Points, and framing a final peace treaty proved difficult. Yet the President was convinced of the righteousness of his cause. Germany signed the Treaty of Versailles under protest as the penalties and burden upon that nation were onerous. Wilson hoped the final section of this treaty would resolve flaws in the treaty by establishing one great international organization to preserve peace: the League of Nations. This constitution or covenant bound member nations to guarantee each other's independence—Wilson's concept of collective security. The President devoted time, energy, rhetorical strategy, and fervor to winning acceptance to this treaty, especially for the League of Nations. Most Americans favored the treaty, the Democrats also favored the treaty, yet Republicans were in the majority in the Senate and they—especially a group called the "Irreconcilables"—were adamantly opposed to the treaty and wanted to focus on civil liberties and progressive reform at home. Other opponents had reservations about certain provisions in the treaty. Wilson refused to compromise with these "Reservationists" as led by Henry Cabot Lodge. In early September 4, 1919, Wilson embarked across the country, beginning in Columbus, Ohio, speaking passionately to win popular support for the treaty. In three weeks, he traveled eight thousand miles and delivered thirty-seven speeches. As the President's train pulled into the station at Des Moines, circling planes dropped flowers on the train. Thousands of local citizens gathered along the streets of the capital city and enthusiastically cheered the smiling President as his motorcade moved toward a packed coliseum of nine thousand people. In the front rows were fathers and mothers of sons lost in the trench warfare of the Great War. This was the very heart of the isolationist Midwest.

*Excerpt:* "The world is desperately in need of settled conditions of peace, and it cannot wait much longer. It is waiting upon us….that is the burdensome thought upon my heart tonight, that the world is waiting for the verdict of the Nation to which it looked for leadership and which it thought would be the last that would ask the world to wait…You know the necessity of peace. Political liberty can exist only when there is peace. Social reform can take place only when there is peace. The settlement of every question that concerns our daily life waits for peace….This [League of Nations] is an unparalleled achievement of thoughtful civilization. To my dying day I shall esteem it, the crowning privilege of my life to have been permitted to put my name to a document like that…nevertheless going up a slow incline to those distant heights upon which will shine at the last the serene light of justice, suffusing a whole world in blissful peace."

*Impact:* The speech would seem like an immediate success, one in which President Wilson could return to his train and bed down with pleasant thoughts and dreams of the success of his speaking tour. This was an audience mobilized in support of the speaker. Everyone present surely knew the speaker's intelligence in matters of history and foreign affairs as well as his passion for peace. On the other hand, the dynamics of heartland USA were not the dynamics of the U. S. Senate. Despite enthusiastic response on this speaking tour, the stress and strain of the tour took its toll. Already weakened by a bout with influenza, Wilson collapsed after an emotional speech in Pueblo, Colorado. He was taken back to Washington. On October 2, Wilson suffered a massive stroke that paralyzed his left side and left him temporarily blind and psychologically unstable. Wilson's wife Edith and his physician kept the illness secret from the public, Congress, and even the vice president and cabinet members. Rumors circulated that Edith Wilson was running the administration, but mainly government was immobilized. Woodrow Wilson never fully recovered. In February 1920, Wilson partially recovered, but he remained suspicious, quarrelsome, and uncompromising. On March 20, 1920, the Senate finally rejected the Paris Treaty and the League Covenant.

*Contemporary Application:* A political career that began to rise because of the effectiveness and popularity of a speaking tour on general subjects might come to a tragic ending by another speaking tour that failed to achieve its purpose on one specific subject.

*Connection to Today:* The idea of an international community that would provide a forum for resolution of conflict between nations and also promote collective security has always been a viable and important concept in today's modern world. The failure of the League of Nations may have laid the groundwork for success in founding the United Nations.

# 50. Robert M. LaFollette, Free Speech in Wartime, October 6, 1917

*Speaker:* Robert M. LaFollette (1855–1925) was a Progressive, effective attorney, practical politician, senatorial debater, campaign speaker, and Chautauqua speaker. He was educated at the University of Wisconsin and was admitted to the bar in 1880. He was known for his commitment to the rights of the common person as opposed to what he called "special privilege." He believed in the common sense and good judgment of the rank-and-file people when they are given all the facts. LaFollette served in several political offices—county district attorney (1881–1884); governor of Wisconsin (1901–1905); member of the U. S. House of Representatives (1885–1891); U. S. senator (1906–1925); and a remarkably successful third party nominee for president—and the common denominator in all these roles was excellence, fervor, and courage in rhetoric and public address. For his devotion to progressive causes and fervent oratory, LaFollette was known as "Fighting Bob" and as a speaker who could dramatize his message effectively. Progressive causes included limiting corporate power, strengthening organized labor, and offering social welfare protection to the weak. The Progressives' campaign began in the 1890s and succeeded best in Wisconsin, where LaFollette's eloquence stirred citizens to mobilize against the state's corrupt politicians and the special privileges the Republican Party had granted to private utilities and railroads. As governor, LaFollette secured for Wisconsin both a direct primary and a tax law that stripped the railroad corporations of tax exemptions they had long enjoyed. Through the Progressives' success in Wisconsin, the "Wisconsin idea" found quick adoption in Ohio, Indiana, New York, and Colorado; New York seemed second only to Wisconsin in the vigor and breadth of its Progressive movement. Though a ceremonial speaker and at times a lecturer, for a quarter century LaFollette's permanent reputation as a spell-binding orator rests almost entirely on his political speaking. Incidentally, this speaker had a reputation for being "long-winded" in speeches and lectures; he was popular at courthouse steps and county fairs where listeners were free to wander away when they felt they had heard enough.

*Occasion*: Unlike William Jennings Bryan, Robert LaFollette did not emerge into national prominence by delivering a single great speech. He spoke on a wide variety of topics relevant to the public interest, and one of his greatest passions was free speech. As the Great War was being waged in Europe, German-Americans became objects of popular hatred and American patriots attempted to expunge every trace of German influence from American culture. While some repression seemed frivolous and silly (giving up German foods or calling sauerkraut "liberty cabbage" and banning Beethoven's symphonies), other repression was endemic to the American heritage of freedom. In the Espionage, Sabotage, and Sedition Acts passed in 1917 and 1918, Congress gave the Wilson administration sweeping powers to silence and even imprison dissenters. These acts went far beyond outlawing behavior that no nation at war could be expected to tolerate (such as sabotage or spying), but citizens could be prosecuted for uttering or writing any statement construed as profaning the Constitution, the military, or the flag—indeed these acts constituted the most drastic restrictions of free speech at the national level since the Alien and Sedition Acts of 1798! LaFollette's opponents in Congress manipulated the schedule so they could speak after him and not allow for any rebuttal. The public, sensing drama, packed the viewing galleries, and the majority of senators made sure they were present to hear all the speeches. In an atmosphere of supercharged patriotism, LaFollette rose to address his colleagues in the Senate. The Senator then read in an unemotional, detached manner the address he had prepared defending free speech in wartime.

*Excerpt*: "In time of war, the Congress must maintain the right of free speech. More than in times of peace it is necessary that the channels for free public discussion shall be open and unclogged...to discuss in an orderly way frankly and publicly and without fear, from the platform and through the press, every important phase of this war; its causes, and the manner in which it should be conducted, and the terms upon which peace should be made….I am contending, Mr. President, for the great fundamental right of the sovereign people of this country to make their voice heard and have that voice heeded."

*Impact:* Upon the speaker's conclusion a spontaneous outburst of applause had to be gaveled into order. Some senators, however, did publicly attack LaFollette and his ideas following the presentation. This address was hailed as "a classic argument for free speech during time of war"—LaFollette had reinforced his reputation for being courageously uncompromising in his political and moral convictions. While the Senator is far better remembered for his crusading for Progressivism, in this address he enhanced his reputation for support of civil liberties. Though not elected president, it was the man in the White House— Woodrow Wilson—who bore responsibility for this climate of repression. Wilson did little to halt persecution of radicals or halt a campaign to exclude Socialist Party publications from the mail, nor did he intervene to prevent the aging Socialist leader Eugene Debs from going to jail. LaFollette courageously opposed both the entrance of the U. S. into World War I and the nation's participation in the League of Nations. Wilson called LaFollette one of the "little band of willful men" who had hurt the nation, but another generation of historians and Senators has selected LaFollette as one of the most outstanding members of the upper chamber. Besides an impressive run for president in the Progressive Party in 1924 (winning Wisconsin and seventeen percent of the national vote), LaFollette is remembered for his powerful advocacy of child labor laws, social security, women's suffrage, and other progressive reforms.

*Contemporary Application:* An eloquent person of courage, even if advocating minority causes at the time, may ultimately be honored as a leading light that pointed the way to equal justice and greater liberty.

# 51. William Borah, On the League of Nations, November 19, 1919

*Speaker:* William Borah (1865-1940) was frequently called the maverick or rogue, long before Sarah Palin was born, and bad boy of the Republican Party; he was often labeled the "great American enigma." Born in Illinois, he was admitted to the bar in 1889, and the following year he moved to Boise, Idaho, where he set up law practice and attracted national attention with his summation for the people in the Coeur d'Alene mining riots. He was elected to the U. S. Senate in 1907, and thus began a career of spearheading opposition against many of the major issues that faced the Congress. He frequently denounced the World Court and was strongly opposed to the entrance of the U. S. into the League of Nations, the latter he considered to be the greatest gratification of his twenty-eight years in the Senate. In his struggle with Woodrow Wilson over the League, Borah was one of the leaders of the "Irreconcilables," playing the leading role in keeping the United States out of the League. Senator Borah opposed a women's suffrage amendment and advocated a Prohibition amendment, both on the grounds of states' rights. Though he often broke with the Republican Party on matters of principle, he never identified himself with a third party movement. Occasionally, Borah did vote and speak with the majority, but his reputation will always be based on his opposition to majority proposals. At age seventy-one, Borah sought the nomination for Republican candidate for the presidency in 1936, but he won only a few delegates and later refused to support the candidacy of Alf Landon, who eventually lost in a landslide election to incumbent Franklin D. Roosevelt.

*Occasion:* Throughout 1919 William Borah presented major speeches against the League of Nations. He felt that if the United States were to join the League a change in the Constitution would be necessary, that the nation would become embroiled in European conflicts, and that the League would abrogate the policy of both Washington and Monroe. To Borah, the League was a step toward internationalism and a start toward sterilizing nationalism. The Versailles Treaty which contained the Covenant of the League was officially given to the Senate on July 10, 1919. Borah studied it and pronounced it dangerous and unsettling, and he felt it had been negotiated with secret diplomacy that led an uninformed public to war. On November 19, after months of Senate argument, Borah delivered this masterful address—a lengthy speech that recited a litany of persuasive arguments for outright rejection of the treaty.

*Excerpt:* "Mr. President, there is another and even a more commanding reason why I shall record my vote against this treaty. It imperils what I conceive to be the underlying, the very first principles of this Republic. It is in conflict with the right of our people to govern themselves free from all restraint, legal or moral, of foreign powers....Call us little Americans if you will, but leave us the consolation and the pride which the term American, however modified, still imparts.... We have sought nothing save the tranquility of our own people and the honor and independence of our own Republic....If we have erred it is because we have placed too high an estimate upon the wisdom of Washington and Jefferson, too exalted an opinion upon the patriotism of the sainted Lincoln.... Sir, we are told that this treaty means peace. Even so, I would not pay the price. ... Peace upon any other basis than national independence, peace purchased at the cost of any part of our national integrity, is fit only for slaves, and even when purchased at such a price it is a delusion, for it cannot last. But your treaty does not mean peace—far, very far, from it. If we are to judge the future by the past it means war. Is there any guaranty of peace other than the guaranty which comes of the control of the war-making power by the people?....Autocracy which has bathed the world in blood for centuries reigns supreme. Democracy is everywhere excluded. This, you say, means peace...The people of our beloved country will finally speak...America will continue her mission in the cause of peace, of freedom, and of civilization."

*Impact:* The speech must be rendered a success for the main reason that the treaty was eventually rejected by the Senate. The "irreconcilables" and the "reservationists" combined to defeat the treaty. In the final vote on March 19, 1920, the treaty was defeated by a margin of seven votes. During the period of debate on the treaty, Borah was considered a chief architect of its defeat, having delivered twenty-five major debate addresses on the subject, as well as many other speeches in the political campaigns. Henry Cabot Lodge was also considered a vigorous and effective advocate for treaty rejection, thus on the shoulders of both Borah and Lodge rested the major responsibility for final Senate action and the commitment of the nation to an isolationist policy for that generation. After Borah's address to the Senate, Lodge concluded: "When I find myself with tears in my eyes, I know I am hearing a great speech." The power in his speaking was both humility and complete sincerity of convictions. As World War II approached, Borah opposed relaxing the nation's neutrality, and delivered numerous speeches in opposition to Roosevelt's actions that led the nation closer to joining the Allied war effort. His last major speech was given in the Senate on October 2, 1939, in defense of the embargo on arms. "I look upon the present war in Europe as nothing more than another chapter in the bloody volume of European power politics," he declared. The "Great Negator" died expecting that peace would be restored in Europe in the spring of 1940.

*Contemporary Application:* Coming from an eloquent speaker, the rhetoric of protest can be highly persuasive, yet history may reveal that such a speaker can be disastrously wrong.

# 52. Clarence Darrow, Plea in Defense of Loeb and Leopold, August 22, 1924

*Speaker:* Few, if any, attorneys in U. S. history have been more self-assured while standing on the courtroom floor, better skilled in the art of debating, or was better known than any other defense attorney of his time than Clarence Darrow (1857–1938). Based in Chicago, Darrow held several important legal positions within the city. When socialist Eugene V. Debs was indicted on charges of conspiracy in 1895, following the American Railway Union strike (Pullman strike), Darrow resigned as general attorney for another railway system in order to accept Debs' defense. From 1895 to 1913, he was defense attorney in labor cases principally, representing the United Mine Workers in 1902, William Haywood in 1907, and the McNamara brothers in 1910-11. He gained fame first as a labor lawyer and then a defense attorney, especially in two nationally celebrated cases: Richard Loeb and Nathan Leopold on a charge of murder and John Scopes on a charge of violating the Tennessee "anti-evolution" law. In the early twentieth century, Darrow established himself as the preeminent trial attorney of his time. He debated and lectured widely, especially during his later years. How difficult it would be to rank Darrow as a "great orator" in any history of American public address! He was nontraditional and a nonconformist in his thinking and rhetoric, and a "devil's advocate" by profession. In his career, Darrow defended some two thousand cases in court, winning most of them. Millions of Americans knew his name and face, and thousands heard him speak. Indeed, he was the champion of the "common man," always pledging to fight for the underdog; he was often referred to as "attorney for the damned." In his skillful courtroom rhetoric, Darrow buttressed his arguments with commonsense observations and humorous aphorisms. In the *Scopes* case, Darrow employed an interplay of cogent argument, disgust, and sarcasm. He came to strongly oppose the death penalty. In his lifetime of law career, Darrow defended a hundred clients charged with murder—not one was sentenced to death.

*Occasion:* In 1924 Richard Loeb and Nathan Leopold, two wealthy, well-educated young men of Chicago, confessed to the murder of fourteen-year-old Robert Franks. Their parents at once engaged Darrow for the defense. At this time he was already considered even by his opponents as the nation's most eloquent and persuasive criminal attorney. Since the young defendants (eighteen and nineteen years old) had already confessed, Darrow did not seek acquittal. The two young men confessed the hideous crime, committed to see if they could get away with "the perfect crime." Darrow set out to spare the defendants from execution by hanging. In his closing statement, Darrow argued directly to Judge John R. Caverly and, indirectly, to a nation held spellbound by this unfolding courtroom drama.

*Excerpt:* "The easy thing and the popular thing to do is to hang my clients. I know it. Men and women who do not think will applaud. The cruel and the thoughtless will approve. It will be easy today; but in Chicago, and reaching out over the length and breadth of the land, more and more fathers and mothers, the humane, the kind, and the hopeful, who are gaining an understanding and asking questions not only about these poor boys but about their own, these will join in no acclaim at the death of my clients. But, Your Honor, what they shall ask may not count. I know the easy way. I know Your Honor stands between the future and the past. I know the future is with me, and what I stand for here; not merely for the lives of these two unfortunate lads, but for all boys and all girls; for all of the young, and as far as possible, for all of the old. I am pleading for life, understanding, charity, kindness, and the infinite mercy that considers all. I am pleading that we overcome cruelty with kindness and hatred with love. I know the future is on my side."

*Impact:* Darrow believed passionately that punishing two young defendants by hanging was far more horrifying than any crime they might possibly have committed. His argument touched millions, for he appeared as spokesperson, not merely for Loeb and Leopold, but for all misguided and unhappy children who act out in terrible ways and then must be judged by representatives of society. His summation speech, leaving the judge in tears, remains perhaps the most persuasive and eloquent argument made against capital punishment in court or any other forum. Sentenced to life in prison, Loeb would ultimately be killed by another prisoner; Leopold was granted parole after thirty-three years behind bars and moved to Puerto Rico.

*Contemporary Application:* One who speaks courageously and eloquently on behalf of the downtrodden and despised will gain the respect of future generations.

*Interesting Fact:* Less than a year after the sentencing, Darrow participated in the second of his two most famous cases—a case that has become one of the nation's most notorious, the *State of Tennessee v. John T. Scopes.* Scopes was a young high school science teacher in Dayton, Tennessee, who was arrested for violating the Butler Act, a statue prohibiting the teaching of Darwin's theory of evolution (or any other theory that challenged the biblical narrative of creation). Assisting with the prosecution was three-time Democratic nominee for president, William Jennings Bryan, a Christian fundamentalist who had lobbied for such legislation. That trial did not produce a great plea from Darrow, but it had great significance personally, giving him the opportunity to attack a pet bugaboo of his boyhood—organized religion—before the eyes of the world. And he considered Bryan as the perfect opponent for such engagement. Darrow's incisive and telling cross-examination of Bryan, who seemed arrogant in taking the stand as an expert on the Bible, would be immortalized by Jerome Lawrence and Robert Lee's play, *Inherit the Wind,* later turned into a movie in which Spencer Tracy played Darrow.

# 53. Franklin D. Roosevelt, The Banking Crisis [First Fireside Chat], March 12, 1933

*Speaker:* Franklin Roosevelt instituted a new strategy for reaching the American people by going directly to them on a regular basis with the medium of network radio broadcasting. This president had so many qualities of an effective speaker. His logic was convincing even though, like many politicians, he oversimplified complex problems. Roosevelt was strong with *ethos*, source credibility, by having succeeded in political life despite a terrible disease that he suffered and endured; by identifying with the audience's religious ideals; by visiting his constituencies often; by constantly reiterating a philosophy of social justice. The nature of the "fireside chats" demonstrated that Roosevelt could adapt to mass media, especially by perfecting a conversational manner of delivery. That conversational method gave the impression of informality, spontaneity, sincerity, and genuine friendship. Frequently he would say, "You and I know…." and he could use simple analogies and illustrations. For example, when he was urging Congress to pass the Lend Lease Act to help Great Britain with war supplies, he compared it to a good neighbor lending a water hose to a person whose house was on fire. He projected the Aristotelian concept of good will and implied he had nothing to hide. He knew how to tap into strong emotional appeals: self-preservation, welfare, altruism, duty, and patriotism, to name a few. In style (word choice and arrangement), he sought clarity and simplicity. His speeches had a definite oral quality. Some of FDR's trite phrases were "crystal clear," "simple as ABC," "shenanigans," "botch," "jazz," and "chisel." He once stated the American government was a "three horse team." He made frequent use of personal pronouns. While his hand gestures were necessarily limited, his facial expressions were almost unlimited.

He had a directness that communicated a sense of sympathy and authority. In vocal expression, FDR's flow of words was slow and distinct—never did he sound hurried. His pronunciation was much like other educated folk of the East, such as JFK ("r's" were often silent). In sum, few public servants in the Western world have demonstrated greater respect for the power of effective public speaking or worked harder to be effective in persuasion for the achievement of what one believed to be the national good than did Franklin D. Roosevelt.

*Occasion:* A true banking crisis existed in the nation and the public's confidence in the system had been shaken. On the day of Roosevelt's inauguration, thirty-eight states had closed their banks, and banks operated on a limited basis in the other states. Also, on that morning, the New York Stock Exchange was closed; other markets and boards of trade had shut their doors. The general public held so little confidence in the banking and finance community, and there was a general belief that only a new president could improve this dismal situation. The President's admonition that only fear need be feared was too vague to instill confidence; after all, Hoover had been making much the same vague encouragement. The Inaugural Address had given a general philosophy for the New Deal, but it was time to implement specific legislation and explain it to the American people. On March 9, Roosevelt sent his banking message to Congress, and lawmakers found his proposal an exceptionally conservative document—no radical reforms, such as nationalization of all banks, but an emergency measure extending government assistance to private bankers to reopen their banks. This was FDR's first "fireside chat" with many to follow. A day earlier the President had announced his purpose was "to convey to the people themselves a clear picture of the situation in Washington itself whenever there is danger of any confusion as to what the government is undertaking." This "chat" was delivered on a Sunday evening with an estimated sixty million people sitting around their radios to hear what this new president wanted to do to help them.

*Excerpt:* "Your government does not intend that the history of the past few years shall be repeated. We do not want and will not have another epidemic of bank failures….We had a bad banking situation….There is an element in the readjustment of our financial system more important than currency, more important than gold, and that is the confidence of the people. Confidence and courage are the essential of success in carrying out our plan. You people must have faith; you must not be stampeded by rumors or guesses. Let us unite in banishing fear. We have provided the machinery to restore our financial system; it is up to you to support and make it work. It is your problem no less than mine. Together we cannot fail."

*Impact:* The President was able in large measure to restore confidence in both the government and the banking system. He discussed upcoming government action and explained it in highly understandable language much like a father would talk to his children. In warm and reassuring tones, the President assured all citizens it was now safe to return their savings to the banks. The next day, newspapers acclaimed the speech as effective and reassuring, and banks reopened. The speech brought a shift in confidence as indicated by the fact people were now more eager to deposit funds than to withdraw funds. And the President had established a new strategy of talking directly to the American public—Roosevelt was the first president to master the technique of reaching and communicating directly over the radio. During the war years, the "fireside chat" was especially important in keeping the public informed and reassured of eventual Allied success in waging the battle against Hitler and the Axis powers. Surely, had Roosevelt served as chief executive in our own times, he would have done equally as well in speaking over television, whether doing public speeches, debates, or interviews.

*Contemporary Application:* Genuineness and sincerity on a delicate subject, yet delivered in a conversational manner, will command attention and restore confidence, especially when the speaker's credibility is high.

# 54. Lou Gehrig, Farewell to Baseball, July 4, 1939

*Speaker*: The New York Yankees first baseman was one of the most outstanding players not simply to wear the traditional pinstripes but ever to play the game. Lou Gehrig (1903-1941) was nicknamed the "Iron Horse," and while his career batting average was an outstanding .340, his stellar achievement was playing a record 2,130 consecutive games. For a long time, many baseball fans felt that record for endurance could never be broken, yet it was indeed broken by the Baltimore Orioles' Cal Ripken, Jr., in September 1995. Gehrig always insisted he was not a headline guy and that he was not a public speaker. His feats on the playing field did, indeed, make headlines. In batting production, he shared Yankee leadership with his famed teammate Babe Ruth. The Babe's flamboyant antics meant he usually garnered more headlines and attention than the modest Gehrig. Had Gehrig stayed healthy, we might now be debating if he or Ted Williams was the greatest hitter of all time. Even today, Lou Gehrig is considered by sports fans and historians as the ultimate example of courage, class, and consistency.

*Occasion*: Gehrig had removed himself from the active roster six weeks earlier in the 1939 season due to the rapid progress of a neuromuscular disorder called amyotrophic lateral sclerosis. The Independence Day doubleheader with the Washington Senators was selected as the occasion to honor the retired star. Almost 62,000 fans gathered in Yankee Stadium, including Mayor LaGuardia and former teammates from the 1927 Yankees World Series championship team. Microphones were set up on the field for speeches to honor the retiree, yet Gehrig had to be coaxed to make a speech on the occasion. His wife Eleanor stated that the night before the speech he wrote out, but did not rehearse, his remarks. And, then, when he spoke, he did not use any notes but seemed to speak completely from his heart.

*Excerpt:* "Fans, for the past two weeks you have been reading about a bad break I got. Yet today I consider myself the luckiest man on the face of the earth. I have been in baseball for seventeen years and have never received anything but kindness and encouragement from you fans. Look at these grand men. Which of you wouldn't consider it the highlight of his career just to associate with them for one day? Sure, I'm lucky....So I close in saying that I might have had a tough break, but I have an awful lot to live for."

*Impact:* This surely is the greatest speech in all baseball history, perhaps, though arguably, all sports history. One biographer, Marty Appel, called Gehrig "a player for the ages" and added "his speech was a baseball moment that had nothing to do with playing. It was baseball's Gettysburg Address" (*USA Today*, July 4, 2014). As Gehrig's voice echoed throughout the grounds and storied stadium, there were few dry eyes. Many in subsequent generations have seen that bit of old black-and-white newsreel footage that shows the Yankee star at his most tender public moment.

*Contemporary Application:* One need not be a forceful, dynamic, confident speaker to sway an audience. A strong sense of ethical character and a reputation for humility, sincerity, and undaunted courage in the midst of a career suddenly abbreviated by injury or disease will touch human hearts. No one expects a famous athlete to be a great public speaker, though many speak on the banquet tour after retirement from their sport. Clearly, this Yankee star communicated his deep gratitude for what the game of baseball had given him.

*Connection to Today:* Lou Gehrig's simple description of himself—"Luckiest Man on the Face of the Earth"—lives on in sports lore. The disease that he so courageously fought now bears his name. Gehrig died two years later. "Tonight I stand here, overwhelmed, as my name is linked with the great and courageous Lou Gehrig," Ripken told the crowd in 1995 after he broke Gehrig's record.

"I'm truly humbled to have our names spoken in the same breath." A year or so after Gehrig's death, the 1942 movie, *The Pride of the Yankees*, starring Gary Cooper as the Yankee star, was released.

*Interesting facts:* Sports is such a huge part of the American culture, little wonder that there are many inspirational speeches made by sports figures. The best ones have elements in common, primarily passion of the heart for both the game and for life, family, and supporters, and, then, most are brief and to the point. Sometimes, these famous speeches get immortalized in movie form, such as Knute Rockne attempting to inspire his Fighting Irish before the players took the field against the mighty Army team; eight years earlier the great Notre Dame star George Gipp had died and his final words to Rockne were "Win one for the Gipper." The speech to the U. S. Olympic Hockey team by Coach Herb Brooks before it took the ice in the semi-final match against the highly-favored Soviets has been immortalized in the movie *Miracle* where Kurt Russell re-enacts Brooks' speech; the incredible upset has been called "Miracle on Ice." Two of the most inspirational sports speeches were presented at the ESPY Awards. The first ever ESPY Award, the Arthur Ashe Courage and Humanitarian Award, went to Coach Jim Valvano, who, while fighting bone cancer, delivered an inspiring speech. A most inspiring and passionate address at the 2016 ESPY Awards was delivered by Craig Sager, who received the Jimmy V Award for Perseverance. The award was presented by Vice President Joe Biden at the formal event in Los Angeles; Biden's son Beau had died from cancer a few months earlier. Wearing a strikingly vibrant sport coat, Sager, who had worked with Turner Sports for thirty-four years, seventeen of which had been covering NBA basketball, delivered most effectively a passionate and attention-riveting address that demonstrated gratitude and appreciation for life, family, friends, and fans. He made heart-felt application for all: "Time is not something that can be bought, it cannot be wagered with God, and it is not in endless supply. Time is simply how you live your life." Sager died on December 15, 2016, at age 65.

# 55. Franklin D. Roosevelt, Four Freedoms Address, January 6, 1941

*Speaker:* Franklin Roosevelt could seize an ordinary speaking occasion, in this case the 1941 State of the Union Address, to present an extraordinary address. Certainly, Roosevelt was a pragmatic politician, yet he was driven by idealism and his own worldview. Early in his political career, FDR, as a state senator and later as governor of New York, was concerned in the broadest sense with human rights and freedoms. His thinking on this crucially important subject developed further in response to rapidly moving developments outside the borders of the nation he served. The President began preparation for this speech almost three weeks before delivery and, typically, he gained assistance on major policy addresses from advisers and speechwriters Samuel Rosenman, Harry Hopkins, and Robert Sherwood. This speech went through seven drafts before final presentation, and the "Four Freedoms" passage, which gives the address its fame, did not appear until the fourth draft. As always, Roosevelt spoke in bold and direct language, and part of his brilliance was an ability to make the complex seem simple and understandable by ordinary citizens.

*Occasion:* The immediate audience, of course, was the joint houses of Congress, but the larger audience was the entire nation through radio broadcast as well as the political leaders and citizens of allied European nations. The conflict which began in Europe was spreading, and one by one the nations of Europe were being pounded into surrender by Hitler's war machine. Only months earlier, nations such as France, Austria, Poland, Czechoslovakia, Denmark, Norway, and the Netherlands had fallen to the Nazis. During these tense, uncertain months, the fall of Great Britain seemed a real possibility. The new British Prime Minister, Winston Churchill, pled with the U. S. for emergency assistance, but the American public remained essentially isolationist, disdaining the thought of thousands of American young men dying in still another European war. The President's speech purpose was to win the support of Congress and prepare the nation for involvement in this war through assistance to the British.

*Excerpt:* "In the future days, which we seek to make secure, we look forward to a world founded upon four essential human freedoms. The first is freedom of speech and expression–everywhere in the world. The second is freedom of every person to worship God in his own way–everywhere in the world. The third is freedom from want–which, translated into world terms, means economic understandings which will secure to every nation a healthy peacetime life for its inhabitants-everywhere in the world. The fourth is freedom from fear–which, translated into world terms, means a world-wide reduction of armaments to such a point and in such a thorough fashion that no nation will be in a position to commit an act of physical aggression against any neighbor–anywhere in the world....That is no vision of a distant millennium. It is a definite basis for a kind of world attainable in our own time and generation. That kind of world is the very antithesis of the so-called new order of tyranny which the dictators seek to create with the crash of a bomb. To that new order we oppose the greater conception–the moral order. A good society is able to face schemes of world domination and foreign revolutions alike without fear....This nation has placed its destiny in the hands and heads and hearts of its millions of free men and women; and its faith in freedom under the guidance of God. Freedom means the supremacy of human rights everywhere. Our support goes to those who struggle to gain those rights and keep them. Our strength is our unity of purpose. To that high concept there can be no end save victory."

*Impact:* The Congress listened carefully as the President addressed only one major topic in his traditional State of the Union Address. The address became one of the most important speeches of the twentieth century—the ideals enunciated became foundational principles that evolved into the Atlantic Charter declared by Winston Churchill and Roosevelt in August 1941 and the Universal Declaration of Human Rights adopted by the United Nations in 1948 through the work of Eleanor Roosevelt. The speech sparked an important debate in Congress, though it eventually prepared the way for passage of Roosevelt's proposed Lend-Lease program that enabled the U. S. to supply airplanes, trucks, tanks, and food to imperiled allies. Roosevelt's pre-speech rhetorical strategy had been using a creative analogy, comparing the "loan" of war materiel to the British to be no different in principle than a compassionate neighbor loaning a garden hose to the man next door to put out a fire destroying his own home. In the literature of great American rhetoric, Roosevelt coined an enduring phrase when he spoke of the U. S. as being "the great arsenal of democracy." This address is listed as number five in Bill Moyers' "Ten Great Presidential Speeches."

*Contemporary Application:* Themes of "liberty" and "freedom" seem foundational in all kinds of political rhetoric as well as great constitutional documents of our history. These words seem omnipresent in times of national or international crisis. Though noble sounding, realistically there are ambiguities, vagaries, nuances, and partisanship that are typically masked by the rhetorical use of these abstract, yet richly meaningful terms.

*Interesting Fact:* As World War II continued, famed popular artist Norman Rockwell painted a series of portraits that illustrated the four freedoms, appearing in the *Saturday Evening Post* in early 1943. These paintings were the most memorable images of American freedom during that war. They seemed to reassure Americans that the goals of international war went beyond just defeating the Axis powers, but war was a struggle to preserve and protect basic American liberties. Rockwell claimed the President's speech inspired him to do the paintings, which eventually went on national tour to raise money for the war effort. Some Americans said that the paintings had helped them understand for the first time what the war was all about.

# 56. Charles Lindberg, Against Entry into the War, April 23, 1941

*Speaker:* Perhaps no one of his generation had come close to garnering the popularity and adulation granted a national hero than Charles Lindberg (1902–1974), the young pilot who, in 1927, became the first individual to cross the Atlantic Ocean in a solo flight. In the *Spirit of St. Louis*, a single engine white monoplane built on a shoestring budget, Lindberg flew nonstop and without sleep, fighting weather and fatigue, for thirty-four hours from the time he took off from Long Island until he landed at Le Bourget Airport in Paris. Thousands of Parisians were waiting for his landing at the airstrip and began charging his plane as soon as it landed—a hero's welcome almost unparalleled! When he returned to New York City, an estimated one million admirers lined the route of the parade in his honor. Americans loved adventurers and Lindberg became the most famous and adored man in the U. S., mobbed by crowds everywhere he visited. In the 20s, the airplane was one of the newest and most exciting inventions of the time, and the young pilot had demonstrated individual initiative and deep conviction. These traits were important in building the sterling ethos that Lindberg enjoyed as a public speaker. *Time*, a new mass circulation magazine, named the aviator as its first "Man of the Year" (for 1927) and more awards were coming by leaders and organizations that valued Americanism and the image of individualism. Lindberg had written an autobiography, and, from July 20 to October 23, 1927, he visited eighty-two cities in all forty-eight states on a book promotion tour; in the tour he delivered one hundred and forty-seven speeches and rode thirteen-hundred miles in parades. Later he toured and spoke in various cities in Central America and South America. Sadly, in 1932 his infant son was kidnapped and murdered in what was labeled "the crime of the century," and the publicity and media attention led Lindberg and wife Anne Morrow to leave the country secretly in a "voluntary exile" in Europe from 1935 to 1939. In later years, Lindberg was a writer, international explorer, inventor, conservationist, and environmentalist.

*Occasion:* As war clouds loomed in Europe in the 1930s, thoughtful Americans dreaded the thought of another world war and the possibility of the nation being drawn into it. In 1940 a group of isolationists organized the America First Committee to protest their nation's drift toward intervention in another European war. In fact, after the election of 1940, Roosevelt and his advisers edged the U. S. toward stronger support of Britain and put pressure on Japan. In January 1941 FDR proposed the Lend-Lease program, which allowed Britain to "borrow" military equipment for the duration of the world (as previously noted, the President used a clever analogy of lending a garden hose to a neighbor who had a house on fire). The Lend Lease Act triggered intense political debate. Majority opinion seemed to support the President. The America First Committee attracted individuals of all political persuasions (including isolationists and pacifists), including socialist organizer Norman Thomas, conservative Senator Robert Taft of Ohio, liberal educator Robert Hutchens, but the most prominent figure was Charles Lindberg. Lindberg toured the nation and campaigned vigorously at mass rallies, making speeches against U. S. involvement in the war and claiming that Lend-Lease would allow the President to declare anything a "defense article." This speech was delivered in New York and, like other important speeches of that era, the address was broadcast over the radio to a larger audience.

*Excerpt:* "The time has come when those of us who believe in an independent American destiny must band together and organize for strength. We have been led toward war by a minority of our people. This minority has power. It has influence. It has a loud voice. But it does not represent the American people."

*Impact:* Lindberg drew an audience that largely supported his isolationist ideas, or at least was willing to consider his ideas. After all, here was an

American hero who had accomplished a great feat even if he had later become controversial. Yet Lindberg's involvement in non-interventionism did impair his credibility as he was labeled by some critics as anti-Semitic and fascist. Roosevelt did make disparaging comments about the America First Committee and about Lindberg, specifically. After this same Lindberg speech had been presented in April in Des Moines, Roosevelt wrote to Henry Stimson: "When I read Lindberg's speech I felt it could not have been better put if it had been written by Goebbels [Nazi minister of propaganda under Hitler] himself. What a pity the youngster has completely abandoned his belief in our form of government and has accepted Nazi methods because apparently they are efficient." As a rhetorical critic, one might validly rate this and other Lindberg speeches advocating non-participation as being failures in that they did not achieve the speaker's purpose; the same critic might also rate them as effective in making the strongest possible case for a minority viewpoint that needed to be discussed in the public arena.

*Contemporary Application:* A person who becomes a highly respected figure due to heroic achievement in one field may become prominent as a speaker in another field. However, that person's public respect and "hero status" might become diminished if he or she advocates an unpopular position and then becomes easily discredited by the verdict of history.

*Interesting Fact:* On December 8, 1941, the day after the Japanese attack on Pearl Harbor, Lindberg abruptly ended his isolationism and noted that had he been in Congress he would have voted for a declaration for war. He volunteered to serve his country "any way [he] could," but Roosevelt and his Cabinet—still furious over Lindberg's isolationist speeches and verbal attacks on the administration—refused his offer. Lindberg, humiliated, then worked for Henry Ford, who used his factories and assembly lines to build bombers and other weapons of war for the government.

# 57. Franklin D. Roosevelt, Keeping Political Faith, September 23, 1944

*Speaker:* President Franklin Roosevelt had been nominated for that unprecedented fourth term almost totally because the nation was at war and, the majority of Americans at least, trusted their president. Yet FDR seemed reluctant to campaign once nominated. The Republican nominee was Thomas Dewey, who began attacks claiming the President was a tyrant. Friends and political advisers encouraged FDR to launch the campaign for that fourth term, but he delayed long enough to deepen speculation about his health, his loss of political acumen, and his enthusiasm for continuing to serve in the White House. Indeed, Roosevelt had been sick and then treated by his personal physician. He had also lost about fifteen pounds, which only added a little more grist to the rumor mill. His personal physician did make a public statement reassuring the nation the President's health was "good, very good." The campaign did not cure what ailed him physically, but it rekindled his fighting spirit, as campaigns always did. After hearing some of the Republican Dewey's attacks on him as well as claims for himself that he was a heroic racket-buster, FDR was ready for a good fight. In anticipating the Teamsters' dinner, he told advisers with a smile: "I expect to have a lot of fun with that one."

*Occasion:* Roosevelt and Democrats in general have been friends of the U. S. labor movement. This speech was a meeting with Dan Tobin, Teamster president, and one thousand members of the Brotherhood of Teamsters gathered at the Hotel Statler in Washington; the speech was also broadcast live on network radio to the entire nation. The President's purpose was to praise labor, dispel personal rumors, answer attacks against his administration, and, just in general, agitate the Republicans. Ultimately, of course, the President hoped to win re-election.

*Excerpt:* "These Republican leaders have not been content with attacks on me, or my wife, or on my sons. No, not content with that, they now include my little dog, Fala. Well, of course, I don't resent attacks, and my family doesn't resent attacks, but Fala does resent them. You know, Fala is Scotch, and being a Scottie, as soon as he learned that the Republican fiction writers had concocted a story that I had left him behind on the Aleutian Islands and sent a destroyer back to find him—at a cost to the taxpayers of two or three, or eight or twenty million dollars—his Scotch soul was furious. He has not been the same dog since. I am accustomed to hearing malicious falsehoods about my self—such as that old, worm-eaten chestnut that I have represented myself as indispensable. But I think I have a right to object to libelous statements about my dog."

*Impact:* President Roosevelt achieved his goals with such a surprising sense of both humor and satire. "Imitation may be the sincerest form of flattery," he told the Teamsters, "but I am afraid that in this case it is the most obvious common or garden variety of fraud." Many Republicans were calling him a tyrant. "They have imported the propaganda technique invented by the dictators abroad." The most shameless of critics had said he had left the United States unprepared for war. "I doubt that even Goebbels [the famed Nazi propagandist] would have tried that one." These statements were prior to his move into the Fala story, the most memorable highlight of this and almost any other campaign speech. The immediate audience loved the speech—one of the greatest campaign speeches in American history and it reveals the old master at his best! This speech showed the President had now jumped back into the 1944 campaign with his old zeal and passion and that he had not lost his sense of humor. His remarks were interrupted over fifty times with applause and laughter. At the end, FDR received a five-minute standing ovation.

*Contemporary Application:* The use of humor and satire can be an effective strategy in certain speaking situations, and almost all listeners enjoy a humorous story about a dog or other pet. Since a pet can't speak for itself, the pet's owner is pretty much free to interpret its behavior in any way he or she chooses.

*Connection to Today:* Most presidents since FDR are known for owning a family dog. True, presidential dogs have been different breeds and called by different names. These dogs and other pets often show up for "photo ops" on the White House lawn and are used to humanize the president and his family, no matter how unpopular that president may be. In recent years, the president in office has "forgiven" a designated white turkey and spared it from the hatchet right before Thanksgiving.

*Interesting Fact:* Franklin Roosevelt's adroit use of Fala to win over the audience in a humorous way might well have provided Richard Nixon with a clue on how to exploit the story of his young daughters' cocker spaniel named Checkers in a televised speech to save his spot on the 1952 Republican ticket.

# 58. George Marshall, On European Recovery, June 5, 1947

*Speaker:* George Catlett Marshall (1880–1959) was an immensely respected and popular American statesman and soldier serving as a leader in key roles during World War II and the Cold War. Hailed as the "organizer of victory" by Winston Churchill, he was chief of staff of the U. S. Army, secretary of state, and secretary of defense in working with President Harry S. Truman. As chief of staff and military adviser to Franklin D. Roosevelt, Marshall organized the largest military expansion in U.S. history, inheriting an outmoded, poorly equipped army of 189,000 men; and he coordinated the large-scale expansion and modernization of the U.S. Army. Though he had never actually led troops in combat, Marshall was a skilled organizer with a talent for inspiring other officers. Many of the American generals who were given top commands during the war were either picked or recommended by Marshall, including Dwight D. Eisenhower, George S. Patton, and Omar Bradley. Marshall possessed high credibility among American audiences, and a shrewd President Truman allowed Marshall's name to be given to the massive economic recovery plan. Unlike Truman, Marshall was widely respected and admired by members of both political parties.

*Occasion:* World War II had ended, but now there was a delicate peace to be maintained. Any hope for an era of postwar cooperation and goodwill between the two new superpowers of the world, the United States and the Soviet Union, quickly evaporated. The map of Europe had been redrawn and, in Churchill's famous metaphor, an Iron Curtain had descended across Eastern Europe as the Soviets had established a ring of Socialist states around its borders. All of Europe seemed to be in chaos, but Greece and Turkey seemed in peril, and there was concern that, one by one, European nations would fall to the

Communists. Major cities were in shambles, both physically and economically; poverty and starvation were rampant. On March 12, 1947, President Harry Truman appeared before Congress, delivering the foundational statement for the Truman Doctrine. His sweeping rhetoric contended the United States should aid all "free people" being subjected to threat of tyranny. Yet there needed to be a specific plan to implement the doctrine. Assistant Secretary of State Dean Acheson presented the first public outline of the plan in a speech on May 8, 1947, but it went almost entirely unnoticed. Secretary Marshall was invited to deliver the commencement address at Harvard University, and he used the occasion to deliver an explanation of this most important plan for economic aid to Europe. However, the main audience to be reached was European rather than at home. The European audience was deemed just as important as the American audience, and Dean Acheson, as Under Secretary of State and a chief architect of the plan, was dispatched to contact the European media, especially the British media, and the speech was read in its entirety on the British Broadcasting Company.

*Excerpt:* "The world situation is very serious…The modern system of the division of labor upon which the exchange of products is based is in danger of breaking down….Aside from the demoralizing effect on the world at large and the possibilities of disturbances arising as a result of the desperation of the people concerned, the consequences to the economy of the United States should be apparent to all. It is logical that the United States should do whatever it is able to do to assist in the return of normal economic health to the world, without which there can be no political stability and no assured peace. Our policy is not directed against any country, but against hunger, poverty, desperation and chaos. Any government that is willing to assist in recovery will find full co-operation on the part of the USA. Its purpose should be the revival of a working economy in the world so as to permit the emergence of political and social conditions in which free institutions can exist….It is logical that the United States should do whatever it is able to do to assist in the return to normal economic health in the world."

*Impact:* Marshall spoke as usual in a soft voice that may have seemed almost inaudible to some listeners; some claimed he seldom looked up at his audience. Yet all listeners were aware that his call was a bold one that embraced a radical concept that would impact all of Europe. The address seemed more a proposal than a plan as it contained virtually no details and no numbers. Marshall challenged European leaders to cooperate and coordinate in their recovery, creating their own plan and being able to count on the U.S. to provide adequate funding. The administration felt that the plan would likely be unpopular among many Americans, and the speech was also directed at a European audience. The speaker emphasized that the goal was humanitarian as, indeed, blizzards and cold in all of Europe had created frightening shortages of winter wheat, coal, electricity, and even food in most nations. The plan did spawn extensive debate that lasted through the winter of 1947–48, but congressmen who visited Europe returned with reports of destitution, suffering, even starvation. By any measure, the Marshall Plan was remarkably successful, funneling $13.34 billion in aid to Western Europe between 1948 and 1952. This speech has always been considered the "opening bell" for the implementation of the Truman Doctrine and "Marshall Plan," considered by many to be the greatest act of humanitarian aid ever implemented. The assistance was welcomed eagerly by European nations. It hastened an impressive recovery that included a quadrupling of industrial production, improved standards of living, and enhanced political stability, thus undermining the appeal of communist parties in Western Europe. Marshall was awarded the Nobel Peace Prize for this plan in 1953.

*Contemporary Application:* Military leaders are not typically known for their skills in public speaking, but in the American tradition the outstanding ones are accorded high credibility, especially when making an important policy statement.

# 59. Eleanor Roosevelt, Universal Declaration of Human Rights, September 28, 1948

*Speaker:* Eleanor Roosevelt (1884–1962) played many roles in her long career of public service: first lady of the U. S., humanitarian, philanthropist, reformer, advocate, public lecturer, teacher, campaigner, politician, political adviser, fund raiser, negotiator, and writer. Skill and confidence in public speaking were at the heart of most of these roles, and she presented literally thousands of speeches over a wide range of topics and to a wide range of audiences in both the United States and overseas in her productive lifetime. She was the longest serving first lady in American history, residing with her husband Franklin in the White House from March 1933 until April 1945. While widely and universally respected in the post-White House years, she was a most controversial first lady, especially for her activism and outspokenness on so many unpopular causes and issues. She spoke out on issues that impacted the American labor force, racial and ethnic minorities, the poor and disadvantaged, and women. She was the first female to address a national political convention, and her address to the 1940 Democratic Convention was the turning point in the delegates' willingness to nominate her husband for an unprecedented third term in office. She held 348 press conferences over the twelve years in the White House, wrote a syndicated newspaper column ("My Day"), and published sixty articles in national magazines. She visited American troops overseas during the war and attracted huge audiences. Her outspoken support for laboring people and civil rights often evoked opposition and even scorn, especially in the South. Political cartoons often caricatured her, usually affectionately but often scornfully, as a tall woman (at 5' 11" she and Michelle Obama have been the tallest first ladies) who was less than attractive in appearance with protruding upper teeth, flying fur piece around her neck, and an ever-present hat. She spoke with a high-pitched voice and, more often than not, without notes due to her confidence and deep knowledge of the subjects for which she was passionate. One writer for the *New Yorker* wrote of her speaking without notes yet with "telling sincerity." When the United Nations seemed tarnished in image and effectiveness, she toured the country proclaiming its mission and purpose in the world. In the study of American rhetoric, surely Eleanor Roosevelt arguably earned the distinction of being the nation's most outstanding female orator.

*Occasion:* The former First Lady had traveled to France to speak on behalf of the United Nations and this Universal Declaration. She had already established credibility as an advocate for the U. N., having been appointed by President Truman as a delegate to the U.N. General Assembly in December 1945, having traveled the nation on behalf of the U. N., and, in April 1946, becoming the first chairperson of the U.N. Commission on Human Rights. The speaker adapted her opening remarks to a French audience "where the Declaration of the Rights of Men had been drafted and proclaimed" and "the great slogans of the French Revolution 'liberty, equality, and fraternity' fired the imagination of men."

*Excerpt:* "We must not be confused about what freedom is. Basic human rights are simple and easily understood: freedom of speech and a free press; freedom of religion and worship; freedom of assembly and the right of petition; the right of men to be secure in their homes and free from unreasonable search and seizure and from arbitrary arrest and punishment….We must not be deluded by the efforts of the forces of reaction to prostitute the great words of our free tradition and thereby to confuse the struggle. Democracy, freedom, human rights have come to have a definite meaning to the people of the world which we must not allow any nation to so change that they are made synonymous with suppression and dictatorship."

*Impact:* This speech, as well as others Mrs. Roosevelt made on behalf of the Declaration, became a major factor in the successful adoption of the Declaration by the U. N. General Assembly on December 10, 1948. The vote was unanimous except for eight abstentions, six from Soviet bloc countries. Mrs. Roosevelt advanced her reputation as a worldwide humanitarian, someone who looked out over the world and saw, most of all, people who were displaced, poor, suffering, and abused. She spoke often on behalf of those people, and she defended the right of refugees to settle wherever they chose. "We stand today at the threshold of a great event both in the life of the United Nations and in the life of mankind. This declaration may well become the international Magna Carta for all men everywhere," she declared. "We hope its proclamation by the General Assembly will be an event comparable to the proclamation in 1789 [the French Declaration of the Rights of Citizens], the adoption of the Bill of Rights by the people of the U.S., and the adoption of comparable declarations at different times in other countries." Eleanor Roosevelt possessed a lifelong commitment to peace and human rights and is without doubt the person most critical to the creation of this Universal Declaration, the most basic document on human rights. She also considered her advocacy of human rights to be the crowning achievement in her legacy. Little wonder President Harry Truman honored her with the title "First Lady of the World."

*Contemporary Application:* When a person gains a position that provides a platform, an activist possessing a strong sense of credibility can sway masses of people and speak for those who have no real voice. Mrs. Roosevelt's commitment to the poor and disadvantaged as well as to those displaced by war or who had been objects of abuse or persecution was never doubted or questioned. She thought of no one as an enemy and was unselfishly committed to social justice.

*Connection to Today:* Over a half century has passed since this eloquent speech, yet the cause of human rights remains crucially important in a world of belligerent nations that find new reasons to make war and develop new technology and weapons to inflict pain.

# 60. Harry S. Truman, The Do-Nothing Congress, October 7, 1948

*Speaker:* Quite early on the morning of April 12, 1945, a former senator from Missouri, who had served as vice president for only eighty-two days, was summoned to the White House where he was met by First Lady Eleanor Roosevelt. Mrs. Roosevelt put her arm on his shoulder and told him, "Harry, the President is dead." Within a few hours, Harry S. Truman (1884–1972) was sworn in as the nation's new commander-in-chief. To his many critics, Truman was nothing but an "accidental president," yet this ordinary man from Missouri served as the thirty-third president from 1945 to 1953 and was a key decision-maker for some of the momentous events in American history. As a speaker, Truman possessed strong *ethos* with his ability to identify with the woman in the grocery store and the man on the street. His speaking style was simple, direct, personal, and unaffected, in contrast to the dry formal presentations of his chief opponent in this election. His most important White House addresses were speeches that announced the death of Franklin D. Roosevelt, the destruction of Hiroshima, and the implementation of the Truman Doctrine and the Fair Deal. For these formal addresses, the President used ghostwriters such as George Elsey, Clark Clifford, and William Hillman. Stump speaking, on the other hand, was the kind of oratory for which Truman was known best. He always spoke extemporaneously with plain language when campaigning and those speeches brought enthusiastic response. In the 1948 campaign, like Demosthenes of ancient times, Truman focused on a villain, but in this case it was a "group" or "collective villain"—the "do nothing" Eightieth Congress.

*Occasion:* Since Truman struggled with civil rights, Palestine, and the eightieth Congress in early 1948, few people gave him much chance of winning the election ahead. He faced open opposition from a number of onetime Democrats, many turning to Henry Wallace for president on a Progressive Party ticket. Several prominent citizens, such as two sons of Franklin D. Roosevelt, publicly endorsed Dwight Eisenhower for the Democratic presidential nomination. Other leading Democrats joined a "Stop Truman" movement. A minority party, the Dixiecrats, nominated Strom Thurmond, a young, energetic, and vigorous campaigner, who tried to focus on states' rights and yet was perceived as a staunch supporter of racial segregation. Beyond the South, Thurmond had little appeal, and Wallace's views on foreign policy alarmed many Democrats. Truman won the nomination and then squared off against Thomas Dewey, a seasoned campaigner and office-holder, having twice been elected governor of New York where he was generally popular. Almost all pundits gave Truman no chance to win, and Dewey's overconfidence and generally bland speeches seemed to inspire very few voters. By contrast, Truman launched a spirited and energetic campaign. The campaign began with an electrifying late night acceptance speech after his nomination by the party delegates. Soon, the candidate launched an extraordinarily energetic campaign, typically on trains that "whistle-stopped" across the nation. Standing on the back of the train, Truman assailed Congress, after which he asked audiences if they would like to meet his family; then he introduced Bess, his wife, whom he called "the boss," and Margaret, his daughter. Between September and election day, the Truman entourage traveled a record 31,700 miles across the nation, and the candidate delivered 275 short speeches. The speech excerpted here is a typical one, delivered in Elizabeth, New Jersey, on October 7.

*Excerpt:* "The Republicans are trying to hide the truth from you in a great many ways. They don't want you to know the truth about the issues in this campaign. The big fundamental issue in this campaign is the people against the special interests. The Democratic Party stands for the people. The Republican Party stands, and always has stood, for special interests. They have proved that conclusively in the record that they made in this 'do-nothing Congress.'"

*Impact:* Harry Truman perfected the art of stump speaking and there is no better example of his effectiveness than this famous "whistle-stop" campaign and the surprising victory he won over Thomas Dewey (and Henry Wallace and Strom Thurmond, too). Truman's speeches constantly reminded listeners of all the programs that he supported that conservative Republicans opposed: higher minimum wage, more public housing, increased Social Security, more progressive taxation. He also emphasized his toughness, including his Berlin Airlift against the Soviets. And the speaker relished presenting partisan attacks on his opponents. By the time his train had reached the West Coast, people were shouting, "Give 'em hell, Harry." Truman's speeches stirred great enthusiasm, sometimes an audience would shout "Pour it on." Late on election night, the *Chicago Tribune* published their election edition with the headline: **DEWEY DEFEATS TRUMAN.** When the results were tallied, Truman garnered 49.6 percent of the popular vote and Dewey 45.1 percent. It was a highly satisfying victory for Truman and the Democratic Party, which regained control of Congress.

*Contemporary Application:* Dynamism is always a major factor in creating strong *ethos* with an audience. Truman is a model in speaking with enthusiasm, directness, energy, and simplicity in word choice. These are traits that will create effectiveness for any public speaker.

*Interesting Irony:* When Truman served in office, he was one of the most unpopular presidents in history; he was often the butt of cruel jokes. His ratings remained low even in the weeks after his tenure ended. In subsequent years, however, with the nation facing the Watergate scandal and the Vietnam War, Truman's popularity and ratings underwent a major upswing, with some rating him in the top five or six of all American presidents. Truman became a political folk hero, a president who exemplified deep integrity, plain speaking, and constant accountability. He is now remembered as a president who "pulled off" one of the greatest political upsets in history and who presided over the end of one great war and the beginning of the Cold War. He has been an inspiration to underdogs in a political campaign. (Incidentally, the "S" between his first and last name does not stand for some other name and some writers do not put a period after the S.)

# 61. Douglas MacArthur, Farewell Address to Congress, April 19, 1951

*Speaker:* General Douglas MacArthur (1880–1964) was one of the most famous generals of World War II, and also served in World War I and the Korean War in a sometimes controversial career spanning almost fifty years. Developments in the Korean War were crucial to determining the end of McArthur's career. Just as there was strong fear in Washington and the nation as a whole about monolithic Communism and its spread to weaker nations, troops from communist North Korea poured across the thirty-eighth parallel into South Korea on June 25, 1950. President Truman received U. N. approval for U. S. forces to be deployed as "police action," along with a small number of troops from other nations. Americans assumed Moscow was orchestrating the communist invasion. Fresh U. S. troops were sent to the battle line and under MacArthur's brilliant leadership at the South's capital city of Seoul, the communist invaders were turned back. Containment had succeeded, the aim of the American involvement. The issue then became: Should American commanders now shift to rolling back communism by proceeding north of the thirty-eighth parallel? Despite Truman's determination to keep the conflict a limited war, MacArthur ignored signals that the Chinese would not allow U. S. soldiers to come to their border at the Yalu River. Some 200,000 Chinese soldiers struck hard, driving U. S. soldiers back three hundred miles, the longest retreat in U. S. history. MacArthur wanted to strike back against the People's Republic, and feuded with Truman as well as General Omar Bradley, who called engagement with China "the wrong war, at the wrong place, at the wrong time, with the wrong enemy." Still, U. S. forces rained down bombs with great destruction on North Korea. MacArthur still wanted to take the fight to the Chinese, even to their mainland, deploying any weapons in the arsenal. Finally, on April 10, 1951, the General was summarily fired by President

Truman from his post as Allied Commander of United Nations forces in the Far East. The President knew the immense popularity of MacArthur, but also knew his own [Truman's] responsibility as Commander-in-Chief of all U. S. military forces.

*Occasion:* General Douglas MacArthur returned home, fired by a president, who, unlike Eisenhower, did not have major military leadership on his resume. The General returned as a war hero, and New York welcomed him with a ticker-tape parade that drew a crowd nearly twice as large as the one that had greeted General Dwight Eisenhower at the end of the Second World War. One poll showed that less than thirty percent of the U. S. public supported Truman's actions. Many believed, as did the General, that Truman had acquiesced to a "no win" containment policy. And for a brief period of time, MacArthur seemed a genuine presidential possibility for 1952 (ironically, another general was elected). It seemed appropriate for this popular general to be granted an opportunity to address a joint-session of Congress, and almost fifty million fellow citizens by national television and radio broadcast, and express his mind and heart in concluding an illustrious career. The House was packed and there was a great deal of interest in the speech. This was a scene of high drama.

*Excerpt:* "Once war is forced upon us, there is no other alternative than to apply every available means to bring it to a swift end.…War's very object is victory, not prolonged indecision.…In war there is no substitute for victory.…I am closing my fifty-two years of military service. When I joined the Army, even before the turn of the century, it was the fulfillment of all of my boyish hopes and dreams. The world has turned over many times since I took the oath on the plain at West Point, and the hopes and dreams have long since vanished, but I still remember the refrain of one of the most popular barrack ballads of that day which proclaimed most proudly that 'old soldiers never die; they just fade away.'…And like the old soldier of that ballad, I now close my military career and just fade away, an old soldier who tried to do his duty as God gave him the light to see that duty. Good Bye."

*Impact:* One can imagine the deposed General feeling gratified and exonerated after presenting this speech to Congress and the nation. It was a special occasion, indeed—here was a veteran of fifty-two years of distinguished military service explaining in a humble way how he had acted with God's guidance and honorable intent for the good of the nation he loved. MacArthur spent the bulk of his speaking time in explaining and justifying his military decisions in the field. As such a successful commander in the Far East theater of World War II, and the general to whom the Japanese signed their surrender, MacArthur enjoyed immense *ethos* with the larger audience. There were reports of misty eyes and outright weeping among audience members. The speaker definitely did not disappoint his admirers. He spoke for thirty-four minutes and was interrupted by applause thirty times. MacArthur ended with dramatics, giving American rhetoric one of its most memorable lines—"Old soldiers never die, they just fade away." The outpouring of admiration reflected the speaker's charisma. However, immediately after the speech, a minority of Democratic senators acknowledged the persuasive appeal of the speech, yet cautioned that the perspective of time would prove Truman had chosen the more prudent course for the U. S. military and for the nation. Truman has been exonerated, and the old saying proved prophetic in this speaker's case— MacArthur simply lost national influence and slowly faded from the American scene. Truman had succeeded in preserving a most important constitutional principle of civilian control over the military.

*Contemporary Application:* A speaker may elicit a strong, emotional, immediate response, yet receive a delayed and more critical judgment from history.

*Connection to today:* The Korean conflict was simply a dress rehearsal for the Vietnam War, for which Americans still pay consequences for a long, protracted war.

# 62. Adlai Stevenson, Democratic Nomination Acceptance Speech, July 26, 1952

*Speaker:* Adlai Stevenson (1900–1965) may be little more than a footnote in the general history surveys for future generations, yet this one-time governor of Illinois, two-time presidential nominee, and American diplomat was one of the most intelligent and eloquent men ever to run for the office of chief executive. Stevenson was an Illinois attorney, who was educated at Princeton and Northwestern, and gained popular respect for his skills at communicating with all kinds of audiences. He achieved distinction as an orator through intellectual demeanor, use of candor, picturesque language, and support for liberal causes and expression of them through both humor and common sense. Though his administration as governor was tarnished by scandal, he emerged as a politician who had communicated an image of exceptional giftedness and intelligence. As a man of piety, intelligence, and wisdom, Stevenson possessed strong *ethos*, especially among Democratic partisans. Republican opponents attacked him for alleged softness on communism and lampooned his intelligence as being proof he was an "egghead." The GOP's staunchly anticommunist vice-presidential candidate, Senator Richard Nixon of California, called Stevenson "Adlai the appeaser" and charged him with holding a Ph. D. from "Dean Acheson's Cowardly College of Communist Containment." Some Republicans even questioned the manliness of the Democratic contender, a soft-spoken gentleman who remained unmarried following his 1949 divorce. Yet, as a man of integrity, Stevenson declared, "Better we lose the election, than mislead the people" (which in the minds of many American voters was exactly what the Republican ticket, especially Nixon, was guilty of doing). Stevenson was re-nominated as Democratic candidate in 1956, but lost again to Eisenhower in yet another landslide. President John F. Kennedy appointed him as ambassador to the United Nations, where he served from 1961 to 1965, when he died in London. Likely Stevenson will be remembered as much as an orator as a politician, an orator who raised the level of political discourse.

*Occasion:* Even Stevenson as the Democratic candidate knew he did not have a prayer against the Republican candidate Dwight D. Eisenhower in the 1952 presidential campaign. "Who did I think I was," he later joked, "running against George Washington?" Not only was Stevenson competing against the man who brought victory to the U.S. and Allies in World War II, but he was attempting to restore popularity and support for his party after the retirement of Harry Truman, whose approval ratings were at an abysmal twenty-three percent. The war in Korea was dragging on and any ceasefire had not been called at that point, and Senator Joe McCarthy's anti-communist witch-hunts and demagogic rhetoric stirred trepidation in the hearts and minds of many Americans. This would not have been a good time for any Democrat to run for president. Stevenson himself did not want to run, but at the Chicago convention's opening he gave such a rousing address that the delegates drafted him as the party's nominee. The convention delegates had no other viable candidate, so Stevenson, who had not campaigned in the primaries, accepted the nomination and addressed the weary delegates at 3:00 A. M.

*Excerpt:* "I hope and pray that we Democrats, win or lose, can campaign not as a crusade to exterminate the opposing party…but as a great opportunity to educate and elevate a people whose destiny is leadership….The ordeal of the twentieth century—the bloodiest, most turbulent era of the Christian age—is far from over. Sacrifice, patience, understanding and implacable purpose may be our lot for years to come."

*Impact:* Standing before the weary delegates, Adlai Stevenson spoke with passion, candor, forthrightness, dignity, and humility in a pledge to fight to win with all his heart and soul. Humility is often evident in sincere remarks, when, for example, he stated "I accept your nomination and your program. I should have preferred to hear those words uttered by a stronger, a wiser, a better man than myself...I have asked the Merciful Father, the Father of us all, to let this cup pass from me. But from such dreadful responsibility one does not shrink in fear, in self-interest, or in false humility...better men than me were at hand for this mighty task." This address enhanced Stevenson's popularity among Democratic partisans, yet neither was this speech nor scores of other candidate speeches in the subsequent months able to stem the tide against the popular opponent. A popular GOP campaign tapped into its own candidate's soaring charisma with a brief declaration: "I Like IKE," and so did millions of voters. The first military leader to gain the presidency since Ulysses S. Grant (1869-77), Eisenhower achieved a great personal victory in 1952, rolling up almost seven million more votes than the Stevenson-Sparkman ticket and dominating the Electoral College by a margin of 442 to 89. The election gave the Republicans the presidency for the first time in twenty years.

*Contemporary Application:* Intelligence and communication skill may not always win over a mass audience. Other factors come to play in determining whether one is remembered as a great speaker who effectively wielded a mighty influence on the flow of history. Though arguable who, Eisenhower or Stevenson, was the best candidate to lead the nation, sometimes the best person does not win.

*Interesting Fact:* Stevenson has been credited with giving the model concession speech that exemplifies honor, graciousness, humility, and even humor. In his concession speech, the Democratic candidate addressed his supporters on November 5, 1952, in the ballroom of the Leland hotel in Springfield, Illinois: "The people have rendered their verdict and I gladly accept it....We vote as many, but we pray as one....Someone asked me how I felt, and I was reminded of a story that a fellow townsman used to tell—Abraham Lincoln. They asked him how he felt once after an unsuccessful election. He said he felt like a little boy who had stubbed his toe in the dark. He said that he was too old to cry, but it hurt too much to laugh."

## 63. Richard Nixon, Fund Crisis Address a.k.a. "The Checkers Speech," September 23, 1952

*Speaker:* Richard M. Nixon (1913–1994) enjoyed a spectacular rise in national politics of the mid-1940s and early 50s. Elected to Congress in 1946, he quickly established himself as a militant anti-Communist while serving on the House Un-American Activities Committee. In 1950 he was elected to the Senate and became an outspoken critic of President Truman's conduct of the Korean War and "wasteful spending" by the Democrats. At the 1952 Republican National Convention, this young senator was chosen to be the running mate of presidential candidate Dwight D. Eisenhower, a selection based on three factors: (1) youth (Nixon was thirty-nine); (2) reputation as a staunch foe of communism; (3) political base in the populous state of California. The Eisenhower camp envisioned Nixon as opposition "hit man," doing the hatchet rhetoric while the General at the top of the ticket would be respected for taking the high road. Nixon's hatchet-man campaigning style did cause pain for the Democrats, thus little wonder his opponents sought a way to inflict injury.

*Occasion:* Early in the '52 campaign, a sensational headline appeared in the *New York Post* stating, "Secret Rich Men's Trust Fund Keeps Nixon in Style Far Beyond His Salary." Amid the shock and outrage that followed, many Republicans, some disliking the young senator from the outset, as well as some newspaper editorials, urged Eisenhower to dump Nixon from the ticket before it was too late—all the while Eisenhower remained damagingly quiet. Nixon, however, in a brilliant political maneuver, received Eisenhower's permission to take his case directly to the American people via the new medium of television. During a nationwide broadcast that emanated from Hollywood's El Capitan Theater, with his wife Pat sitting stoically nearby, Nixon offered a full explanation of his finances and his legal use of funds. Pitching the speech at the right emotional level was his biggest challenge. For the first time in his career, and by no means the last time, he aimed words not at intellectuals or elites, but at the mass audience he would later call "the great silent majority."

*Excerpt*: "Pat and I have the satisfaction that every dime that we have got is honestly ours. I should say this, that Pat doesn't have a mink coat. But she does have a respectable Republican cloth coat, and I always tell her she would look good in anything. One other thing I probably should tell you, because if I don't they will probably be saying this about me, too. We did get something, a gift, after the election. A man down in Texas heard Pat on the radio mention the fact that our two youngsters would like to have a dog, and, believe it or not, the day before we left on this campaign trip we got a message from Union Station in Baltimore, saying they had a package for us. We went down to get it. You know what it was? It was a little cocker spaniel dog, in a crate that he had sent all the way from Texas, black and white, spotted, and our little girl Tricia, the six year old, named it Checkers. And you know, the kids, like all kids, loved the dog, and I just want to say this, right now, that regardless of what they say about it, we are going to keep it."

*Impact*: Nixon might well have been driven to include his passage about the family pet dog by a memory of how Franklin Roosevelt so skillfully and successfully (albeit for humor) referenced his pet dog Fala in the most important campaign speech of 1944. There was also strong emotion in his voice, a tone of defiance against those who unfairly accused him; then he extolled the greatness of Eisenhower. Nixon at first thought the speech a failure, but the effect of the "Checkers" broadcast was extraordinary. The candidate had touched the hearts of Middle America, typified by cameramen in the studio who were crying. Within minutes of the telecast, telegrams and telephone calls poured into various Republican offices demanding Nixon remain on the ticket. Although it would forever be known as Nixon's "Checkers Speech," it was actually a political triumph for Nixon at the time of presentation. Eisenhower requested

Nixon to come to West Virginia where he was campaigning and greeted Nixon at the airport with, "Dick, you're my boy." The Republicans then marched to a landslide election victory. The speech has been criticized by rhetorical critics as being maudlin, even demagogic, in exploitation of emotional proof. Yet, had Nixon not given such a persuasive speech, he would not have secured his place on this winning ticket and one could only speculate the direction his political career might have taken. Though much praised as well as much scorned, the speech is important for another reason—this was the first American political address to be delivered live for a national audience (sixty million viewed it), and marks the beginning of the political use of television. The large viewing audience was not surpassed until the first Kennedy-Nixon presidential debate in 1960.

*Contemporary Application:* The strategy of a powerful emotional appeal can sway an audience and render a speech memorable. And emotion based on one's family, especially children and even pets, always seems to touch the heart strings of viewers and listeners. On the other hand, if emotion is over-played, a speaker may be considered more of a demagogue than a statesperson.

*Connection to Today:* The speech became known only as the "Checkers Speech," and has since become an idiom for an emotionally-charged political speech. Richard Nixon was the only president to resign from the office of U. S. presidency, and he remains, perhaps, the most complex and enigmatic man who has ever served in that high office. Some of that complexity is captured in the movie *Frost/Nixon*, the story of how a British journalist secured and conducted the most famous television interview in presidential history.

# 64. Dwight D. Eisenhower, Farewell Address, January 17, 1961

*Speaker:* Dwight D. Eisenhower (1890–1969) epitomized the American success story, achieving the pinnacle of American executive power. He served as supreme commander of Allied military forces in World War II, and returned home as a military hero. He had a brief stint as president of Columbia University, and, then, his landslide election victory in 1952 set the stage for the first full two-term Republican presidency since that of Ulysses S. Grant. While known as an effective leader, he was never a renowned orator. Intellectuals and liberals found it easy to attack and satirize his vagueness, verbal gaffes, and blandness. Yet, millions continued to "like Ike," and his *ethos* (source credibility) was always high. He accepted the New Deal legacy and seemed to believe that the government should be run like a big business. The decade of the 50s was a time of stability, despite racial tensions seething under the surface, and a time of prosperity, economic growth, and religiosity. Growth and expansion happened continually, and television was more and more an integral part of Americans' lives. Liberals and activists complained about Eisenhower's avoidance of racial issues, his basic conservatism in domestic affairs, and even his rambling syntax in news conferences. Eisenhower seemed more of a "caretaker" president than an activist. To appreciate the Eisenhower Administration, it is appropriate to think of the events that did not happen: The President did not dismantle New Deal social welfare programs; he exerted American military power around the globe but avoided war; he knew how to keep disagreement private and to delegate authority; he avoided major political scandal.

*Occasion:* After eight years in the White House, preceded by a nearly forty-year military career, President Dwight D. Eisenhower, also known by the nickname "Ike," delivered his Farewell Address via television from the Oval Office, January 17, 1961, three days before he left office. The President was leaving the office as the nation's oldest chief executive and was soon to be succeeded by the youngest man ever to be elected president. Eisenhower spoke about the Cold War, the role of the United States armed forces, and government spending that he believed was unjustified, but the speech is most noted for its warning about unwarranted influence by the "military-industrial complex."

*Excerpt:* "This conjunction of an immense military establishment and a large arms industry is new in the American experience. The total influence— economic, political, even spiritual—is felt in every city, every Statehouse, every office of the Federal government. We recognize the imperative need for this development. Yet we must not fail to comprehend its grave implications. Our toil, resources and livelihood are all involved; so is the very structure of our society. In the councils of government, we must guard against the acquisition of unwarranted influence, whether sought or unsought, by the military-industrial complex. The potential for the disastrous rise of misplaced power exists and will persist. We must never let the weight of this combination endanger our liberties or democratic processes. We should take nothing for granted. Only an alert and knowledgeable citizenry can compel the proper meshing of the huge industrial and military machinery of defense with our peaceful methods and goals, so that security and liberty may prosper together."

*Impact:* Eisenhower's ethical appeal was always strong. He was perceived as a man of good moral character and good will for his audience, the American people. His audience thought of him as a smiling grandfather, but definitely a wise and caring grandfather. Therefore, his warnings to the nation upon departing office carried a sense of authority. He had definitely seen a shift in American politics, and the shift seemed alarming to him. The Cold War and the arms race combined for potential abuse or corruption. Warnings about the corruption of power have been a part of political philosophy for centuries.

One might recall Lord Acton's proverb: "Power corrupts, and absolute power corrupts absolutely." Yet the President saw a newer and greater dimension and possibility for corruption with political authorities having big business connections, combined with a massive military budget, in which decisions must be made about new arms, new technology, new gadgetry, and human resources. Liberals may have been surprised and amazed at the warnings at that time. Historians now would contend that this warning from Eisenhower was perhaps the wisest statement he ever uttered.

*Contemporary Application: Ethos* is one of Aristotle's three major forms of proof; it would be difficult to overestimate the persuasive power of strong *ethos*. Eisenhower delivered few memorable public speeches, but his strong *ethos* rendered his speeches persuasive.

*Connection to Today:* Huge government military contracts since the time this speech was delivered keep this crucially-important issue alive, whether or not very many people have given serious heed to Eisenhower's warning. Might a president's decision to wage military action be influenced by the possibility of lucrative government contracts for administration-friendly corporations and companies manufacturing weapons and supplies?

*Interesting Fact:* There is an interesting parallel with this Farewell Address by a modern president and the Farewell Address of our very first president, George Washington. Each president wisely gave warnings to the American people. The Farewell Address seemingly is becoming an American oratorical tradition. Barack Obama delivered his Farewell Address on January 10, 2017, in Chicago, shoring up his legacy, extolling the virtues of democracy, and calling for a smooth transition of power to President-elect Donald Trump.

# 65. John F. Kennedy, Address to the Houston
## Ministerial Alliance, September 12, 1960

*Speaker:* Senator John F. Kennedy was the second Roman Catholic to be nominated for the nation's highest office, but none had been elected (Roman Catholic Democratic candidate Alfred Smith lost to Herbert Hoover in 1928).

*Occasion:* The close presidential election campaign of 1960 provided an occasion for a high profile American political leader to address a religious issue. As for their chief executives, Americans had always generally preferred one-time married, Protestant, older white men as prerequisites for the fit candidate to serve in the Oval Office. Indeed, Protestantism had been the *de facto* established religion for many generations after the nation's founding. However, with the growth of Roman Catholic population in the nation, there emerged Catholic political power, especially in the Northeast. By 1960 Roman Catholics dominated most of New England and most urban areas of the nation. Yet, given Bible Belt reservations (not to mention remaining pockets of outright anti-Catholic prejudice and remnants of American nativism), the Senator's chances for victory in a close election were constantly in doubt. Kennedy, his family, and closest advisers realized that the candidate must address the "Roman Catholic issue" forthrightly. While Kennedy had often made comments on the role of religion in voters' political behavior, contending that specific religious affiliation should be incidental rather than foremost, the candidate did not address the issue in specific clarity until this speech. In this address before the Greater Houston Ministerial Alliance, Kennedy pronounced his own vision of the separation of church and state. He claimed to have no "divided loyalty" between his commitment to his church and his commitment to his nation, as his opponents claimed. Early in the address he articulated his vision.

*Excerpt:* "I believe in an America that is officially neither Catholic, Protestant, nor Jewish—where no public official either requests or accepts instructions on public policy from the pope, the National Council of Churches, or any other ecclesiastical source—where no religious body seeks to impose its will directly or indirectly upon the general populace or the public acts of its officials—and where religious liberty is so indivisible that an act against our church is treated as an act against all."

*Impact:* The address turned out to be crucial to Kennedy's winning key votes, especially in the Bible Belt states. Conceivably, in an election that turned out to be so close, this speech made a difference in his election victory. In his personal address, JFK cited Thomas Jefferson's *Virginia Statute of Religious Freedom* and contended that in another day a finger of suspicion could be pointed toward a Jew, a Quaker, a Unitarian, or even a Baptist. This was a skillful rhetorical strategy since Southern Baptist clergy outnumbered clergy of other affiliations in the immediate, live audience. On the other hand, Kennedy knew a secondary audience for this speech was a large Roman Catholic population that might be sensitive to the candidate's discounting his faith for the purpose of political expedience. As historian-theologian Shaun Casey notes, "Kennedy sensed he was walking a tightrope" in attempting to address both audiences without alienating either (*The Making of a Catholic President,* Oxford University Press, 2009, pp. 164-76). Note that the candidate affirmed his Catholic faith at the outset of his remarks, while contending that faith would not be a hindrance in discharging the constitutional duties of the high office. Kennedy stated that questions about his religion were not the real issue and that he needed to state again "not what kind of church I believe in....but what kind of America I believe in." While the speech did not lay the religion issue to rest, it was a landmark address that tended to neutralize religious objection to the Democratic nominee. JFK's narrow victory over Richard Nixon was claimed as a sign of the end of religious politics in the United States, but that would be only partially true.

*Contemporary Application:* This address is a model of rhetorical strategy in handling a hostile audience. To be certain, the audience was not hostile personally to the candidate, only hostile to the idea a Catholic should serve in the nation's highest office.

*Interesting Fact:* Republican Mitt Romney delivered a similar speech, "Faith in America," on December 6, 2007, in which he attempted to lay to rest concerns about a Mormon serving as U. S. president. Romney did not receive his party's nomination until the 2012 election campaign; by then, there seemed very little concern about Romney's faith.

*Connection to Today:* We may think of religious leaders presenting addresses, sermons, essays, and articles on political themes. However, political leaders also address religious themes and employ religious language. For example, Thomas Jefferson often spoke or wrote about his religious beliefs. Though Abraham Lincoln said almost nothing about his faith publicly, we can draw inferences, especially from his correspondence and a few scattered public comments, about his views of God and divine providence in time of national crisis. Most U. S. presidents have dropped little insights into speeches and conversation about their personal faith. At this point in time, it is difficult to conceive of an avowed atheist or even an agnostic being elected to the nation's highest office. In 2016 Donald Trump was clearly "non-churched" and came across as unfamiliar with Holy Scriptures, but the evangelical "right" apparently did not consider that a deficiency that would diminish his qualification as a candidate.

# 66. John F. Kennedy, Cuban Missile Address, October 22, 1962

*Speaker:* The young President John F. Kennedy was soon facing the most serious foreign policy crisis of his young presidency. The President had already faced mild threats from the communist leader Nikita Khrushchev, and he had bungled the Bay of Pigs invasion and publicly admitted his error. Another dramatic confrontation loomed in Berlin, where the Berlin wall became a symbol of communist repression.

*Occasion:* In the fall of 1962, the Soviet Union, fulfilling a request from Fidel Castro, began sending sophisticated weapons to the island nation of Cuba. On October 14, an American U-2 plane conclusively photographed the installation of nuclear missiles in Cuba, only ninety miles from the U. S. coast of Florida. National security analysts estimated the missiles were capable of a strike against several population centers along the east coast and within two or three minutes could kill eighty million Americans. Secretary of Defense Robert McNamara and other advisers analyzed and debated the merits of various responses the Administration could make to the crisis. After tense strategy sessions with his top advisers, Kennedy rejected a military strike against Cuba that might have taken the U. S. and the Soviet Union into war. Instead, he ordered the U. S. Navy to "quarantine" the island and prevent more missiles from coming into the island and being installed. The Strategic Air Command was put on full alert for a possible nuclear conflict. With all these moves, Kennedy was aware of his need to fully inform the nation of this grave situation, but he knew also his speech would be heard throughout the Western world and in the Soviet Union (with translation, of course). The purpose in the speech was to convince the Soviet premiere that removal of the missiles and warheads was not only in the best interests of the U.S. but the entire world.

Interestingly, until the time of the television broadcast, the American public had no idea of the unfolding drama. Press Secretary Pierre Salinger simply released a statement at noon that the President would talk to the nation on a matter "of the greatest urgency" later that evening.

*Excerpt:* "I call upon Chairman Khrushchev to halt and eliminate this clandestine, reckless and provocative threat to world peace and stable relations between our two nations. I call upon him further to abandon this course of world domination and to join in an historic effort to end the perilous arms race and to transform the history of man....My fellow citizens, let no one doubt that this is a difficult and dangerous effort on which we have set out. No one can see precisely what course it will take or what costs or casualties will be incurred...[We are] aware of our dangers. But the greatest danger of all would be to do nothing....The cost of freedom is always high, and Americans have always paid it. And one path we shall never choose, and that is the path of surrender or submission. Our goal is not the victory of might, but the vindication of right—not peace at the expense of freedom, but both peace and freedom, here in this hemisphere, and, we hope, around the world. God willing, that goal will be achieved."

*Impact:* The speech was delivered in the most somber tones as the President spoke of "this secret, swift, and extraordinary buildup of communist missiles" and also described the missile installation as "a sudden and clandestine decision." Every word of the speech was carefully analyzed for how it might be translated into the Russian language. The speech had several goals. One was informing the American people of the crisis. That goal was achieved, even if it frightened the masses of adult viewers. Second, a more important goal was for Khrushchev to dismantle and remove the missiles from Cuba. There were complicated moves by both governments behind the scene, but Khrushchev offered to remove the missiles from Cuba in exchange for an American pledge not to invade Cuba; the U. S. agreed to this stipulation. On October 28, 1962, Khrushchev ordered the Soviet missiles in Cuba dismantled and the supply ships brought home. The crisis had lasted thirteen days, yet many people, both inside and outside government, looked all around them wistfully and wondered if the world as they knew it would still be there twenty-four hours later.

*Contemporary Application:* Some situations are so crucially important because they are in a crisis context. That is when strategic decisions must be made but must also be clearly and effectively explained to an audience of anyone and everyone who is impacted by the crisis. When the stakes are high and countless millions are anxiously listening, this is when the rhetorical message must be wise, cautious, and well-crafted.

*Connection to Today:* Because the stakes were so high with this speech, and because the strategy proved the proper one, and thus the speech was a success, the address deserves to be in the top ten of all-time great American presidential speeches. Think of how different our nation and our world might have been had the policy and the address failed catastrophically. Interestingly, in 2016 President Barack Obama took action that more formally recognized the Cuban government and opened doors of trade and tourism with the island nation. Later that year, Fidel Castro died. An era seemed to come to an end.

# 67. Martin Luther King, Jr., Letter from a Birmingham Jail, April 16, 1963

*Speaker:* Martin Luther King was as much a Baptist preacher as he was a civil rights reform speaker, and he typically merged the two roles in developing themes of slavery, injustice, liberation, and freedom. King's sermons and addresses eventually created different kinds of audiences, some all-black and others racially mixed. He knew how to adapt to his audiences quite effectively. He could speak with an air of intellectualism as he adapted themes from leading preachers and thinkers of his day for the purpose of explaining black demands for full freedom. His major themes were the superiority of love; the need for passive resistance in the midst of human injustice; an appeal to God and to "higher law;" and the power of redemptive love. And by the early 60s, clearly King had emerged as the moral leader of Southern black activism.

*Occasion:* The Supreme Court, in the famous *Brown v. Board of Education* decision (1954), had called for desegregation of public schools and, by application, of all public institutions and businesses. Racial integration met with massive resistance by Southern whites. Instead of relying on public officials to speed the process of desegregation, African-Americans took up the battle themselves. In 1963 the Southern Christian Leadership Council began a series of civil rights protests in Birmingham, Alabama. The established political leaders liked to talk about "law 'n order," a code phrase for opposition to these demonstrations, though, of course, the demonstrations were protected as "free speech" under the First Amendment. Many whites, even clergymen, contended they were not opposed to racial equality and desegregation, but that they feared the protesters would become violent and destructive of lives and property. During the Birmingham demonstrations and on Good Friday, Dr. King was arrested, incarcerated for violating a state court order prohibiting public demonstrations without a permit, and held incommunicado for twenty-four hours in solitary confinement. Eight local white clergymen published an attack in a Birmingham newspaper, calling King a trouble-maker and a communist and criticizing his tactics as "unwise and untimely." The clergymen seemed to make an attempt to shame King as a minister for setting an example of law-breaking. Not long thereafter, King's response letter was reprinted in several national periodicals and distributed across the nation in single reprints. King's audience was not simply the eight clergymen critical of him—it was intended for all clergy and laity, for black and white citizens, in both North and South, in essence, for anyone interested and concerned about civil rights and strategies of social justice.

*Excerpt:* "We know through painful experience that freedom is never voluntarily given by the oppressor; it must be demanded by the oppressed....For years now I have heard the word 'Wait!!' It rings in the ear of every Negro with piercing familiarity. This 'Wait' has almost always meant 'Never.' We must come to see, with one of our distinguished jurists, that 'justice too long delayed is justice denied.'...One may ask: 'How can you advocate breaking some laws and obeying others?' The answer lies in the fact that there are two types of laws: just and unjust....One has not only a legal but a moral responsibility to obey just laws. Conversely, one has a moral responsibility to disobey unjust laws. I would agree with St. Augustine who said that 'an unjust law is no law at all.'.....A just law is a man-made code that squares with the moral law or the law of God. An unjust law is a code that is out of harmony with the moral law."

*Impact:* The preacher-essayist weaves a powerful argument for Christian people using civil disobedience as a weapon against humanly-devised laws that conflict with the higher law of God and enlightened human reason. Christian ministers and other readers could not miss the examples of civil disobedience that King draws from varied biblical narratives in both the Old and New Testaments. He also turned to Socrates, Aquinas, Buber, and Tillich to support his position. How much the intended audience was stirred by this message is impossible to say. Yet the long range impact of this message has been vindicated as one of the greatest essays in American history, serving analogously as the *95 Theses* nailed to the door of the white church.

*Interesting Fact:* This document joins an elite and varied canon of great literature produced in prison by a profound, incarcerated thinker, thus proving the body might be shackled but the mind can remain forever free. (Also included in that canon of literature would be writings of Dietrich Bonhoeffer, John Bunyan, Malcolm X, and others.) One might also think of Emile Zola's 1898 letter to the President of the French Republic denouncing the Dreyfus decision and Thomas Mann's 1937 public letter to the Dean of the University of Bonn. Indeed, the public letter has long been used by politicians, reformers, writers, and prisoners. Attesting to its enduring value, this essay is reprinted in numerous anthologies of readings for high school and college students. The essay is both briefer and more powerful than Henry David Thoreau's classic essay of the nineteenth century on the same subject. King's arguments have stood the test of time.

*Contemporary Application:* Clearly, this is not a speech in the traditional sense, but is indeed a rhetorical effort. Rhetoric can be written as well as spoken if the message attempts to persuade a specific audience at a specific point in time. Actually, this "letter" or essay reads and sounds like a sermon—undoubtedly, Dr. King had preached every word and shared every idea in this essay in previous sermons and reform speeches.

*Connection to Today:* The abstract principle of justice is always crucially important and relevant. And race relations and the need for peaceful means of protest remain still very much issues in twenty-first century USA. The issue of civil disobedience is a perennial one. All thoughtful citizens likely have occasion to consider compliance or non-compliance to a law they believe to be unfair or unjust.

# 68. John F. Kennedy, Address at the Berlin Wall, June 26, 1963

*Speaker:* John F. Kennedy was the nation's youngest president and had promised vigorous action in foreign policy. He raised the defense budget despite the fact that the alleged "missile gap" with the Soviets did not exist, and supported military assistance programs, as well as covert action plans. One of his most popular initiatives was the Peace Corps, a new program that sent Americans, especially young people, to Third World nations to work on development projects that might undercut communism's appeal. The worst fiasco of the Kennedy presidency had been the ill-conceived CIA mission against Cuba in an effort to oust Fidel Castro. The speaker certainly had credibility (*ethos*) as an advocate for freedom and democracy and a foe of communist repression.

*Occasion:* When World War II ended, the Allies had split Germany, and the capital city of Berlin, into four occupation zones. Due to the steady flow of immigrants from East Germany into West Berlin, a migration that was both economically draining and embarrassing to the German communist regime, on the night of August 12-13, 1961, the communists began to erect first a barbed-wire fence and then a massive concrete wall to separate East Berlin from West Berlin. Patrolled by armed guards, East Germans attempting to escape into the West were shot down. The Berlin Wall became a symbol of both communist repression and the postwar division of Europe between East and West. Many hopeful escapees were killed trying to cross the border to the West. President Kennedy visited Europe in 1963, and this speech was scheduled as the high point of his trip. The speaker faced an adoring crowd of more than 400,000. Although he spoke two miles from the famous wall, he had seen it earlier in the day, and when he began to speak he sounded angry. "Two thousand years ago," he began, "the proudest boast was "*Civitas*

*Romanus sum.*" Today, in the world of freedom, the proudest boast is "*Ich bin ein Berliner.*"

*Excerpt:* "Freedom has many difficulties and democracy is not perfect, but we have never had to put a wall up to keep our people in, to prevent them from leaving us....This generation of Germans has earned the right to be free, including the right to unite their families and their nation in lasting peace with good will to all people. You live in a defended island of freedom, but your life is part of the main. So let me ask you, as I close, to lift your eyes beyond the dangers of today to the hope of tomorrow, beyond the freedom merely of this city of Berlin, or your country of Germany, to the advance of freedom everywhere, beyond yourselves and ourselves to all mankind. Freedom is indivisible, and when one man is enslaved, all are not free. When all are free, then we can look forward to that day when this city will be joined as one—and this country, and this great continent of Europe—in a peaceful and hopeful glow. When that day finally comes, as it will, the people of West Berlin can take sober satisfaction in the fact that they were in the front lines for almost two decades. All free men, wherever they may live, are citizens of Berlin, and, therefore, as a free man, I take pride in the words "*Ich bin ein Berliner.*"

*Impact:* Kennedy received a rousing reception from the large crowd that shared complete emotional unity. The crowd roared with approval and Kennedy delighted in the occasion and continued: "There are many people in the world who really don't understand, or say they don't, what is the great issue between the free world and the communist world....Let them come to Berlin!' He continued to invoke that refrain, ending with, "*Lass'sie nach Berlin kommen!* Let them come to Berlin!" The crowd was chanting "KEN-NE-DY!" This speech, and the exclamation in German "I am a Berliner," provided a memorable image of JFK's presidency. The speech was truly one of Kennedy's most successful and noted addresses during his all-too-brief tenure as the U. S. chief executive.

*Little Known Fact:* Kennedy's speech was typed on index cards he carried in his suit coat pocket, but he did not include almost half the speech he actually uttered. The cards did bear his handwritten phonetic pronunciations for the German phrases he had practiced. After the speech, presidential advisor McGeorge Bundy told the President the speech "went a little too far." The President seemed to agree and they edited the tone of his next speech to make it seem more conciliatory. After the speech, Kennedy and his entourage flew to Ireland to visit his ancestral homeland, and he told aides of his excitement and satisfaction with his Berlin visit and speech. Less than five months later, the President was dead.

*Contemporary Application:* There can be stunning effectiveness when a speaker so identifies with one's audience by speaking their language and proudly claiming to be one of them. Kennedy displayed a unique rhetorical strategy by speaking a German phrase in his introduction and returning to the same phrase in the conclusion of the address.

*Connection to Today:* In 1987 a Republican president, Ronald Reagan, also delivered one of his most courageous speeches nearby in Berlin at the Brandenburg Gate. On November 9, 1989, the East German government opened the Berlin Wall in a paradoxical effort to stop the exodus of people fleeing their repressive society across the border. During that remarkable year, the East European Communist regimes collapsed. Throughout Europe and the rest of the western world, the opening of the Berlin Wall was celebrated as symbolic of the end of the Cold War. At this writing, there has been commemoration of the twenty-fifth anniversary of the fall of the Wall.

# 69. Malcolm X, The Ballot or the Bullet, April 3, 1964

*Speaker:* Malcolm X (1925–1965; born Malcolm Little in Omaha, Nebraska), though not specifically a political or religious speaker, presented compelling speeches often dealing with political and religious themes; ultimately, of course, the cause of civil rights is deeply religious and moral. *The Autobiography of Malcolm X* is a classic recounting of Malcolm's prison experiences (having been arrested for burglary), his exposure to the teachings of Elijah Muhammad, leader of the Nation of Islam, and his powerful conversion to the Nation of Islam. The NOI, also called Black Muslims, aspired to create a self-reliant, highly disciplined, and proud community that would be a separate "nation" for African-Americans. Malcolm then sought a new name and a new identity. He took the surname X to symbolize his original African family name, lost through slavery. He soon emerged as the Black Muslims' leading evangelist, and wielded much influence among young urban black men. Some of his strongest rhetoric was waged against those he called the "Negro preachers" who, he believed, had conspired in brainwashing the black man and woman to accept the control of the white man. Malcolm X believed that Islam and Christianity were fundamentally different—that Christianity enslaves people and Islam liberates and unites them. His message was more strident than King's, and he argued publicly that spiritual integrity for blacks must begin by throwing off a white-dominated religious system that perpetuated the status quo. In 1964 Malcolm X broke with the NOI, made a pilgrimage to Mecca, and was transformed by meeting Islamic peoples of all colors. He returned to the U. S. and abandoned his black separatist views. On February 21, 1965, he was gunned down during a speech in Harlem's Audubon Ballroom. Actor and activist Ossie Davis delivered the eulogy of Malcolm and described him as "our shining prince." Malcolm X's interesting, courageous, and authentic life has earned him a solid place in American history.

*Occasion:* The speech was presented at a special event before an audience of hundreds at Cory Methodist Church in Cleveland, Ohio. Malcolm X claimed the speech was not meant to discuss religion, though indeed he did discuss religion and his delivery had a sermonic tone.

*Excerpt:* "Now in speaking like this, it doesn't mean that we're anti-white, but it does mean we're anti-exploitation, we're anti-degradation, we're anti-oppression. And if the white man doesn't want us to be anti-him, let him stop oppressing and exploiting and degrading us. Whether we are Christians or Muslims or nationalists or agnostics or atheists, we must first learn to forget our differences. If we have differences, let us differ in the closet; when we come out in front, let us not have anything to argue about until we get finished arguing with the man. If the late President Kennedy could get together with Khrushchev and exchange some wheat, we certainly have more in common with each other than Kennedy and Khrushchev had with each other….If we don't do something real soon, I think you'll have to agree that we're going to be forced either to use the ballot or the bullet. It's one or the other in 1964. It isn't that time is running out -- time has run out!....I'm not standing here speaking to you as an American, or a patriot, or a flag-saluter, or a flag-waver—no, not I. I'm speaking as a victim of this American system. And I see America through the eyes of the victim. I don't see any American dream; I see an American nightmare."

*Impact:* The speech deserves to be honored in the top four or five great addresses presented by African-American speakers, and perhaps in the top ten or twenty of all American speeches. Malcolm possessed a great skill for directness and bluntness in stating his case for direct action, even violence if necessary, and for interpreting historical evidence to support his claims. Though he had a sympathetic audience, Malcolm was adept at using humor, sarcasm, and irony to reinforce his points and hold attention. He boldly labeled Billy Graham a "white nationalist," noting by contrast that he [Malcolm] was a "black nationalist." Courageously, Malcolm had no compunction about offending the sensitivities, beliefs, and values of white Americans. He challenged President Johnson to make good on his promise to effect more civil and voting rights legislation, and, indeed, that did happen within a few months. Truly, Malcolm X spoke for a rising segment of the African-American population growing impatient with seeming intransigence of King's power of love and nonviolence approach to reform. Through this speech and similar ones, Malcolm stirred a new militancy and pride among black people. Perhaps he was more effective than anyone in his generation in articulating the frustrations, bitterness, and aspirations of younger black people. As much as any other speaker of his time, Malcolm X pointed to a new black consciousness that celebrated the African heritage, black culture, black history, and black self-reliance. In many ways, his ideas and leadership were much like those of Marcus Garvey, the leader whom Malcolm's father, a preacher, respected and followed.

*Contemporary Application:* Speakers will be polarizing who bluntly offend majority sensitivities, but if the speaker delivers the truth in a captivating style, then, he or she will be vindicated by history.

*Connection to Today:* Black pride, history, and culture are all celebrated today in a variety of ways. One might wonder what Malcolm X, had he lived to this day, would be saying publicly about the state of race relations in the United States of the twenty-first century.

# 70. Barry Goldwater, Nomination Acceptance Speech, July 16, 1964

*Speaker:* Barry M. Goldwater (1909–1998) was a ruggedly handsome and militant anti-communist who won election to the U. S. Senate in 1952 and emerged as the spokesperson for those Republicans of the 50s who viewed President Eisenhower's policies as not conservative enough. He served five terms as U. S. senator from Arizona (1953–65, 1969–87) and is best remembered as the Republican Party's nominee for president in the 1964 general election against incumbent President Lyndon B. Johnson. Goldwater became a hero of militant conservatives. The Arizona senator believed stronger military measures should be taken against the Soviet Union. He was convinced that by not making "victory the goal of American policy" Eisenhower had endangered national security. Goldwater rejected the legacy of FDR's New Deal, thus denouncing almost all domestic programs, including national civil rights legislation, as threats to individual liberty. He was one of only eight Republican senators who had voted against the Civil Rights Act of 1964, criticizing the statute as an unconstitutional extension of national power into areas reserved for state legislatures and private citizens. Little wonder, as an articulate and charismatic figure during the first half of the 1960s, he was known as "Mr. Conservative"—a conservative with a conscience. His speeches gained national attention though his critics decried his penchant for blurting out ill-considered pronouncements on controversial issues. Thus, Goldwater's *ethos* was strong with conservative Republicans who viewed him as a leader of great, uncompromising principle, but Democrats pictured him as reactionary, unpredictable, and even fanatical.

*Occasion:* Goldwater was the darling of fervent, upper-middle class conservatives, who were impressed by his outspoken criticisms of Johnson's policies, and were determined to make him the GOP presidential candidate in 1964. Goldwater's chief opponent for the nomination was Governor Nelson Rockefeller of New York, a liberal who commanded virtually no support in the conservative wing of the party. The convention was a raucous affair in San Francisco. Delegates of both major contenders booed when the other candidate rose to speak. Goldwater further rendered the audience of delegates a more polarized one by naming Rep. William Miller (New York) as his running mate—a congressman almost totally unknown but nearly as reactionary as Goldwater himself. When Goldwater rose to speak, he stood before an ideologically and emotionally polarized audience.

*Excerpt:* "Back in 1858 Abraham Lincoln said this of the Republican Party— and I quote him, because he probably could have said it during the last week or so: 'It was composed of strained, discordant, and even hostile elements in 1858. Yet all of these elements agreed on one paramount objective: To arrest the progress of slavery, and place it in the course of ultimate extinction.' Today, as then, but more urgently and more broadly than then, the task of preserving and enlarging freedom at home and safeguarding it from the forces of tyranny abroad is great enough to challenge all our resources and to require all our strength. Anyone who joins us in all sincerity, we welcome. Those who do not care for our cause, we don't expect to enter our ranks in any case. And let our Republicanism, so focused and so dedicated, not be made fuzzy and futile by unthinking and stupid labels. I would remind you that extremism in the defense of liberty is no vice. And let me remind you also that moderation in the pursuit of justice is no virtue."

*Impact:* While Goldwater's speech could not be considered highly effective by looking at the election results, it is worthy of our listing of 101 noteworthy American speeches. The speaker introduced one of the great lines in American oratory ("Extremism is the pursuit of liberty is no vice" and "Moderation in the pursuit of justice is no virtue"), yet that memorable line was vague and ambiguous. Despite the creative language strategy, the line fed fears that Goldwater might be an "extremist." The speech successfully introduced the Senator to a nation that may have known little or nothing about him. On the other hand, the theme and supporting ideas of the speech did not serve the speaker well, placing him generally on the defensive throughout the presidential campaign. Even some Republicans doubted Goldwater's effectiveness and "fitness" for candidacy, and the GOP was led to a spectacular defeat in November. Johnson carried forty-four states and won more than sixty percent of the popular vote. Goldwater's rhetoric was also a factor in Johnson's supporters producing and airing what was, perhaps, the most controversial spot in campaign history (a little girl picking petals off a daisy and counting "one, two,...." and the frame freezes until she dissolved in a mushroom-shaped cloud and the screen went blank). Nonetheless, this speech advanced an ideology that re-fashioned American conservatism, and the campaign propelled a compelling group of conservatives into national politics, including especially Ronald Reagan, who became the fortieth president of the United States in 1981. Goldwater is credited with sparking that resurgence of the American conservative political movement of the 1960s. Goldwater's rhetoric also resonated with Southern states, laying the groundwork for a "Southern strategy" and the "religious right." Also, Goldwater, despite being trounced in an election he had no chance to win, retained his credibility and respect as a statesman of principle. He is credited with having privately consulted with Richard Nixon during the last days of the Watergate scandal and convincing him to resign for the good of the nation.

*Contemporary Application:* An eloquent but vague declaration in a vital speech will render that address memorable, but runs the risk of requiring the speaker to give persistent explanation to clarify its meaning. The proper choice of words is crucially important for any persuasive speaker or writer. When the rhetorical critic evaluates a speaker's style, which is the third canon of classical rhetoric (word choice and word arrangement), the critic looks for clarity of expression. An effective speaker not simply seeks to be understood, but speaks in such language that he or she cannot possibly be misunderstood.

# 71. Lyndon B. Johnson, Resignation Address to the Nation, March 31, 1968

*Speaker:* Lyndon Johnson was catapulted into the White House by the tragic assassination of John F. Kennedy in November 1963, and then he won a landslide election in 1964 over Barry Goldwater. Many historians contend the Johnson presidency marked the peak of modern liberalism in the United States after the New Deal era. This president is ranked favorably by many historians because of his domestic policies and the passage of landmark legislation, especially in the area of civil rights. As a speaker, Johnson was no spellbinding orator. His manner was a slow, deliberate delivery with a Texas drawl, and he was quite the contrast in speaking manner from his predecessor John F. Kennedy.

*Occasion:* Year 1968 was one of the most difficult years in all American history. The nation had been rocked with race riots, beginning with the Watts riot in the Los Angeles area in 1965, then racial unrest moved to other major U. S. cities, especially in Detroit in 1967. These outbreaks in violence, rooted in economic inequality and racial tension, had spread into many cities, leaving many African-American neighborhoods in ruin. In 1968 several violent events abroad worsened the political polarization in the U. S. The war in Vietnam was obviously worsening and becoming more expensive, both in terms of human loss and revenue. At the end of January, during an alleged truce in observance of *Tet*, the Vietnamese lunar New Year celebration, troops of the National Liberation Front (NLF) and North Vietnamese forces mounted surprise attacks throughout South Vietnam. This *Tet* offensive swept through eight provincial capitals, even seizing the grounds of the U. S. embassy in Saigon for several hours. The media pundits argued whether the U. S. combat response meant "victory" or "defeat." Critics of the administration contended that the *Tet* offensive had caught the U. S. military off guard and ill-prepared to take advantage of enemy losses. Regardless, *Tet* turned out to be a severe psychological defeat for the U. S. because it undercut Johnson's claims about an imminent South Vietnamese-U. S. victory. Anti-war opposition was building at home, and some peace demonstrations turned out to be dangerously volatile and chaotic events captured by television cameras. At many rallies the youthful protesters burned draft cards and chanted: "Hey, hey, LBJ, how many kids did you kill today?" The President was already in political trouble and faced strong criticism from leaders in his own party. Minnesota's liberal Senator Eugene McCarthy decided to challenge Johnson in the presidential primaries and, with enthusiastic college students staffing his campaign, the Senator won an astonishing forty-two percent of the popular vote and twenty of the twenty-four delegates in the New Hampshire primary. With Johnson's vulnerability clearly revealed, Senator Robert F. Kennedy decided to enter the primary race, and this younger brother of the former president inspired great loyalty, especially among African-American and Hispanic voters as well as the white working class. Johnson was indeed facing revolt from within his own party. His *ethos* as a speaker was probably about as low as could be imagined; the press had already sensed a "credibility gap" between what the President was saying and what was actually happening on the ground in Vietnam. The President then decided it was time to address the nation and explain his war policies and his personal intentions for the future.

*Excerpt:* "I would ask all Americans, whatever their personal interests or concern, to guard against divisiveness and all its ugly consequences....Believing this as I do, I have concluded that I should not permit the Presidency to become involved in the partisan divisions that are developing in this political year. With America's sons in the fields far away, with America's future under challenge right here at home, with our hopes and the world's hopes for peace in the balance every day, I do not believe that I should devote an hour or a day of my time to any personal partisan causes or to any duties other than the awesome duties of this office—the Presidency of your country. Accordingly, I shall not seek, and I will not accept, the nomination of my party for another term as your President. But let men everywhere know, however, that a strong, a confident, and a vigilant America stands ready tonight to seek an honorable peace—and stands ready tonight to defend an honored cause—whatever the price, whatever the burden, whatever the sacrifice that duty may require. Thank you for listening."

*Impact:* The early sections of the speech seemed self-congratulatory as Johnson explained his whole-hearted commitment to bringing peace to Vietnam and getting the soldiers home from the bloody conflict. Most of the eighty-five million viewers and listeners in the national audience were likely skeptical of the President's claims and his leadership ability. No viewer or listener was likely prepared for his big announcement at the end of the speech: That he would not run for re-election, that he would halt the bombing of North Vietnam, and his pledge to devote his remaining time in office to seeking an end to the war. The speech was a welcome relief to Johnson critics. And many in the listening audience expressed sympathy and sorrow for a long-time political leader feeling that he must withdraw from the political race. The speech was an important one, of course, because it marked a huge surprise and a huge change in domestic political leadership. Those who were listening only casually to such a lengthy address and with huge skepticism, if not cynicism, immediately were drawn to listen intently as the speech moved to a conclusion. The momentous decision was a statesmanlike act by a man who had been consumed by a war he did not want, had never fully understood, and could not end.

*Contemporary Application:* One who speaks from the heart in times of crisis will long be remembered for sincerity, even when listeners may or may not concur with the speaker's policies.

# 72. Martin Luther King, Jr., "I've Been to the Mountaintop," April 3, 1968

*Speaker:* For his leadership in the Civil Rights Movement, the Reverend Martin Luther King, Jr., was awarded the Nobel Peace Prize in 1964. In the late 60s the term "black power" was becoming more popular among African-Americans. The idea promoted pride in African heritage and culture. Unlearning habits of public deference to whites, most African-Americans began referring to themselves as "black" rather than "Negro." Some black activists curried disfavor with King, thinking his strategy was too slow and too accommodating to mainstream culture. By 1967 King decided he could no longer keep quiet about his growing unease with the American war effort in Vietnam. A storm of criticism greeted his public denunciation of the war, most of it suggesting that he should limit himself to domestic civil rights work. But King no longer believed that events at home and abroad could be separated. He believed the heavy cost of the war had retarded availability of federal funding to fight poverty in Johnson's Great Society, thus he took up the banner of advocacy for the poor, both black and white. None of this new emphasis made his life more secure. Each time King stood to deliver a speech, or even march in a city street or stand in public, surely required a great deal of courage.

*Occasion:* Dr. King became continually concerned about American poverty. In a speech at Riverside Church, New York City, April 4, 1967, King declared: "[Our troops in Vietnam] must know after a short period there that none of the things we claim to be fighting for [such as freedom, justice, and peace] are really involved. Before long they must know that their government has sent them into a struggle among Vietnamese, and the more sophisticated surely realize that we are on the side of the wealthy and the secure while we create a hell for the poor." The year 1968 was a traumatic one. Conservative backlash came to a critical stage. Politicians seized on feelings of working class alienation for political gain. Republican leaders such as Goldwater, Reagan, and Nixon (all later to win their party's nomination for president) gave voice to those resentments and siphoned off votes from Democratic blue-collar strongholds. Governor George Wallace of Alabama became a spokesman for the anger of many "forgotten" whites on both sides of the Mason-Dixon Line. In early April King went to Memphis to support a strike of sanitation workers. Even though he was still committed to the strategy of non-violence, King was perceived as more radical. On the evening before the planned demonstration, there was a gathering of approximately two thousand demonstrators and supporters.

*Excerpt:* "Like anyone, I would like to live a long life. Longevity has its place, but I'm not concerned about that now. I just want to do God's will, and he's allowed me to go up to the mountain, and I've looked over and I've seen the Promised Land. I may not get there with you, but I want you to know tonight that we as a people will get to the Promised Land. So I'm happy tonight. I'm not worried about anything; I'm not fearing any man. Mine eyes have seen the glory of the coming of the Lord."

*Impact:* The famous 1963 "I have a dream" address was prepared in manuscript form, though the speaker supposedly extemporized on some of the memorable passages. This Memphis speech is important for several reasons: First, it seems to be totally extemporized, delivered totally from the heart; second, it is the last speech King ever delivered in his career; third, perhaps most interesting, King spoke prophetically of his own demise, highlighting his prophetic sense of personal destiny. The point of this speech: The Civil Rights Movement would eventually succeed despite the threats on the speaker's life. Had King not been assassinated the next day by a gunman named James Earl Ray, quite likely this speech would have been unheard and unknown by the masses and totally ignored by historians. Less than forty-eight hours after the speech's presentation, King became a martyr for his lifelong cause. Fortunately, this speech was filmed for posterity.

*Contemporary Application:* When attempting the most effective strategy for ending a speech, a speaker should build such a peak of interest and a climax of emotion that he or she need not utter the signpost "Now in conclusion." The rising inflection, the energy, the rhythm, and the emotional expression should leave no doubt the address is nearing its conclusion. King's speeches, especially the famous "I have a dream" speech, demonstrate that strategy. So does this speech.

*Connection to Today:* King wielded a huge impact on modern American history as an effective and courageous spokesman for the causes of justice and human rights.

## 73. Robert F. Kennedy, Remarks on the Occasion of Dr. King's Assassination, April 4, 1968

*Speaker:* Robert Kennedy (1925–1968) was one of the two younger brothers, along with the late Senator Edward Kennedy, of the late President John F. Kennedy. In the spring of 1968, with President Lyndon Johnson having announced he would not seek re-election to another term in high office, Robert Kennedy, perhaps reluctantly, decided to seek the nomination.

*Occasion:* On April 3, 1968, Martin Luther King, Jr., delivered an electrifying speech in which he thundered: "Longevity has its place. But I just want to do God's will. And He's allowed me to go up to the mountain. And I've looked over and I've seen the Promised Land…Mine eyes have seen the glory of the coming of the Lord." These were the words in the climax of the last public speech or sermon King ever delivered. The next day, as he stepped onto the second floor walkway of the Lorraine Motel in Memphis, he was shot and killed by James Earl Ray. When news of the assassination surged through the nation, riots flared in more than seventy-five cities, especially the inner cities of large urban population centers. Senator Kennedy was campaigning for the presidential primary in Indiana and was scheduled to speak at an outdoor rally in a black neighborhood in Indianapolis that evening, just three hours after King had been shot. Kennedy's aides and even the chief of police vigorously urged the Senator to cancel the speaking event in the heart of the Indianapolis inner city neighborhood (bluntly advising him to "get out of Dodge"), fearing for his safety—yet Kennedy insisted on going. He spoke largely impromptu without notes from the back of a flatbed truck in the freezing cold and a howling wind to an audience of approximately one thousand distressed and grieving African-Americans. Deep, raw emotions were being felt by everyone present, and at times Kennedy had to pause, allow emotional outbursts to die down, then resume his remarks, measuring his words thoughtfully.

*Excerpt:* "In this difficult day, in this difficult time for the United States, it is perhaps well to ask what kind of a nation we are and what direction we want to move….We can make an effort, as Martin Luther King did, to understand and to comprehend, and to replace that violence, that stain of bloodshed that has spread across our land, with an effort to understand with compassion and love….For those of you who are black and are tempted to be filled with hatred and distrust at the injustice of such an act, against all white people, I can only say that I feel in my own heart the same kind of feeling. I had a member of my family killed, but he was killed by a white man….What we need in the United States is not division. What we need in the United States is not hatred. What we need in the United States is not violence or lawlessness, but love and wisdom and compassion toward one another, and a feeling of justice toward those who still suffer within our country, whether they be white or they be black. So I shall ask you tonight to return home, to say a prayer for the family of Martin Luther King, that's true, but more importantly, to say a prayer for our own country, which all of us love—a prayer for understanding and that compassion of which I spoke."

*Impact:* The speech was a very brief one, only about five minutes. The oral style of the speech is obvious. Yet it may have been among the most poignant and powerful impromptu speeches in American history. The speech wins high marks if for no other reason than the courage of the speaker. For Senator Kennedy, this was a tender "teachable moment," an opportunity to touch the hearts and minds of listeners bitterly crushed by sadness and disappointment. At times there were screams and wailing among audience members, understandably as African-Americans were experiencing shocking news and raw emotions. Sometimes it is difficult for rhetorical critics to measure the nature of an immediate response to a speech. Not so in this case. While local officials were prepared, and perhaps expecting, the worst (rioting, looting, and destruction of property and perhaps even loss of human life), the crowd of listeners quietly returned to their homes. Over the next few days, there were riots in seventy-six American cities. The toll was staggering: Forty-six people died, 2,500 were injured, 28,000 arrested, and yet Indianapolis remained relatively quiet.

*Interesting Fact:* While both interesting and ironic, it is also profoundly sad and disheartening that within only a few weeks later in that campaign Senator Kennedy would also become a martyred leader, fatally wounded in Los Angeles while celebrating his victory in the important California Democratic primary. The sobering duty then fell to youngest brother Edward to eulogize Robert. That eulogy became one of Edward Kennedy's best known speeches.

*Contemporary Application:* In a crisis situation, whether a national or personal crisis, a wise man or woman who speaks from the heart can truly connect with a compassionate audience and make a real difference in their lives.

*Connection to Today:* True political courage seems almost extinct. Some high political leaders have visited scenes of human tragedies and others have avoided them. Media consultants are paid by political figures to advise whether it is "safe" to be "courageous." Yet, as the astute political observer Joe Klein reminds us, "acts of courage don't come with a money-back guarantee" (*Time*, July 28, 2014, p 19). (Incidentally, Klein, a political columnist for *Time*, was present for this speech and gives a first-hand report on this speech and audience reaction in his book, *Politics Lost*, Doubleday, 2006).

# 74. Edward M. Kennedy, Address to the Nation after Chappaquiddick, July 25, 1969

*Speaker:* Edward Moore Kennedy (1932–2009), serving almost forty-seven years in the U. S. Senate (actually the fourth longest serving member of that august body), earned the nicknames "The Lion in the Senate" and "Democratic Icon." Most of all, "Ted" Kennedy was known as the youngest of four sons of Joseph and Rose Kennedy. Early in that Senate career, Kennedy continued to endure almost unspeakable family tragedy. The oldest brother Joseph had been killed as a fighter pilot in World War II; then, John was assassinated after approximately a thousand days as U. S. president; and, finally, the next younger brother, Robert, was assassinated in Los Angeles in June 1968 while running in the Democratic presidential primary race. Edward Kennedy's public eulogy for Robert has been considered, perhaps, the best among hundreds of speeches delivered during a lifetime of public service. Millions considered Edward to be next in line eventually to win election to the White House, to continue the legacy of the Kennedy clan, and to advance the narrative of Camelot. The tragic event late one night on Chappaquiddick Island dramatically changed that narrative. Kennedy passed on running for high office in 1972 and 1976, but did begin a campaign in 1980 that challenged Jimmy Carter; however, the Massachusetts senator was never able to muster enough support to derail the incumbent and withdrew from the primary race. Kennedy's personal life too often dominated his public image in the 70s and 80s. Considered a powerful, charismatic orator and an unabashed liberal, he devoted himself to liberal causes connected to social justice, especially universal health care. One of his most famous speeches, considered by some as "incendiary rhetoric," entitled "Robert Bork's America," helped defeat the successful confirmation of nominee Bork for the Supreme Court. Kennedy delivered a number of speeches as a rallying cry for modern American liberalism.

*Occasion:* On the night of July 18, 1969, a social event was held on Chappaquiddick Island by six men, all but one married, in honor of six young women, known as "boiler room girls." Each young woman was single; each had served in Robert Kennedy's 1968 campaign. Before the night was over, one of the young women, Mary Jo Kopechne, died by drowning while trapped in Kennedy's Oldsmobile sedan. The automobile had veered off a narrow bridge over a tidal channel while Kennedy was driving. The Senator managed to escape the vehicle, then made several attempts to rescue Kopechne, walked back to the house to report the incident to a cousin and a colleague, and did not report the accident to authorities for another nine hours. Kennedy pleaded guilty to the charge of leaving the scene of an accident causing injury, and later received a two-month suspended jail sentence. Understandably, the story made big headlines in all news media. An initial response was sympathy for Kennedy, but soon the story became a national scandal when details did not seem to square with reality and common sense. There were too many questions, and the Senator was a national figure from America's best known political family. His reputation was at stake, to say the least. Kennedy, with staff writers and advisers, prepared a speech to the nation, and it was broadcast by the television networks from the library of his father's home in Hyannis Port, Massachusetts, and viewed by an estimated thirty-five million.

*Excerpt:* "[After stating his closest companions were solicited to dive in the water in an effort to rescue Ms. Kopechne] All kinds of scrambled thoughts -- all of them confused, some of them irrational, many of them which I cannot recall, and some of which I would not have seriously entertained under normal circumstances -- went through my mind during this period. They were reflected in the various inexplicable, inconsistent, and inconclusive things I said and did, including such questions as whether the girl might still be alive somewhere out of that immediate area, whether some awful curse did actually hang over all the

Kennedys, whether there was some justifiable reason for me to doubt what had happened and to delay my report, whether somehow the awful weight of this incredible incident might in some way pass from my shoulders. I was overcome, I'm frank to say, by a jumble of emotions: grief, fear, doubt, exhaustion, panic, confusion, and shock....These events, the publicity, innuendo, and whispers which have surrounded them and my admission of guilt this morning raises the question in my mind of whether my standing among the people of my State has been so impaired that I should resign my seat in the United States Senate. If at any time the citizens of Massachusetts should lack confidence in their Senator's character, or his ability--with or without justification--he could not in my opinion adequately perform his duties and should not continue in office."

*Impact:* Kennedy's speech presented a dramatic narrative, in many ways like a Greek tragedy, wherein the protagonist presents himself as a victim of fateful circumstances over which he has no control. Some critics consider it "apologetic rhetoric," a *mea culpa* address—in the midst of conceding he left the scene of the accident, still he had done everything humanly possible to save Ms. Kopechne's life. The speaker bares his emotional soul, and he seeks his viewers to identify with the hand that fate has dealt him. As for immediate response, there was overwhelming support expressed favoring Kennedy remaining in office, and he was re-elected the following year with sixty-two percent of the vote. More sobering, the address was a rhetorical act to salvage his reputation, but Kennedy failed to answer important questions convincingly, and the incident continued to damage his reputation nationally.

*Contemporary Application:* A speech may contain such emotional soul-bearing (*pathos*) that successfully projects a common humanity with which listeners identify, but might sadly fail to convince listeners they should trust that speaker to serve the nation in the highest office in time of national or international crisis.

# 75. Gaylord Nelson, A Proposal for the Earth, September 20, 1969

*Speaker:* Gaylord Nelson (1916–2005) was born in Wisconsin where he served the state's citizens in several high offices, including governor. He is best remembered as a liberal Democratic senator who was first elected to the U. S. Senate in 1962 and re-elected in 1968 and 1974, though he was unseated in 1980. In the Senate Nelson was a strong supporter of civil rights and liberties. He was a consumer advocate as well, and was concerned about the nation's population as an important aspect of environmentalism. Indeed, his greatest legacy combined his passion and achievements for the environment. He began to build that legacy while governor of Wisconsin and he was known as the "Conservation Governor," but this gubernatorial role was a dress rehearsal for pushing conservation issues on the national scene. Nelson constantly pushed the environment front and center in Washington politics by drawing from that experience as governor. He had toured parts of the nation that had been recently impacted by seeming environmental disaster, such as the massive tanker oil spill off the coast of California near Santa Barbara. When the chemical disposal that sat above the Cuyahoga River in Cleveland caught on fire, this not only grabbed his attention, but also the attention of just about any American that cared about the environment. In 1969, having observed the success of "teach-ins" on American college and university campuses—an entire class day devoted to the study and protest against the war in Vietnam—Nelson envisioned how powerful and effective a special day for the environment, also with university "teach-ins," might be as strategies for education and action.

*Occasion:* After the booming 50s, Americans began to pay attention to "pollution," a kind of catchall term for the damage that advanced industrial production and new technologies inflicted on natural systems. Rachel Carson's

*Silent Spring* in 1962 gave voice to concerns about the environment, her own study examining the side effects of DDT and other pesticides on animal life. In 1969 Nelson conceived and promoted the idea of a special day devoted to the environment. Just after having toured the oil spill devastation on the coast of Santa Barbara, he was scheduled to speak to a small environmental group in Seattle (also addressing an audience in Denver). He capitalized on this occasion to announce his proposal—he called for a teach-in on every college campus for the next spring, and volunteered to take initial leadership in organizing the event. "I am convinced that the same concern the youth of this nation took in changing the nation's priorities on the war in Vietnam and on civil rights," Nelson declared, "can be shown for the problems in the environment." The audience may not have been a large one, but, fortunately for the cause, there were national media representatives present.

*Excerpt:* "The battle to restore a proper relationship between man and his environment, between man and other living creatures, will require a long, sustained, political, moral and ethical and financial commitment far beyond any commitment ever made by any society in the history of man. Are we able? Yes. Are we willing? That's the unanswered question....If we could tap into the environmental concerns of the general public and infuse the student anti-war energy into the environmental cause, we could generate a demonstration that would force the issue into the national political agenda....This is the time for old-fashioned political action."

*Impact:* One must rate this speech as one of the most important speeches in twentieth century American history, providing the spark for an important national day that has become an academic tradition. Senator Nelson certainly did not "invent" the environmental movement, but this speech set in motion one of the most important strategies in the movement—the establishment of "Earth Day." On that first "Earth Day," twenty million Americans demonstrated for a healthy and sustainable environment—the largest demonstration in U. S. history. This protest against the deterioration of the environment led to the creation of the Environmental Protection Agency and marks the birth of the modern environmental movement. In the turbulent 70s, Americans found one issue they could agree on—a safe and respectable crusade to assimilate and express the idealism and discontent of the 60s and of the decades since the first Earth Day. In this speech Nelson proved the power of an idea whose time had come.

*Contemporary Application:* Even if the immediate audience for a speech on a significant national issue seems small, there will always be a secondary audience if national media are present for the speech and deem it newsworthy. That larger national audience may immediately be impacted. Such is the basis, of course, for modern press conferences.

*Connection to Today:* Earth Day remains an important annual way to raise awareness of local environmental issues each year, and the idea of a special day for the environment has spread to other nations. And the environment will always justifiably remain a perennial issue as humans make their home on Planet Earth. Nelson stated an important principle: "The ultimate test of man's conscience may be his willingness to sacrifice something today for future generations whose words of thanks will not be heard."

# 76. Spiro Agnew, Television News Coverage, November 13, 1969

*Speaker:* Perhaps no vice president has been ranked lower by historians than Spiro Theodore Agnew (1918–1996), and yet he is included here because he raised important questions in his critique of the news media. Agnew was born in Baltimore, drafted in 1941 and served as an officer during World War II, and was elected as the fifty-fifth governor of Maryland, the first Greek-American to hold the position. During the 1968 Republican convention, Agnew, barely known nationally, was selected in private by Richard Nixon and his campaign staff to be the vice presidential running mate; the Nixon-Agnew team beat the incumbent Vice President Hubert Humphrey and his running mate, Edmund Muskie. The attributes of Agnew that appealed to Nixon were his moderate image; his immigrant family background (his father had been a poor immigrant); his strong reputation on law and order; and his political success in a traditionally Democratic state. As a speaker, the graying Agnew had both a distinguished professional appearance and a low key professorial speech delivery. The provocative nature of his content was the trait that maintained attention among intelligent listeners, not any dynamic quality to his delivery. In the use of language, the third canon of classical rhetoric, Agnew scored in a class to himself. Many other speakers, of course, have used alliteration to hold attention (not the least of which, Jesse Jackson), but none surpassed Agnew in alliteration to polarize an audience—creating adulation or scorn and very little between these extremes. Many of the alliterative epithets have been attributed to ghostwriters William Safire and Pat Buchanan, though undoubtedly Agnew wrote many of them himself. (See the chapter "Hall of Shame" for some Agnew alliterative epithets.)

*Occasion:* The broader context for this speech was the turbulent decade of the 60s. Richard Nixon was in the first year of his term of office, and the war in Viet Nam, already quite costly in every way, had become increasingly unpopular. In his campaigning, Nixon claimed to possess a "secret plan" to end the war, but no end seemed in sight. Indeed, each night's national news telecast gave major time and emphasis to the growing anti-war movement, especially among college and university youth. The speaker was already known for his sharp, acerbic criticism of the youth protest movement as well as his clever use of language. Thus, Agnew seemed the perfect spokesperson for a message that Nixon and his staff wanted the media and the general public to hear. The message was that the major network news media possess too much power, an influence that rivals, if not surpasses, the influence of the White House. The administration gave full advance publicity to this speech, thus the news media were prepared to grant coverage. Though the venue did not seem so large—the Des Moines Midwest Regional Republican Committee Meeting—there was a much wider audience nationwide as the three major networks covered the speech live.

*Excerpt:* "Now the upshot of all this controversy is that a narrow and distorted picture of America often emerges from the televised news. A single, dramatic piece of the mosaic becomes in the minds of millions the entire picture...The American who relies upon television for his news might conclude that the majority of American students are embittered radicals; that the majority of black Americans feel no regard for their country; that violence and lawlessness are the rule rather than the exception on the American campus. We know that none of these conclusions is true. Perhaps the place to start looking for a credibility gap is not in the offices of the Government in Washington but in the studios of the networks in New York. Television may have destroyed the old stereotypes, but has it not created new ones in their places?....Tonight I've raised questions. I've made no attempt to suggest the answers. The answers must come from the media men. They are challenged to turn their critical powers on themselves."

*Impact:* This speech was well received by a highly partisan audience, but it was also welcomed by conservative Americans who agreed with the Vice President. Agnew came across as a man of reason. In the address, he dropped names such as Winston Churchill, David Brinkley, and Will Rogers, and he supported main points with quotes from a variety of authorities: network executive Fred Friendly, columnist Walter Lippmann, Justice Byron White, and historian Theodore White. Agnew succeeded in the sense that he enhanced national discussion of an important topic; understandably, he put television news people on the defensive. Given the wide publicity of the speech, the message played a major role in establishing Agnew's reputation as the major voice for the "silent majority," Nixon's term for a majority of citizens who would agree with his domestic and foreign policy views but did not use loud voices or unruly public demonstrations to gain media attention. To liberals, Agnew had his own bias against the "Left," and he certainly had his own ax to grind in the speech. Nonetheless, the address raised important questions about network news representation and fairness and is rated by *American Rhetoric* as one of the one hundred great speeches of the twentieth century.

*Contemporary Application:* A political speaker may seem a quiet, respectful, professorial type, and yet still polarize an audience with one's position and language.

*Interesting fact:* Much evidence reveals Richard Nixon almost immediately became displeased with Agnew as vice president and eventually sought ways for him to be removed from the position. In late 1973 Agnew was shown to have accepted kickbacks from contractors while governor of Maryland and even while vice president. On October 10 he was forced to resign after pleading no contest to a charge of tax evasion. Spiro Agnew became only the second vice president to resign from office, the other being John Calhoun, and the only one to resign due to criminal charges. In the midst of his own Watergate scandal issues, Nixon named House GOP leader Gerald Ford as the new vice president.

# 77. Richard M. Nixon, Resignation and Farewell Address, August 8, 1974

*Speaker:* Richard M. Nixon was one of the most controversial presidents in American history. He had served as vice president in the 50s under President Eisenhower, was narrowly defeated by John Kennedy for president in 1960, ran unsuccessfully for governor of California in 1962, and made a political comeback as the Republican presidential winner in 1968. Nixon won an easy victory for re-election in November 1972, receiving the Electoral College votes of all but one state and the District of Columbia. Throughout his term in office, Nixon was widely popular with the majority of middle-class Americans, and was viewed suspiciously by many Democrats. Nixon was one of the most brilliant men to serve in the White House. He loved political combat and was tough and cunning, but there were reminders of the "old Nixon"—the political loner, who ruminated about taking revenge against his enemies (an "enemies list" was created with hundreds of names from several fields). Indeed, Nixon seemed to be his own greatest foe.

*Occasion:* During the 1972 election campaign, five men had been caught breaking into the Democratic Party Headquarters in the Watergate Hotel in Washington. An informant from the FBI ("Deep Throat") passed on information to *Washington Post* reporters Carl Bernstein and Bob Woodward that the crooks had links to the Nixon White House. Eventually, there were hearings in special judiciary committees in the Senate (1973) and the House (1974). Information about the President's taping system emerged as well as evidence that important taped evidence had been erased. Nixon fired one special prosecutor (Archibald Cox) and discovered his replacement (Ron Jaworsky) cut him no special favors. The "smoking gun" tape, released on August 5, made it obvious that the President had known about the plot from the beginning and had actively attempted to stop the FBI investigation. Nixon made the decision to resign. Realistically he had no better choice at this point, but knew he owed it to his staff and friends to offer explanation, if not confession. In somber yet composed tones, and with wife Pat and daughter Tricia at his side, the President delivered his farewell. His immediate audience was composed of family, close friends, advisers, and staff, yet the speech was also televised live for the entire nation. This was a moment of relief for an exhausted citizenry, and Nixon's *ethos* was perhaps higher for this speech than at any time since the scandal broke.

*Excerpt:* "I have never been a quitter. To leave office before my term is completed is abhorrent to every instinct in my body. But as President, I must put the interest of America first....Sometimes I have succeeded and sometimes I have failed, but always I have taken heart from what Theodore Roosevelt once said about the man in the arena, 'whose face is marred by dust and sweat and blood, who strives valiantly, who errs and comes short again and again because there is not effort without error and shortcoming, but who does actually strive to do the deed, who knows the great enthusiasms, the great devotions, who spends himself in a worthy cause, who at the best knows in the end the triumphs of high achievements and who at the worse, if he fails, at least fails while daring greatly.' I pledge to you tonight that as long as I have a breath of life in my body, I shall continue in that spirit. I shall continue to work for the great causes to which I have been dedicated throughout my years as a Congressman, a Senator, a Vice President, and President, the cause of peace not just for America but among all nations, prosperity, justice, and opportunity for all our people....I have done my very best in all the days since to be true to that pledge...In leaving office, I do so with a prayer: May God's grace be with you in all the days ahead."

*Impact:* This may have been the best speech ever delivered by Richard Nixon, presented in the immediate environment of people who could feel empathy and appreciation. Though many in the wider television audience could not have changed their opinion of Nixon's complicity in the scandal, they surely were impressed by a tone of acceptance and humility. The speaker did not express blame or bitterness, but instead expressed "regret for any injuries done," and contended that with Gerald Ford "the leadership of the nation will be in good hands." In the end, Richard Nixon seemingly understood his downfall: "Always give your best, never get discouraged, never be petty; always remember, others may hate you, but those who hate you don't win unless you hate them, and then you destroy yourself."

*Contemporary Application:* If a person is controversial due to alleged wrongdoing, one's legacy can only be enhanced by speaking to the public in tones marked by contrition, humility, and understanding. Defiance and accusation may bring temporary relief, but ill-serve that person both at the time of delivery and in long-range effect. Americans may celebrate President Nixon's achievements and contributions to our national history, such as opening formal relations with China and his New Federalism policies, but also favorably consider the words he delivered before leaving Washington and flying off into permanent exile.

*Little Known Fact:* In 2005 "Deep Throat" was finally identified as FBI Deputy Director William Mark Felt, Sr.

*Connection to Today:* Though two presidents have been impeached and remained in office, Richard Nixon remains the only president to have resigned from the office. On August 9 Gerald Ford, who had never even been elected to the vice presidency, became the nation's thirty-eighth president. Those who lived through the Watergate scandal still debate the relative seriousness of Nixon's duplicity and other offenses. The national media seem to have affixed the Watergate label to nearly every political scandal of the post-Nixon era. The suffix "gate" has been attached to grave constitutional wrongdoings as well as to obviously trivial political misdeeds and episodes.

# 78. Gerald Ford, On Pardoning Richard M. Nixon, September 8, 1974

*Speaker:* Gerald Ford (1913– 2006) was one of those unique political leaders in U. S. history who became the first person to serve as both vice president and president without being elected to either office. He replaced Vice President Spiro Agnew, who had resigned in 1973 and pleaded "no contest" to charges of bribery and income tax evasion as the Watergate scandal was gathering steam. Then, when Richard Nixon resigned the presidency in 1974, he was sworn into office. Ford was a genial, unpretentious former University of Michigan football star, who preferred his public entries be accompanied by the fight song of his alma mater rather than "Hail to the Chief." Historians rate Ford as competent but unimaginative. He had served many years with distinction as GOP leader in the U. S. House of Representatives and was a humble, soft-spoken leader who, in the wake of the Vietnam War and Watergate scandal, sought to "heal the land," as he put it. His desire to re-establish the presidency as a focus of national unity proved to be limited. As a speaker, Ford came into office with high positive *ethos*, a man who had served thirteen terms as a representative from Michigan's fifth congressional district without any serious charge of scandal. His speech delivery seemed rather unemotional, slow in rate, and deliberate in expression. Safe to safe, while Ford's audiences could be informed, they were seldom, if ever, deeply stirred.

*Occasion:* The nation had endured several years of highly publicized Watergate investigation. President Nixon's approval ratings had dipped low. Infuriated by Nixon's excessive abuse of power, many in Congress and in the nation deeply desired and anticipated the time when he would be tried in a court of law. However, Nixon's hand-picked successor, facing a number of domestic issues that had been put "on hold," was determined to put criminal justice issues to rest for once and all. President Ford braced himself and prepared a brief speech that he knew would be calamitous and unleash a firestorm, yet, in his opinion, it was best for the country. The new president then needed to make his case to the American people. On a Sunday morning, exactly thirty days after he took office, the White House summoned reporters for a mysterious announcement by the new president. His main argument was that many more months, perhaps even years, would be required, "before Richard Nixon could obtain a fair trial by jury in any jurisdiction in the United States"….[and] I deeply believe in equal justice for all Americans."

*Excerpt:* "As President, my primary concern must always be the greatest good of all the people of the United States whose servant I am. As a man, my first consideration is to be true to my own convictions and my own conscience. My conscience tells me clearly and certainly that I cannot prolong the bad dreams that continue to reopen a chapter that is closed. My conscience tells me that only I, as President, have the constitutional power to firmly shut and seal this book. My conscience tells me it is my duty, not merely to proclaim domestic tranquility but to use every means that I have to insure it. I do believe that the buck stops here, that I cannot rely upon public opinion polls to tell me what is right. I do believe that right makes might and that if I am wrong, ten angels swearing I was right would make no difference. I do believe, with all my heart and mind and spirit, that I, not as President but as a humble servant of God, will receive justice without mercy if I fail to show mercy….Now, therefore, I, Gerald R. Ford, President of the United States, pursuant to the pardon power conferred upon me by Article II, Section 2, of the Constitution, have granted and by these presents do grant a full, free, and absolute pardon unto Richard Nixon for all offenses against the United States which he, Richard Nixon, has committed or may have committed or taken part in during the period from January 20, 1969 through August 9, 1974."

*Impact:* The Nixon pardon was highly controversial, as to be expected. Ford's popularity began to tumble almost immediately. Critics derided the move and claimed a "corrupt bargain" had been struck. They claimed Ford's pardon was granted in exchange for Nixon's resignation that elevated Ford to the presidency. Ford's first press secretary and close friend Jerald terHorst resigned his post in protest. Insiders believed that Ford decided to pardon Nixon for various reasons, primarily the friendship he and Nixon shared mutually. Regardless, the controversy was one of the major reasons Ford lost the election in 1976, an observation with which Ford agreed. *The New York Times* stated editorially that the Nixon pardon was a "profoundly unwise, divisive and unjust act" that in a stroke had destroyed the new president's "credibility as a man of judgment, candor and competence." On October 17, 1974, Ford testified before Congress on the pardon. He was the first sitting president to testify before the House since Lincoln. Decades later, the John F. Kennedy Library Foundation presented its 2001 Profile in Courage Award to Gerald Ford for his 1974 pardon. In pardoning Nixon, said the Foundation, Ford placed his love of country ahead of his own political future and brought needed closure to the divisive Watergate affair. The late Senator Ted Kennedy said that he had initially been opposed to the pardon of Nixon, but later stated that history had proved Ford to have made the correct decision. Ford left politics after losing the 1976 presidential election to Democrat Jimmy Carter.

*Contemporary Application:* The speech that seems divisive at the moment of delivery and faces acerbic criticism, because it attempts to justify a highly unpopular and consequential decision, may well be judged by history to be a courageous, unifying address that deserved presentation.

*Interesting Little Known Fact:* Ford lived longer than any other U. S. president (ninety-three years and 165 days), while his 895-day presidency remains the shortest term of all presidents who did not die in office.

# 79. Barbara Jordan, "Who Then Will Speak for the Common Good?" Keynote Address, Democratic National Convention, July 12, 1976

*Speaker:* Barbara Jordan (1936–1996) has been called "the Jackie Robinson of Texas politics." She was the first African-American elected to the Texas Senate after Reconstruction, the first black female elected to the U. S. House of Representatives, and the first black woman to deliver a keynote address at a Democratic National Convention. Born in Houston, her father was a Baptist minister. She graduated from Texas Southern, and then earned a law degree from Boston University School of Law (1959) and returned to Texas for private law practice. When elected to Congress (1972), President Lyndon Johnson helped her secure a position on the House Judiciary Committee. She first came to national prominence as a powerful and eloquent speaker with her impassioned, influential televised speech before the committee in 1974 supporting the impeachment process of President Richard Nixon. In casting a "yes" vote, Jordan stated empathically, "My faith in the Constitution is whole, it is complete, it is total." Jordan's speaking style seemed to come naturally. She was a college debater, then, in her career she accepted a wide variety of speaking opportunities. As a somewhat larger black woman, she had been called "Aunt Jemima" both by friends and enemies, a name she did not like but which gave her opportunity to counter racial stereotypes. As an orator, Jordan spoke with confidence and an authoritative, thunderous voice that could captivate large audiences.

*Occasion:* In 1976 Representative Jordan had been mentioned as a possible running mate of Jimmy Carter, but instead became the first African-American woman to deliver the keynote address at the DNC. Given the years of Vietnam conflict, and then the drawn-out Watergate scandal, there was much disillusionment about government and public officials. And there was continuing interest in civil rights. Many Democrats perceived incumbent President Ford as less than a strong candidate, thus the Democratic National Convention was an opportunity to initiate a strong campaign to return a Democrat to the White House.

*Excerpt* (Peroration): "In this election year we must define the common good and begin again to shape a common good and begin again to shape a common future. Let each person do his or her part. If one citizen is unwilling to participate, all of us are going to suffer. For the American idea, though it is shared by all of us, is realized in each one of us... If we as public officials propose, we must produce. If we say to the American people it is time for you to be sacrificial; sacrifice. If the public official says that, we (public officials) must be the first to give. We must be. And again, if we make mistakes, we must be willing to admit them. We have to do that. What we have to do is strike a balance between the idea, the belief, that government ought to do nothing.... Let there be no illusions about the difficulty of forming this kind of a national community. It's tough, difficult, not easy. But a spirit of harmony will survive in America only if each of us remembers that we share a common destiny."

*Impact:* Representative Jordan impressed the national television audience with an eloquence rooted in intelligence, insight, and in her thunderous, dynamic delivery. Her range of topics was diverse, but civil rights was ever in the forefront. She told listeners at the outset of the speech, "My presence here . . . is one additional bit of evidence that the American dream need not forever be deferred." Millions heard, and were impressed, with Barbara Jordan's oratory for the first time. "I turned on my television set and thought I was listening to God," one awed young woman said. "It sounds," Congressman Andrew Young of Georgia stated, "like the heavens have opened up." The religious parallels are apt, because the voice was an evangelical voice, a voice designed to bring to the fold the presence of the Lord. For that voice, for much of her ambition, and for her exacting standards of excellence, she was indebted to her father, according to many who knew her family. Her speech was so successful at the convention that it led the audience to deeper support for Carter's presidential campaign.

*Contemporary Application:* A woman with supreme self-confidence, natural gifts of voice and delivery, and, most of all, the courage of her convictions, will gain and maintain an audience's attention and respect.

*Connection to Today:* Jordan's speech addressed themes of unity, equality, accountability, and American ideals. The congresswoman stated that the nation must form a willingness to "share the responsibility for upholding the common good" and that everyone "must define the 'common good' and begin again to shape a common future." These themes, and the unifying image she projected, are just as relevant today as they were in 1976.

# 80. Jimmy Carter, Crisis in Confidence Address, July 15, 1979

*Speaker*: In the bicentennial year 1976, Governor James Earl Carter (b. 1924) defeated President Gerald Ford, the latter appointed and ratified by Congress to complete the term of Richard Nixon, the only president to resign the high office. The nation had tired of war and scandal. Both Viet Nam and Watergate had taken their toll on Americans' confidence in their governmental leaders. Jimmy Carter, governor of Georgia and peanut farmer from Plains, projected an image of optimism, integrity, and intelligence, and was granted much good will early in his administration. He had already unabashedly made clear his roots in the Southern Baptist Church, had taught Sunday School in his local Baptist congregation, even owned up to the sin of having lust in his heart on some occasion(s), his surprise and unusual confession coming in perhaps the most famous interview ever published in *Playboy* magazine.

*Occasion*: In the summer of 1979 Carter's approval ratings took a nosedive, dropping even lower than Nixon's ratings during the heat of Watergate. The President had accomplished a stellar achievement in foreign policy with the historic Camp David Accords, which established peace between Egypt and Israel. But then came a short list of major crises that amounted to plain "bad luck" for Carter—the Soviets invaded Afghanistan, subsequently Carter took the controversial policy decision of canceling U. S. participation in the summer Olympics scheduled for Moscow; the economy was reeling with unemployment in the double digits; inflation lingered in the double digits; the interest rate reached an astronomical twenty percent; and oil and gas appeared to be in short demand for Americans (the oil producing nations [OPEC] jacked up oil prices over one hundred percent). While Carter's evangelical piety, idealism, and "outsider status" appealed to voters in November 1976, now that status seemed to convey a sense of the President being overwhelmed and inept. A slow crisis seemed to be developing. The President felt the need to address the nation's citizens and confront their anxieties and concerns head on. "I want to talk to you right now about a fundamental threat to American democracy," the President began in a radio and television speech now called the "Crisis of Confidence Address." Stating there was no threat to political and civil liberties, and that the United States was strong militarily and economically, Carter noted that the crisis was invisible in ordinary way—it was a "crisis of confidence." He then noted that Americans are losing faith in their government and losing faith in the future. Noting that Americans were once proud of hard work, strong families, faith in God, and close-knit communities, now moral virtue seemed in decline. President Carter's speech purpose was to identify and describe that crisis and to point to a path away from crisis.

*Excerpt:* "It is a crisis of confidence. It is a crisis that strikes at the very heart and soul and spirit of our national will. We can see this crisis in the growing doubt about the meaning of our own lives and in the loss of a unity of purpose for our nation. The erosion of our confidence in the future is threatening to destroy the social and political fabric of America....Too many of us now tend to worship self-indulgence and consumption. Human identity is no longer defined by what one does, but by what one owns....We are at a turning point in our history. There are two paths to choose....I will do my best, but I will not do it alone. Let your voice be heard....With God's help and for the sake of our nation, it is time for us to join hands in America."

*Impact:* An estimated sixty million Americans saw or heard the address. Some cultural observers have panned the speech as overly simplistic and a misguided effort to inspire a troubled nation. Critics were harsher, calling it the "malaise speech," even though "malaise" was not a word used in the address. Nonetheless, the speech bumped the President's approval rating by eleven percent. One could thus make the case that this speech deserved to go down in history as one of the greatest presidential speeches in history. On the other hand, the new success was short-lived. Carter was fated to be a one-term president, especially after a revolution led by the Ayatollah Khomeini with his Iranian fundamentalists, who stormed the U. S. embassy in Teheran and took fifty-two Americans hostage. Though it was a nationally-televised address and cast a moral tone, the speech is hardly known or remembered today by anyone in the general public.

*Contemporary Application:* Theodore Roosevelt was the president who first used the term "bully pulpit," referencing the U. S. chief executive's unique position of influence to sway or mold the general American populace along political or moral issues. Yes, the president can function as a preacher when talking about policies and values, and the president can inform, explain, instruct, admonish, inspire, or even scold the American audience. Yet a president in that role needs to speak wisely and humbly.

*Connection to Today:* Carter's basic analysis and insights were sound, but a lower sense of *ethos* meant the address was given little credibility by the immediate audience. On the other hand, the basic themes of community and moral fabric of a nation are just as relevant in the twenty-first century—and perhaps even more so—as they were in the 1970s. After the divisive presidential election of 2016, the nation seems as much divided and at crisis point as in any time in modern history. Former President Carter and his wife attended Donald Trump's Inauguration in January 2017; Carter has served the longest as an ex-president as any president in our history.

# 81. Ronald Reagan, Nomination Acceptance Speech, July 17, 1980

*Speaker*: Ronald Wilson Reagan (1911–2004) ushered in major political change with his election mandate in 1980. A product of small-town Illinois, Reagan succeeded in Hollywood in the late 1930s while playing lead as a romantic actor, who, politically, supported the liberal policies of FDR. He moved rapidly to the political right as a spokesperson for General Electric, having hosted General Electric Theater. In both those roles (G. E. spokesperson and president of Screen Actors Guild from 1947 to 1952), Reagan made hundreds of speeches, most celebrating the achievements of corporate America and emphasizing the dangers of big government and the dangers of liberalism. He ran successfully for governor of California in 1966 and served for two terms in office. And when Reagan sought higher office, the 69-year-old one-time actor breezed through the primaries. With a common touch, the candidate tapped into the nostalgia of a simpler past. While Carter spoke of living within limits, Reagan insisted that "we are too great a nation to limit ourselves to small dreams." His Hollywood background and experiences as a corporate representative to the general public made Reagan experienced at communicating in public forums and in using popular films to illustrate his points. He was clearly conservative and some of his strongest support came from anti-Communist stalwarts of both parties. His buoyant and upbeat personality (in public he was almost always smiling and often waving), along with his irrepressible sense of humor, rendered Reagan popular with the majority. The television media loved the photogenic Reagan. The 1980 election was about more than Reagan's infectious personality (so much like FDR's personality)—it revealed the nation's renewed interest in conservative ideas.

*Occasion:* While President Jimmy Carter predicted in a July 15, 1979, speech that America would regain its confidence, ironically the nation's renewed sense of security and strength was not inspired by Carter but by his political opponent in the 1980 election—the former governor of California, Ronald Reagan. Even his political opponents conceded that Reagan exuded a sense of confidence and contagious optimism about the future—qualities that even a good, honest man like Carter with a terrific smile still could not match. The former governor and campaigner delivered a stunning impromptu speech at the Republican Convention four years earlier when Gerald Ford was nominated, but this convention in Detroit was the occasion for Reagan to accept the nomination and once again project his image for the future of the nation.

*Excerpt:* "The American people, the most generous on earth, who created the highest standard of living, are not going to accept the notion that we can only make a better world for others by moving backwards ourselves. And those who believe we can have no business leading our nation. I will not stand by and watch this great country destroy itself under mediocre leadership that drifts from one crisis to the next, eroding our national will and purpose….We need a rebirth of the American tradition of leadership at every level of government and in private life as well…No American should vote until he or she has asked: is the United States stronger and more respected now than it was three-and-a-half years ago? Is the world safer, a safer place in which to live?"

*Impact:* The speech was a stunning success, at least to the Republicans, and it kicked off a successful campaign that projected Reagan into the White House. Reagan was convincing to his audience when he castigated "Democratic Party leadership" for "this unprecedented calamity which has befallen us." Though Democratic opponents attempted to characterize their opponent as a trigger-happy nuclear cowboy who was unsympathetic to the plight of the poor, Reagan remained upbeat and stuck with his script which promised to cut taxes, reduce government, and rebuild the military. The speech at this convention was one of the most masterful performances of his political career. It clearly established Reagan as a national political leader.

*Contemporary Application:* There are so many lessons to be learned from Reagan's career, but one is that *derived ethos* can be a positive factor in a speaker's success—that is the source credibility that is enhanced as the speaker actually delivers the speech with great skill, confidence, and assurance.

*Connection to Today:* The most memorable presidents since 1900 have been excellent communicators—Teddy Roosevelt, who invented the "bully pulpit;" Woodrow Wilson, who expressed idealism and democratic sentiment; Franklin Roosevelt, who inspired hope and confidence during the two greatest challenges of the middle of the century (the Great Depression and World War II); and both John Kennedy and Barack Obama, who, though a half century apart, used television to inspire a young generation and promote civil rights and equality. And, then, there is Ronald Reagan, whose confidence and skill in public speaking earned him the nicknames of "the Great Communicator" and "the Communicator-in-Chief." Republicans running for high office today take pride in connecting their ideology and convictions with those of Reagan, who clearly has become more popular and respected in terms of his legacy than when he was actually serving in office.

# 82. Mario Cuomo, Keynote Address to the 1984 Democratic National Convention, July 17, 1984

*Speaker:* Mario Cuomo (1932–2015) was born in the Queens borough of New York to a family of Italian origin, and he served as the fifty-second governor for the state between 1983 and 1994. Cuomo was widely known for his liberal political views, though as a Roman Catholic he opposed abortion. Highly regarded as a skilled orator and in much demand as a public speaker, this speech introduced him to the nation; however, he seemed hesitant and reticent about seeking any higher office after he was defeated for a fourth term as governor by George Pataki (Republican). One stance that especially hurt Cuomo was his opposition to the death penalty. As a private practice attorney, he turned down the opportunity for a nomination to an appointment on the Supreme Court. As a "reluctant politician," he was dubbed by some as "Hamlet on the Hudson." An older son, Andrew, married and later divorced Kerry Kennedy, a daughter of Ethel and the late Robert Kennedy, and has been active in political life, known for holding the same office as did his dad (governor of New York). His youngest son, Chris, has been a journalist on ABC and CNN. In his later years, Cuomo developed some favorite speech themes, and was outspoken about the unfair stereotyping of Italian-Americans in the entertainment media (he hated the movie *The Godfather*); he criticized the Giants of the NFL for building their home stadium in New Jersey (he thus attended home games of the Buffalo Bills as New York's only professional football team).

*Occasion:* "Four years ago we raised a banner of bold colors. We proclaimed a dream of an America that would be a shining city on a hill"….Well, now it's all coming together"—thus proclaimed Ronald Reagan in a 1984 re-election speech. Those words did strike a chord with many in the general public. Compared to some of the agonizing economic realities of the Carter Administration, employment was up, prices had stabilized, and runaway inflation had been halted. Reagan had already established himself as a popular president, and the Democratic Party's candidate for president was Walter Mondale, a man of integrity and compassion, but lacking the charisma of Reagan or a Kennedy and, as Carter's vice president, seemed tied to policies that failed. Democrats were not encouraged, but they rolled the dice, much like John McCain in 2008, and nominated a woman for the second slot on the ticket.

*Excerpt:* "[President Reagan] said, 'Why, this country is a shining city on a hill.' And the President is right. In many ways we are a shining city on a hill. But the hard truth is that not everyone is sharing in this city's splendor and glory. A shining city is perhaps all the President sees from the portico of the White House and the veranda of his ranch, where everyone seems to be doing well. But there's another city; there's another part to the shining city; the part where some people can't pay their mortgages, and most young people can't afford one; where students can't afford the education they need, and middle-class parents watch the dreams they hold for their children evaporate. In this part of the city there are more poor than ever, more families in trouble, more and more people who need help but can't find it.... There are ghettos where thousands of young people, without a job or an education, give their lives away to drug dealers every day. There is despair, Mr. President, in the faces that you don't see, in the places that you don't visit in your shining city. In fact, Mr. President, this is a nation -- Mr. President you ought to know that this nation is more a 'Tale of Two Cities' than it is just a 'Shining City on a Hill.'"

*Impact:* Though this was an extremely difficult speaking situation with Democrats already realistically facing another humiliating defeat, one of two huge highlights of this convention was Cuomo's keynote address. In a voice that resonated with clarity, urgency, and power, the defiant governor urged

Americans to look beneath the shiny gloss of the Reagan campaign rhetoric and see the realities of suffering and despair glossed over by the incumbent president. This memorable speech enhanced Cuomo's *ethos* for his many speeches to follow. Reporters who covered the governor from Queens in the 1980s treated him with almost rock star reverence, recalling his speeches the way others remember concerts. They would exchange stories of how the power of his oratory could sway even the most hostile audiences. After this convention, Cuomo was considered a front-runner for the presidential nomination in both 1988 and 1992, but he declined to seek the nomination. Incidentally, the other convention highlight was the introduction of Geraldine Ferraro as vice presidential nominee and her acceptance speech. Cuomo's performance is simply remembered as "the speech," and it placed him on the national political map. On his death, political observer David Colton commented that Cuomo was "the ultimate Democrat, a fierce liberal who nonetheless earned the respect of his political opponents, then and now....Many, maybe most Americans, never agreed with Mario Cuomo's compassionate vision. But when he spoke, the nation at least stopped and listened" (*USA Today*, Jan. 2, 2015).

*Contemporary Application:* Great oratory can emerge from a losing side. Besides Cuomo, Democratic nominee Adlai Stevenson, twice defeated for president in the 50s, was an intelligent and gifted speaker.

*Little Known Facts:* Mario Cuomo was the first and the final guest on the long-running (1985–2010) talk show *Larry King Live*. His son Andrew eulogized his father during his Inaugural address on the first day of 2015, the day Mario Cuomo died. Days later, son Andrew delivered an eloquent eulogy for his dad: "At his core, at his best, he was a philosopher and he was a poet and he was an advocate and he was a crusader....Mario Cuomo was the keynote speaker for our better angels."

# 83. Geraldine Ferraro, Nomination Acceptance Speech, July 19, 1984

*Speaker:* Geraldine Ferraro (1935–2011), though likely an unfamiliar name to many in the current generation, played an important role in advancing women's position of leadership in American politics. She was an attorney who entered politics as a Democrat, then was elected to the U. S. House of Representatives. While previously women had declared themselves a candidate for president on a major party ticket, before 1984 no woman had been placed on such a ticket. Ferraro's accomplishments were historic, as she was the first woman nominated by a major party for the vice-presidential role, as Senator Walter Mondale's running mate. Not until two dozen years later when presidential nominee John McCain selected Sarah Palin, governor of Alaska, for vice president on the Republican ticket was such a nomination repeated. After the convention, Ferraro had an active speaking schedule. As a speaker she came across as an attractive, intelligent, and energetic communicator. Nor did she disappoint in the vice presidential debate with George H. W. Bush, the man who four years later would head the Republican ticket and serve one term as president. Mondale and Ferraro were running on a platform calling for "the eradication of discrimination in all aspects of American life." Mondale also proposed higher taxes to fund his agenda. Republicans labeled Mondale's support for civil rights groups and labor unions as a vestige of the old politics of "special interests" and his tax proposal as a return to wasteful spending of earlier Democrats. Republicans also attempted to tie Ferraro to special interests, in this case claiming the Democrats were kowtowing to feminist and pro-choice groups. During the campaign, questions were raised about her husband's financial dealings and the candidate's financial disclosures, serving as a distraction from the issues that Mondale and Ferraro wanted to discuss. Reagan, then 73, limited campaign appearances to well-orchestrated events and was benefitted by a textbook perfect campaign. The election ended with Mondale and Ferraro carrying only his home state of Minnesota and the District of Columbia. Ferraro remained active in politics though she was defeated in two attempts at election to the U. S. Senate. Her voice was still respected. She died of a blood cancer in 2011. At her funeral Senator Barbara Mikulski declared, "Ms. Ferraro's candidacy took down the 'men-only' sign at the White House."

*Occasion:* When the Democrats met in San Francisco in 1984 to nominate their leading candidates, most of them were fully aware of an uphill battle against the highly popular Republican president Ronald Reagan. The nation was in a reasonably sound financial situation and, despite problems, "Reagonomics" helped the national economy recover from the trauma of the 1970s. The Democrats had no potential candidate who could match the popularity of Reagan, and it seemed both natural and an orderly act of succession for them to turn to Senator Walter Mondale, Jimmy Carter's vice president. Mondale stirred few passions and his candidacy would need major assistance, thus he made the surprising move—turning to Representative Ferraro as his running mate and as the first woman to stand for president or vice president on a major party ticket. The decision was enthusiastically received by convention members, and now, Ferraro, the impressive Italian-American female, stood to address a highly partisan and excited audience of thousands in the arena and millions of viewers around the nation following the proceedings by television. The occasion was indeed historic.

*Excerpt:* "Tonight, the daughter of a woman whose highest goal was a future for her children talks to our nation's oldest party about a future for us all. Tonight, the daughter of working Americans tells all Americans that the future is within our reach, if we're willing to reach for it. Tonight, the daughter of an immigrant from Italy has been chosen to run for President in the new land my father came to love. Our faith that we can shape a better future is what the American dream is all about."

*Impact:* Ferraro's address was enthusiastically received, as might be expected by such a partisan audience. And yet, the moment and the occasion were historic, a point not lost by the speaker or most Americans at home viewing the proceedings. Some critics claimed that Ferraro "played it safe" in this address and in her debate with Vice President Bush, that she was too traditional and too masculine in her style. The speaker acknowledged that fact and expounded on what most new candidates discuss in acceptance speeches—their roots, their heritage, and their connection to the American dream. Thus the speaker did not overreach, but ideally fulfilled both her goal and the audience expectation, allowing the historic occasion provide the inescapable and memorable context. This speech is listed by *American Rhetoric* as one of the one hundred greatest speeches of the twentieth century. The nomination and the address then introduced Congresswoman Ferraro to the entire nation, thus enhancing her credibility and visibility on issues she addressed in the future.

*Practical Application:* A pioneer in the areas of civil rights or social justice will earn a place in history, and that pioneer's words and achievements will be part of a grand legacy even if one falls short of being elected to a higher office or acknowledged by the general public.

*Connection to Today:* Geraldine Ferraro was indeed a pioneer for women in national politics at the highest level. Her nomination, along with Reagan's appointment of Sandra Day O'Connor to be the first woman justice on the U. S. Supreme Court in 1981, seemed to pave the way for other women to be appointed or nominated and accepted. In 1993 Clinton appointed the second woman to the Supreme Court, Judge Ruth Bader Ginsberg. Clinton also appointed Janet Reno as the first woman to serve as attorney general and Madeleine Albright the first to serve as secretary of state. George W. Bush continued to break ground in naming Condoleezza Rice as national security adviser in 2001 and secretary of state in 2005. And, of course, Hillary Clinton was nominated for president by the 2016 Democratic National Convention and garnered almost three million more popular votes than the Electoral College winner.

# 84. Ronald Reagan, Eulogy for Challenger Astronauts, January 28, 1986

*Speaker:* President Reagan was immersed in crises from the moment he entered the White House, some of which of his own "making"—budget battles, tax battles, the Falklands, the Philippines, the war in Lebanon, the Beirut hostage crisis, the assassination of Egyptian President Anwar Sadat, the truck bombing of the American marine barracks in Beirut killing 241 men, the hijacking of airliners, and the shooting down of a Korean airliner in international airspace. All of these crises elicited public comments, usually a speech, directly to the American people. Until 9/11 with George W. Bush in office, no president seemed to have a greater burden of catastrophic events to explain to the nation and put into perspective than Ronald Reagan. Perhaps his most eloquent speech followed still another crisis and honored the memory of seven astronauts killed in a space shuttle.

*Occasion:* "Shuttle Mission 51-L" was known by most Americans as "the flight with the teacher," the teacher being 37-year-old Christa McAuliffe, the first civilian to venture into space. She had been chosen out of eleven thousand volunteers to join the six astronauts on the *Challenger*. The flight was dubbed "the ultimate field trip," and NASA heavily promoted the mission and millions of school children tuned in to watch the historic event live on January 28, 1986. At 11:39 A. M., the *Challenger* lifted off the pad and headed skyward on a cloudless, picture-perfect, but cold day. Suddenly, even inconceivably, the shuttle exploded into a massive fireball leaving behind a billowy cloud of smoke. Shock and disbelief melded into grief. Immediately, for everyone watching, there was the clear perception that no one on board could have survived the explosion. President Reagan was scheduled to present the State of the Union Address to Congress and the nation that evening, but he realized there was far more on the minds of Americans than political agenda and budgets. Instead, he chose to speak from the heart to the nation, and he focused on the seven crew members who had lost their lives—the first American astronauts ever to die in flight.

*Excerpt:* [Peroration] "There's a coincidence today. On this day 390 years ago, the great explorer Sir Francis Drake died off the coast of Panama. In his lifetime the great frontiers were the oceans, and an historian later said, 'He lived by sea, died on it, and was buried in it.' Well, today we can say of the *Challenger* crew, their dedication was, like Drake's, complete. The crew of the space shuttle *Challenger* honored us by the manner in which they lived their lives. We will never forget them, nor the last time we saw them, this morning, as they prepared for their journey and waved good-bye and 'slipped the surly bonds of earth' to 'touch the face of God.'"

*Impact: Challenger's* explosion was truly an extraordinary visual event, viewed over and over again with sadness on American television. The images watched by millions spurred intense national grief. Yet the very moment in which words fail will melt away into other moments very quickly in which words are needed. Someone needed to speak for the nation and someone needed to speak to the nation. The President is the person who assumed that responsibility as head of government but representative of all the people of the nation. No one could have performed this role better than Ronald Reagan. First, he consoled the children, helping them reframe the tragedy so that it was a meaningful lesson to be learned rather than a tragic event for which to be bitter and cynical. The President spoke as a loving father: "I know it's hard to understand, but sometimes painful things like this happen. It's all part of the process of exploration and discovery. It's all part of taking a chance and expanding man's horizons. The future doesn't belong to the fainthearted. It belongs to the brave. The *Challenger* crew was pulling us into the future, and we'll continue to follow them." The President's tone of voice and entire manner were appropriate for the somber occasion. The speaker also addressed the families of the seven:

"We cannot bear, as you do, the full impact of this tragedy. But we feel the loss, and we're thinking about you so very much. Your loved ones were daring and brave." Reagan's best statement was in the conclusion (see excerpt above). He could have recalled the image of the exploding shuttle but that could leave viewers thinking only of the tragedy. Instead, he replaced that awful image with one seen less often but conveying a sense of courage and hope—the waving astronauts waving to bystanders as they walked to get onboard the shuttle. NBC kept showing that more positive picture while playing the President's eloquent words. Ronald Reagan truly gave meaning to the nation's grief.

*Contemporary Application:* Sometimes an eloquent eulogy can be more powerful and impact more lives than any campaign speech, legislative debate, classroom lecture, pious prayer, or spiritual sermon.

*Little Known Fact:* Peggy Noonan was a special assistant to President Reagan from 1984 to 1986, then left Washington, D. C., for her native New York, where her writings were published in book, magazine, and essay forms. Noonan was the ghostwriter who crafted this brief, inspiring message to the nation by Reagan. Noonan believes the secret to Reagan's general presidential success was his character: honesty, courage, persistence, and patience in the face of setbacks. She shares her reflections on Reagan and his leadership style in her book, *When Character Was King: A Story of Ronald Reagan* (Penguin Books, 2001). Noonan continues to write and be available for media interviews.

*Connection to Today:* Character became an issue in the 2016 presidential election campaign. Many thoughtful citizens questioned whether Donald Trump possessed the moral character and temperament to serve in the nation's highest office. Interestingly, Republicans today often speak of themselves as being in "the party of Lincoln and Reagan," using these former presidents as a standard for other Republicans. Identification with esteemed leaders typically serves as an effective rhetorical strategy.

# 85. Jesse Jackson, Address to the Democratic National Convention, July 20, 1988

*Speaker:* Jesse Jackson was born in 1941 in Greenville, South Carolina, and grew up in poverty. "I was born in the slum, but the slum was not born in me," he told the 1988 Democratic National Convention. "I wasn't born in the hospital….I was born in the bed at home." Jackson attended the University of Illinois, then transferred to the historically black Agricultural and Technical College of North Carolina. He was ordained as a Baptist minister in 1968, having done biblical and theological studies at the Chicago Theological Seminary. Jackson marched with Martin Luther King, Jr., in Selma, Alabama, and became associated with the Southern Christian Leadership Conference. With Chicago as a base of operations, he became active in national politics in the 1980s. He directed a voter registration drive that helped elect the city's first black mayor. He ran for the Democratic presidential nomination in 1984, the first black candidate to launch a serious bid for the presidency. He campaigned again for the Democratic nomination in 1988, and on "Super Tuesday," a day in early March when twenty-one caucuses and primaries took place nationwide, Jackson either won or came in second in sixteen of those states. Four months later he still was focused on the White House (and jokingly assured voters he would keep the name White House if he were elected), but Massachusetts governor Michael Dukakis was the frontrunner and the eventual candidate who later ran an ineffective national campaign.

*Occasion:* The 1988 Democratic National Convention and a national television coverage constituted the audience for this address. Jesse Jackson had already established himself nationally as a prominent black spokesperson for political issues. Most voters knew of Jackson's association with Dr. King. Furthermore,

Jackson had been a charismatic and dynamic speaker, whose style is within the tradition of African-American preaching.

*Excerpt:* "Common ground. America's not a blanket woven from one thread, one color, one cloth….Wherever you are tonight, I challenge you to hope and to dream. Don't submerge you dream. Dream above all else….We must never surrender to inequality….You must not surrender. You may or may not get there, but just know that you're qualified and you hold on and hold out. We must never surrender. America will get better and better. Keep hope alive. Keep hope alive. Keep hope alive. I love you very much. I love you very much."

*Impact:* This speech reaffirmed the image of Jesse Jackson as a confident, forceful, dynamic orator. The address was the emotional high point of the campaign, and it signaled the coming of age of African-Americans as a significant force in American politics. In the address, Jackson drew from his Christian roots and biblical training, quoting from Scripture and adapting Scripture. In fact, Jackson came across as a preacher delivering a sermon ("The Bible teaches when lions and lambs lie down together, none will be afraid and there will be peace in the valley. It sounds impossible. Lions eat lambs. Lambs sensibly flee from lions. But even lions and lambs find common ground. Why? Because neither lions nor lambs want the forest to catch on fire. Neither lions nor lambs want acid rain to fall. Neither lions nor lambs can survive nuclear war. If lions and lambs can find common ground, surely, we can as well, as civilized people.") Jackson proved that he was and still remains a master at alliteration, repetition, and other "plays" on words. ("Left wing. Right wing. Progress will not come through boundless liberalism nor static conservatism, but at the critical mass of mutual survival. It takes two wings to fly. Whether you're a hawk or a dove, you're just a bird living in the same environment, in the same world.") To his credit, Jackson resisted rehashing his quarrels with Dukakis, beginning his speech with a tribute: "Tonight, I salute Governor Dukakis. He has run a well-managed and a dignified campaign. No matter how tired or how tried, he always resisted the temptation to stoop to demagoguery. I've watched a good mind fast at work, with steel nerves, guiding his campaign out of the crowded field without appeal to the worst in us." While Jackson has never had the stature of his mentor, Dr. King, he has mastered the art of blending African-American preaching with passionate political speaking.

*Contemporary Application:* Dynamic, passionate delivery of a speech is so important, and the impact of the speech is enhanced with memorable stylistic devices. Jesse Jackson uses so many stylistic strategies effectively; in this speech there is repetition of the two words "Common Ground" that serves as reminder of his theme as well as a transition device.

*Connection to Today:* The Reverend Jesse Jackson continues to draw national media attention with speeches and comments regarding rights of all kinds of minorities, his "rainbow coalition." Seems fair to say that Jackson's influence on the American political scene has waned in recent years due, perhaps, to the elevation of Barack Obama to the presidency and personal and family issues.

# 86. George H. W. Bush, Call for Intervention in Kuwait, January 8, 1992

*Speaker:* George Herbert Walker Bush (b. 1924) almost seemed destined to be the U. S. president in 1988. Born into a prominent Republican family and educated at Yale University, a combat pilot in World War II, Bush had moved from Connecticut to Texas and entered the lucrative oil business as a young man. Yet his heart for political life and public service surpassed his interest in oil. Given his passion for public life and his intellectual and communication gifts, Bush served in many government roles, compiling a lengthy political resume, including time in the House of Representatives and a stint as director of the CIA. He served eight years as vice president for President Ronald Reagan. Given Reagan's leadership and popularity, Cold War détente boosted the presidential prospects of Bush as heir apparent to Reagan in the White House. Easily gaining the Republican nomination, Bush made a controversial choice for his running mate—youthful Senator Dan Quayle from Indiana, better known for his verbal blunders than his legislative skills. The election of 1988, the last of the Cold War era, became best known for negative campaigning, especially by Republican strategists who depicted Governor Michael Dukakis in a negative light, using the infamous "race card" to charge their opponent with being soft on crime. Bush did emerge the winner, but by a relatively narrow margin. As a speaker, Bush spoke with skill and confidence. Though hailing from the Lone Star state, this president did not have the slow Southern drawl that characterized Lyndon B. Johnson and some other Southern politicians. He had the ability to coin memorable phrases, such as his slogan about a "kinder, gentler America" and his metaphor for simple deeds of compassion, "a thousand points of light." A number of factors combined to render Bush vulnerable when he was nominated for re-election in 1992. Bush's Democratic challenger, Governor William Jefferson

Clinton of Arkansas, focused on economic issues and addressed concerns that cut across partisan lines. The 1992 election brought decisive victory for Clinton and defeat for a man who had served honorably.

*Occasion:* On August 2, 1990, Iraq's President Saddam Hussein seized the small neighboring oil-rich country of Kuwait, a move that caught the U. S. off guard. The quick conquest gave Iraq control of twenty percent of the world's oil production and reserves. Then concern arose over the possibility that Iraq's next target might be Saudi Arabia, the largest oil producer in the Middle East and a long-time ally of the U. S. Within weeks, the U. S. moved tens of thousands of soldiers and hundreds of aircraft into Saudi territory—a golden opportunity for the President to assert the U. S.'s world influence. The importance of Middle Eastern oil helped to enlist France and Great Britain as military allies and to secure billions of dollars from Japan and Germany, and the collapse of the Soviet Union meant the Russians would not interfere with U. S. plans. Bush convinced the United Nations to adopt a series of tough resolutions that culminated in November 1990 with Security Council Resolution 678 authorizing "all necessary means" to liberate Kuwait. Bush probably had decided on war weeks earlier. Now, the time had come for President Bush to explain to the nation and the Western world the reasons for U. S. military action and ask the Congress for official support via a joint resolution.

*Excerpt:* "Iraq must withdraw from Kuwait completely, immediately, and without condition. Kuwait's legitimate government must be restored. The security and stability of the Persian Gulf must be assured. And American citizens abroad must be protected....Out of these troubled times, our fifth objective – a new world order – can emerge: a new era – freer from the threat of terror, stronger in the pursuit of justice, and more secure in the quest for peace. An era in which the nations of the world, East and West, North and South, can prosper and live in harmony.... A world where the rule of law supplants the rule of the jungle. A world in which nations recognize the shared responsibility for freedom and justice. A world where the strong respect the rights of the weak."

*Impact:* President Bush's speech to Congress was televised for the entire nation. In somber tones, the President offered a series of justifications for American action. Foremost was the desire to punish armed aggression and the presumed imperative to protect Iraq's other neighbors. In reality, there was scant evidence of Iraqi preparations for nefarious intentions against the Saudis or any other nation, and effective economic sanctions and effective diplomatic pressure might also have brought withdrawal from Kuwait. The President spoke in terms of moral obligation of a great nation; however, his policy-makers spoke frankly about the economic threat that Hussein's aggression posed for the oil-dependent economies of the U. S. and its coalition allies. The speech predicted "a new world order," a vague and careless phrase, if the war were successful. The speech was successful in winning the support of Congress. Using the macho figure of speech "Operation Desert Storm," Bush launched the massive air attack one day after the U.N.'s January 15 deadline for Iraqi withdrawal from Kuwait. After six weeks of aerial bombardment, General Colin Powell ordered a ground offensive on February 24 that decimated Iraqi armies over the next four days, and U. S. casualties were relatively light (148 deaths in battle). Despite the immediate success of the speech, critics may rightly question the long-range validity of the case the speaker made for war and the wisdom of a military intervention that laid the groundwork for even more costly war in this volatile region of the world. In one sense, the U. S. won the war but not the peace—chaos and instability were just beginning.

*Connection to Today:* Ironically, one of Bush's sons, George W. Bush, would feel compelled to make a similar foreign policy decision regarding Iraq and Hussein. Americans now live with the consequences of both Bush decisions.

*Contemporary Application:* If a president plans to go to war and is addressing a nation for support, the appeal to moral obligation and international justice will typically render the president's case persuasive and effective.

# 87. Hillary Clinton, Address to the United Nations World Conference on Women, September 5, 1995

*Speaker:* Hillary Rodham Clinton (b. 1947) has been a public servant in diverse roles in state and local government for almost four decades. In these roles, she has made hundreds of public speeches and interview appearances before a wide range of audiences, not all of them especially friendly. She bears comparison with another controversial first lady who broke the mold of what a president's wife should be like: Eleanor Roosevelt. Clinton attended the academically-elite Wellesley College in the Boston area, and immediately became involved as a spokesperson in social justice issues. She was the first student commencement speaker at Wellesley in 1969, and she dared to offer an impromptu critique of the main address by Republican Senator Edward Brooke (Rodham was a Republican at that time). Her commencement speech was celebrated for its direct incisiveness: "We are, all of us, exploring a world that none of us even understands, and attempting to create within that uncertainty....And so our questions—our questions about our institutions, about our colleges, about our churches, about our government—continue." *Life* magazine then acknowledged her notoriety and published a picture of Rodham wearing striped pants and thick glasses with a headline borrowed from her speech: PROTEST IS AN ATTEMPT TO FORGE AN IDENTITY. Rodham Clinton went on to Yale Law School, graduating in 1973. As a young woman, she immersed herself in justice causes for women and children, and this speech was just another expression of that lifelong passion.

*Occasion:* The address was presented to the first United Nations Conference on Women in Bejing in September 1995. Delegates to this conference came from over 180 countries. As one would expect, a large number of women were in the audience. As First Lady of the world's most powerful nation, Clinton had already achieved high *ethos* for this audience. She built on her initial *ethos* by referencing women she had met and encountered in nations around the world. "I have met new mothers in Indonesia, who come together regularly in their village to discuss nutrition, family planning, and baby care. I have met working parents in Denmark who talk about the comfort they feel in knowing that their children can be cared for in safe, and nurturing after-school centers," Clinton declared. Then she referenced meeting women in South Africa who struggled against apartheid, in India, and in Bangladesh (where women were taking out loans to buy cows or rickshaws), as well as meeting doctors and nurses in Belarus and Ukraine, "keeping children alive in the aftermath of Chernobyl." The speaker was effectively using a rhetorical strategy known as identification.

*Excerpt:* "Those of us who have the opportunity to be here have the responsibility to speak for those who could not. As an American, I want to speak for those women in my own country, women who are raising children on the minimum wage, women who can't afford health care or child care, women whose lives are threatened by violence, including violence in their own homes. I want to speak up for mothers who are fighting for good schools, safe neighborhoods, and clean air; for older women, some of them widows, who find that, after raising their families, their skills and life experiences are not valued in the marketplace; for women who are working all night as nurses, hotel clerks, or fast food chefs so that they can be at home during the day with their children; and for women everywhere who simply don't have time to do everything they are called upon to do each and every day. Speaking to you today, I speak for them, just as each of us speaks for women around the world who are denied the chance to go to school, or see a doctor, or own property, or have a say about the direction of their lives, simply because they are women. The truth is that most women around the world work both inside and outside the home, usually by necessity. We need to understand there is no one formula for how women should lead our lives. That is why we must respect the choices that each woman makes for herself and her family. Every woman deserves the chance to realize her own God-given potential. But we must recognize that women will never gain full dignity until their human rights are respected and protected."

*Impact:* The 2,500 delegates gave the U. S. First Lady a warm and rousing reception. The speaker had announced that her purpose was "a celebration of contributions that women make to all aspects of life." The iconic speech was both a celebration and a declaration of the priority of women's rights. Not only would it be unlikely to find any negative comments about the speech, but, to the contrary, the speech was hailed as a major success—an eloquent woman speaking *to* women and speaking *about* women. Magazine editor Tina Brown called this address "the speech that launched a movement" and a speech that "remains the battle cry for women." Such praise for the address seems overstated, especially in light of the courageous oratory of a few nineteenth century women reform speakers, yet Clinton clearly established herself as chief spokesperson of *this* generation for universal women's rights. After this speech, Clinton delivered other addresses and gave interviews often on this subject, often repeating the chief thesis of the Bejing speech which became the defining battle cry for women—"If there is one message that echoes forth from this conference, it is that human rights are women's rights … And women's rights are human rights." This is likely the "sound bite" for which she is best known in the more than two decades since this speech.

*Contemporary Application:* Women's issues have always been crucially important in virtually every culture and, typically, a passionate female speaker carries greater *ethos* and conviction in addressing them than any male speaker.

# 88. Bill Clinton, Address to the Nation After Testimony, August 17, 1998

*Speaker:* Bill Clinton (b. 1946) came into the nation's highest office by representing the Baby Boomer generation and defeating an incumbent. During his administration the nation enjoyed more peace and economic well-being than at any time in its history. Yet in the years 1998 and 1999, American citizens were riveted by revelations about the President's personal behavior and private life, his possible extramarital affairs, and doubts about his integrity and fitness for high office. After years of exhaustive probes on the Whitewater land deal and other purported deeds going back to the 1970s, Independent Counsel Kenneth Starr found a witness named Linda Tripp, whose secret taping of conversations with a former White House intern named Monica Lewinsky pumped new life into a dying, irrelevant investigation.

*Occasion:* Earlier in the day of this televised speech to the nation, Clinton had become the first sitting president to give testimony before a grand jury in which he, the President, was the focus of the grand jury investigation. This testimony was the latest in a long chain of legal entanglements resulting from a sweeping investigation by Kenneth Starr as well as a private lawsuit concerning alleged sexual harassment committed by Clinton before he became president. The issue in this hearing was whether Clinton had lied about the Lewinsky affair during a deposition for a sexual harassment suit brought against him by Paula Jones. Clinton denied he had lied under oath, but he did confess to having an "inappropriate sexual relationship" with Lewinsky. Knowing the admission would leak to the public, the President decided to tell the nation that, despite previous denials, he and Lewinsky had engaged in a sexual relationship. Sixty-seven million Americans tuned in to hear the President explain his action and express remorse for what he had done. Clinton appeared stony-faced and solemn, understandably, as a humiliated man making a confession.

*Excerpt:* "This afternoon in this room, from this chair, I testified before the Office of Independent Counsel and the grand jury. I answered their questions truthfully, including questions about my private life—questions no American citizen would ever want to answer....Indeed, I did have a relationship with Miss Lewinsky that was not appropriate. In fact, it was wrong. It constituted a critical lapse in judgment and a personal failure on my part for which I am solely and completely responsible. But I told the grand jury today and I say to you now that at no time did I ask anyone to lie, to hide or destroy evidence or to take any other unlawful action....This has gone on too long, cost too much and hurt too many innocent people. Now, this matter is between me, the two people I love most -- my wife and our daughter -- and our God. I must put it right, and I am prepared to do whatever it takes to do so. Nothing is more important to me personally. But it is private, and I intend to reclaim my family life for my family. It's nobody's business but ours. Even presidents have private lives. It is time to stop the pursuit of personal destruction and the prying into private lives and get on with our national life. Our country has been distracted by this matter for too long, and I take my responsibility for my part in all of this. That is all I can do. Now it is time -- in fact, it is past time to move on."

*Impact:* Clearly, the purpose of this *mea culpa* speech had the goal of getting the nation, and especially the Republican-led Congress, to drop at last their obsession with Clinton's private life, thus putting an end to the scandal, and to move on with the nation's business. This may have been the strongest and most public acknowledgement of a private wrongdoing by any president in office in the history of the Republic. Most confessions of marital infidelity are made privately to angry spouses and bewildered children, but Bill Clinton confessed his affair to the entire nation. Those who saw and heard the speech would not have forgotten it. And the speech was a brief one, lasting only four minutes. Democratic supporters judged it as "heart-felt," as Clinton took responsibility for his action without specifying what specific conduct for which he was apologizing. Some critics wanted more confession and contrition and claimed that Clinton resorted to vagueness and ambiguity. One critic, Herbert W. Simons, labeled the speech "such a pathetically effete rhetorical performance." In fairness, the speech seemed highly personal, credible, and contrite. And by this time, polls indicate, most Americans were tired of the whole affair and wanted to move on. The Republican leaders who controlled Congress, however, decided Clinton's statements and misstatements justified them in initiating the process of impeachment. Clinton was acquitted by the Senate in February 1999.

*Contemporary Application:* When a speaker bares his or her soul and offers public confession and contrition, friends and supporters will empathize and support that speaker. On the other hand, those who greatly dislike and detest the speaker are seldom moved by heart-felt confession and will continue their opposition.

*Little Known Fact:* There are two drafts of this speech for students of American public address to consider. The first draft expressed more contrition and contained this passage: "What I did was wrong—and there is no excuse for it….I want to apologize to all of you, my fellow citizens. I hope you can find it in your heart to accept that apology." This speech, however, was replaced by one less contrite and sterner in tone. Why? Unbeknown to many of his closest advisers, the President was planning a military strike against Osama bin Laden for his role in the embassy bombing in Africa, and the President did not want either the U. S. or himself to appear weak before conducting the attack; the strike was carried out on August 21. Also, perhaps personal reasons influenced the tone of each draft.

# 89. Elie Wiesel, The Perils of Indifference, April 12, 1999

*Speaker:* Elie Wiesel (1928–2016), born in Transylvania (a part of Romania), was a noted Jewish writer, professor, political activist, and Nobel Laureate. He made Holocaust education his mission in life after surviving the Auschwitz and Buchenwald death camps. Having been a journalist, he was the author of fifty-seven books, including the best known *Night*, which tell his experiences as a prisoner at those infamous death camps. Most prisoners in these camps were compelled to work and simply survive under some of the most appalling conditions. Wiesel lost both parents and a younger sister Tzipora in the camps. In 1955 Wiesel moved to Washington D. C. and became a U. S. citizen. He was awarded the Nobel Peace Prize in 1986 for courageously speaking out against violence, oppression, and racism. He received the Congressional Gold Medal in 1985 and was given numerous other awards as well as honorary degrees. He continued to speak out on various causes related to social injustice. Wiesel was a popular speaker in various venues, especially in college and university settings, and he taught classes at Boston University and City University of New York. He voiced support for various humanitarian causes around the globe, and was especially concerned about the crisis of Darfar. He worked for Jewish reconciliation with Germany; in 2009 he toured Buchenwald with German Chancellor Angela Merkel, each making public statements. As a speaker, Wiesel seemed mild-mannered and controlled, at times almost monotone, though his passion was evident. Given the experiences he had lived through and survived, he possessed immense respect and credibility even before uttering a word to any audience. Rabbi David Wolpe eulogized Wiesel by calling him "one of the most eloquent voices in the history of witness," and noted that "hearing Wiesel speak was like listening to the whisper of eternity. His voice had a haunting magic, speaking words that were wrung from the suffering of his own soul and his indelible witness to the sufferings of others.... His voice was as large as history, and as gentle as reaching out to a child and never forgetting him" (*Time*, July 25, 2016). President Obama called Wiesel "the conscience of the world."

*Occasion:* Elie Wiesel presented this impassioned speech in the East Room of the White House on April 12, 1999, as part of the Millennium Lecture series, hosted by President Bill Clinton and First Lady Hillary Rodham Clinton. At the White House event, Wiesel was introduced by Hillary Clinton, who made sad reference to seeing mistreatment of children in Kosovo.

*Excerpt:* "What is indifference? Etymologically, the word means 'no difference.' A strange and unnatural state in which the lines blur between light and darkness, dusk and dawn, crime and punishment, cruelty and compassion, good and evil....Can one possibly view indifference as a virtue? Is it necessary at times to practice it simply to keep one's sanity, live normally, enjoy a fine meal and a glass of wine, as the world around us experiences harrowing upheavals? Of course, indifference can be tempting—more than that, seductive. It is so much easier to look away from victims. It is so much easier to avoid such rude interruptions to our work, our dreams, our hopes. It is, after all, awkward, troublesome, to be involved in another person's pain and despair. Yet, for the person who is indifferent, his or her neighbors are of no consequence. And, therefore, their lives are meaningless. Their hidden or even visible anguish is of no interest. Indifference reduces the other to an abstraction....Rooted in our tradition, some of us felt that to be abandoned by humanity then was not the ultimate. We felt that to be abandoned by God was worse than to be punished by Him. Better an unjust God than an indifferent one. For us to be ignored by God was a harsher punishment than to be a victim of His anger. Man can live far from God--not outside God. God is wherever we are. Even in suffering? Even in suffering. In a way, to be indifferent to that suffering is what makes the human being inhuman. Indifference, after all, is more dangerous than anger and hatred. Anger can at times be creative...Indifference is never creative. Even hatred at times may elicit a response. You fight it. You denounce it. You disarm it. Indifference elicits no response. Indifference is not a response."

*Impact:* The speech was warmly received by the audience. Such warm reception was typical for almost all of Weisel's speeches. The speaker used *pathos*, or emotion, to engage the feelings of all the listeners. He drew the audience into the experience (identification) by using the personal pronouns of "we" and "us." His tone was serious, even grave, and sorrowful, but there was no anger in his voice. Everyone was intensely listening, and possibly no one in the audience had heard an entire message on the topic of indifference presented so powerfully. The power of his rhetoric did not reside in the delivery, of course, but in the power of his courageous life experience and the content of his speech. Weisel dared to discuss theology from a personal and existential perspective. Theology is a topic of near universal interest, but Weisel challenged the audience to empathize with the way he came to see God. This speech possesses both immediate and universal application to any kind of social injustice in any age. Little wonder the speech was included in the "Great Speeches Collection" of *The History Place.*

*Contemporary Application:* A speaker who has lived out existentially the truth of one's message will possess tremendous credibility before any audience of mature thinkers and learners. A deep life experience during an epochal period of crisis, when shared passionately before an audience, can be insightful and provocative.

*Interesting Fact:* In 1978 President Carter appointed Wiesel to lead the President's Commission on the Holocaust that proposed a museum in Washington. The museum opened in April 1998 and has welcomed over thirty-eight million visitors.

# 90. George W. Bush, War Message to Saddam and to the American People, March 17, 2003

*Speaker:* George W. Bush (b. 1946) was the nation's forty-third president, the eldest son of George H. W. and Barbara Bush. He is a graduate of Yale University and Harvard Business School, and, more interestingly, the second president to be the son of a former president, the other being John Quincy Adams, son of John Adams. On November 8, 2000, the day after the election, Americans woke up to the news that neither Republican Bush nor Democrat Albert Gore, Jr., had a majority of votes in the Electoral College. A series of events followed: Protests about voting irregularities and malfunctioning voting equipment, recounts involving hanging chads, and the Supreme Court finally preempting the state process and ordering a halt to the recount in Florida on December 12 by a margin of five to four—the result made Bush the winner in Florida by a few hundred votes. Eight months into Bush's first term, terrorists hijacked four commercial jetliners on the morning of September 11 and used them as high-octane, human-guided missiles; two planes toppled the twin towers of the World Trade Center, another ripped into the Pentagon in Washington, and courageous action by some passengers on a fourth plane (which crashed in Pennsylvania) prevented a second attack in the nation's capital. Calling these attacks "acts of war," the President, donning the mantle of a war-time president, responded by launching his own "war on terror." Government response was a hodge-podge of security measures, including the Patriot Act, giving federal authorities substantial new capacity to conduct criminal investigations. First conducted in Afghanistan, the war claimed some successes; however, U.S.-led coalition forces failed to secure the countryside or capture bin Laden and his top lieutenants. As a speaker, Bush was not the orator that were many of his predecessors; often he bungled pronunciation and articulation of words and used confusing syntax. Nonetheless, immediately after the attacks, he projected an image of both toughness and compassion, best illustrated by visiting "Ground Zero" soon after the attack and taking the "bull horn" and making impromptu remarks to convey understanding and support.

*Occasion:* Throughout the first Bush term, the White House kept the nation, particularly through the media, focused on its war on terrorism. In January 2002, in the first State of the Union Address after 9/11, Bush named Iraq, along with Iran and North Korea, as part of the "Axis of Evil." Months passed. As Al Qaeda reorganized and bin Laden dropped from sight, Bush shifted his attention to Iraq and Saddam Hussein, the old nemesis of his father, who controlled one of the richest oil basins on the globe. Bush and "neocon" advisers favored a unilateral war against Hussein. They claimed that Hussein, based on his avoiding inspections, was both aiding terrorists and stockpiling weapons of mass destruction. Bush sought support of Western European nations, but only Great Britain and several smaller nations agreed to be part of what Bush called "the coalition of the willing." Clearly, the Bush administration had made a decision to strike Iraq, but the plan needed to be sold to a skeptical Congress and the nation at large.

*Excerpt:* "For more than a decade, the United States and other nations have pursued patient and honorable efforts to disarm the Iraqi regime without war. ….Yet, the only way to reduce the harm and duration of war is to apply the full force and might of our military, and we are prepared to do so….The terrorist threat to America and the world will be diminished the moment that Saddam Hussein is disarmed." [Two nights later:] "My fellow citizens, at this hour American and coalition forces are in the early stages of military operations to disarm Iraq, to free its people and to defend the world from grave danger….The people of the United States and our friends and allies will not live at the mercy of an outlaw regime that threatens the peace with weapons of mass murder."

*Impact:* If the purpose of the speech was to explain the President's rationale for taking military action against Iraq, the speech succeeded. With many citizens viewing the speech, his *ethos* (credibility) had remained high since 9/11. Bush sought the image of a fair leader, offering the ruthless dictator one last opportunity to renounce his evil plans and surrender. On the other hand, did the speech make a convincing case that persuaded those doubting the wisdom of the unilateral strike or completely opposing such a strike? Clearly, no! Indeed, it was a "hard sell"—convincing citizens there was justification for invading a sovereign nation that had not attacked or even threatened the United States. From the perspective of history, Bush did not possess credible evidence to support claims that Iraq had sponsored the 9/11 terrorism or that Hussein was building weapons of mass destruction. In effect, he declared one small, possibly dangerous nation to be the greatest threat and menace the United States faced. The ground and air assault against Iraq was launched on March 20, 2003. The Iraq War was a military success and, on May 1, 2003, Bush declared that U. S. and British forces now controlled Iraq and major combat operations were over. The smiling President made happy announcements after landing on an aircraft carrier and speaking in front of a banner with large letters: "Mission Accomplished." It matters not who ordered and financed the banner or who made it. The end had not arrived—it was just beginning!

*Contemporary Application:* A president determined to wage war will find reasons to justify such a crucial decision, but then must explain the reasons convincingly to the very citizens who bear both the financial and human cost of military engagement. If the reasons are not convincing, the nation will be divided and polarized.

*Interesting fact:* Paradoxically, George Bush was both one of the most popular and one of the most unpopular presidents in our history. After the 9/11 attacks he received the highest recorded approval ratings, and by the end of his second administration, especially after the 2008 financial crisis, he received the lowest approval ratings.

# 91. Barack Obama, 2004 Democratic Convention Keynote, July 27, 2004

*Speaker:* Barack Obama (b. August 4, 1961) is a graduate of Columbia University and Harvard Law School, who had served as a community organizer in his home state of Illinois. He had served eight years in the Illinois state senate, from 1997 to 2004, and that term was coming to an end on Election Day for the U. S. Senate. Obama won a landslide victory in the March 2004 Democratic primary for the Senate, and that made him an overnight rising star in the national Democratic Party. Understandably, the soon-to-be Democratic candidate for president, John Kerry, was impressed by the youthful political leader and selected him over several other strong speakers to deliver the keynote address at the national convention. Kerry had considered several candidates, including Bill Richardson, to deliver the keynote, but wanted someone who could create a real buzz in the media.

*Occasion:* The national convention was held at the FleetCenter in Boston, home to the NHL Bruins and NBA Celtics. Obama's speech was delivered on July 27, 2004, but was not carried on the major networks, instead only by C-Span and the cable news networks. Written in a hotel in Springfield, Illinois, the first draft was done in long hand. In wrestling with wording, Obama played former keynote addresses to generate ideas, but also drew rhetorical themes, such as his diverse family background, from former stump speeches. His advisers were concerned about his potential effectiveness as this was the first time Obama had used a teleprompter. He practiced his speech in the locker rooms of the Bruins and Celtics.

*Excerpt:* "There is not a liberal America and a conservative America — there is the United States of America. There is not a black America and a white America and Latino America and Asian America — there's the United States of America….The pundits like to slice-and-dice our country into Red States and Blue States; Red States for Republicans, Blue States for Democrats. But I've got news for them, too: We worship an awesome God in the Blue States, and we don't like federal agents poking around in our libraries in the Red States. We coach Little League in the Blue States, and, yes, we've got some gay friends in the Red States. There are patriots who opposed the war in Iraq and there are patriots who supported the war in Iraq….Hope! Hope in the face of difficulty! Hope in the face of uncertainty! The audacity of hope! In the end, that is God's greatest gift to us, the bedrock of this nation. A belief in things not seen. A belief that there are better days ahead."

*Impact:* The address was presented in just under twenty minutes to a live audience of around nine million viewers. Before this address, Obama enjoyed very little name recognition outside his home state of Illinois. Just as Abraham Lincoln gained national recognition with his "president-making speech" at Cooper Union in 1860, Barack Obama's "president-making speech" was this keynote, even if his own nomination for president came four years later. Immediately after the speech, a flood of positive response from noted media personalities followed. Cable news host Chris Matthews exclaimed: "I have to tell you, a little chill in my legs right now. That is an amazing moment in history right there. It is surely an amazing moment. A keynoter like I have never heard." He added prophetically: "I have seen the first black president there. And the reason I say that is because I think the immigrant experience combined with the African background, combined with the incredible education, combined with his beautiful speech, not every politician gets help with the speech, but that speech was a piece of work." On PBS columnist David Brooks exclaimed, "This is why you go to conventions, to watch a speech like this!" The highly regarded NBC anchor Tom Brokaw asked rhetorically whether Obama or Kerry would be the man more remembered from the convention, while CNN's Jeff Greenfield called it "one of the really great keynote speeches of the last quarter-century." So the speech catapulted Obama into the spotlight as a national figure, one often interviewed and quoted in the next four years—all prelude and preparation for seeking the Democratic presidential nomination four years later.

*Contemporary Application:* Obama presented some of the themes and some of the style he would later employ rhetorically as president. This speech demonstrates the power of the spoken word presented with amazing effectiveness. Seeking a simple explanation for the "overnight" meteoric rise of Barack Obama to the nation's highest office (remember that he had not even completed one term in a national office when he was elected), it would surely be Obama's effectiveness and persuasiveness as a public speaker.

*Connection to Today:* Barack Obama being such a contemporary figure, it is important to understand how such a person ascends to power by using communication and persuasion skills. And the theme of "one America" rather than an America of "red states" and "blue states" is one that Obama has used in subsequent speeches as president, one being the 2015 State of the Union Address.

# 92. Steve Jobs, Stanford University Commencement Address, June 12, 2005

*Speaker:* Steve Jobs (1955–2011) will be remembered as one of the most powerful and creative inventers of his time, and he was able to translate that creativity into becoming one of the most powerful and creative orators and marketers of our time. Jobs often shared his personal story before audiences. He dropped out of Reed College to pursue what he loved. He started the Apple Computer, Incorporated, in 1976 with a friend in his own garage and then, within ten years, turned the company into a two billion dollar corporation with over four thousand employees. Without embarrassment, Jobs narrated the personal story of being fired from his own company, then starting two new companies, and then returning a decade later to his former company and setting it on a course that became legendary for its creative technology and extended market. In his later speeches, Jobs openly spoke of the pancreatic cancer that ultimately claimed his life. As a speaker, Jobs possessed tremendous *ethos* as a man who dared to dream and dared to venture and risk everything to innovate and watch for the results. Some have praised Jobs' inventiveness and creativity and spoken of him as "the Thomas Edison of our time." As a speaker, Jobs spoke directly and conversationally, and he could employ the language of the youth culture, at times using slang to punctuate his points. He typically used visuals in his presentations. Jobs was not at all reluctant to share personal life—both successes and failures—and he was able to glean important lessons from the pivotal moments in his life.

*Occasion:* Commencement addresses have long been a tradition at American graduation ceremonies, and Jobs' speech in 2005 was presented at one of the most academically distinguished universities in the nation. Approximately 23,000 were present on this ceremonial occasion.

*Excerpt:* "No one wants to die. Even people who want to go to heaven don't want to die to get there. And yet death is the destination we all share. No one has ever escaped it. And that is as it should be, because death is very likely the single best invention of Life. It is Life's change agent. It clears out the old to make way for the new. Right now the new is you, but someday not too long from now, you will gradually become the old and be cleared away. Sorry to be so dramatic, but it is quite true. Your time is limited, so don't waste it living someone else's life. Don't be trapped by dogma — which is living with the results of other people's thinking. Don't let the noise of others' opinions drown out your own inner voice. And most important, have the courage to follow your heart and intuition. They somehow already know what you truly want to become. Everything else is secondary."

*Impact:* This inspiring speech has received near legendary status, primarily from its being seen and heard over *YouTube* by almost twenty million viewers. The address resonated far beyond the Stanford audience, which gave him a standing ovation, with a masterful mix of practical insight, universally applicable pieces of wisdom, and personal anecdotes. The speech is perhaps most relevant to Millennials, who live in a world Jobs helped create—a world in which young people increasingly look to non-traditional and entrepreneurial career paths (not to mention a world dominated by Apple products). In this speech and others Jobs delivered, three basic lessons are highlighted: (1) Drop out by dropping in, and the passion for a task is the key to one's success (Jobs had a passion for calligraphy and that was carried over to devising the way certain fonts looked on his computer invention; (2) The best tasting medicine is failure (Jobs was fired from the company that he started but it was "the best tasting medicine" to free him from high expectations and allow him to super charge his personal growth); (3) Knowing you will die releases you from fear. (A sense of mortality releases one from the fear of incompetence and the fear of failure.) The irony of the speech is that Jobs told the audience of his pancreatic cancer and his subsequent surgery, but also announced he was cancer-free. Sadly, as we all know, the cancer returned and robbed him of many other opportunities to address an audience, not to mention how many new products he might have either invented or improved. The overwhelming viral response to the commencement address is a testament to just how much of a mark Jobs left on the world, and especially on young aspiring innovators. Some professors, especially in schools of business, will play the speech to new students with the beginning of a semester. Others have admitted seeing the speech many times for inspiration. Jobs was a living manifestation of the spirit of innovation that characterizes the Millennial generation. He ended this speech with a brief, emphatic, bit of advice: "Stay hungry. Stay foolish."

*Contemporary Application:* Jobs' audiences always seemed enthusiastic and interested in what the speaker presented. Audiences will listen carefully and be inspired by words of advice presented by a speaker whose legendary achievements are known and respected universally. And the words of such an inventive and creative person constitute part of that legacy that lives on for future generations.

*Interesting Fact:* Jobs' last speech was at the March, 2011, I-Pad 2 event. He had already taken a medical leave of absence and people wondered if he would be strong enough even to make an appearance. In this last speech, the rhetorical flourishes were not attempted. Jobs spoke in a weaker and gravelly voice, yet was able to underscore one last time a favorite theme—computer technology must always be wedded to the humanities.

*Another Interesting Fact:* The movie *Jobs* featuring actor Ashton Kutcher in the title role provides a reasonably accurate biographical depiction of Jobs' life from his days at Reed College until his return to Apple Computer, Inc.

# 93 (Tie). Hillary Clinton, Concession Speech, June 7, 2008

*Speaker:* Hillary Rodham Clinton has served in many important offices in her lifetime: A practicing attorney in the Rose Law Firm, the Arkansas first lady, the first lady of the U. S. from 1993 to 2001, a U. S. senator (the only former first lady to run for elective office and the first female senator to serve from New York), a leading candidate for the Democratic presidential nomination in 2008 (winning far more primaries and more votes than any former female running for high office in American history), and the sixty-seventh U. S. secretary of state serving under President Obama. Clinton made history by becoming the official candidate for the Democratic nomination for president in 2016, the first female to win high nomination in a major political party. In these roles she has delivered a large amount of speeches to varied audiences. As first lady she was deeply invested in the Clinton health plan that was ultimately defeated by Congress. As senator, she voted to approve George Bush's request for funding to fight the war in Iraq, though she generally opposed his domestic policies; she later visited U. S. troops in Iraq and Afghanistan and soon became a critic of the conduct of the war. As secretary of state, Clinton met with world leaders and discussed vital issues and generally supported Obama's foreign policy agenda. Uprising in the Middle East, terrorism in Benghazi, Syria, and continuation of fighting and terrorism in certain Middle Eastern countries challenged the Secretary and all U. S. political leaders, for that matter, as to causes and possible courses of response and future policy.

*Occasion:* As she proceeded in the 2008 presidential campaign, by September polling in the first six states holding Democratic contests showed Clinton was leading in all of them, with races being closest in Iowa and South Carolina. By the following month, national polls showed Clinton far ahead of Democratic competitors. At the end of October, Clinton suffered a rare poor debate performance against Obama, Edwards, and other opponents. Obama's message of change began to resonate with the Democratic electorate better than Clinton's message of experience. The race tightened considerably with Clinton losing her lead in some polls by December. On Super Tuesday, Clinton won the largest states, such as California, New York, New Jersey, and Massachusetts, while Obama won more states. Following the final primaries on June 3, Obama had gained enough delegates to become the presumptive nominee. By campaign's end, Clinton had won 1,640 pledged delegates compared to Obama's 1,763, thus the time had arrived for the candidate to make a concession speech (her critics thinking she should have conceded much earlier). The setting for this speech was a low stage in the light-filled, colonnaded atrium of the National Building Museum. There was a crowd of mostly women, some with small children, many with tears in their eyes, and, with a crowd of people in front of her and around her and on the sides, and her immediate family on the platform, she seemed to be "floating in a sea of love," according to one commentator.

*Excerpt:* "You can be so proud that, from now on, it will be unremarkable for a woman to win primary state victories - unremarkable to have a woman in a close race to be our nominee, unremarkable to think that a woman can be the president of the United States. And that is truly remarkable, my friends. To those who are disappointed that we couldn't go all of the way, especially the young people who put so much into this campaign, it would break my heart if, in falling short of my goal, I in any way discouraged any of you from pursuing yours. Always aim high, work hard and care deeply about what you believe in. And, when you stumble, keep faith. And, when you're knocked down, get right back up and never listen to anyone who says you can't or shouldn't go on. As we gather here today in this historic, magnificent building, the fiftieth woman to leave this earth is orbiting overhead. If we can blast fifty women into space, we will someday launch a woman into the White House. Although we weren't able to shatter that highest, hardest glass ceiling this time, thanks to you, it's got about eighteen million cracks in it, and the light is shining through like never before, filling us all with the hope and the sure knowledge that the path will be a little easier next time."

*Impact:* This speech could be called both celebration and a "self-celebration," and might be appropriately entitled "Eighteen Million Cracks in the Glass Ceiling." Fair to say, this speech was the finest and most eloquent of the entire nomination campaign. Clinton rose to the occasion with an infectious smile, an air of confidence, and a joyful delivery in the midst of conceding defeat. The tone of the address was upbeat, inspirational, encouraging, and magnanimous in gratitude and respect for one and all who participated in the process. To heighten suspense, Clinton delayed till near the end of the address to acknowledge Obama as the presumptive candidate and that strategy kept attention focused on her persona and agenda, especially the progress of women in American political life. "During the campaign it was her opponent who owned the lofty rhetoric," declared op-ed journalist Dana Milbank. "But on the day she finally conceded defeat, it was Hillary Clinton's words that soared." Columnist and politico Pat Buchanan noted that Clinton laid aside the divisiveness of earlier campaign comments and delivered the "model concession speech, which said goodbye but embraced her opponent," and another observer labeled the speaker as "Hillary the healer."

*Contemporary Application:* The loser in a big election often seems to do his or her most effective speech in concession, making some observers wonder why the same effectiveness had not been demonstrated in earlier addresses—perhaps because most of us identify compassionately with the honorable and gracious loser.

# 93 (Tie). Al Gore, Concession Speech, December 13, 2000

*Speaker:* Al Gore (b. 1948) came incredibly close to becoming president of the United States. In fact, with much evidence, a strong case can be made that Gore was actually elected president but, then, not inaugurated. Instead, he will be remembered as a politician and an environmentalist from Tennessee, a young man who served in the Congress both as a representative (1977-85) and a senator (1985-93) and then as the forty-fifth vice president from 1993 to 2001 under President Bill Clinton. Though he has strong roots in the Volunteer State, Gore was born in Washington because his father, Albert Gore, Sr., was also a long time congressman, a Democrat and a liberal from a Southern state. As a youngster, Gore resided and attended school in Washington though he spent summers working on his parents' farm in Carthage, Tennessee. He was drawn to political journalism, though destined to a career in politics. At a time when his dad, the late senator, was known so well and heavily criticized for being a "dove" on the Vietnam War, the junior Gore enlisted in the U. S. Army to help his father's re-election chances in 1970 (Senator Gore lost that election anyway to challenger Bill Brock). As senator, Gore developed an interest in progressive causes, especially environmentalism and internet technology. He wrote *Earth in the Balance*, a text that became the first book by a current U. S. senator that became a *New York Times* best-seller since Senator John F. Kennedy's *Profiles in Courage*. Gore pushed legislative support for development of the Internet and popularized the term "Information Super Highway," synonymous with the Internet. As a speaker, Gore did avoid the stereotype of political speakers with the Southern drawl. On the other hand, his oral style became stereotyped almost as passionless and slow in the flow of words, thus some pundits lampooned the style as boring and sleep-inducing. When Gore was named to join the Clinton ticket in 1992, the two, each being in his forties, became known as "the Baby Boomer" ticket. Gore's image was boosted by wife Elizabeth, always known as Tipper, an intelligent person with Christian values and a commitment to imparting solid values in raising children. After the 2000 election, Gore became more involved in environmental issues; he was also a critic of George W. Bush's war in Iraq. Though his involvement in environmentalism has been heavily criticized and even lampooned by the "far right," Gore was awarded a Nobel Peace prize on December 10, 2007, for his study, *An Inconvenient Truth*, a work that was turned into a well-attended movie. In recent months, Gore has visibly aged and has pursued a low profile politically, and he has been active on the speaker circuit for forums (such as TED Talks), and dinners. One speakers' bureau describes Gore as "an environmental, business, and tech visionary and activist." The former vice president did make a few public appearances with Hillary Clinton in the 2016 election campaign, with the candidate touting Gore's achievements in environmental education.

*Occasion:* On the evening of November 7, 2000, CBS-TV made a horrendous mistake—the network projected Gore the winner of Florida and thus winner of the presidency. Later, CBS reversed itself and announced Bush the winner. Gore called Bush to concede, then later in the evening called Bush again to retract his concession. The dispute was headline news for several weeks and the partisan rancor involved protests over voter irregularities, malfunctioning voting equipment, dimpled and hanging "chads" produced by incomplete puncturing of punch card ballots, and the despised "butterfly ballot" that was difficult for some voters to decipher. This seemed a period in which democracy in America was on hold. A state recount was underway when the U. S. Supreme Court finally preempted the process on December 12 in *Bush v. Gore*, a politically-charged 5-4 decision, and ordered a halt to the recount. The final results nationally showed Gore had won 508,683 more votes than Bush, but Bush became the forty-third president of the U.S. by winning the Electoral College tally by 271 to Gore's 266 votes. The decision did little to ease the intense partisan fighting. Observers wondered if Gore would press his fight for the White House in other legal directions. This speech would answer that question.

*Excerpt:* "Almost a century and a half ago, Senator Stephen Douglas told Abraham Lincoln, who had just defeated him for the presidency, 'Partisan feeling must yield to patriotism. I'm with you, Mr. President, and God bless you.' Well, in that same spirit, I say to President-elect Bush that what remains of partisan rancor must now be put aside, and may God bless his stewardship of this country. Neither he nor I anticipated this long and difficult road. Certainly neither of us wanted it to happen. Yet it came, and now it has ended, resolved, as it must be resolved, through the honored institutions of our democracy....Now the U.S. Supreme Court has spoken. Let there be no doubt, while I *strongly* disagree with the court's decision, I accept it....And tonight, for the sake of our unity as a people and the strength of our democracy, I offer my concession. I also accept my responsibility, which I will discharge unconditionally, to honor the new President-elect and do everything possible to help him bring Americans together in fulfillment of the great vision that our Declaration of Independence defines and that our Constitution affirms and defends.... I know that many of my supporters are disappointed. I am too. But our disappointment must be overcome by our love of country. And I say to our fellow members of the world community, let no one see this contest as a sign of American weakness."

*Impact:* Al Gore made the decision to be magnanimous as a peacemaker. Millions viewed the address made from his office, perhaps most wondering if the former vice president would cast blame on Florida officials, claim that he had been robbed of high office, and/or that he might continue his fight all the way to the House of Representatives if necessary. Instead, Gore found his deep passion that was expressed in simple, yet heart-felt tones. He thanked his family, the Liebermans, his supporters, and extended an olive branch as well as a helping hand and a pledge of cooperation to President-elect Bush. With the themes of gratitude, acceptance, cooperation, and understanding, this seven-minute address was clearly the best speech Gore has ever presented. Nothing could have healed the bitter wounds of this hotly contested national election any more effectively than these brief remarks to the nation, and millions saw a genuine humanity and humility they had never seen before.

*Contemporary Application:* The rhetoric of graciousness, good will, humility, unity, and patriotism will be long admired and appreciated by the masses of fellow citizens while the rhetoric of personal vanity, anger, bitterness, and partisanship serve only to deepen division and animosity. The former exhibits genuine statesmanship and the latter demonstrates petty, self-serving partisanship.

*Connection to Today:* In the last presidential debate of 2016, Donald Trump refused to pledge gracious support for the winner if he should lose the election to Hillary Clinton. Many viewers seemed shocked at such refusal. The next day, Trump surrogates cited Gore's original retraction of concession (on Election Day) as a case in point. The analogy was not an apt one, however. Trump had been making claims the upcoming election was "rigged" by deliberate voter fraud, while Gore's concern was the proper tally of votes already cast in the one state that had become the most crucial one in determining the outcome.

# 94. Sarah Palin, Acceptance Speech, September 4, 2008

*Speaker:* Sarah Palin (b. 1964) might have seemed the most unlikely candidate for a vice presidential nomination in 2008, however John McCain selected the one-time Alaska governor to complement the Republican ticket in its campaign against the Democrats' ticket of Senators Barack Obama and Joe Biden. Palin's candidacy was announced by McCain at Wright State University on August 29; she was selected over possible running mates such as Mitt Romney, Mike Huckabee, and Joe Lieberman. Barely known outside her home state, Palin's background included local television sportscasting, serving as mayor of Wasilla, and serving as the ninth governor (and youngest and first female in that office) for Alaska. In her own rhetoric, Palin projected an image of a small-town woman, a fighter who is tough on powerful interests that would exploit ordinary people, able to get things done, and an outsider to Washington D. C. When being introduced as the new candidate, Palin declared: "Hillary left eighteen million cracks in the highest, hardest ceiling in America. But it turns out that women in America aren't finished yet, and we can shatter that glass ceiling once and for all."

*Occasion:* This was the most important speech of Sarah Palin's life, a speech she presented under a large magnifying glass held up by all kinds of party leaders and voters. The setting was the Xcel Energy Center in St. Paul, Minnesota, with thousands of convention-goers anticipating the energy and enthusiasm of the traditional closing night with stirring nominating speeches, music, and colorful hoopla. Palin's role was historic, being the first woman ever to accept the Republican nomination for vice president and the first Alaskan on the ticket of a major party. Adding to the pressure, McCain had been losing in the polls to candidate Obama. Serious questions remained in the eyes of most political observers about Palin's fitness to serve as president should the ticket win. With a television viewing audience around thirty-eight million, this was the candidate's best opportunity to make a lasting impression.

*Excerpt:* "I guess a small-town mayor is sort of like a 'community organizer,' except that you have actual responsibilities. I might add that in small towns, we don't quite know what to make of a candidate who lavishes praise on working people when they are listening, and then talks about how bitterly they cling to their religion and guns when those people aren't listening. We tend to prefer candidates who don't talk about us one way in Scranton and another way in San Francisco. As for my running mate, you can be certain that wherever he goes, and whoever is listening, John McCain is the same man. I'm not a member of the permanent political establishment. And I've learned quickly…that if you're not a member in good standing of the Washington elite, then some in the media consider a candidate unqualified for that reason alone. But here's a little news flash for all those reporters and commentators: I'm not going to Washington to seek their good opinion. I'm going to Washington to serve the people of this country. Americans expect us to go to Washington for the right reasons, and not just to mingle with the right people. Politics isn't just a game of clashing parties and competing interests. The right reason is to challenge the status quo, to serve the common good, and to leave this nation better than we found it….But listening to him [Obama] speak, it's easy to forget this is a man who has authored two memoirs, but not a single major law or reform—not even in the state senate."

*Impact:* The speaker fulfilled several roles in her acceptance speech: Introducing herself and her family (performed quite capably); establishing her own reputation as a tough fighter for justice (the nickname "Sarah Barracuda" emerged); promotion of McCain ("Our nominee for president is a true profile in courage, and people like that are hard to come by"); and unleashing an attack on the Democratic nominee. The attack on Obama was both scathing and personal, often biting in sarcasm. Obama was depicted as untested and inexperienced, and yet even worse: hypocritical and inept. A purist might complain about the propaganda and overgeneralization in Palin's speech, while a realist accepts campaign rhetoric as frequently replete with bombast and over-simplifications. Regardless, among Republican rank-and-file members, Palin's oration, interrupted several times by enthusiastic applause and even laughter (some of her most popular lines oozed biting sarcasm), was more than a rousing success—it was a sensation that seemed fitting a rock star! Palin's gender connected with Republican women easily. Her winsome personality, continual smile and facial expressions, and her seeming confidence demonstrated in dynamic delivery, appealed to all Republicans and a number of undecided voters. After the speech, this ticket enjoyed a spike in the polls, a lead of six points. Palin became a media sensation and received intense national attention, even appearing on the cover of both *Time* and *Newsweek*. Her career as a national political figure was just beginning.

*Little Known Facts:* The speech was penned by Matthew Scully, a former Bush speechwriter. Palin supporters contend that early in the speech the teleprompter malfunctioned, and the candidate delivered most of the speech from memory, thus giving evidence to her skill, confidence, and grace under pressure as a public speaker. Palin's next test was the vice presidential debate with Biden, in which she performed effectively because the public's expectations were lowered.

*Contemporary Application:* A stirring, passionate speech on the national stage can catapult a candidate from total obscurity into the national limelight.

*Little Known Fact:* Palin carried a prepared concession speech to deliver on election night, but McCain vetoed its presentation citing a lack of precedent for a vice presidential candidate.

*Connection to Today:* Palin is still active in American politics, especially with the Tea Party. She introduced "bridge to nowhere" into the political lexicon, and is remembered for an uproarious answer to "What is the difference between a hockey mom and a pit bull?" Answer: "lipstick." She gained additional publicity in early 2016 by endorsing Donald Trump for the Republican presidential candidacy.

# 95. Barack Obama, First Inaugural Address, January 20, 2009

*Speaker:* On November 4, 2008, Barack H. Obama was elected as the first African-American president of the United States. A number of factors came into play in his winning a narrow victory over Senator Hillary Clinton in the Democratic primary campaign. George W. Bush, the sitting president, had dropped dramatically in approval ratings, and his policy in the Middle East was considered ineffective and wasteful by millions of voters who wanted a change. By the time of his election, Obama had clearly established himself as an effective orator, and, many commentators noted, it was the power of his oratory that was the key factor in winning both his party's nomination and the general election. "Obama won the presidency with words," Henry Allen of the *Washington Post* (January 20, 2009) observed. "He is an orator, a rare thing in a time when educated people, a lot of them Obama supporters, have been taught to distrust old-fashioned eloquence."

*Occasion:* President Barack Obama's first Inauguration in January 2009 was like none previously—from the diverse hundreds of thousands who were drawn to Washington for the ceremony to the immense funding required to finance the event, the intense media coverage worldwide, and the giddiness and goodwill expressed by the most diverse group of Americans ever gathered in Washington. Even if the honeymoon with the forty-fourth president ended early, as most presidential and political honeymoons seem to do, the Inaugural event remained memorable. This was the largest audience for any speaking event held in the nation's history, easily eclipsing the size of the audience for King's famous "I Have a Dream" speech at the 1963 March on Washington gathering. "A New Birth of Freedom," a phrase from Lincoln's

Gettysburg Address, served as the theme for the Inaugural, and there was also a commemoration of the two-hundredth anniversary of Lincoln's birth.

*Excerpt:* "We remain a young nation, but in the words of Scripture, the time has come to set aside childish things. The time has come to reaffirm our enduring spirit; to choose our better history; to carry forward that precious gift, that noble idea, passed on from generation to generation: the God-given promise that all are equal, all are free, and all deserve a chance to pursue their full measure of happiness….In reaffirming the greatness of our nation, we understand that greatness is never a given. It must be earned. Our journey has never been one of short-cuts or settling for less. It has not been the path for the faint-hearted—for those who prefer leisure over work, or seek only the pleasures of riches and fame. Rather, it has been the risk-takers, the doers, the makers of things—some celebrated but more often men and women obscure in their labor, who have carried us up the long, rugged path towards prosperity and freedom."

*Impact:* The speech, as well as the entire Inaugural event, was a resounding and joyful success for the nation as a whole. The context of the entire Inauguration was irrepressible diversity, a nation of people who want their beliefs acknowledged in the most important ritual of American civil religion. And while Obama drew from a biblical allusion ("setting aside childish things"), for the first time in history a president reached out to secularists and called the United States "a nation of Christians and Muslims, Jews and Hindus—and nonbelievers." This addition (referencing nonbelievers), though subtle, was historic. What Obama did *not* say also spoke volumes, conveying a sense of humility about oneself and the nation he loved. There was no sense of American triumphalism or national arrogance about the past. No mention of Manifest Destiny in international affairs. No hint that America is the most righteous nation on earth and that a few other threatening nations are evil. No sense that God established a special covenant with America, that America was the special "light unto the nations" of the world, that America was basically good and has always done right by all its citizens, that God has blessed America more than any other nation in the world, that American might makes right, and that America's enemies must be punished or at least live in fear of reprisal. There was none of this grandiose rhetoric. Instead, there was a sense that we must learn from experiences of the past, and yet a belief that the American dream still exists. Thus, the American civil religion had been either laid to rest or, more likely, substantially redefined for a new generation. That is why this Inaugural Address, along with a select few other Inaugural Addresses, belongs in our list of 101 best American public addresses.

*Contemporary Application:* Change is inevitable, whether change in a society or change in individuals. Today's audiences have become more multi-cultural and diverse by almost any standard. To be effective, the public speaker must be audience-centered, analyzing both the demographics of one's audience and the situation in which a speech is to be delivered, and then the speaker must adapt to that audience.

*Connection to Today:* President Obama's election to the presidency, and then his re-election in 2012, remind us that political oratory still matters in U. S. politics. Obama's oratorical skill and the wide diversity of so many audiences that he has faced during his political career places him in the select company of a small group of American presidents who are remembered as great speakers: Abraham Lincoln, Theodore Roosevelt, Franklin Roosevelt, and Ronald Reagan. Like Theodore Roosevelt, Obama has seized his high position on the "bully pulpit" to educate and admonish all kinds of audiences on all kinds of issues, especially race relations and the plague of gun violence. He has also demonstrated that a great speaker must adapt one's style to be effective in the electronic era, that the old-fashioned podium-pounding, arm-flailing, and stem-winding oratorical style of a century ago will no longer work with the cool medium of television. Selecting and ranking the best Obama speeches is a challenge indeed!

# 96. Barack Obama, A New Beginning, June 4, 2009

*Speaker:* Shortly into his term of office, Barack Obama made good on a promise made in his campaign. Acting on the spirit of his Inaugural to reach out to the Muslim world "to extend a hand," the new president went to Egypt and presented one of the most important speeches of his life—"A New Beginning," delivered at the Major Reception Hall at the University of Cairo. For all important speeches, Obama spoke by reading from a teleprompter

*Occasion:* In the context of strained and suspicious relations between the U. S. citizenry and citizens of the Middle Eastern nations, also in the context of the U. S. military fighting wars in Afghanistan and Iraq, President Obama's speech was highly appropriate for the audience. On the other hand, the speech also dealt with delicate issues on which Americans and Muslim nations vehemently disagree. The President called for improved mutual understanding and relations between the Islamic world and the West, and he stated that both sides should do more to confront violent extremism.

*Excerpt:* "Although I believe that the Iraqi people are ultimately better off without the tyranny of Saddam Hussein, I also believe that events in Iraq have reminded America of the need to use diplomacy and build international consensus to resolve our problems whenever possible.... [Though] America does not presume to know what is best for everyone, I do have an unyielding belief that all people yearn for certain things: the ability to speak your mind and have a say in how you are governed; confidence in the rule of law and the equal administration of justice; government that is transparent and doesn't steal from the people; the freedom to live as you choose."

*Impact:* The speech was undauntedly bold and courageous, and it certainly helped Obama's presidency get off to a good start. The President clearly adapted to his foreign audience, thus enhancing his ethical appeal as the speech continued. The rhetorical strategies in the address were skillfully used, surely disarming much, if not all, hostility against the speaker among Muslims in the audience. Obama cited Muslim contributions to Western civilization, such as algebra, navigational tools, Islamic architecture, even the fountain pen, and he noted the presence of over 1,200 Islamic mosques in the United States. Obama also quoted from a passage in the *Qur'an* on which people of any monotheistic religion could agree: "Be conscious of God and always speak the truth." He called for peace between the Israelis and Palestinians. Choosing his words carefully, the President never used the word "terror" or "terrorism" in his speech. Clearly, President Obama's speech was both political and religious in nature, not a speech of contrition. The speaker did not apologize for any U. S. action or attitudes in the past, the fact that the President's major opponent in the 2012 presidential campaign called the visit in Cairo the beginning of an "apology tour" notwithstanding. That label ("apology tour") continued to be placed on the speech by some leading Republican candidates in the 2016 presidential campaign. Nonetheless, the speech captured a vision of the future with tolerance and understanding. And clearly, if we concede the importance of words in our history, this was one of the most important speeches in modern American history. Arab leaders mostly gave the President and the speech high marks, but some just dismissed it as "mere rhetoric." A few delegates in the U. S. Congress did not like or appreciate certain parts of the speech.

*Contemporary Application:* When the president of the United States dares to speak on the subject of another religion besides the Christian faith, and especially delivering it in a foreign nation, one can expect controversy and misunderstanding.

*Connection to Today:* Many Americans are still deeply concerned about the U. S. role in Muslim-dominated nations. There seem to be so many misunderstandings of different cultures, including religion, and heritages. Religious zeal seems to drive so much extremist behavior, even terrorism. Proper understanding of other religions and their adherents would be so beneficial for people in all nations.

*Interesting Fact:* By the time of the 2016 presidential primary race, clearly the issue of the Islamic religion and Muslims in general remained a topic of debate and a subject of misunderstanding. Donald Trump, the Republican primary candidate and eventual nominee for president, had won support by pledging a ban on Muslims entering the country "until we can figure out what the hell is going on." Trump also promised to conduct surveillance on mosques. In a speech similar in purpose to the Cairo address, delivered on February 3, 2016, President Obama visited the Islamic Society of Baltimore and spoke on the same themes. This was his first visit to an American mosque and he used the occasion to condemn "inexcusable political rhetoric against Muslim Americans that has no place in our country." Once again, Obama recognized the contributions of Muslim citizens and appealed to Muslims around the world to help combat the extremist ideologies of terrorist groups like the Islamic State. "The first thing I want to say is two words that Muslim Americans don't hear often enough," the President said: "Thank you. Thank you for serving your community. Thank you for lifting up the lives of your neighbors and for helping keep us strong and united as one American family." The speech was delivered within a few days of the San Bernardino terrorist killings, and Obama acknowledged that Muslims in general are often stigmatized by the violent actions of a few extremists. "We've seen children bullied, we've seen mosques vandalized. It's not who we are. We're one American family. And when any part of our family begins to feel separate or second class or targeted, it tears at the very fabric of our nation," the President declared. The Baltimore speech came amid an eight-day stretch during which Obama spoke to Muslim, Jewish, and Christian audiences.

# 97. Joe Biden, Personal Address on Grief, May 25, 2012

*Speaker:* Former Delaware Senator Joe Biden (b. 1942) was elected the forty-seventh U.S. vice president with President Barack Obama in 2008, earning a second term in 2012. Born into a blue collar family in Pennsylvania, at age thirteen his family moved to Delaware. Upon graduation from the University of Delaware, he attended the Syracuse University Law School. Biden briefly worked as an attorney before turning to politics. In November 1972, in a tight race against a popular incumbent with a large turnout, Biden won an upset victory to become the fifth-youngest U.S. senator in history, beginning a tenure as Delaware's longest-serving senator. A week before that Christmas, Biden's wife and three children were involved in a terrible car accident while out shopping for a Christmas tree. The accident killed his wife and daughter, and severely injured both of his sons, Beau and Hunter. Biden seemed inconsolable to those who knew him best, and he confessed to having considered suicide. Passing on the traditional group swearing in of new senators, he took the oath of office in a hospital chapel near his son's hospital room. From 1973 to 2009 Biden served a distinguished Senate career. During his time in the upper chamber, Biden won respect as one of the body's leading foreign policy experts, serving as chairman of the Committee on Foreign Relations. In addition to foreign policy, Biden was an outspoken proponent of tougher crime laws. In 1987, Supreme Court nominee Robert Bork's failure to receive confirmation was largely attributed to strong questioning by Biden, who was then chairman of the Senate Judiciary Committee. In 1987 he dropped out of a race for the presidential nomination when reports surfaced he had plagiarized a speech. His presidential campaign twenty years later never gained sufficient traction in a contest that was dominated by Hillary Clinton and Barack Obama. However, Democratic nominee Barack Obama later selected him as his running mate. Biden is unquestionably one of the most important political figures in recent history, having taken a lead in financial and fiscal issues with Congressional leaders and serving as a national leader in the debate over gun control. On May 30, 2015, Biden suffered still another personal loss when his son Beau died at the age of forty-six, after battling brain cancer. Following this tragedy, Biden considered a run for the presidency, but he put the speculation about a possible presidential run to rest in October 2015 when he announced that he would not seek the 2016 Democratic nomination; in January 2016 he told the press that "every day" he regretted not running in the presidential race. As a speaker, Biden uses the conversational manner of delivery. Perhaps his most visible role on speech occasions has been standing close by President Obama's side and looking earnest and engaged when the President delivered an important address. Biden has sometimes been lampooned for his loquaciousness, blurting out verbose, impertinent, and/ or historically inaccurate statements without first engaging his mind and, in hearings, asking long and convoluted questions. On the other hand, after the 2016 election, Joe Biden seems to enjoy a widespread respect and affection from American people, especially Democrats, as a kind of non-controversial elder statesman.

*Occasion:* This occasion was the opening session of the eighteenth annual TAPS National Military Survivor Seminar. TAPS is an acronym for "Tragedy Assistance Program for Survivors." And the Vice President was selected as featured speaker.

*Excerpt:* "And I remember looking up and saying, 'God,' I was, as if I was talking to God myself, 'You can't be good, how can you be good?'…. There was still something gigantic missing. And just when you think, 'Maybe I'm going to make it,' you're riding down the road and you pass a field, and you see a flower and it reminds you. Or you hear a tune on the radio. Or you just look up in the night. You know, you think, 'Maybe I'm not going to make it, man.' Because you feel at that moment the way you felt the day you got the news….It was the first time in my career, in my life, I realized someone could go out -- and I probably shouldn't say this with the press here, but no, but it's more important, you're more important. For the first time in my life, I understood how someone could consciously decide to commit suicide. Not because they were deranged, not because they were nuts, because they had been to the top of the mountain, and they just knew in their heart they would never get there again....It can and will get better. There will come a day -- I promise you, and your parents as well -- when the thought of your son or daughter, or your husband or wife, brings a smile to your lips before it brings a tear to your eye. It will happen."

*Impact:* Vice President Biden enjoyed rapport and emotional support from the moment he stepped to the podium. No audience could have been more supportive. No topic could have been more sensitive. And yet, as a high ranking political official, he enjoyed credibility with families who had lost loved ones in government service. The speaker bared his heart and soul, discussing dark thoughts and doubts about God he could not rid his mind of in the wake of the terrible accident that robbed him of his wife and daughter. There is no doubt of the genuineness and warmth conveyed in the speaker's voice and manner. It is seemingly impossible to think of another government official or even some theologian or preacher who could have spoken more meaningfully or empathetically to this particular audience on this sensitive topic.

*Contemporary Application:* This personal, heartfelt speech illustrates that speakers and writers can be the greatest comfort and blessing when they have lived the truth of their message and speak directly and honestly from personal experience.

*Little Known Fact:* As a child Biden struggled with a stutter, and kids called him "Dash" and "Joe Impedimenta" to mock him. Eventually, he overcame his speech impediment by memorizing long passages of poetry and reciting them out loud in front of the mirror.

# 98. Bill Clinton, Address to the Democratic National Convention, September 5, 2012

*Speaker:* William Jefferson Clinton, always known as Bill, the forty-second president of the U. S., the first Democratic chief executive in twelve years, and the first chief executive from the Baby Boomer generation, brought an image of vitality, youth, and cultural diversity to Washington (the Inaugural celebration included different balls for different musical tastes, one featuring rock n' roll from the Vietnam era; Clinton also named Madeleine Albright as the nation's first female secretary of state). Clinton is an alumnus of Georgetown University and earned a Rhodes scholarship to attend the University of Oxford. At age forty-six, he was the third youngest president, defeating incumbent George H. W. Bush. His major failure was the inability to pass major health care reform. During his years in office, President Clinton presided over the nation during an era of more peace, prosperity, and economic expansion and well-being than at any other time in the nation's history; unemployment was at an all-time low in modern times as well as the inflation rate being the lowest in thirty years; there was a reduced welfare roll, high home ownership, and a national budget surplus. Clinton became the first Democrat to be elected to a second term since Franklin D. Roosevelt. Year 1998 was not kind to the Clinton family as the President was impeached for perjury before a grand jury and for obstruction of justice during a lawsuit. Both related to a scandal involving a White House intern. Yet Clinton left office with the highest approval rating of any U. S. president since World War II. Since his tenure ended, Clinton has been involved in public speaking and humanitarian causes, creating the William J. Clinton Foundation to address international issues. Affectionately called the "Do-gooder-in-Chief" by President Obama, Clinton has been involved in several humanitarian projects, the best known being the rebuilding of Haiti after the devastation wreaked by the 2009 earthquake. As a speaker, Clinton was never the traditional spell-binding orator with a deep voice and dramatic gestures, but he modeled the conversational manner at its best—confidence, earnestness, animation, facial expression, sincerity, and a sense of "I feel your pain" empathy for listeners.

*Occasion:* There was no doubt that the 2012 Democratic National Convention in Charlotte, North Carolina, would be nominating Barack Obama for a second term, but there was doubt about whether he could win re-election in light of strong Republican attacks against his performance in the previous four years. Any convention audience is mobilized in terms of partisanship, though not every national convention has the opportunity to see and hear a popular ex-president. Clinton was allotted a half hour to make the major nominating speech for Obama. Knowing that Obama and Clinton were not close personal friends, many party regulars felt anticipation about the case the forty-second president would make for the forty-fourth president. While the immediate audience was composed of thousands in the arena, the television audience was composed of millions and included party "regulars" to be energized as well as a larger general audience of centrist voters who had not decided which candidate would receive their vote.

*Excerpt:* "I want to nominate a man whose own life has known its fair share of adversity and uncertainty. I want to nominate a man who ran for president to change the course of an already weak economy and then just six weeks before his election, saw it suffer the biggest collapse since the Great Depression; a man who stopped the slide into depression and put us on the long road to recovery....I want to nominate a man who's cool on the outside, but who burns for America on the inside....And by the way....I want a man who had the good sense to marry Michelle Obama. I want Barack Obama to be the next president of the United States. And I proudly nominate him to be the standard-bearer of the Democratic Party."

*Impact:* Clinton's forty-eight minute speech is, indeed, a model convention address that demonstrated why the ex-president has been such an effective political leader for so many years. Arguably, this was the best convention speech ever delivered, at least in the electronic era, and arguably remains the best speech Bill Clinton has delivered. Effective rhetorical elements were numerous, from the choice of words to the style of delivery. Here was a respected political leader thoroughly enjoying himself: clapping, laughing, smiling, incorporating humor, speaking respectfully of everyone, and, most of all, playing the role of a wise and experienced teacher or loving father merely instructing his pupils. With strong *ethos*, Clinton demonstrated the power of "identification" and "connection" with his audience, often using phrases such as "you and I know," "y'all know," or "we Democrats." At one point Clinton declared: "We believe 'we're all in this together' is a far better philosophy than 'you're all on your own.'" Indeed, the speech contained many such sound bites. When Clinton made claims about the economy or Obama's health plan, he explained and supported them by using reasoning and statistics. Again, as a master of the conversational style he would often ask, and then answer, rhetorical questions. The response for this speech was overwhelmingly positive, with many interruptions of cheers and applause. To use the old cliché, Bill Clinton "brought the house down." The following day, one critic, John Harris, wrote in *Politico*: "Clinton knows a thing or two about blending argument, language, and performance to achieve the biggest thing for any first-term president, which is becoming a second-term president." "There is simply no one better," former presidential speechwriter David Gergen declared. "This is the most effective and influential speech Clinton has given since leaving the presidency. He told the Obama story better than Obama ever did." Indeed, this speech may well have been the moment that re-elected Obama for a second term.

*Contemporary Application:* A speaker possessing high *ethos* with a special audience and a compelling conversational manner of delivery can mobilize and energize millions of listeners with a single dynamic, compelling address.

## 99. Michelle Obama, King College Prep School Commencement, June 9, 2015

*Speaker:* Not many U. S. first ladies display high competence and versatility in the art of public speaking, but Michelle Obama (b. 1964) must surely be ranked among the most effective. As with many first ladies, she has used her speaking skills to support the career of her husband since the beginning of his political career, and yet later turned to embrace a variety of public concerns in the life of the nation and its diverse communities. Michelle Obama was the nation's forty-fourth first lady (and first African-American first lady) and the wife of President Barack Obama. She attended Princeton University, graduating *cum laude* in 1985, and then earned her J. D. degree from Harvard Law School in 1988. After marriage to Barack Obama in 1992, she began a career in public service with her main emphasis on improving all standards in local community life. Since 2004 Obama has delivered many public speeches supporting the goals and purposes espoused by her husband. During her years as first lady, the national media, understandably, have given much attention to her life as wife and mother to two children, Malia and Sasha, and to her clothing and grooming fashion. Yet, more importantly, Obama has addressed all kinds of audiences, emphasizing national goals, human values, and public service. Since 2010 she has led a fight against childhood obesity and has emphasized health, wellness, and exercise for all ages, but especially youth. Michelle Obama is an outstanding public speaker who models the conversational manner at its best—confidence, genuineness, sincerity, animation, warmth, friendliness, vivid expressiveness in face and body, good eye contact, and attention to feedback. She has addressed the Democratic National Convention in 2008, 2012, and 2016. Her speech to the Democratic National Convention in 2012 was surely one of her best, if not *the* best, speech she has ever delivered and maybe her most important speech—it introduced the human side of her husband at a time when his candidacy needed a boost. "Barack knows the American dream because he has lived it," she declared. The "American dream" is a favorite theme of hers, and Michelle Obama's favorability ratings have always remained high, often higher than her husband's ratings.

*Occasion:* Michelle Obama returned to her hometown to honor 177 graduates at King College Prep School and their families and friends. All the graduates had already been accepted into a college program. To African-American youth, especially, she had high credibility. Obama had already established her deep concern about street violence and its effect on youth. On March 10, 2013, she had joined Mayor Rahm Emanuel in his goal to raise $50 million for programs to support "at risk" youth in Chicago. In an address at the Hilton Chicago, she demonstrated the seriousness of the problem and urged audience members to contribute to programs providing resources for youth. The commencement audience was an opportunity to speak directly to Chicago youth. In the audience, there was one empty chair that was draped in purple for a missing honor student, Hadiya Pendleton. While the overall tone was one of celebration, there were somber moments of reflection on lessons to be learned.

*Excerpt:* "I know the struggles many of you face, how you walk the long way home to avoid the gangs; how you fight to concentrate on your schoolwork when there's too much noise at home; how you keep it together when your family's having a hard time making ends meet. But more importantly, I know the strength of this community....I know that many of you have already dealt with some serious losses in your lives. Maybe you've lost someone you love, someone you desperately wish could be here with you tonight. And I know that many of you are thinking about Hadiya right now and feeling the hole that she's left in your hearts... I want you to understand that every scar that you have is a reminder not just that you got hurt, but that you survived. If Hadiya's friends and family could survive their heartbreak and pain, if they could found organizations to honor her unfulfilled dreams, if they could inspire folks across this country to wear orange to protest gun violence, then I know you all can live your life with the same determination and joy that Hadiya lived her life. I know you all can dig deep and keep on fighting to fulfill your own dreams.... You embody all of the courage and love, all of the hunger and hope that have always defined these communities -- our communities. And I am so proud of you all, and I stay inspired because of you, and I can't wait to see everything you all achieve in the years ahead."

*Impact:* Michelle Obama received a warm reception throughout her entire presentation, beginning with a warm hug given by the female who introduced her. She created common ground with her audience by noting the Southside of Chicago was also her home, that she was born and raised in the same city as her listeners. Once again, as in some previous addresses, Obama personalized her remarks by referencing the story of Hadiya Pendleton, who was a fifteen-year-old student at King College Prep where the commencement was presented. She spoke of the closeness of the Pendleton family, the excellence of Hadiya as a student, and how, just one week after performing at the President's Inauguration, she went to a park with some friends and got shot in the back because some kid thought she was in a gang. Everyone in the audience, young and old, would have known that story. And everyone present would have known struggles of all kinds. Obama received good attention and came across with the sincerity and credibility that no other speaker, unless the President himself, could have achieved.

*Connection to Today:* In the presidential campaign of 2016, Michelle Obama became the most effective surrogate for candidate Hillary Clinton, making a number of speaking appearances in various battleground states. Her address at the 2016 Democratic National Convention was, by far, the best address of the entire occasion. She was often quoted about Clinton's strategy in dealing with a political opponent who seemed to relish personal insult against his opponents:

"When they go low, we go high." The First Lady never mentioned Republican candidate Donald Trump by name in her speeches, yet always spoke with great passion about the issues at stake. Some observers have contended that Michelle Obama would be an excellent presidential candidate in the future, should she desire to run for high office; she has disclaimed any interest in political office.

*Contemporary Application:* Approach your audience with confidence, connect with your eyes with all listeners, speak sincerely and from your heart, and tell your own story. The audience will embrace you. This natural strategy, combined with intelligence and speaking skill, constitutes the key to Michelle Obama's effectiveness with audiences.

# 100. Barack Obama, Eulogy for Clementa Pinckney, June 26, 2015

*Speaker:* President Barack Obama was an obvious choice to present a eulogy on this occasion. No longer subject to a presidential election vote, the President was free to speak his mind on a number of topics for which he cared deeply.

*Occasion:* On June 17, 2015, a 21-year-old man entered the Emmanuel African Methodist Episcopal Church in downtown Charleston, South Carolina, sat through a Bible class, then later pulled out his weapon and began shooting parishioners with the intent to kill. Nine were killed in the senseless carnage, including the senior pastor, the Rev. Clementa Pinckney, also a state senator. Emmanuel A.M.E. is one of the oldest African-American congregations in the U.S. (founded in 1816), and has long been a site for community organization around civil rights. Conducted at the T. D. Arena at the College of Charleston, the funeral service was a long one with musical numbers by the choir and various speakers honoring Pinckney. Approximately three hours into the service, Obama stood to address both the immediate audience and a worldwide audience reached by C-Span and CNN. The speaker's purpose seemed to be threefold: (1) To honor the life and legacy of Rev. Pinckney; (2) To place the AME Church tragedy in perspective by interpreting the issues that emerged from the tragedy (grief and pain, injustice, racism, gun violence, role of the black church in American history, and even Confederate iconography); and (3) To bring unity through hope and healing, both to the church and the city of Charleston, yet, in a larger sense, to the entire nation.

*Excerpt:* "As a nation, out of this terrible tragedy, God has visited grace upon us, for he has allowed us to see where we've been blind. He has given us the chance, where we've been lost, to find our best selves. We may not have earned it, this grace, with our rancor and complacency, and short-sightedness and fear of each other -- but we got it all the same. He gave it to us anyway. He's once more given us grace. But it is up to us now to make the most of it, to receive it with gratitude, and to prove ourselves worthy of this gift....By taking down that flag, we express God's grace. But I don't think God wants us to stop there....We don't earn grace. We're all sinners. We don't deserve it. But God gives it to us anyway. And we choose how to receive it. It's our decision how to honor it. None of us can or should expect a transformation in race relations overnight....But it would be a betrayal of everything Reverend Pinckney stood for, I believe, if we allowed ourselves to slip into a comfortable silence again.... To settle for symbolic gestures without following up with the hard work of more lasting change -- that's how we lose our way again. ...Clem understood that justice grows out of recognition of ourselves in each other. That my liberty depends on you being free, too. That history can't be a sword to justify injustice, or a shield against progress, but must be a manual for how to avoid repeating the mistakes of the past -- how to break the cycle. A roadway toward a better world. He knew that the path of grace involves an open mind -- but, more importantly, an open heart....That reservoir of goodness. If we can find that grace, anything is possible. If we can tap into that grace, everything can change....Amazing grace. Amazing grace. [Obama begins to sing] -- Amazing grace -- how sweet the sound, that saved a wretch like me; I once was lost, but now I'm found; was blind but now I see. Clementa Pinckney found that grace."

*Impact:* One might justifiably conclude that this eulogy was the most moving, effective, and inspirational speech that President Obama has ever delivered. The Chief Executive so masterfully melded the theological and political elements of the address. The most effective rhetorical strategy was Obama's development of the theme of God's grace and using that theme, not only to express his own humility, but as a framework for understanding changes that America needed to make if the nation rises above social diseases such as racism, poverty, hatred, and gun violence. The President used the word "grace" thirty-five times, and, as he ended his remarks, he declared that Rev. Pinckney had found that grace and then, one by one, he called the names of each church member who had been killed, stating by calling personal names that each Christian martyr had found God's grace—a powerful use of repetition. Finally, to the astonishment of millions, after thirty-five minutes of "preaching," he broke out into movingly (if not perfectly) singing, *a cappella* style, that most familiar hymn of the Christian faith: "Amazing Grace," interestingly enough, the great Christian anthem written by a former slave-trader-turned-abolitionist. As for the immediate audience, the address was interrupted numerous times by applause. A number of journalists and editorialists also concurred that the oration was the best that Obama had ever presented. "Obama at his best," declared one; another called it "Obama's most accomplished single oratorical performance." In years past, Obama had been the campaigner and also the politician seeking votes. For other speeches, the President had been Professor Obama. On this day, however, as a church and a nation wept over precious innocent lives having been lost through a crime of hatred, the President became Reverend Obama, assuming the roles of theologian, minister, and pastor, and seemingly ever humble throughout every moment of fulfilling these important roles for the occasion.

*Contemporary Application:* There are deep moments of crisis and perplexity that occur in the life of a nation, and these moments provide opportunities in which the nation's highest elected leader can address the nation in terms of the spiritual and the transcendent.

*Interesting Fact:* Though Obama's eulogy was thoroughly "Christian," and "God" was mentioned often, the name of "Jesus" was not mentioned once.

# 101. Hillary Clinton, Nomination Acceptance Speech, July 28, 2016

*Speaker:* Given such a diverse and long record of public service and political activism in the U.S., one could make the case that, at this moment in time, Hillary Rodham Clinton was the one person best qualified to become chief executive of the nation. By this time, her face and voice were so familiar to millions. She had made hundreds if not thousands of public appearances, delivering both long and brief speeches and countless interviews. Could any American be better known? Herein lies the paradox of the speaker: Many felt she was a mystery woman, a bundle of inconsistencies and "unknowns" despite daily media attention. Clinton had fought long and hard during a grueling primary campaign against Senator Bernie Sanders, whose campaign gathered momentum as the primary season wound down. As a public speaker, Clinton is not the blue-ribbon orator that is Barack Obama; her rhetoric seldom takes flight into the rarefied air of pure eloquence. However, she projects her own sense of rhetorical excellence: unshakable confidence; strong voice, vivid facial expressions, active body language; command of material; and solid content. She projects an image of the "doer," the experienced one, the pragmatist, the master of details, the unrelenting fighter, and the one who makes things happen. The flip side: a severely damaged *ethos*. Clinton was seen as a polarizing figure. Over two-thirds of American voters viewed her as dishonest and untrustworthy. Her Republican opponents had hammered her, even blamed her, over the loss of four Americans at the diplomatic compound in Benghazi, Libya. Her decision to set up a private email server in her home and conduct official, state department business on that server constituted the biggest detrimental factor in both her judgment and credibility.

*Occasion:* The occasion was indeed historic—the Democratic National Convention conducted in the Wells Fargo Center in Philadelphia, birthplace city of our nationhood, a fact frequently referenced by convention speakers. This was a primetime address and it was, indeed, the most important speech of Hillary Clinton's long career in politics. Two nights earlier, she had won the delegate voting to become the first female in the nation's history to be nominated by a major party for the presidency. Traditionally, the candidate then is expected to address the party and the nation and accept the nomination and then the general campaign has officially begun. Besides the shadow of controversy over the party's chairwoman and her immediate resignation under duress, the convention went about as well as Clinton could have imagined. Three nights earlier, the President's wife, Michelle Obama, presented a sterling performance in addressing the delegates and making the case for electing Clinton. Noting how much the nation has changed for the better, the First Lady stated: "I wake up every morning in a house that was built by slaves. And I watch my daughters, two beautiful, intelligent, black young women playing with their dogs in the White House lawn." (One could argue this was the best address of the entire week). The following night, Bill Clinton spoke, the first ever speech about a nominee spouse by a male. Using his highly effective conversational manner, Bill presented the personal side of Hillary as both wife and mom. The following evening, President Obama presented another of his soaring rhetorical efforts, making the bold assertion that absolutely no one, not even himself or Bill Clinton, was better qualified to be president than Hillary. Night after night, there had been a speaker line-up of some of the biggest names in the Democratic Party, including Joe Biden—a stark contrast from the Republican convention in which several prominent party leaders shunned attendance. The nominee received a warm and sweet introduction by daughter Chelsea. The stage could not have been set more dramatically for this historic moment.

*Excerpt:* [Clinton accepted the nomination] …"With humility, determination, and boundless confidence in America's promise…When any barrier falls in

America, it clears the way for everyone. When there are no ceilings, the sky's the limit…America's destiny is ours to choose."

*Impact:* As with most national conventions, the in-house audience was highly partisan in favor of the party and usually the candidate, as well. A reported thirty-four million watched via television, one million less than viewed Trump's acceptance speech. In this case, there was a large segment of delegates who felt disappointment that Bernie Sanders came so close but did not garner enough votes to win nomination. Nonetheless, Clinton reached out to this distrustful and reluctant group as warmly and effectively as possible with gracious compliments and reassurance ("I've heard you. Your cause is our cause"). There did not seem to be a central theme to this address that provided a frame of reference for all the assertions and supporting data, certainly no memorable line to repeat (or for the crowd to chant) such as King's "I have a dream!" The candidate made a number of references to her Republican opponent, mentioning Trump's name twenty-two times, and projected an image of a wealthy business mogul who got rich by stiffing workers and reneging on contracts, a man who peddles fear and lacks the temperament to be commander-in-chief. "A man you can bait with a tweet," she warned, "is not a man we can trust with nuclear weapons." She showed no contrition over personal controversies that had lowered the trust-level—indeed what *words* alone could have reassured all listeners that she could be believed and trusted? Instead, Clinton projected a self-image of someone who is practical, policy-driven, persistent, and who may get knocked down but always gets back up to fight another day on behalf of the middle class, the poor, and all minority and ethnic groups. While she did discuss policy proposals in a general way, this self-introduction as someone of strong character, unrelenting determination, common-sense agenda, and graceful demeanor rendered this address successful. But how successful? Election Day provided evidence that one historical moment—one historical nomination—and a strong convention address are not enough to win a national election, at least in the Electoral College. On December 19, 2016, the Electoral College confirmed the electoral vote tally and officially elected Donald J. Trump the forty-fifth president of the United States.

*Contemporary Application:* The long and winding road to women's equality in American political life has been traveled by courageous and eloquent women whose words stirred audiences. Michelle Obama and Hillary Clinton may be the latest examples of female oratorical excellence, but there surely will be others in the immediate future.

# Alternative 101. Donald J. Trump, Inaugural Address, January 20, 2017

(*Author's note*: At this point, no claim is made that this Inaugural Address is one of the greatest speeches in American history, but that this address was, indeed, *representative* of Trump's political thinking and speaking at this point in time. The reader may decide whether this speech or the previous one cited, Hillary Clinton's nomination acceptance speech, deserves to be the 101st speech to be cited. Completion of this book was postponed until this speech could be viewed and evaluated. Due to the importance and recency of this speech, more space is allotted to its coverage. Additional detail about Trump's presidential primary and candidate debating and speaking is discussed in chapters 2 and 6 of this study.)

*Speaker*: What Donald J. Trump (b. 1946) has been able to accomplish in the months of 2015 and 2016 is nothing short of amazing, to use one of his favorite words. Prior to his serious entry into national politics, Trump compiled an impressive resume as private citizen. He built a global real estate empire and earned billions of dollars. With a base in New York, he earned a moniker of "real estate mogul" and his name appeared on all kinds of buildings, resorts, leisure and vacation facilities, and that famous name also is emblazoned on his own private Boeing jet. His media appearances have been virtually innumerable, and he enhanced his reputation as host and star of his own network reality show, "The Apprentice." Though not distinguished as a spell-binding orator, Trump does demonstrate an effective conversational style of delivery. He faces all kinds of audiences with confidence. He enjoys being introduced with generous praise, and sometimes enters the speaking stage with show business fanfare, then walks to the podium and immediately adjusts the microphone pedestal by raising or lowering it an inch or so. He is always dressed in professional business attire that typically includes a solid, colorful silk tie and, in beginning a speech, usually expresses gratitude for any friendly audience. He gestures with both arms and hands throughout a speech, typically making a small circle with tips of thumb and index finger joined or giving a two thumbs-up gesture. Of much more importance, however, is the man's image. With friendly audiences he projects a sense of a leader who is confident, bold, tough, shrewd, unafraid, and unapologetic. His surrogates and defenders declare that Trump has a deft skill set in negotiating deals and understanding the ordinary person, and that, while he has offended many while gaining his stronghold on a large segment of the voting citizenry, everyone should simply "allow Trump to be Trump." At seventy, Trump became the oldest man assuming the high office as America's forty-fifth president.

*Occasion*: The presidential Inaugural Address has always been that quadrennial moment in the nation's history wherein the newly sworn-in chief executive, whether a first termer or an incumbent, strives for an eloquence that produces inspiration and aspiration for the entire nation. This solemn occasion seeks to strike that delicate balance between national heritage and the pledge of a new start. As an impressive ritual of American civil religion, the Inaugural event is intended to be nonpartisan, honoring and strengthening the conviction that what we Americans share is greater and runs deeper than what divides us. The election campaign is over, though it is hardly forgotten, and the "nuts and bolts" of public policy will be discussed days later in the State of the Union Address to the Congress. Such pomp and ceremony call for "soaring rhetoric," and even some of the most unpopular and controversial presidents have been able to achieve it. The occasion is tailor-made for some of the most memorable lines a president can utter, whether that president personally penned the lines or a ghost-writer fortuitously authored them. No wonder Ronald Reagan in his 1981 Inaugural Address called the Inauguration ceremony "both commonplace and miraculous."

This Inaugural occasion followed one of the most divisive, inflammatory, bitter, fractured and controversial presidential campaigns in recent history. The President-elect faced this speaking moment with damaged *ethos* and self-inflicted wounds. Many of his previous off-the-cuff comments—times when he strayed from the teleprompter's prepared script—plus a number of negative, 140-character Twitter comments, seemed to disparage large and important segments of American citizens. Some observers contended the election results were "tainted" by Russian interference and the subsequent release of private Democratic Party email messages. Standing on the west front of the Capitol, Trump addressed the largest audience of his life and presented the most important speech of his life. Many of those directly in front of him were his avid supporters, some wearing the campaign caps saying "Make America Great Again," and a handful, unfortunately, were booing and jeering Senate Minority Leader Chuck Schumer's call for respect of American diversity in his brief speech just before the oath of office was administered. And, of course, there were millions viewing the ceremony via television both in this nation and in the Western world. Yet the new President addressed the audience with a disapproval rating lower than the 46% of the vote he carried November 8. The challenge and goal for the speaker was to bring together a sense of hope, encouragement, and unity as one great nation of diverse citizens. The audience size that gathered was a large one, but modest compared to the Inaugurations of Barack Obama (a fact disputed the next day by the Trump staff). Everyone was aware there was an unprecedented influx of people who flocked to the nation's capital to protest his inauguration. Also, some sixty Democratic members of Congress chose to boycott the ceremony for reasons of their own. When Trump rose to speak, a light rain began to fall, but the speaker was not deterred or distracted—he had an audience of admirers in front of him and was surrounded by his wife, Melania, five children, their spouses, and grandchildren, and he had just been sworn in with the thirty-five word oath of office as administered by Chief Justice John Roberts. He was now, indeed, the new President of the nation as well as the proverbial "leader of the free world."

*Excerpt*: [After acknowledging former Presidents Carter, Bush, and Obama on the dais] "January 20, 1917, will be remembered as the day the people became the rulers of this nation again....For too long, a small group in our nation's capital has reaped the rewards of government while the people have borne the cost....For too many of our citizens, a different reality exists: Mothers and children trapped in poverty in our inner cities; rusted out factories scattered like tombstones across the landscape of our nation; an education system, flush with cash, but which leaves our young and beautiful students deprived of knowledge; and the crime and gangs and drugs that have stolen too many lives and robbed our country of so much unrealized potential. The American carnage stops right here and stops right now....At the bedrock of our politics will be a total allegiance to the United States of America, and through our loyalty to our country, we will rediscover our loyalty to each other. When you open your heart to patriotism, there is no room for prejudice...Together we will make America strong again. We will make America wealthy again. We will make America safe again. And, yes, together, we will make American great again."

*Impact*: As the 2016 presidential campaign was so unprecedented, in so many ways this sixteen-minute Inaugural Address was as well. Indeed, it is difficult to place a label on the speech. This was not a typical conservative Republican speech, though the President was elected as a Republican. Most observers labeled it a robust "nationalist" and "populist message" that was totally anti-government in tone. The picture he painted (with a broad brush) of the nation he would now lead was dire and gloomy. By one count, there were a dozen or so negative words and terms that had never been used in an Inaugural Address, such as "tombstones across the landscape" and "American carnage." Yet the new President concluded with a declaration of promise and hope of making America great again by putting "America first." He made a gesture toward unity, declaring: "When America is united, America is totally unstoppable."

One standard used by the rhetorical critic to determine greatness is the immediate response to a speech. On the positive side: For his millions of voters and supporters, President Trump sincerely and courageously delivered a stirring and candid assessment of the current political and cultural landscape of the USA. Though the speech was much like his nomination acceptance speech in its theme and tone, the presentation has been labeled his best rhetorical effort. He spoke with passion and his words were received as "heart-felt" by his supporters, especially when speaking of the "forgotten" men and women who would no longer be forgotten and ignored. The President enhanced his appeal as a forthright, courageous communicator of truth and relevance. Prior to this moment in history, to his followers Donald Trump projected an image of a man who can gets things done, and that strength of purpose and skill-set proven in the business and corporate world would be put to effective use in government. Perhaps Trump is, as he claimed in the address, leading "a historic movement the likes of which the world has never seen before."

On the negative side, however, the rhetorical critic must be fair and objective in pointing to some important weaknesses and omissions. First, it might be questioned as to whether the speaker accurately described the nation he was elected to serve. While there have been notorious and sensational instances of violent crime, the crime rate in the nation has been decreasing. Also, the economy has shown a recovery with an unemployment rate that is low by contemporary standards. And the U. S. military is stronger and more capable than the speaker seemed to allow. Second, there were broad and sweeping claims of what goals would be accomplished, none any greater, perhaps, than a pledge to eliminate "radical Islamic terrorism"—those three words never used by President Obama received enthusiastic applause. The stated priorities of bringing back jobs from foreign lands and securing the borders were simply promised without any nuanced hint of a policy strategy for accomplishing these goals. Third, though Congressional leaders sat behind him, there was no mention of appreciation for Congress or any expressed intention to work harmoniously with Republican and Democratic leaders in the legislative branch of government to achieve those goals. Despite proposing an FDR-style public works campaign to rebuild U. S. infrastructure, the new President did not suggest he needed anyone's help in accomplishing his grand goals. Fourth, and perhaps most important, the address was largely a polished presentation of the speaker's standard campaign speech. There was not the slightest mention of the millions of dedicated citizens who chose to vote for Hillary Clinton or another candidate, no gracious mention of the Democratic Party nor Clinton (who had amassed nearly three million more votes than Trump) as a hard-working, worthy opponent, and nothing positive or complimentary to utter about members of Congress. With a stinging criticism of government in recent years, it seemed to one observer that the new President was "trashing" everyone who was sitting behind him. At least there was no recognition of sincere efforts of many hard-working, well-intentioned men and women in public service. There was no sense of appreciation and healing for those who were hurt, offended, or afraid because of campaign rhetoric or the election results. By contrast, the brief speech that Trump delivered at the end of Election Day was much more gracious and noble, complimenting his opponent and declaring his desire to be president of all the American people—those passages did not make their way into this Inaugural Address.

Of course, perhaps the best standard to be met by a great speech is the long-range effect for lasting good upon the immediate audience and for generations to come. Manifestly, this address cannot be evaluated by that standard at this time. Perhaps indeed, President Trump is leading a movement that will re-shape the political and cultural life of the nation for good. Every newly-elected leader in such a crucially important position of power and authority deserves an opportunity to "rise above" all the doubts and negative criticism and accomplish great deeds. If such success happens, this Inaugural Address may be judged as one of the great speeches in our history. If that does not happen, well, let's not conjure some gloomy scenario for the future. How interesting indeed will be the narrative and judgment of future historians on this period in our nation's history!

*Contemporary Application*: Inauguration ceremonies are special moments in the life of the nation. The opportunity to recognize the differences between citizens politically, as well as all other kinds of differences, and then to witness a peaceful transfer of leadership power constitute a profound and memorable experience. People may disagree in deeply emotional ways, and yet the oratory of the ceremony can beckon them to ideals, hopes, and dreams that are far greater than their differences. Most of all, we must remember that speeches are important and publicly-uttered words matter deeply—they are tools that can bring hope and healing or sew strife and division!

*Interesting Fact*: There have been other occasions when a U. S. president-elect came to power when the nation was bitterly divided. President-elect Lincoln faced such a crisis with the secession threats and acrimonious sectional passions of 1861 that he had to sneak into Washington for fear of Confederate assassins. Richard Nixon's second Inauguration came in 1973 as the controversial and costly war in Vietnam raged on. Anger was a common ingredient among citizens in both 1861 and 1973, but Nixon, unlike Lincoln and Trump, had been re-elected in a landslide. Other new presidents have clashed with their predecessors.

# PART THREE

## FILLING GAPS IN THE AMERICAN RHETORICAL LANDSCAPE

# I. Not Quite a Traditional Public Speech, Yet Instructional, Persuasive, and Often Inspirational, Nonetheless

The history of the United States has been enriched, even altered, by a number of varied written documents with different styles and different goals of the author. Also, there have been official statements, songs, poems, or lesser known speeches that have made their mark on American history. Some of these written documents and oral declarations were meant to persuade, others to inspire, most of them to persuade in one way or the other. Over the years, many have been sung or recited without any serious thought as to meaning or origin of the text. The most important written document intended to persuade is listed first in this study—the Declaration of Independence. Much of the argumentation and supporting evidence had been stated in numerous political addresses and sermons prior to the Declaration, and the Declaration itself is indeed a rhetorical effort, as was Martin Luther King's "Letter from a Birmingham Jail."

The following written pieces were aimed at a more general reading audience, with some exception, and are simply cited here with a brief description of contents. (A few non-traditional spoken pieces are also included.) As we will see, some of these writers, poets, and composers were also public speakers whose speeches touched on the same themes of which they wrote. Indeed, passion and patriotism cannot be restricted to any one literary genre. Avoiding possible controversy over ranking them in order of importance and influence, they are simply listed in chronological order.

## The Mayflower Compact (1620)

*We whose names are underwritten…doe by these presents solemnly and mutualy in the presence of God, and one of another, covenant and combine our selves togeather into a civill body politick.*

After sixty-six days at sea, on November 11, 1620, the sailing ship *Mayflower* approached land with its passenger load of one hundred and two pilgrims. Though their destination was the area of the mouth of the Hudson River, rough seas pushed them to what is now Provincetown Harbor off Cape Cod. It seemed wise not to sail on to the intended point of debarkation. About a third of the passengers were members of an English separatist congregation that had withdrawn from the Church of England. They had first sought refuge in Leyden, the Netherlands, as an environment to practice religious freedom; this liberal environment, however, did not seem the best one to maintain religious beliefs and practices and safeguard the family as English rather than Dutch. These colonists, also called the Pilgrims, had negotiated an agreement with the Virginia Company of London to locate at a place of their choice with the company's vast holdings and to govern themselves.

Thoughtful Americans have always seen merit and security in drawing up documents or covenants and pledging themselves to uphold and maintain their commitments. Forty-one *Mayflower* male passengers signed a covenant later known as the "*Mayflower* Compact" while still on board their ship. The signers pledged to create a body politic that would be based on the consent of the governed and the rule of law; and they all agreed to submit to the laws framed by the new body politic. The compact was signed by heads of family, adult bachelors, and most hired manservants aboard the ship. Women had no political rights, thus were not asked or expected to sign. Both separatists and non-separatists signed.

On the day after Christmas, the one hundred and two colonist adventurers disembarked at what is now Plymouth, and those who had signed the compact became the governing body of the Plymouth colony with the power to pass laws, elect officers, and admit new voting members. Indeed, self-government and the rule of law had been established in the New World—at least a world that was new to the settlers. The "*Mayflower* Compact" has been considered by historians as the first constitution written in North America.

## Benjamin Franklin, *Poor Richard's Almanac* (1733–1758)

*Early to bed and early to rise, makes a man healthy, wealthy, and wise.*
*Fish and visitors stink in three days.*
*He that lies down with the dogs, shall rise up with the fleas.*
*One today is worth two tomorrows.*
*No gains without pains.*

Benjamin Franklin (1705–1790) was truly one of the most remarkable Americans who ever lived: author, printer, editor, civic leader, philosopher, scientist, politician, inventor, humorist, entrepreneur, shopkeeper, statesman, diplomat, counselor, and public servant—have we left out any role? He wore all those hats. All the labels fit, though, interestingly, he was not known as a stirring orator. Nonetheless, he garnered so much respect and admiration that when he spoke, people listened. Though born in Boston as the fifteenth of a candle maker's seventeen children, and failing to get along with a half-brother named James, he moved to Philadelphia and found employment as a printer, quickly gaining the confidence of the most powerful men in that community. After a trip to London in 1724, Franklin returned to Philadelphia and began a diverse, multi-faceted career of professional and community service in so many roles—too many to discuss in detail here. He served in the Second Continental Congress, served on the committee formed to draft the Declaration, and was sent to Paris to negotiate an alliance with the French. During his lifetime, he was truly one of the most famous men in the world.

Franklin's almanacs, published pseudonymously in Philadelphia as the work of a fictional Richard Saunders (thus, "Poor Richard") appeared annually from 1733 to 1758. The almanacs were immensely popular among colonists and they contained a variety of information much like their successors—weather predictions, calendars, advice, recipes, and other useful information. Poor Richard's proverbs, maxims, and adages were sometimes original from a man who lived a full and fascinating life, and sometimes they were not, but they served as a vehicle for Franklin's open-minded, pragmatic, cheerful philosophy and wit. Franklin is so frequently quoted in every successive generation of Americans. Quite likely, some of his proverbs and wise sayings are better known than ones in the Bible's Book of Proverbs.

## Thomas Paine, *Common Sense* (1776)

*But Britain is the parent company, say some. Then the more shame upon her conduct. Even brutes do not devour their young, nor savages make war upon their families…small islands not capable of protecting themselves are the proper objects for kingdoms to take under their care; but there is something very absurd in supposing a continent to be perpetually governed by an island. In no instance hath nature made the satellite larger than its primary planet…*

*it is evident they belong to different systems. England to Europe: America to itself...O ye that love mankind! Ye that dare oppose not only tyranny but the tyrant, stand forth!*

Thomas Paine (1737–1809) was born in England to a poor Quaker-Anglican family and left school at thirteen to work with his father as a corset maker. After meeting with Benjamin Franklin in London, he came to the colonies in late 1774 and secured an editing job with the *Pennsylvania Magazine*. Of course, this was a time in which tensions between the colonies and the mother country were building to a high point, and Paine was all too anxious to leap into the fray. After the Lexington and Concord military scuffles between the patriots and England, on April 17, 1775, Paine concluded that the revolt need not focus on unjust taxation alone but advocate full independence. He then spelled out his arguments in *Common Sense*, an anonymously-penned fifty-page pamphlet that was published January 10, 1776.

Paine portrayed the American Revolution as a world event, an epoch-making step in the history of humankind. The author laid out his arguments for independence in simple, yet eloquent, and, at times, melodramatic prose. He reduced the idea of hereditary succession of kings to an absurdity, refuted all arguments for reconciliation with England, and argued the economic benefits of independence. The little book was an immediate sensation with more than 100,000 copies printed and sold within three months and possibly as many as a half million altogether, to a colonial population of around two and a half million people—truly a literary and political success. *Common Sense* demonstrated the power of written rhetoric to persuade mass public opinion and build the case for total independence from Great Britain.

## Thomas Jefferson, A Bill for Establishing Religious Freedom in Virginia (1779)

*We the General Assembly of Virginia do enact that no man shall be compelled to frequent or support any religious worship, place, or ministry whatsoever, nor shall be enforced, restrained, molested, or burthened in his body or goods, or shall otherwise suffer, on account of his religious opinions or beliefs.*

Thomas Jefferson, a product of Enlightenment philosophy, was more radical in his beliefs about freedom than either Franklin or Washington. He was passionately committed to the principle of the free mind, inveighing against "every form of tyranny over the mind of man." He was cognizant of the human costs of religious prejudice, even and especially from loyal Christian activists and soldiers, who had created hatred and bloodshed for centuries. In 1779 Jefferson offered this statute for religious freedom in the Virginia legislature though it was not officially adopted till several years later. Nonetheless, it was landmark legislation guaranteeing every citizen the freedom to worship in the church of one's choice and ending state support for the Episcopal Church in Virginia. The bill, passed thanks to the efforts of James Madison, is important as a precursor of the First Amendment to our Constitution, which prohibits the Congress from establishing a religion or interfering with the free exercise of religion. Jefferson had also once produced an edited version of the New Testament Gospels (*a.k.a. The Jefferson Bible*) in which he highlighted the moral and ethical teaching of Jesus while deleting any reference to divinity or miracles.

Interestingly, the epitaph Jefferson wrote for his tombstone reads: "Here was buried Thomas Jefferson, author of the Declaration of Independence, of the statute of Virginia for Religious Freedom, and father of the University of Virginia." Apparently, he did not think his eight years as president of the nation merited mention.

## James Madison, Alexander Hamilton, and John Jay, *The Federalist Papers*, 1787–1788

*A Republic, by which I mean a Government in which the scheme of representation takes place, opens a different prospect, and promises the cure for which we are seeking. Let us examine the points in which it varies from pure Democracy, and we shall comprehend both the nature of the cure, and the efficacy which it must derive from the Union.*—James Madison, *Federalist Paper* No. 10 (1787)

References to the U. S. Constitution by a wide range of contemporary American political leaders and office-seekers seem as common as preachers' references to the Holy Bible. Even though both political leaders and ordinary citizens have varying interpretations of the meaning of the Constitution or some of its provisions, the document is treated as sacrosanct, almost as American Ten Commandments divinely inspired and etched in stone. So it is difficult to imagine that the current Constitution was almost aborted before it could be born and accepted by the new nation. In fact, when the Founders left

Philadelphia in 1787 having completed the drafting of this document, the country was almost evenly divided between those favoring a strong national government (citizens who came to be known as Federalists) and those who favored a limited national government and stronger states' rights (the Anti-Federalists). A total of nine states had to ratify the new Constitution before it could become the official law of the nation. Delaware, Pennsylvania, and New Jersey instantly ratified the document, but the issue was hotly contested in two important key states: Virginia and New York.

The greatest political debate in the history of this new nation occurred during the fall and winter of 1787 and 1788. The issue: The merits of the newly proposed national Constitution. This debate engaged some of the most brilliant political philosophers of the generation and their rhetoric raised issues about the promise and the perils of a strong national government that have confronted subsequent generations. The Anti-Federalists, composed of loyal Americans and staunch patriots (many were Revolutionary leaders and veterans, such as Patrick Henry and Samuel Adams) feared a new breed of elected monarchy at the expense of individual liberties. To these patriots, a stable republican government was based on a small, homogeneous population; a huge nation with strong national power seemed an unlikely candidate for lasting success.

To convince New York voters to ratify, Alexander Hamilton, James Madison, and John Jay collaborated on a series of essays collectively called *The Federalist Papers*, published in various newspapers in New York under the pseudonym "Publius." The Anti-Federalists marshalled telling arguments, for sure, against giving the new national government too much power. *The Federalist Papers*, however, constituted a brilliant logical defense of the proposed Constitution. Eighty-five of these essays were published, and now these are considered among the most significant political documents in American history, surpassed only by the Declaration of Independence and the U. S. Constitution itself.

*The Federalist Papers* did sway concerned citizens in New York, for sure, but their immediate influence on ratification might be questioned. Perhaps of greater impact was the pro-ratification stance of America's two most prominent men, Benjamin Franklin and George Washington, combined with the addition of a Bill of Rights which assuaged concerns about national power intruding on personal liberties.

The most important essay, perhaps, is Number Ten, which pierced to the very heart of the most compelling Anti-Federalist argument: The nation is too big and diverse to be regulated by a central government. James Madison challenged this traditional thought, arguing that because the United States is so large, no single interest group or faction could possibly dominate the national government. A chief theme of the *Federalist* essays was the efficacy of a checks and balances system that would stymie the greed and lust for power in a big nation-state. Interestingly, the vote for ratification was so close in most of the new states and aggressive speechmaking and private negotiating and "buttonholing" for key votes all combined with this written rhetoric to carry the day for the new Constitution.

## *Virginia and Kentucky Resolutions* (1798)

In the early days of the Republic, federal power was dominated by Federalists. In 1788 opponents of the Constitution had warned that granting extensive powers to the national government would endanger freedom. As the next decade passed, and Federalists controlled all branches of government, their prediction seemed validated. A system of checks and balances, along with the Bill of Rights, did not seem to guarantee protection of individual liberties. There was renewed interest, with a sense of urgency, in the doctrine of states' rights.

Recognizing they were holding a minority point of view in political philosophy, Thomas Jefferson and James Madison anonymously wrote manifestos on states' rights known as the *Virginia and Kentucky Resolutions*, adopted respectively by the legislatures of those states in 1798. Madison repudiated his position at the constitutional convention, arguing that state legislatures never surrendered their right to judge the constitutionality of federal legislation and actions, and that they retained an authority called *interposition* to protect the liberties of their citizens. Jefferson's resolution for Kentucky went even further by declaring that ultimate authority rested with the states, not the national government. True, no other state adopted these resolutions, but their passage was an early warning of the great potential for disunion as early as the late 1790s.

These resolutions, by two outstanding political thinkers of that generation, provided the ideological foundation for John Calhoun, specifically, and for supporters of the Confederacy during the later years of secession and Civil War.

## Francis Scott Key, The Defense of Fort McHenry/"The Star Spangled Banner" (1814)

*Oh, say, does that star-spangled banner yet wave*
*O'er the land of the free, and the home of the brave!*

Over two centuries have passed now since a Washington attorney, along with a government official named John S. Skinner, were detained on a truce-seeking and prisoner exchange mission and confined to a British troop ship during its assault on an American fort guarding Baltimore. Just two weeks earlier the British had burned down Washington D. C. and threatened to do the same to Baltimore, or at least burn the fort protecting the harbor. Key and Skinner sailed with that British fleet and watched helplessly as the British first invaded near Baltimore, then bombarded Ft. McHenry during the night of September 13 and 14. Key became the person of national destiny and history. Through the haze and smoke of bombardment, they could dimly see a huge American flag waving over the fort's ramparts. When the bombardment ended and dawn was arriving, Key and Skinner focused their gaze to see if the flag was still flying over the fort, a clear indication that forces in the very young nation—only twenty-seven years old—had not surrendered to the British. To their relief, the stars and stripes were still waving. While awaiting their release, Key began collecting his thoughts and making notes for a poem, and on the evening of September 16, he composed the poem in a Baltimore hotel, recreating the events and the joy of what that meant to him and others.

The next day the poem, entitled "Defense of Fort McHenry," was circulated in Baltimore. A month later, the poem was retitled "The Star Spangled Banner" and set to the tune "To Anacreon in Heaven," which supposedly was well known to Key and, indeed, the poet may have had that melody in mind when he wrote it. Days later, the song was performed in the Baltimore Theater. The song was not destined to become our national anthem until another one hundred and seventeen years later, accomplished by an executive order by President Woodrow Wilson in 1916, and then adopted by Congress in 1931.

Since this momentous military event and the poem that celebrated it, the flag has taken on a near-sacred meaning. Before the night of September 13, 1814, the flag had been thought of solely in terms of utilitarian value—a marker raised to identify government buildings and military installations. After the British navy's failure to capture the fort, the American flag was destined to become a symbol of liberty, freedom, and perseverance for American citizens and their military. That flag has necessarily been redesigned over the decades to add new stars, but seldom if ever has it been raised at momentous times in history without eliciting chill bumps and tears. Rather than simply a marker, it has the aura of sacred cloth—raised in parades, sporting events, cemeteries, battlefields, dedications, school campuses, conferences, and meetings of all kinds. And so often in its raising, Key's words are put to music, and loyal citizens may sing along or perhaps even pledge their allegiance to that flag and "to the nation for which it stands."

Key's poetic words are truly ones that inspire, even if still there remains a bit of irony. One irony is that American youngsters and older folk too can utter the words being sung, but have no idea of the historical context and origin of the song or even the meaning of some of the words, such as "ramparts" and "star spangled." The vast majority could not quote two lines from any other stanza of the song or even know that there are three other stanzas. Most Americans may not be aware of how long the poem and music were performed along with many popular patriotic songs, such as "Hail, Columbia" and "America," without actually being a national anthem. "The Star Spangled Banner" gained favor with Union troops during the Civil War and became more popular in subsequent decades. Around the turn of the century, Army and Naval leadership set regulations that required its being played as part of flag raising and lowering and other color rituals. This all combined to enhance sentiment that the poetic song needed official status.

Yes, this American national anthem has garnered more than its share of critics. A chief criticism has been the difficulty of the musical score for most people to sing, for both the general public and even professional singers. Other critics claim the song is low quality poetry, far too militaristic and, hence, does not capture the essence of the nation, and deals only with a one-day incident in a little known and almost inconsequential war. Why not choose "America the Beautiful" in its place?

From the perspective of the rhetorical critic, none of these criticisms is relevant to understanding the evocative power of this anthem. When one listens to a video replay of the late Whitney Houston's rendition of the anthem, or stands in a throng of almost 100,000 in a football stadium and hears the anthem with a uniformed color guard raising the American flag and Air Force jets flying a timed maneuver over the stadium at the crescendo of the anthem, then no cognitive experience is occurring—the tearful, goose-bumpy, patriotic feeling is all that matters!

Now, an addendum: "The Star Spangled Banner" has been a standard ritual before nearly all professional sporting events in this nation since World War II, and professional sports leaders have made a determined effort to associate their franchises with love of the nation. None has succeeded with quite as much color and pageantry than the National Football League, whose product in American stadiums is the most-viewed sport in the nation. Little wonder there was such controversy when San Francisco Forty-Niners quarterback Colin Kaepernick, in pre-season and regular games, refused to stand and salute while that anthem was being played and/or sung during pre-game ceremonies. At first, Kaepernick's protest of police killings of unarmed black men was widely criticized as an act of selfish, unpatriotic, and immature behavior; critics claimed this athlete had chosen the wrong venue for protest, however sincere he may have been. Within a few weeks, however, other players joined him in this style of protest—from professional football players to high school players. Then, thoughtful observers reminded the general public of other black athletes, from Muhammad Ali to the U. S. Olympic athletes in the 1968 games in Mexico City, who had gone against the grain of public opinion to protest a war, protest social injustice, or simply offer a black power salute.

Protesters have contended they are not simply rejecting the nation itself but using the most effective venue available to send a memorable message. The bottom line for students of rhetoric and public address: Whether locking arms, holding up a fist, taking a knee—communication is all about the effective use of symbols and symbols have meaning!

## Alexis de Tocqueville, *Democracy in America* (1835)

Alexis Charles Henri Clerel de Tocqueville (1805–1859) was a young French magistrate and aristocrat who arrived in America in 1831 with his friend Gustave de Beaumont for the purpose of examining American democracy. They entertained the desire to understand how the American experience could possibly shape the developing democratic spirit in France and the rest of Europe. Tocqueville and Beaumont spent nine months traveling the nation, gathering facts and interviewing Americans from President Andrew Jackson to frontier people and Indians.

When Tocqueville visited the United States, more than two-thirds of all Americans lived on farms, and only ten percent lived in cities or towns with populations larger than 2,500. The overwhelming majority of white males owned property and worked for themselves rather than for wages. Tocqueville was impressed with the relative absence of extremes of both great wealth and great poverty. The modest prosperity of the large middle class provided evidence of equality

When Tocqueville returned home, he put together his report on his visit, his personal observations, and his personal explorations, and the book appeared in two volumes and was entitled *Democracy in America*. Tocqueville made equality the central theme of his insightful report. With his keen insight into the American character, the book became a classic and has been studied as a basic analysis of the American character in the early nineteenth century.

Tocqueville admired the republican system, but he found a number of shortcomings. He wrote about the "general equality of condition among the people" he encountered. He noted there were class differences but the lines were not as rigidly or permanently drawn as class lines were drawn in Europe. He felt the young nation ran the risk of a social leveling that would result in a reign of mediocrity, conformity, and the "tyranny of the majority." Perhaps he was never more "off base" than in his assessment of the presidency as a weak office or that the Union would fall as a result of regional conflict. He was quite astute in his observation that the young nation had an addiction to the pragmatic rather than philosophical matters and that Americans possessed a single-minded and relentless pursuit of wealth. He also forecast a future competition would arise between the United States and Russia. He was also sensitive and even prophetic in his observation that Indians who were being forced off their native homelands would "have no longer a country, and soon will not be a people."

Much changed in the generations after Tocqueville toured the country and wrote about his observations and analysis. The North began to industrialize, urban areas grew much faster than rural areas, and the gap between the wealthy and poor began to widen radically. The Civil War demonstrated how deeply sectionalism ran in the young nation. By the 1890s, no American could deny that Tocqueville's republic of equality had passed away. Nonetheless, *Democracy in America* has given for every generation since the 1830s an insightful look at political and social life in the new nation. As an aside, Tocqueville returned to France, but with Napoleon's coup he decided he could not bring himself to serve under a usurper and despot, and thus retired from political life and returned to his castle. After bouts with tuberculosis, he eventually succumbed to the disease.

# Henry David Thoreau, *Civil Disobedience* (1849)

*Under a government which imprisons any unjustly, the true place for a just man is also in prison.*

Perhaps all of us can imagine a man or woman who is quite gifted with artistic ability and keen insights into the human nature or the natural world, one who is able to think, study, and write, and yet that person earns only a meager remuneration for expression of these ideas. Such was the case of Henry David Thoreau (1817–1862), a gifted philosopher, essayist, poet, naturalist, and reformer. Yet he was not solely a "Poet-Naturist"—he was one of the most profound scholars of his day and widely educated (Greek was his second language and oriental philosophers and religious leaders were known to him through French and German versions). Since his death, Thoreau has been elevated as a patron saint for two movements: civil disobedience and environmentalism.

Thoreau was born in Concord, Massachusetts, and graduated from Harvard College. After a few years teaching school, he determined to make poetry and writing about nature his calling and life work. Along with Ralph Waldo Emerson, whom he respected, Thoreau was a leading figure in the American transcendentalist movement. This movement shunned absolutism and authoritarianism and elevated intuition and personal sensory experience over reason and logic. The movement valued individual integrity and wholeness, which moved followers to meaningful societal reform.

Thoreau's publications did not sell sufficiently to provide the author a livable wage, thus he supplemented his income by working in his family pencil-making business. In 1845, at the age of twenty-eight, he determined to liberate himself from so many mundane concerns of ordinary life and, with Emerson's support, built a small cabin on the land that Emerson owned on Walden Pond, a couple of miles from Concord. Like the Shakers and early Quakers, Thoreau had chosen simplicity and thrift as spiritual values.

While living at Walden Pond, a year later, the local constable approached Thoreau about paying his Massachusetts state poll tax of $1.50, a citizen's duty that had been neglected for several years. Thoreau respectfully refused payment. The constable then locked him up for the night in the local jail. The next day, an unidentified person, likely a family member (probably his aunt Maria), paid the tax, and he was released the next morning.

As with many other thoughtful American citizens, including Abraham Lincoln, Thoreau objected both to the practice of slavery and to the nation waging an imperialist war against Mexico. Thus, he prepared a lecture that he presented to audiences and later turned the lecture into an essay to explain his non-compliance. The essay was entitled "Resistance to Civil Government" and it was published in 1849. Thoreau described his action as a moral protest against immoral government practices: the return of escaped slaves, the war against Mexico, and the treatment of American Indians. Interestingly, there is no evidence that Thoreau ever used the expression "civil disobedience" in his life. He did not invoke the federal Constitution to sanction the violation of a state stature, and the only "higher laws" that he cared about were the eternal principles of morality.

At the time of publication, this essay attracted little attention. Decades passed. By the end of the nineteenth century, however, "On Civil Disobedience" had become a classic document with an international following. The essay has been read and admired by respected thinkers and reformers throughout the twentieth century, including Leo Tolstoy, and Mohandas K. Gandhi, who read it while serving as a lawyer in South Africa, Martin Luther King, opponents of South African apartheid, and others who have used its guiding principles in their own civil disobedience and passive resistance to unjust laws. Thus, seminal ideas have a way of trickling down to other generations and into the minds of thinkers and reformers, thereby laying an ideological foundation in the fight for social justice. Yes, we may rightly draw a link between this seminal American essay and the fight for Indian independence from Great Britain as well as the American Civil Rights Movement.

In the two years at Walden Pond, Thoreau possessed the time to think about what was important in life and to write his reflections. "I went to the woods because I wished to live deliberately," he wrote in his essay "Walden," "to front only the essential facts of life, and see if I could not learn what it had to teach, and not, when I came to die, discover that I had not lived." And what drove this passion? From the same essay is, perhaps, his most familiar quotation: "The mass of men lead lives of quiet desperation. What is called resignation is confirmed desperation."

## Harriet Beecher Stowe, *Uncle Tom's Cabin* (1852)

In a time when slavery was too often discussed in dry, almost academic terminology that seemed to circumvent people's deepest emotions, a story appeared in serial form in the *National Era*, an abolitionist journal. In 1852 a Boston publisher bought out the book in its complete form and published the novel, at once simplistic and often melodramatic, but also deeply affecting. The novel was soon to have a great impact on the nation, citizens of both the North and the South. *Uncle Tom's Cabin, or Life Among the Lowly* was destined to touch the masses with a story that humanized the issue of slavery as no amount of congressional debate or abolitionist literature was able to accomplish.

Harriett Beecher Stowe (1811–1896) was the daughter, wife, and sister of Protestant clergymen. Her father, Lyman Beecher, was a noted Calvinist minister who moved his family to Cincinnati, where he headed Lane Seminary; there, Harriett Beecher met and married Calvin Stowe, a professor of biblical literature. One brother became one of the nation's best known and loved ministers, Henry Ward Beecher, and sister Catharine was a courageous reform activist and speaker. The seminary was a hotbed of abolitionist sentiment, and a trip to Kentucky just across the Ohio River provided the young woman with her only firsthand glimpse of slavery. Yet she had heard others tell firsthand experiences and possessed a terrific sense of imagination to write a gripping story that stirred strong emotions in the reader.

The story begins with a Kentucky slave holder reluctantly forced by financial ruin to sell some of his slaves. Among them are the son of two mulatto slaves, George and Eliza Harris, and an older slave, Tom. Eliza escapes across an ice-filled Ohio River, clutching her son as slave catchers and their bloodhounds pursue them. Tom submits to being sold to a New Orleans master, but later winds up on a plantation owned by Simon Legree, a vicious and sadistic master. Tom is a devout Christian who attempts to maintain his dignity through all the degradations he suffers in hopes of being reunited with his family. Thus, Tom remains obedient and loyal until Legree asks him to whip another slave; Tom refuses, then Legree beats him to death. Similar themes get played out in the 2014 "Best Picture" *12 Years a Slave*.

The story, while based on caricatures just like many movies on slavery, aimed to evoke emotions in readers. Stowe put a human face on human bondage. She did not offer abstractions or academic argument, but described characters who seemed real. The major themes of American slavery all emerged: the denial of freedom; the broken family; the Christian martyr; the strength of family love and commitment; the evidence of widespread interracial and extramarital sex; and the wrestling with conscience.

For Southerners, *Uncle Tom's Cabin* was a damnable lie, political propaganda disguised as legitimate literature. Some Southerners retaliated with plays and novels of their own wherein no slave families were broken up, no slaves were killed, and all masters were the paradigm of compassionate Christian behavior. For Northerners, the book was eye-opening, too. The novel put a vivid face on slavery; it changed people's moral perception about this "peculiar institution" in an era of deep Protestant piety. The rhetoric of abolitionism no longer seemed extremist as many northerners had previously considered. Black Northerners praised the novel, and Frederick Douglass embraced it as a literary work "plainly marked by the finger of God" on behalf of African-Americans.

Sales of the book reached 300,000 within a year. Once foreign translations were published throughout Europe, sales soon afterward exceeded one and a half million, a staggering number for the mid-nineteenth century. And while sales can be estimated fairly accurately, the emotional impact is not calculated so easily. One anecdote sums up that impact: In 1862 President Lincoln met Harriett Beecher Stowe, during the midst of the Civil War conflict, and reportedly exclaimed, "So you're the woman that wrote the book that made this great war." Safe to say, no other literary work since Thomas Paine's *Common Sense* had wielded the political and social impact of *Uncle Tom's Cabin*.

## John Brown, Last Statement to the Court, November 2, 1859

*I believe to have interfered as I have done...in behalf of His despised poor, I did no wrong, but right.*

The above declaration captured the essence of a final statement to the court and the general public from the nation's best known abolitionist zealot, who considered himself anointed by the Lord to avenge the sins of slaveholders.

John Brown (1800–1859) was born in Connecticut, but his large family (he fathered twenty children) moved from place to place in several states and sought a successful vocation in several lines of work—farmer, merchant, tanner, wool merchant, and land speculator. Yet the abiding passion of his life was personal hatred of slavery. Brown had never shared the commitment of most abolitionists to nonviolence. His "God" was the deity who drove the moneychangers out of the temple, who drowned Pharaoh's army in the Red Sea, who drove the Canaanites out of the Promised Land; and his favorite scripture was Hebrews 9: 22—"Without the shedding of blood, there is no remission of sin." To Brown, bondage was "a most barbarous, unprovoked, and unjustifiable war" of masters against slaves.

Brown felt called by God to migrate to Kansas, joining several of his sons, when he learned of civil strife over slavery in that territory and of the murder of several free-state settlers and the sack of Lawrence. Armed conflict between the two factions, pro-slavery and free-staters, gave rise to the term "Bleeding Kansas." In retaliation of crimes against free-staters, Brown led four of his sons and three other men to a pro-slavery settlement at Pottawatomie Creek on the night of May 24-25, where Brown dragged five settlers from their cabins and split open their heads with broadswords. To him, this was Old Testament-style retribution—an eye for an eye. He conducted another raid two years later in Missouri, where he killed a slaveholder and liberated eleven slaves, fleeing with them to Canada.

Brown spent months studying guerilla warfare and the history of slave insurrections, so he decided to take his war against slavery into "Babylon"—the South. In October 1859, with a small militia of five black men and seventeen whites (including three of his sons), Brown seized the arsenal at Harpers Ferry, Virginia (now West Virginia). Brown expected to arm the local slaves, who would join his rebellion, but none did. The raiders were captured in a bloody battle with state and federal troops led, interestingly enough, by Colonel Robert E. Lee and Lieutenant J. E. B. Stuart. The raid was a tactical miscalculation. Four townsmen, one marine, and ten of Brown's men (including two of his sons) were killed—and not a single slave was liberated.

The raid had lasted for thirty-six hours, but its repercussion resounded for years. In that sense, perhaps the raid was an emotional success for Brown, even if an alarm bell for Southerners who feared that Brown had other cohorts willing to step to the forefront and lead any number of slave insurrections. The raid certainly captured the nation's attention. Brown was convicted of treason, murder, and fomenting insurrection. Five of his fellow guerilla soldiers escaped, but the rest were either killed during the raid or hanged. Brown was convicted on November 2nd and hanged a month later.

Brown's final statement to the court, delivered when the sentence was pronounced, was reprinted the next day in the *New York Herald*. Radical abolitionists treated it almost as though it were sacred scripture. Many Northerners, impressed by Brown's dignified bearing and eloquence during his trial, considered him a martyr to freedom.

"I see a book kissed, which I suppose to be a Bible, or at least the New Testament, which teaches me that all things whatsoever I would that men should do to me, I should do even so to them," Brown declared to the court. "It teaches me further to remember them that are in bonds as bound with them. I endeavored to act up to that instruction. I say I am yet too young to understand that God is any respecter persons. I believe that to have interfered as I have done, as I have always freely admitted I have done, in behalf of his despised poor, I did no wrong, but right. Now, if it is deemed necessary that I should forfeit my life for the furtherance of the ends of justice, and mingle my blood further with the blood of my children and with the blood of millions in this slave country whose rights are disregarded by wicked, cruel, and unjust enactments, I say, let it be done." Brown closed his statement by saying he felt "entirely satisfied with the treatment I have received on my trial."

On the day of his execution, John Brown was hailed as a saint and a hero throughout the North, as bells tolled in hundreds of Northern towns, guns fired salutes, and ministers preached sermons of commemoration. "The death of no man in America has ever produced so profound a sensation," commented one Northern citizen, and the literary genius and philosopher Ralph Waldo Emerson declared Brown had made "the gallows as glorious as the cross." Meantime, in the South, every Yankee was deemed a possible "John Brown" and every slave who acted suspiciously seemed to be an insurrectionist. Political leaders in the South instructed their constituents to be ready to defend themselves. Indeed the crisis seemed moving inexorably toward war.

## Julia Ward Howell, "Battle Hymn of the Republic" (1861)

*Mine eyes have seen the glory of the coming of the Lord;*
*He is trampling out the vintage where the grapes of wrath are stored;*
*He hath loosed the fateful lightning of His terrible swift sword.*
*His truth is marching on. Glory, glory, hallelujah!*

One November day in 1861, Julia Ward Howe (1819–1919) visited Washington D. C. with her husband, Dr. Samuel Gridley Howe, a prominent Massachusetts reformer. The Howes observed army maneuvers south of the Potomac and had joined the soldiers in singing the popular "John Brown's Body." A companion suggested she write new lyrics for the marching song. According to Howe's account, she rose before dawn, located a pen and paper, and was inspired to write "Battle Hymn of the Republic" while the couple's infant daughter slept nearby. To people such as Howe and Harriett Beecher Stowe, the Civil War was a righteous cause in which the Almighty God was using this terrible carnage and pain to exact justice for national sins and eventually free men and women who were still in bondage. The poem was published anonymously in *The Atlantic Monthly* in February 1862. The song soon elicited great praise from literary figures such as Henry Wadsworth Longfellow, William Cullen Bryant, and Ralph Waldo Emerson.

The significance of this hymn: It was immediately embraced by the Union army as its marching song and has been sung by American troops in the Spanish-American War, World War I, and World War II. It was the only Civil War song that eventually rose above sectionalism to become a truly national song. The song has been played and sung innumerable times in churches and patriotic gatherings, and could easily vie for a national anthem. The words are familiar to many who sing it, but who have no knowledge as to the overall message of the song or the context in which the song was written and first played and sung. Most who sing it might say that, in some providential sense, the Almighty God is carrying out justice and truth through a terrible military conflict. The song is still referenced in literature, films, and other facets of popular culture. The song's popularity and durability can be attributed not simply to its upbeat music, but to lyrics that are simultaneously religious, patriotic, and celebrative of a freedom and liberty worthy of men dying "to make men free."

*Little Known Facts:* "Battle Hymn of the Republic" has been played in the funerals of several presidents, as well as that of Sir Winston Churchill. The last words of Martin Luther King's last public sermon before his death were "Mine eyes have seen the glory of the coming of the Lord." The most recent occasion for the song's being played and sung was the conclusion of a moving memorial service honoring five Dallas police officers who were ambushed during a protest march; the service, addressed by President Obama, was conducted July 12, 2016.

## Helen Hunt Jackson, *A Century of Dishonor* (1881)

*Cheating, robbing, breaking promises—these three are clearly things which must cease to be done. One more thing, also, and that is the refusal of the protection of the law to the Indian's rights of property, "of life, liberty, and the pursuit of happiness." When these four things have ceased to be done, time, statesmanship, philanthropy, and Christianity can slowly and surely do the rest. Till these four things have ceased to be done, statesmanship and philanthropy alike must work in vain, and even Christianity can reap but small harvest.*

Helen Hunt Jackson (1830–1885) was born in Amherst, Massachusetts, and became a conventional wife and mother during early adulthood. Her father taught philosophy and Latin at Amherst College, and she was a neighbor and lifelong friend of Emily Dickinson. She was truly a well-educated young lady when she married an army officer, Edward B. Hunt, and the couple gave birth to two sons. Eleven years later, however,

Helen Hunt experienced a series of sad losses, from the death of her first son, the death of her husband in an accident, and the death of the second son. In her despair, she began writing poems and essays for magazine publications. In 1875 she married William S. Jackson, and the couple settled in Colorado Springs. Jackson had a reformer's heart, and living in the West was a factor in her developing an intense interest in Native Americans.

Jackson embarked on thorough research of the subject of U. S. government and Indian affairs. Though there was talk in the 1870s of bringing reform to the Indian policies, a number of sad and tragic events occurred: pursuit and relocation of the Nez Perces in 1877; the uprooting of the Ponea tribe to make room for new Sioux reservations the same year, and the desperate flight in 1878 of some three hundred Northern Cheyenne from a reservation in Indian Territory. Hunt described these tragic events in moving terms in her book, *A Century of Dishonor*. "The tale of the wrongs, the oppressions, the murders of the Pacific-slope Indians in the last thirty years," she wrote "is too monstrous to be believed."

In the late nineteenth century, members of Congress generally reflected the view of most Americans: They wanted to "civilize" Indians and have them live peaceful and sedentary lives on fixed plots of land, be self-supporting, practice Christianity, accept their living conditions, yet be ready to comply with any ordinance to relocate to another piece of real estate if demanded by "progress." Hunt exposed this injustice with poignant and eloquent language. In quoting a commission report to President Grant: "The history of the Government connections with the Indians is a shameful record of broken treaties and unfulfilled promises. The history of the border, white man's connection with the Indians is a sickening record of murder, outrage, robbery, and wrongs committed by the former, as the rule, and occasional savage outbreaks and unspeakably barbarous deeds of retaliation, as the exception." Jackson sent a copy of *A Century of Dishonor* to every member of Congress.

## The Pledge of Allegiance (1892)

In any book purporting to discuss American oral communication, consider, then, there is a brief statement that has been uttered in unison by literally millions of citizens over the past century and even longer. The authorship of the pledge has been disputed. Surely every reader has recited these thirty-one words on numerous occasions. The pledge first appeared in a magazine, *The Youth's Companion*, on September 8, 1892, as part of a national commemoration of the four-hundredth anniversary of Christopher Columbus' voyage to the "New World," at least a world new to him and other Europeans. James B. Upham and Francis Bellamy, both being editors of *The Youth's Companion*, claimed credit. A report from the U. S. Library of Congress in 1957 supported Bellamy as the author.

Soon after appearing in the magazine, the pledge was widely adopted for use in patriotic rituals in schools. Originally it was recited as: "I pledge allegiance to my Flag and the Republic for which it stands: one nation indivisible, with liberty and justice for all." In 1924 the words "the flag of the United States of America" were substituted for "my flag." In 1942 the United States government accorded official recognition to the pledge. President Dwight D. Eisenhower led Congress to pass legislation that added the phrase "under God" after the words "one nation..." This change came in the midst of a Cold War where many Americans felt the nation was in a major ideological battle with "godless communism," and this was one way to affirm and declare the religious and spiritual commitment of American citizenry.

The pledge has been the subject of debate and controversy. A few Christians believe that the pledge can be an act of idolatry because only God deserves such a pledge of allegiance; a larger group of Christians believe the pledge, along with display of a flag, should not be recited during a church service (even if July Fourth falls on a Sunday as did the bicentennial). Then, many atheists object to the phrase "one nation *under God*" for understandable reasons. Like many rituals, the recitation of the pledge may have little substantive impact on the behavior of those who recite it, but it may give a reassuring feeling that the right ritual was done at the appropriate moment.

## John Marshall Harlan, Dissent From *Plessy v. Ferguson* (1896)

*In view of the Constitution, in the eye of the law, there is in this country no superior, dominant, ruling class of citizens. There is no caste here. Our Constitution is color-blind, and neither knows nor tolerates classes among citizens.*

Although the Declaration of Independence had heralded the premise as "self-evident" truth that "all men are created equal," it soon became obvious, in the words of George Orwell, "some men are created more equal than others." Racial inequality was attacked in several ways in the nineteenth century, including the Emancipation Proclamation, the

Thirteenth Amendment that outlawed slavery in 1865, and the Fourteenth Amendment in 1868. Despite these enactments, neither the myth of white supremacy nor the fact of color prejudice was wiped out. After radical Republican Reconstruction, whites regained control of Southern legislatures and enacted Jim Crow laws to enforce racial segregation and discrimination. When it came to civil rights in race relations, both the law and common practice followed the doctrine of "separate but equal."

An important test case occurred when *Plessy v. Ferguson* came to the highest court in the nation. At issue was the constitutionality of a Louisiana law mandating racial segregation of rail passengers in transportation. Eight of the nine Supreme Court justices upheld the state law, arguing that there was nothing wrong with racial segregation so long as the facilities provided for the races were equal, and if "colored persons" chose to believe that "enforced separation of the two races stamps the colored race with a badge of inferiority, it is not by reason of anything found in the act, but solely because the colored race chooses to put that construction on it."

The only Supreme Court justice to dissent from the *Plessy* decision was John Marshall Harlan (1833–1911). Harlan achieved a reputation of being a forceful dissenter, especially on matters related to civil rights. His famous dissent should have been the majority opinion, but it took another half century and the arrival of the Warren Court for that decision to be over-turned. Yet that famous dissent, especially the quotation above ("Our Constitution is color-blind"), took on a life of its own by inspiring future generations to fight for social justice.

## John Philip Sousa, "Stars and Stripes Forever" (1896)

John Philip Sousa (1854–1932), rightfully earning the label "March King," possessed at least two big loves in his life: his native land, the U.S.A., and band music. He grew up in the nation's capital during the Civil War, and he loved hearing the marches of the military band; in fact, his father played the trombone in the U. S. Marine Band. Playing in the Marine Band was a dream for Sousa, and he enlisted actually as a violinist and later became the band leader. His passion was the composition of inspiring music, and he often used his sense of imagination of military action to evoke inspiration to write the music. By the 1890s Sousa had composed enough marches to earn that label of "March King." Altogether, Sousa wrote 135 marches and many other musical works.

As for the setting when he composed this classic piece, Sousa was returning home from a European vacation in 1896 when he learned his band manager had died. Though saddened, he felt a "rhythmic beat" in his brain. Within a short time after getting home from this voyage, he wrote down the music for "Stars and Stripes Forever." Sousa always felt patriotic, but after being out of the country for weeks and then returning, the sight of "stars and stripes" seemed to him like "the most glorious sight in the world." This march became an instant hit, and, when played, most audiences would stand as though it was the actual national anthem. The number is considered Sousa's *magnum opus* of all his musical compositions, and he played it for the last time on the day he died. This prolific composer died during the Great Depression, and one might imagine how uplifting the number might have been to many citizens discouraged and despondent about the nation's economic condition.

Yes, let's concede it is quite a stretch to include this musical composition in a book on American rhetoric. Music alone is not rhetoric. Music may accompany rhetorical events, but music *per se* is not rhetoric! However, good rhetoric can inspire, and, there are actual lyrics that Sousa wrote for this march, albeit precious few Americans know the lyrics. And this number has been played at almost every Fourth of July patriotic event where music is part of the program. It is often played at the conclusion of a major presidential address where music is part of the program, whereas "Hail to the Chief" is played when the president is introduced. The composition is indeed a classic, and in 1987 an act of Congress made this piece the official "National March of the United States of America."

## Margaret Sanger, *Birth Control Review* (1914) and *Woman and the New Race* (1920)

"No woman can call herself free who does not own and control her own body," wrote Margaret Sanger (1883–1966) in *Woman and the New Race*. "No woman can call herself free until she can choose consciously whether she will or will not be a mother." Sanger devoted her entire career, which involved active public speaking and writing and publishing, to promoting women's sexual and reproductive freedom.

Sanger founded the American Birth Control League (later renamed Planned Parenthood Federation), and established America's first birth control clinic in Brooklyn on October 16, 1916. The police raided the clinic soon after its opening and arrested Sanger for violating New York's Comstock Law, which forbade distribution of birth control information. She was imprisoned for thirty days and confined to the work house, then released, and she immediately resumed her mission of speaking, writing, and distributing information about sexual freedom and birth control. Sanger traveled all over the world to speak out publicly on the importance of birth control. The passion of her calling was evident in her insightful and courageous words.

What was Sanger's driving force? One might imagine she was motivated by the loss of her mother, an Irish Catholic who birthed eleven children and died at the age of fifty. In her many public speeches of the 1920s, Sanger passionately voiced her opposition to the Catholic Church and to Christian churches in general for their teachings about sex. "The sex instinct in the human race is too strong to be bound by the dictates of any church," she declared. "The Church's failure, its century after century of failure, is now evident on every side....The teachings of the church have driven sex underground in secret channels....How is any progress to be made, how is any human expression or education possible when women and men are taught to combat and resist their natural impulses and to despise their bodily functions?"

In arguing "birth control is an ethical necessity for humanity today because it places in our hands a new instrument of self-expression and self-realization," Sanger was an activist and courageous feminist in a time when feminism was hardly recognized as a movement. The year 2016 has brought substantial evidence that feminism in the U. S. has placed a huge crack in the glass ceiling.

## Irving Berlin, "God Bless America" (1938)

*God bless America, land that I love; stand beside her and guide her, through the night with a light from above.*

Irving Berlin's greatest contribution to Americana and American heritage, undoubtedly, was a song that was written in 1917 for his Army musical, *Yip, Yip, Yaphank.* The irony, however, is that he did not use the song as it remained packed away for twenty-one years. Then, a popular singer and entertainer with a great operatic voice asked Berlin for a patriotic song for a national radio broadcast in 1938. The composer merely pulled out the song he had written two decades earlier, and it was virtually an overnight sensation. Both political parties played it at their national conventions in 1940.

Interestingly, Irving Berlin (1888–1989) was born in Russia and was brought to the United States five years later by his parents. Upon the death of his father when he was only eight years old, Berlin left school, sold newspapers, then later sang for tips in bars on New York's Lower East Side. At nineteen, his name was printed mistakenly as I. Berlin and attached to his first song, and he decided to retain the mistaken name throughout a long career of songwriting of over 1,500 songs. "God Bless America" and "White Christmas" are surely his most popular and best loved compositions.

So understandable are these lyrics and so endearing is the melody! Over the years, it has been called America's "unofficial national anthem," especially since "The Star Spangled Banner" has difficult—and almost non-understandable—lyrics and a challenging musical score. "God Bless America" is played at numerous patriotic and other public events, including major league baseball parks during the traditional "seventh inning stretch" for fans. Berlin assigned royalties for the song to a special fund that supports Boy Scouts and Girl Scouts.

## Woody Guthrie, "This Land is Your Land" (1940)

When folk singer Woody Guthrie was feeling angry, frustrated, and sorry for himself, he decided to "take it out" [his negative feelings] on Irving Berlin. He wrote these winsome lyrics in a dingy hotel room near New York Times Square and entitled the song "God Blessed America" with each verse ending "God blessed America for me." The song was intended as a parody and the music taken from a country song by the Carter family, and that song was based on an old Baptist hymn, "Oh My Lovin' Brother."

Guthrie put the song away for a number of years, then he recorded it in 1944, titling it "This Land is Your Land." The song romanticizes natural beauty in the nation ("From California to the New York Island, from the redwood forest to the Gulf Stream waters… endless skyway….golden valley….sparkling sands of her diamond deserts….wheat fields waving"). The Civil Rights Movement included the song as one of its favorite anthems of the 1960s ("As I go walking that freedom highway; nobody living can ever make me turn back, this land was made for you and me"). The song has been joyfully sung by many groups, such as the New Christy Minstrels. With simple melody and romantic lyrics, it, too, as with "God Bless America," has been recommended as a substitute for "The Star Spangled Banner."

# Rachel Carson, *Silent Spring* (1962)

Should it be entitled *The War against Nature* or *At War with Nature*? Thus a marine biologist wrestled with how her book should be entitled. Eight years earlier, Rachel Carson (1907–1964) released her first major book, *The Sea Around Us*, for which she won the National Book Award. Carson eventually settled on the more irenic and poetic title *Silent Spring*, referring to the eerie hush of natural areas that once were vibrant with the sounds of wildlife but now quietened by the devastation wreaked by decades of pesticide use. Carson's picturesque prose and lyrical style attracted millions to her message—a message that celebrated the interconnectedness of the natural world and all living things, plant and animal, that made up that world. The treatise explained vividly how humanly-made chemicals were endangering all life. The book became an instant best-seller and prompted legislation that eventually banned DDT and other deadly pesticides.

Carson was also an effective public speaker, especially appealing to women to understand the role of natural beauty as "a healing release from tension." At every speaking opportunity she underscored how vital a love of nature is to the well-being of both a nation and each of its citizens. Her passion and influence helped to launch the environmental movement.

# Guy Caraway, "We Shall Overcome" (Early 1960s)

A music director at a small Tennessee private training school for industrial and agricultural laborers turned a spiritual called "I Shall Overcome" in 1960 into an anthem for the struggling Civil Rights Movement. Guy Caraway (1927–2015), a folk singer and civil rights activist, is credited with turning the African-American spiritual "We Shall Overcome" into a unifying anthem of the 1960s Civil Rights Movement. The song was adapted by Pete Seeger, Caraway, and others at the Highlander Folk School in Grundy County, Tennessee. Caraway taught the song to activists who led the sit-in movement of the 1960s. According to his wife, he sang it at the first meeting of the Student Nonviolent Coordinating Committee on April 15, 1960. The song included a verse added a year earlier by a thirteen-year-old African-American activist named Mary Ethel Dozier. (She came up with the words "We are not afraid" when the HFS was raided by the sheriff's department while she, Caraway, and others sat in the dark, waiting to learn their fate.) This song is known by most Americans who lived through the Civil Rights Movement of the 60s and 70s, and it has been sung by blacks and whites as a show of unity and encouragement.

## Tom Hayden, *Port Huron Statement* (1962)

The Students for a Democratic Society was formed in 1962 by a loose organization of college and university students who had developed a deep and passionate concern about social injustices in the U. S. and for the future of the nation. Some had been involved in the Civil Rights Movement. Most harbored a deep concern that the nation was not truly democratic and its leaders did not understand the deepest needs of masses of fellow citizens. The foundational statement for SDS was the *Port Huron Statement*, adopted in 1962, which called for grassroots action and participatory democracy. At its organizing meeting in Port Huron, Michigan, SDS adopted this manifesto drafted by Tom Hayden (b. 1939), though he consulted with other like-minded students in its drafting.

The *Port Huron Statement* was a wide-ranging critique of the American society—the dangers of nuclear war, racial injustice, the failure to develop peaceful atomic energy, the Cold War, the maldistribution of wealth, the political apathy of students, consumerism, the impersonal nature of American corporate life, and the bankruptcy of liberal ideology. Somewhat lengthy as a statement, with 25,700 words (sprawling over 124 pages in book form), the document articulated both a critique and then a radical vision of the future. By being "New Left," the SDS did not want the general public to confuse their message and strategy of the "old left" and its squabbles of the 1930s and 1940s.

The statement was truly a seminal moment in the grassroots development of the New Left that drew tens of thousands of university students into its ranks. Its basic thesis is that genuine democracy is "a radical idea." Consider that the *Port Huron Statement* came *before* such movements as gay rights, feminism, Vietnam War protest, and environmentalism. Thus its principles echoed mightily in other student-led movements that soon followed, though the students then (in the 60s) and ones to follow have typically been characterized as radicals. Many of the "radicals" in the movement seemed to join the "Establishment" upon reaching middle age. Tom Hayden was elected to the California legislature in 1982.

# James William Fulbright, *The Arrogance of Power* (1966)

*The more I puzzle over the great wars of history, the more I am inclined to the view that the causes attributed to them—territory, markets, resources, the defense or perpetuation of great principles—were not the root cause at all but rather explanation or excuses for certain unfathomable drives of human nature. For lack of a clear and precise understanding of exactly what these motives are, I refer to them as the "arrogance of power"—as a psychological need that nation seems to have in order to prove that they are bigger, better, or stronger than other nations, that force is the ultimate proof of superiority.*

The Vietnam era was a dark period in American history, and a somewhat recent one, of course. As the war continued deeper into the Johnson years and then into the Nixon years, anti-war sentiment grew stronger and youthful protest demonstrations were larger and more frequent. And, of course, there were many speeches and a few sermons passionately presented in opposition to American involvement in the terrible conflict in Southeast Asia.

How unlikely that a Southern senator, J. William Fulbright (1905–1995), would become the most outspoken opponent in the U. S. Senate of that war! Fulbright served as U. S. senator from Arkansas from January 1945 until his resignation in December 1974, which came after his defeat by challenger Dale Bumpers. He holds the record for the longest-serving chairman of the Senate Foreign Relations Committee, serving from 1959 to 1974. Fulbright was devoted to internationalism and carefully studied the role of the U. S. in the larger world community. From much study and observation, he concluded there were two strands in American history that co-existed in tension: A dominant strand of democratic humanism that sought to lead by example and goodness and a lesser but durable strand of intolerant Puritanism that sought to compel other nations to comply with our will. While initially supporting the Gulf of Tonkin Resolution that gave powers to President Johnson to fight the Vietnam War, he soon became the war's chief dissenter and critic.

While Fulbright did make a number of speeches, his book, *The Arrogance of Power*, stated in plain, ordinary language the case against the continuation of U. S. involvement in Southeast Asia or anywhere else around the globe where the nation had no vital interest. To Fulbright, that war was costly foolishness. The Senator would usually begin his speeches with praise for American citizens' diversity, natural resources and rich territory, the institutions devised by the Founding Fathers, and the wisdom of those political leaders who adapted the Constitution to changing needs of the great nation. Fulbright acknowledged that, for the most part, the nation had made good use of its blessings, but then had reached a point in which a great nation was about to lose its perspective on greatness.

Senator Fulbright clarified that he did not believe the nation was attempting to dominate the world in the manner of a Hitler or Napoleon, but that it was drifting to commitments which, "though benevolent in intent, are so far reaching as to exceed even America's great capacities." The Senator called to task the notion that the U. S. knew infallibly what was best for all other nations and, even it did, whether the nation had resources to inflict our notion of what is best on all other nations, especially some countries on the other side of the globe. He rightly concluded the stakes are high.

Fulbright's writing and speaking brought common sense to a generation willing to question the wisdom of the war in Vietnam, and it encouraged those protesters who were attempting to see U. S. foreign policy in a realistic way. He felt the causes of war may be rooted as much in pathology as in politics. He noted there were many signs of arrogance of power in the way Americans act when they go into foreign countries, which Americans in foreign lands "act as if they own the place" and "in many places they very nearly do." In his speeches and writings, the Senator then cited examples of U. S. arrogance as strong evidence for his contentions.

Fulbright could use simple, home-spun analogies and illustrations to make his point that Americans abroad carry an unconscious knowledge of all that power and its arrogance about knowing what is best for people in other lands. He contended the missionary instinct runs deep whenever people feel they are bigger, stronger, and richer than they actually are. Among his illustrations is the anecdote of the three boy scouts who reported to their scoutmaster that as their good deed for the day they had helped an old lady to cross the street. "That's fine," said the scoutmaster, "but why did it take three of you?" "Well," they explained, "she did not want to go."

Fulbright's passion for humane internationalism fueled his devotion to establish an international exchange program for scholars, eventually resulting in the creation of a fellowship program that bears his name: the Fulbright Scholarship Program. Two quotations from his speeches and writings bear thoughtful reflection: "The citizen who criticizes his country is paying it an implied tribute," and "In a democracy, dissent is an act of faith."

## Statement of Purpose, National Organization of Women (1966)

*We, men and women who herby constitute ourselves as the National Organization of Women, believe that the time has come for a new movement toward true equality for all women in America, and toward a fully equal partnership of the sexes, as part of the world-wide revolution of human rights now taking place within and beyond our national borders.... We believe that women will do most to create a new image of women by acting now, and by speaking out in behalf of their own equality, freedom, and human dignity—not in pleas for special privilege, nor in enmity toward men, who are also victims of the current, half-equality between the sexes—but in an active, self-respecting partnership with men. By so doing, women will develop confidence in their own ability to determine actively, in partnership with men, the conditions of their life, their choices, their future and their society.*

In June 1966, the National Organization of Women was founded in Washington D. C. Then later that year, the first organizing conference was attended by about thirty of the three hundred members. The publication of Betty Friedan's book, *The Feminine Mystique*, three years earlier helped launch the modern women's movement. The book appeared at a time in which growing numbers of women were entering the labor force and when women were making stronger inroads into careers and professions that formerly had been male-dominated. The book aided the formation of NOW as a political lobby for women's interests. "The feminine mystique says that the highest value and the only commitment for women is the fulfillment of their own femininity," Friedan writes in her book, and "the greatest mistake of Western culture, through most of its history, has been the under-valuation of this femininity. It says this femininity is so mysterious and intuitive and close to the creation and origin of life that man-made science may never be able to understand it." Quite naturally, in the 1970s the NOW supported the ERA, the Equal Rights Amendment to the U. S. Constitution. The ERA aroused a torrent of right-wing opposition and failed to gain requisite support for passage.

## Lee Greenwood, "God Bless the U. S. A." (1984)

*And I'm proud to be an American, where at least I know I'm free, and I won't forget the men who died, who gave that right to me. And I'd gladly stand up and defend her still today, cause there ain't no doubt I love this land. God bless the U. S. A.*

In the early 1980s, country music performer Lee Greenwood (b. 1942) felt the nation needed to be more united, so he composed a song about his feelings for his native country. The song "God Bless the U. S. A." was released in 1984 and played at the Republican National Convention that year, a convention that re-nominated Ronald Reagan to run for the presidency. The song especially gained prominence during the Gulf War of 1990-91, and then its popularity skyrocketed after the 9/11 terrorist attacks against the nation.

Greenwood originally placed the performance of this song in the middle of his show as a new song, but then he found most audiences jumping up and applauding as he played the piano and sang the lyrics. So then he moved the song to the end of the show as an encore. There are four cities mentioned in this simple composition—New York City, Los Angeles, Detroit, and Houston—and four other geographical citations—"lakes of Minnesota, "hills of Tennessee," "plains of Texas," and "from sea to shining sea." Members of the audience who either live in these locations or relate to the area in one way or another find this an opportune time to sing heartily or applaud and perhaps let out a cheer.

This song might now be rendered the most popular of modern patriotic songs. It is often played on the Fourth of July along with the best and most well-known of other patriotic hymns and melodies. Some have confessed to goose bumps popping up when hearing the song, but, regardless, with such simple lyrics it is easy to sing along.

## Whitney Houston, "One Moment in Time" (1988)

Every two years, artists and composers are summoned to record a song that will capture the mood of the Summer and Winter Olympic Games. The best numbers continue to be played and sung in a variety of venues. The "gold standard by which all Olympic theme sons should be judged," according to *USA Today* (August 4, 2016), is the late Whitney Houston's "One Moment in Time," written for the 1988 Summer Olympic Games. The special song became a hit in its own right.

"One Moment in Time" ideally encapsulates the spirit of the Games. For these athletes, sometimes it is a matter of a split second of time between either realizing dreams or not being awarded the desired medal. The outcome might be determined by a matter of inches or even millimeters. Both athletes and fans have their favorite events. There is excitement unbounded; the one hundred meter dash, for example, has been labeled as "the most exciting ten seconds in all of sports." Composed as a pop anthem, the song catches an important part of the human spirit at its best: sacrificing totally, giving one's all, facing the pain, and becoming "more than I thought I could be." And then the song builds to a triumphal conclusion with Houston's powerful voice exclaiming "I will be free." The song addresses the human spirit at its best, and will surely remain a timeless American classic.

## Anita Hill, Testimony Regarding Judge Clarence Thomas (1991)

President George H. W. Bush, not unlike other presidents, knew he could enhance his legacy before leaving office with the opportunity to choose wisely a candidate for an open chair on the highest court in the land, the United States Supreme Court. Bush nominated Clarence Thomas to replace Thurgood Marshall, the first African-American to sit on the high court. The selection, however, elicited the disdain of liberals who felt that Thomas' conservative beliefs and unimpressive qualifications were an insult to Marshall's legacy. Nonetheless, Thomas' confirmation was expected to sail through the Senate's Judiciary Committee and then before the entire Senate.

In early October 1991 a startling development impacted the proceedings. Thomas was accused of having sexually harassed a former associate whom he supervised when he was chairman of the Equal Opportunity Council (EEOC). This associate, Anita Hill, was born into a poor African-American family, worked hard to gain an education, attended Yale University Law School, held conservative beliefs and convictions, and was deeply religious. The irony, of course, is that Thomas headed the very agency that supposedly protects workers from sexual harassment.

The Judiciary Committee began televised hearings on October 11. The nation seemed riveted to the real life drama. This was a legal proceeding and a high stakes confrontation. The drama was heightened as to the eventual vote of committee members. Not since the debate on explicit music lyrics in 1985 had the nation viewed testimony as lurid as the Clarence Thomas-Anita Hill hearings.

When Thomas was asked to speak in his own defense, he openly expressed his anger. He claimed he was a "victim of this process," and that his name, integrity, character and family had been harmed. He defended himself claiming "I am not going to allow myself to be further humiliated in order to be confirmed....or to put my private life on display for a prurient interest or other reasons. I will not allow this committee or anyone else to probe into my private life. This is not what America is all about."

Anita Hill impressed millions of citizen-viewers with her courageous, controlled, and calm testimony. She seemed to respectfully report experiences with Thomas from her perspective as she told the history of their working relationship and the ways in which she believed she had been sexually harassed by Thomas. She seemed uncomfortable reporting some of the experiences, perhaps the most memorable one being an allegation that Thomas looked at a can of Coke he was drinking in his office and asked, "Who has put pubic hair in my Coke?" Hill impressed many with her humility, admitting she "may have used poor judgment," and that she had "no personal vendetta against Clarence Thomas," but, as she concluded, "I felt I had to tell the truth. I could not keep silent."

The testimony by both Thomas and Hill were unforgettable for concerned citizen-viewers, and committee members took their votes seriously; some explained carefully the logic of their decisions. The credibility of both "majors" in the drama was an issue. Thomas would eventually be confirmed fifty-two to forty-eight by the Senate—the slimmest number of votes any Supreme Court justice had ever received. Women viewers, especially, did not forget the all-male Judiciary Committee's interrogation of Hill. Thomas has served on the court for over a quarter century. His most recent public appearance was at the Presidential Inauguration of January 2017 in which he administered the oath of office to Vice President Mike Pence.

Readers may surely think of other and more recent instances where the English language was used within the national boundaries—either in public speeches, essays, testimony, poetry, or music—to inspire and move both the immediate audience as well as generations to follow.

# 2. Town Meeting of the Mind—Forums for American Public Address

A number of institutions and forums have developed with the history of American democracy that have given opportunity for men and women to employ and develop their public speaking skills.

In addition to the public and private school classroom setting, the hundreds of thousands of churches and synagogues have provided a setting for public speaking. We see this involvement from the earliest colonial days as nearly every colonist directly participated in the activities of public speaking, either as speaker or audience member, and because this means of communication and expression was more readily available during this period and up until the time of the Revolution than the various means of written communication and publication. As my former major professor George V. Bohman often pointed out: During the colonial period, public speaking at religious, legislative, academic, and popular meetings was plentiful. Speaking occasions afforded much of the public entertainment, even in the earliest days of this culture.

Prior to the Great Awakening and Revolutionary period, opportunities for public speaking had been mostly limited to professional speakers: teachers, preachers, judges, lawyers, and legislators. However, in the New England town meetings, opportunities granted for all who cared to speak and argue for a particular course of action. Women did not usually speak in public, except in the case of itinerant Quaker preachers and a handful of women in other denominations. The Great Awakening, with its emphasis on equalitarian ideas, served as a stimulus to public speaking by untrained men who became lay preachers in new denominations, who gave testimony in public, and who took renewed interest in political activities, especially as concern over British rule increased. In general, the speakers who commanded the greatest influence on colonial thinking were members of the clergy—they were respected for their communication skills, their education, and their religious and spiritual status in the community.

The New England town meeting was the first American institution of popular speaking, discussion, and debate on important issues. The town meeting came into general use in the colonies of Massachusetts Bay, Connecticut, New Hampshire, and Rhode Island. The town meetings served as a setting for radical and merchant leaders and orators to argue for resistance to British policies. Numerous meetings were held all over the colonies to support separate state governments and the Declaration of Independence. On March 25, 1783, the city of Boston adopted a resolution authorizing an annual oration on the Fourth of July instead of the fifth of March, "in which the Orator shall consider the feelings, manner, and principles which led to this great National Event as well as the important and happy effects whether general or domestick [sic], which already have, and will forever continue to flow from this Auspicious Epoch." Thus began the oldest regularly celebrated popular commemoration in the United States of America.

We will note at least three institutions or forums for professional public speaking in our history, all the while acknowledging that there are numerous others, some large and some smaller. Most large cities have speakers' bureaus where skilled orators can be contracted to deliver speeches to general or specialized audiences on all kinds of occasions. Most of the professional speakers seem to deal with motivational and/or inspirational themes.

The beginnings of American lecturing for profit cannot be established with certainty, but origins might be traced to traveling evangelists in the colonial days who traveled by horseback from one community to another to bring glad tidings or simply report news. By "professional," we do not contend that all the speakers were fantastic orators or the best informed ones to stand before audiences, but only that they were reimbursed for their services; their goals in speaking were generally religious, educational and/or inspirational. And in the case of political debate, their purpose was winning support and votes for a cause or candidate.

## The Lyceum and Chautauqua Movements

In 1826 Dr. Josiah Holbrook, an early advocate for free public education, began the lyceum movement by organizing the first lyceum in Millbury, Massachusetts. In less than a decade, there were over three thousand town lyceums that were, in turn, associated with a national lyceum. There was some decline in the lyceum movement, but in 1867 an organization named the Associated Literary Societies was formed, marking the beginning of the lecture business, thus the first commercial lecture bureau. The bureau's purpose was to render some of the more effective Eastern speakers available to Western audiences. James Clark Redpath co-founded the Boston Lyceum Bureau, and it provided a central bureau that could dispatch well-known lecturers to local lyceums.

Just as Holbrook gave the lyceum its initial impetus, then Redpath gave the lyceum its beginning as a major enterprise, rendering well-known lecturers available to almost any community. Redpath drew a ten percent commission and managed most of the American lecturers from 1867 to 1875. Among the more prominent lecturers under his management were Wendell Phillips, William Lloyd Garrison, Charles Sumner, Ralph Waldo Emerson, John Greenleaf Whittier, Susan B. Anthony, Elizabeth Cady Stanton, Anna Dickinson, Henry Ward Beecher, and Charles Dickinson, the English novelist. Some of these speakers collected handsome sums for their rhetorical efforts as they already were known to audiences before their arrival to the local platform. For some of the speakers there was not only an opportunity to earn a living, but also to advocate an important cause, such as women's rights or antislavery. Other speakers were happy to entertain and simply give listeners what they most wanted to hear. Crusading speakers needed to be cautious not to identify people in the audience as agents of evil. Speakers were mostly aware they needed to please the audience, or at least not unduly offend listeners, in order to receive follow-up invitations and recommendations for future bookings in other cities and towns.

In the late nineteenth century, the lecture business enjoyed major growth. Fees increased so that lecturers could receive as much as a thousand dollars for a single performance. Several factors enhanced the lecturing as a big business: the industrial revolution with its comparatively greater prosperity than agricultural pursuits; the growth of the city; the spread of temperance and women's suffrage movement; the improvement in transportation; and the presence of James B. Pond and other bureau managers of great ability.

The business was not limited to lecturers. Various entertainers in acting, music, and opera performed. The system had two types of talent—the lesser light or "simon-pure lecturer" and the "star" of the platform, much like today's rock concerts may include a "warm up" act before the featured star performs. Taken as a whole, the "lesser lights" surely exerted the greater influence, especially on the smaller communities, as they conveyed much needed information and molded public opinion. Yet the "stars" of the platform constituted a virtual "who's who" of the mid- and late-nineteenth century who used the platform to advocate causes in reform and social justice.

In 1874 John Vincent converted a Sunday School summer study course into the Sunday School Institute and Open Air Camp Meeting in which lectures on diverse topics were given at Lake Chautauqua, New York. Chautauqua attracted a great deal of lecturing talent, including William Jennings Bryan, perhaps the most effective and popular orator of his generation; President William McKinley, Theodore Roosevelt, Robert LaFollette, James Bryce, and William Allen White. Traveling Chautauquas were organized around local communities, and by 1906 the business was in full swing. The other "super star" besides Bryan was Russell Conwell, whose famous lecture "Acres of Diamonds" was presented hundreds of times over several years. Interestingly, Mark Twain was one of the greatest masters of the lecture platform.

William Jennings Bryan drew the largest audiences prior to the advent of radio; Bryan was to Chautauqua what Wendell Phillips was to the lyceum. "The Great Commoner" shunned speaking on political topics at Chautauqua and dealt with biblical and inspirational themes. The one lecture for which Bryan was most in demand was entitled "The Prince of Peace," delivered in three thousand circuit tents over two decades up to 1924, the year prior to his death. Bryan often told people he much preferred speaking on religion rather than political issues. In the later years of his life, he had become nationally known as an uncompromising foe of teaching evolution in public schools. Often Bryan had to answer a major question about his thinking—how could he be such a progressive in politics and such a fundamentalist in religion?

By 1917–1920 the Chautauqua movement had settled down to approximately five thousand communities, with annual audiences accumulating to approximately two million. This was an institution of major public education for the masses willing to participate. The bill of fare offered was much like the offerings in general magazines, such as *Reader's Digest*—there were intellectual discourses, humorous presentations, inspirational speeches, and popular discourses. There was a respectable "home, heaven, and mother" moral tone within many of the lectures and only rarely were liberal ideas and prophetic preaching laid before a sizable audience. Franklin D. Roosevelt delivered his famous "I Hate War" speech at Chautauqua on August 14, 1936. Musicians (such as George Gershwin and Duke Ellington), poets (such as Vachel Lindsay) and other artists both spoke and performed before live audiences.

The public platform did open doors of opportunity for females speaking and addressing feminist issues, often to the vocal derision of males in the audience. Susan B. Anthony and Dr. Anna Howard Shaw formed one of the most effective teams in the history of American public address, focusing their rhetorical gifts on the noble cause of women's suffrage. Anthony could draw SRO audiences and on occasion was invited to speak in liberal churches. Julia Ward Howe lectured for thirty years all over the U. S., as did Anna Dickinson, a lyceum lecturer that rivaled Gough and Beecher as lyceum favorites. Eleanor Roosevelt delivered an address in the Chautauqua Amphitheater in 1933. The Lyceum and Chautauqua movements both began with high ideals of education and inspiration, yet both succumbed to the temptation to enhance financial success through increasing popularization. These movements did encounter demise due to a number of factors:

- increasing availability of newspapers
- the advent of radio broadcasting
- the development of motion pictures
- the opera house, and theatrical companies on tour
- the increase in the number of magazines

Radio instituted such features as America's Town Meeting of the Air (in conjunction with Town Hall) and similar forum programs made available to persons with radio.

The public platform and lecture business is very much alive and well in the early twenty-first century. The media that convey the messages, of course, is now much more electronic. Speeches can be downloaded, viewed on television or computer screen, stored electronically, and experienced at one's convenience. All kinds of education and personal enrichment are offered continuously. Speaker bureaus are alive and well, even if proportionate audiences are not as large as in the late nineteenth and early twentieth centuries. Guest speakers are invited on special occasions to universities and churches. Specific speakers are selected for specific audiences. Admittedly, the situation rooms have changed, but the phenomenon continues in one form or another in American adult education. And the lecture platform in its earliest beginnings provided an important medium of American public address from the 1840s to the 1930s, thus contributing immeasurably to the life of the nation.

## Political Discussion and Debate

Public discussion and debate among political opponents have long constituted an established tradition within American political life. Public discussion has been practiced at all levels of government—national, state, and local community. If a candidate for public office within a democracy cannot effectively articulate one's convictions or positions on public policy or public morality issues, that candidate suffers severe disadvantage. Admittedly, many officeholders and candidates have been bumbling, ineffective public speakers. Indeed, political leaders must often face a general audience and in the electronic era the entire environment has been altered in a major way. This survey of public speaking in America must surely include the way major candidates have reached out to the public to be convincing and/or win votes. We begin with a series of debates with which most students of history have some familiarity.

## The Lincoln-Douglas Debates (1858)

Stephen A. Douglas (1813–1861) and Abraham Lincoln (1809–1865) were two men from the same state, each of whom was an astute politician, each possessing skill in stump speaking, each knowing and understanding the positions of the other, each holding similar positions, and each possessing political aspirations. Many hold the view that the Lincoln-Douglas debates were the first presidential debates and that Douglas was trapped into debating against Lincoln, an aspiring politician whose views and skills were unknown. The first view is incorrect, as these debates were held to influence a voting public that would determine who went to the Senate and not to the White House. The second notion is absurd—Lincoln and Douglas knew and respected each other's skills and positions quite well, thus there were no huge surprises to either candidate in this debate.

What may be questioned is the opinion that these debates deserve to be labeled the most famous political debates in American history—indeed a stretch! Lincoln was the candidate who proposed the debates, and Douglas agreed to seven confrontations in various areas of Illinois. The debates matched two powerful minds, two astute logicians, and two hard-hitting speakers with much stump speaking experience—one candidate was nationally known and had achieved remarkable legislative leadership in the Senate and the other candidate was little known outside the region and within the national Republican Party. Both men wanted to debate and the national issues were, indeed, momentous—what should be done about slavery, especially in the territories, and what can prevent the young nation's drift toward civil war? Slavery was the sole issue. Not a word about banks, tariffs, roads, education, internal improvements, corruption, or other standard talking points was ever uttered.

Both Douglas and Lincoln were running for the Senate seat from Illinois in 1858 when Lincoln challenged his opponent to this series of debates across the state. Douglas, though born in Vermont, had moved to Illinois at age twenty, was already a national figure in the Democratic Party, and Lincoln was hardly known outside his home state. Douglas was a gifted orator. Because of short stature was known as "The Little Giant." He was elected to the Senate in 1846 and established a reputation as avid expansionist into the western territories. Western expansion was a popular cause, but the "downside" of this idea involved bitter controversy over whether slavery should be permitted in the new territories.

Slavery in the territories was the major context for discussion about the "peculiar institution." Douglas believed that voters in each territory or state should make the decision about permitting slavery. The Senator had championed the Kansas-Nebraska Act of 1854, which repealed the Missouri Compromise and allowed local option. Lincoln contended that slavery should not be allowed to spread beyond the existing slave states. The aspiring candidate insisted that slavery was morally and politically wrong, but that he would not destroy the Union to rid the young nation of this evil institution. In his publicized "House Divided" address, Lincoln had argued that the nation would not remain "half slave and half free" but would become either totally slave or totally free. Douglas was equally insistent that the survival of the Union, surely just as important to him as it was to Lincoln, required respect for popular sovereignty, even if it led to the spread of slavery.

The debates were huge events in the small Illinois cities in which they were held for a period of almost two months (the cities chosen were selected from the seven Congressional districts in which the candidates had not yet made major addresses, thus Chicago had not been neglected):

- Ottawa (August 21, before approximately 12,000, mostly pro-Lincoln).
- Freeport (August 27, 15,000 stood in a cool drizzle, mostly Republicans).
- Jonesboro (September 15, 14,000 mostly Democrats).
- Charleston (September 18, 12,000 mostly pro-Lincoln).
- Galesburg (October 7, 12,000 Republicans in cold wind).
- Quincy (October 13, largely Douglas supporters from across the river in Missouri).
- Alton (October 15, 6,000 mostly Douglas supporters).

To these seven prairie towns gathered townspeople, clerks, businessmen, lawyers, and especially the farmers. We must not imagine the motley crew that composed the audiences—often sitting and at times even standing in heat or cold, sunshine or rain—sat in polite and dignified attention. Audience members were often participants in the whole process by cheers, groans, shouting questions, or exclamatory comments.

Remember that the election for U. S. Senate would be carried out by the Illinois state legislature in the next session, but the two candidates carried the campaign directly to the voters. Remember, also, that stump speaking was such a powerful magnet to draw listeners in the Middle West. People loved debate, rivalry was strong, and newspaper reports could be so biased in reportage with each reporter coloring his own report. The debates were only one part of the campaign, as altogether Lincoln traveled four thousand miles and made sixty-three speeches and Douglas traveled almost five thousand miles and made fifty-nine longer speeches and seventeen shorter addresses. In every city each side competed to bring the largest flag, the longest parade, and the loudest and best music.

When one reads the transcripts of the debates which were stenographically recorded, clearly one notices that the presentations were not highly polished, stylistic rhetorical presentations. There was rambling and repetition. Both candidates could digress into side issues. Each had his "talking points," to use a modern expression. Lincoln exerted more effort to confine the debate to the chief issues, while Douglas labored to broaden the controversy to cover the emotionally disruptive issue of social and political equality between the races. Douglas also sought to tag Lincoln with the stigmas attached to the radical abolitionists, whose popularity in the Midwest was at ground zero. Douglas attempted to put Lincoln in the camp of "black Republicans," citizens believing in total racial equality. Of course, that was an idea to be debated by another generation. Lincoln did ridicule Douglas for indifference on the morality of slavery; to him, popular sovereignty was pro-slavery.

Did Lincoln have a weakness? Actually, his "House Divided" thesis (that the nation could not remain half slave and half free of slavery) made the contender look like an abolitionist, and an abolitionist had no chance of winning an election outside of New England. Lincoln humbly replied he was "not in favor of anything," and that he was making "a prediction only—it may have been a foolish one, perhaps."

Did Douglas have a weakness? Indeed so, a weakness that Lincoln exploited at Freeport. Douglas' dilemma was to denounce the court decision in *Dred Scott* which protected slaves when brought into any new territory from slaveholding states, thus denouncing the highest court in the land, or to renounce his "popular sovereignty" philosophy. The "popular sovereignty" doctrine was Douglas' "baby," one on which he had based his later political career, and the *Dred Scott* decision was a major decree by the high court in interpretation of the U. S. Constitution. Lincoln sprang this trap and repeated the dilemma in subsequent debates, and Douglas' only retort was that the whole point was moot since slavery would not thrive outside a cotton and tobacco culture. Lincoln made clear that slavery was evil, a moral principle he could not get Douglas to admit.

How easily the importance of these debates can be exaggerated! They contributed nothing new to political philosophy, and neither candidate hardly qualified as a model of debating skill. However, there is significance in the historic debates: First, they provided a model for political debate for future generations. Second, the debates introduced Abraham Lincoln to the national audience, and he was able to present himself as a moderate Republican to party regulars rather than an extremist, radical candidate. Furthermore, each candidate was able to spend time testing his ideas with the general public and analyzing weaknesses and flaws in arguments.

Lincoln won the popular vote, but lost the election held in the Illinois state legislature. Subsequent events in the next two years proved more favorable to the contender. Lincoln advanced his career by losing the state election; his stature was elevated in the eyes of fellow Republicans and he became a national figure. Douglas began to lose favor with the Southern Democrats for his stand against the pro-slavery Lecompton Constitution. Yet Lincoln and Douglas continued their rivalry in the subsequent two years, and the larger prize for Lincoln was the Republican Party's nomination for president in 1860 and his eventual defeat of Douglas in the national arena. Without these debates, most likely Lincoln would not have been the president.

## Presidential Debates

On September 26, 1960, a tradition began that has established itself as one of the most significant and anticipated events of the quadrennial presidential election campaigns—the presidential debates. The U. S. Constitution does not require presidential candidates to debate, and the first debate was often compared to the Lincoln-Douglas debates that served as something of a model. After the important 1960 election, sixteen more years passed before presidential debating by major candidates was resumed and the tradition began to be established. When the debates resumed in 1976, a new precedent was established in that an incumbent president running for a second term might also be expected to debate (in contrast simply to two new challengers who had not served in the highest office). An ABC poll in 2016 showed nearly a quarter of Americans say the debates would have a major impact on their choice for president.

The rules and logistics for the debates are negotiated well in advance by the candidates and their advisers. A number of venues and formats have been utilized. Audiences have almost always been respectful, as admission to the immediate debate venue is carefully considered and controlled. College and university campuses serve as the most typical venue; Saint Anselm College has hosted four debates and Washington University in St. Louis has hosted three debates and one vice presidential debate; Belmont University in Nashville has hosted one. A brief survey of the debates and election outcome:

**Kennedy-Nixon (1960).** This was the first presidential debate and, as moderated by respected news anchor Howard K. Smith, the candidates were the Democratic nominee John F. Kennedy and the Republican nominee Richard M. Nixon. The first debate drew over sixty-six million viewers out of a U. S. population of almost 180 million, making it at the time the most-watched broadcast in U. S. history. Three more debates were conducted in this series (October 7, October 13, and October 21).

The two candidates came across in such different styles. In the first encounter, Nixon actually gave better replies, according to many historians, but his nervousness and a bad makeup appearance were negative factors to many viewers. Try as he might, Nixon seemed wooden, uncomfortable, and self-conscious. Americans who listened by radio deemed that Nixon, a trained debater since high school, had "won" the debate. The majority of the millions who watched on television, however, seemed more attracted by the charisma of the Democratic nominee. Nixon reportedly had hurt his knee campaigning and also had a chest cold and, refusing to allow application of heavy make-up, looked unshaven and haggard; additionally, he sounded hoarse. Kennedy, by contrast, arrived tan from California and seemed cool and controlled. The Democratic nominee did indeed have chronic and severe health problems, which his entourage effectively concealed, and yet he projected self-confidence, vigor, and energy, if not deep experience.

What was the impact of this first presidential debate? Some observers contended it made the difference in who won the election, that Nixon was ahead in the race till the debates, and that Kennedy emerged as the front runner after the debates. The race was close from beginning until its very end on election night and the morning after, being one of the closest elections in American history. Kennedy's victory depended on his appeal in northern industrial states with large Roman Catholic populations and his ability to hold much of the traditionally Democratic South. The home state of his running mate, Texas, was vital to the success of the ticket.

While the debate may not have changed many minds, it served the Democratic ticket an important function—lifting Kennedy from lesser-known status as challenger and presenting an upgraded image of a young political leader who was capable of leading the free world. The remainder of the campaign inspired many younger and middle age voters who found Kennedy personally charming, intelligent, poised, handsome, youthfully energetic, and even magnetic in charisma. In calling for change (sound like Obama and other recent office-seekers?), the Massachusetts senator appealed to the idealistic hopes of young and old alike.

Though Nixon ran a skilled campaign, Kennedy outpolled him by only about 100,000 popular votes. JFK's victory in the Electoral College rested on razor-thin margins in several states, including Illinois wherein a suspicious vote tally was submitted. Nixon seemed convinced that debating was not in his best interest, at least in a close election, and thus not necessary in a one-sided campaign where a landslide is likely. Consequently, there were no presidential debates in 1964 (when Lyndon Johnson won in a landslide victory over Barry Goldwater), 1968 (when Nixon returned to national prominence in a close victory over Hubert Humphrey), and 1972 (when Nixon maintained a ridiculously large lead over a left-leaning, anti-war Senator George McGovern and won every state but Massachusetts).

**Ford-Carter (1976).** Governor Jimmy Carter of Georgia was a relative newcomer to the national political scene as the Democratic nominee and Gerald Ford had become, in a sense by default, the president of the U. S. after resignation by Richard Nixon in August 1974. Debates were held on September 23, and October 6 and 22. Carter, with his perpetual smile and reputation as a humble peanut farmer who taught Sunday School in the Baptist Church at Plains, Georgia, projected an image of integrity, humility, and intelligence. Ford's image as a fair and honest man had been impaired by such an early presidential pardon of Richard Nixon for any crimes he may have committed in the Watergate scandal. The most damaging mistake that Ford made was an utterance in the second debate: "There is no Soviet domination of Eastern Europe and there never will be under a Ford administration"—a mistake that the moderator granted opportunity for him to correct right there on the spot. Carter respectfully pointed out that one could not convince the Eastern Europeans that there was no Soviet domination. The gaffe was consequential for Ford, irreparably damaging his credibility in international relations and putting his momentum in a stall. Even today it is still considered the one single, biggest intellectual and verbal miscue in presidential debate history. Carter won the close election.

**Carter-Reagan (1980).** This debate on October 28 was consequential as an embattled President Carter entered the debates with a thin margin and by the conclusion of the debates the challenger had taken a lead—all on his way to a landslide victory. Ronald Reagan attempted to transfer his own optimistic vision of a rejuvenated U. S. to the voting public. His stock arguments, such as opposition to big government spending and cuts in domestic spending, were punctuated with humorous quips and "aside" comments. Reagan repeatedly asked the question: "Are you better off now than you were four years ago?" and his campaign coined a term, "misery index," that added the rate of inflation to that of unemployment. While Carter could still seem likeable and knowledgeable, his seventy-year-old opponent was skilled in direct, optimistic, and expressive communication. The GOP ticket captured the Electoral College tally by a 489 to 49 margin. Carter conceded defeat even before the West Coast voting booths had officially closed.

**Reagan-Mondale (1984).** There were two debates between President Reagan and the Democratic challenger, Walter Mondale, on October 7 and 21, using different formats. Reagan was a popular president and it is doubtful he could have been defeated for a second term by any living person on the face of the globe. The incumbent was a master of both imagery and rhetoric, and could casually and effectively pose for pictures inspired by his Hollywood westerns—a rugged individual from whom the strongest foes would shrink. While Mondale, who may have seemed more intelligent, seemed to offer something for everybody, Reagan's directness, simplicity (perhaps even over-simplification), optimism, and sense of humor, all seemed to capture the moment. As the older gentleman who was deemed too old by some voters to serve in office, Reagan defused the "age issue" by saying he would not exploit the issue in the debates by referencing "my opponent's youth and inexperience." This prepared humorous line was received with hilarity by all viewers and is one of the most memorable lines in debate history. Mondale made history himself by choosing as his running mate Representative Geraldine Ferraro of New York, the first woman to win nomination for president or vice president on a major party ticket. Seems fair to say that the debates had no major consequence on the voting behavior of the American public—the campaign ended with Mondale carrying only his home state of Minnesota and the District of Columbia.

**Bush-Dukakis (1988).** There were two debates between the former Vice President George Herbert Walker Bush and the Massachusetts Governor Michael Dukakis (September 25 and October 13). As heir apparent from the Reagan era, Bush easily secured the Republican nomination. Dukakis seemed short on larger ideas of any kind, and he stirred little enthusiasm for himself while promising to bring honesty and competence to the White House, recently stained by the Iran-Contra affair. The debates had little impact on the expected Bush victory, but they are remembered most for the answer given by Governor Dukakis on the very first question of the first debate. Dukakis was known for his opposition to capital punishment, and reporter Bernard Shaw asked him if he would change his position on capital punishment if he came home to discover his wife, Kitty, had been brutally raped and murdered. Dukakis ignored the emotional depths of the question and, rather than making a personal statement (or even claiming the question was stated in an insensitive way), he seemed to launch into a "canned" and detached recital of stock arguments in his opposition to the death penalty. Actually, neither candidate thrilled large numbers of potential voters, and the turnout in November seemed to confirm this—the lowest turnout, percentage-wise, for any national election since 1924.

**Bush-Clinton-Perot (1992).** There were three presidential debates in 1992 (October 11, 15, and 19). Self-financed Texas billionaire businessman Ross Perot, despite a humorously quirky style of straight talk, merited a spot in the debates due to his polling appeal. George H. W. Bush was, of course, re-nominated for re-election, and the Democratic challenger, Governor William Jefferson ("Bill") Clinton, stressed economic issues and images of his relative youth. The debates introduced Clinton to voters who had known little about him. Perot, with his visual aids and emphasis on budget and spending, added humor to the proceedings, and Bush seemed, at times, over-confident, self-assured, and perhaps even bored (at one point the television camera caught him looking at his wrist watch while another nominee was speaking). Clinton won a surprisingly easy victory, garnering forty-three percent of the popular vote but winning 370 electoral votes by carrying thirty-two states and the District of Columbia. Bush gained a majority only among white Protestants in the South.

**Clinton-Dole (1996).** Two debates were conducted between incumbent Bill Clinton and Kansas Senator Robert Dole (October 6 and 16). Clinton and Al Gore defeated the Republican team of Dole and Jack Kemp by about the same margin they had beaten George H. W. Bush and Dan Quayle in 1992. The debates had negligible impact on the election outcome.

**Gore-Bush (2000).** Three debates between Senator Al Gore of Tennessee and Texas Governor George W. Bush, son of the nation's forty-first president, played a role in introducing each candidate to the voting public (October 3, 11, and 17). To many observers, Gore came across as knowledgeable and intelligent, but Bush came across as more likable. In an early debate, Gore demonstrated with his body and facial (nonverbal) language his deep personal disbelief and exasperation in what his opponent was saying— all perceived as disrespectful to Bush. Bush promised "compassionate conservatism," while Gore seemed to struggle to articulate any coherent theme, all the while distancing himself from the controversial Clinton. Voter turnout was comparatively low, but in Y2K the election produced a near dead heat between Republicans Bush and Richard (Dick) Cheney and Democrats Gore and Senator Joseph Lieberman of Connecticut. Gore carried the popular vote by 500,000 votes, but the identity of Clinton's successor hinged on the twenty-five electoral votes from Florida where Bush's brother Jeb served as governor. After weeks of wrangling and maneuvering by party leaders on both sides, the U. S. Supreme Court in two 5-4 opinions, in essence, chose the new president. Legally outflanked, Gore graciously conceded political defeat.

**Bush-Kerry (2004).** Three debates were conducted between incumbent George W. Bush and challenger John Kerry (September 30, October 5 and 8). Kerry, a senator from Massachusetts, impressed voters with his intelligence and reminded some of another senator from Massachusetts of the previous generation who had the same initials and was elected to the White House. Kerry had served in Vietnam during the 60s and then became an antiwar activist. Bush had the advantage of incumbency and developed the theme of "staying the course" in Iraq as central to the broader mission to fight terrorism and spread liberty and democracy in the Middle East. Bush defeated Kerry and his Democratic running mate, Senator John Edwards of North Carolina, by less than three percent of the popular vote and gained only fifteen more electoral ballots. The debates further introduced John Kerry to the nation.

**Obama-McCain (2008).** Two new faces appeared as major party candidates in 2008, both U. S. senators: Barack Obama from Illinois, and John McCain, long-time senator from Arizona. Three debates (September 26, October 7 and 15) granted Obama an opportunity to advance his theme of "change," while McCain emphasized his experience in the military (having been a courageous prisoner of war in Vietnam) and in the U. S. Congress. The nation seemed desirous to move past an unpopular George W. Bush, and Obama won a decisive victory with 365 electoral votes to McCain's 173 electoral votes—the largest percentage of popular votes for a Democrat since LBJ won in 1964 (Obama garnered 69.5 million popular votes). Interestingly, this was the first election in which neither candidate was born in the contiguous United States.

**Obama-Romney (2012).** Three debates between the incumbent president and former governor of Massachusetts, Mitt Romney, served to introduce the latter to the general voting public (October 3, 16, and 22). Obama was generally considered to have been poorly prepared for the first debate, and Romney excelled in rhetorical presentation. Obama performed more effectively in the other two debates, yet most of all was able to enjoy the benefits of incumbency. Romney did give a memorable phrase, "binders full of women"—a reference to a long list of female candidates for cabinet positions under Romney when he was governor of Massachusetts. Obama won with 332 electoral votes to Romney's 206 votes.

**Clinton-Trump (2016).** The 2016 presidential election campaign pitted two of the most unpopular candidates in U. S. history against each other—Democrat Hillary Clinton and Republican Donald Trump. Former Secretary of State Hillary Clinton seemed to have waited her turn for the Democratic nomination (having served in various positions, elective and appointive, as well as being a close runner-up to the nomination eight years earlier), and accomplished a great historic achievement in becoming the first female to be nominated for president by a major party. The nomination of Trump as Republican nominee seemed a most unlikely and unusual turn of events—the candidate had never served a day in elective or appointive public office nor had he served in the U. S. military. Thus, with a record viewing audience expected, and the event broadcast live with no opportunity to "edit" mistakes (as true with all the presidential debates), this was truly a "high risk" television event for the candidates.

The televised debates between Trump and Clinton were highly contentious. The first debate, held September 26 at Hofstra University, was moderated by Lester Holt of

NBC News. More than eighty million viewers tuned in this Monday evening debate, a record for such an event. Though Trump claimed "victory" the following day, based on polls cast on the internet, most analysts as well as scientific polling that was completed later in the week declared Secretary Clinton to have won overwhelmingly. The Secretary attacked Trump for his business practices; his questioning President Obama's citizenship (Trump's instigation of the "birther" issue which seemed an attempt to de-legitimize President Obama's qualification to serve in high office); his past comments about women, Mexicans, and Muslims; his temperament to serve as chief executive; and his refusal to release his tax returns.

The first debate was Trump's first one-on-one debate, as the Republican primary debates featured multiple candidates. The Trump team said their candidate had not conducted practice debate sessions in preparation, and that, along with Trump's other innate weaknesses, were soon obvious to viewers. By one count, he interrupted either Clinton or moderator Holt fifty-five times, compared to eleven interruptions by Clinton. While Hillary Clinton came across as informed, poised, dignified, courteous, and respectful, the New York businessman, by contrast, occasionally interrupted rudely, huffed, puffed, sighed, sniffled, and swilled water. Some viewers could not point to his offering one solid proposal during the course of ninety minutes. Trump suggested that finding a way to avoid all income taxes was "smart" and that rooting for the housing crash was merely a matter of successful business practice. Toward the end of the debate, Clinton found opportunity to present a well-prepared case study of an occasion in which Trump openly ridiculed a Miss Universe winner who had gained, in his opinion, too much weight, and thus he called her "Miss Piggy" and "Miss Housekeeping" (because she is Hispanic, originally from Venezuela). Trump continued to engage himself in this story for several days following, contending he had done only good favors for this beauty contestant.

The second debate, conducted in a town hall format in St. Louis on Sunday evening, October 9, was preceded by a news cycle of immense proportion. Two days earlier, a videotape was released to the national media in which Trump, apparently unaware of being recorded in 2005 as part of a television show, talks about being able to "do anything" to women because he is famous and admits he often grabs and kisses women who attract him without any warning. Trump spoke of himself as being a "star" and a "magnet," and that when he grabbed women's genitals they could not resist him. A firestorm of immense proportion emerged. Many prominent Republican leaders, including governors and congressmen, announced publicly that it was time for "Trump to step down as candidate." "This is who Donald Trump is," said Clinton in the opening of the second debate. "It's not only women and it's not only this video. He has also targeted immigrants, African-Americans, Latinos, people with disabilities, POWs, Muslims, and so many others." Trump responded by offering another quick apology and then took aim at Bill Clinton, declaring there has never been anyone in "the history of politics that's been so abusive to women," and then stated that Hillary Clinton had "attacked those same women and attacked them viciously."

Heightening the tension of this debate, Trump had invited four of the Clintons' accusers and alleged victims to sit in the audience, and occasionally television cameras panned their row during this contentious second round of debates. Trump attacks came rapidly. The candidate called Hillary Clinton a liar, stated that if elected he would appoint a special prosecutor to investigate her private email server as secretary of state, and even said she would then be "in jail." This was "red meat" for his hard-core supporters. The debate was filled with interruptions and wild generalizations, thus, fascinatingly, the last questioner asked the candidates if either of them saw something good and positive in the opponent each faced. Two days before this debate, many political pundits believed Trump's candidacy was "dead in the waters" and that he would be compelled to step down. After the militant encounter with his Democratic opponent, though the bar was set low for him, the same pundits believed he had redeemed his candidacy. One political scientist offered his conclusion that each candidate had won the debate, but each one won for different reasons—Clinton on public policy analysis and Trump because the bar was set so low for him to clear and rescue his candidacy.

Like an exciting serial movie or drama series, interest heightened for the third encounter between Trump and Clinton. This third and final debate, held at the University of Las Vegas on Wednesday evening, October 19, drew an audience of 71.6 million viewers, the third highest audience for any presidential debate. In this final debate, the candidates fought over the issues of abortion, guns, and nominees to the Supreme Court. They had far different visions of the nation as they spoke about the Second Amendment—Clinton spoke of "reasonable regulation" to keep guns away from "people who shouldn't have guns" and Trump saw that amendment under "absolute siege" and warned that if Clinton is elected "it will be a very, very small replica of what it is now." The Democratic nominee made clear that on the abortion issue she defended a woman's "right to choose," and Trump berated her for supporting late-term abortions. Clinton said that Trump was using "scare rhetoric" in discussing the topic. On immigration policy, Clinton took aim at Trump's long ballyhooed pledge to "build a wall along the border with Mexico," and Trump asserted rather indelicately: "We have some bad hombres here and we're gonna get 'em out."

Donald Trump performed reasonably well through the early segments and issue discussions, according to some observers, yet often a debate is remembered for some defining moment that overshadows everything else that is said. In days prior to the debate, Trump had been advancing the idea that the election was "rigged" against him by the liberal media and the political establishment. When moderator Chris Wallace of Fox News asked him that if he were defeated in the general election that he would abide in good faith with the results of the election, Trump twice refused to promise to accept the outcome: "I will look at it at the time" and then noted he might keep the media and the viewers "in suspense." This one statement was widely interpreted by Democratic voters as a threat to the democratic process and presented a huge challenge for Trump surrogates to explain and justify.

Though Donald Trump seemed to break nearly every rule of candidacy and campaigning, at least according to loyal Democrats, and though he lost the popular vote by almost three million votes, he won the election in the all-important electoral tally, 306 electoral votes to Hillary Clinton's 232 electoral votes.


## Vice Presidential Debates

Since 1976 the vice presidential candidates have met for debate and discussion one time during the election cycle. These debates are largely uneventful events, they do not draw as large an audience as the presidential debates, and they have little, if any, impact on the election outcome. The first vice presidential debate featured President Gerald Ford's political partner, Bob Dole, and Democratic challenger Walter Mondale, Jimmy Carter's running mate.

The most memorable exchange came when Senator Dole blamed the Democratic Party for global warfare ("All Democrat wars, all in this century"), and Mondale's terse reply declared simply, "Senator Dole has earned his reputation as a hatchet man." By contrast, one may remember a most restrained, respectful, and reasonable dialogue on the issues when candidates Dick Cheney and Joseph Lieberman met for "debate" in 2000. Some observers gave extra attention to how a male candidate would relate to the female candidate of the other party, such as in 1984 when George H. W. Bush debated Geraldine Ferraro or in 2008 when Joe Biden debated Sarah Palin, the latter using a memorable folksy style of interacting with Biden. The latter drew an audience of about seventy million television viewers, the largest audience for a vice presidential debate. "Can I call you Joe?" the first term Alaska governor asked during the opening handshake.

One vice presidential candidate exchange stands out as more memorable than all others. In 1988 the first George Bush was widely criticized for having selected a young and relatively inexperienced Senator Dan Quayle to serve as running mate on the Republican ticket. Understandably, the issue of experience came up in the VP debate between Quayle and Senator Lloyd Bentsen, a senator from Texas with a long, distinguished tenure in the upper chamber. When asked whether lack of experience would be a problem for Quayle, the junior senator glibly replied that he had as much experience as had John F. Kennedy when Kennedy ran for president. Immediately, with a very calm and fatherly demeanor, Bentsen looked directly at Quayle and slowly declared: "Senator, I served with Jack Kennedy. I knew Jack Kennedy. Jack Kennedy was a friend of mine. Senator, you're not Jack Kennedy." The audience applauded while an embarrassed Quayle muttered some words of disapproval for Bentsen's statement, but clearly the senior senator had won both the point and the audience. Bentsen's reply has been arguably called the most famous put-down in political history.

The only three-candidate vice presidential debate is one remembered for its third man, James Stockdale, Ross Perot's running mate. Flanked by candidates Quayle and Democratic challenger Al Gore, the respected and retired admiral opened with a much parodied line: "Who am I? Why am I here?"

On October 4, 2016, the GOP vice presidential candidate, Indiana governor Mike Pense, and Democratic candidate for vice president, Virginia Senator Tim Kaine, engaged in a heated and contentious debate, each attempting to defend and win votes for the top person on his ticket, Donald Trump and Hillary Clinton respectively. Pense's purpose was to defend Trump after the latter's "tweetstorm" against a former beauty queen who had gained, in the opinion of the nominee, too much weight, and to explain why Trump may not have paid federal income taxes for close to two decades. "Donald Trump is a businessman, not a career politician," the Governor explained. Kaine reviewed all the major insults Trump had hurled against minorities, especially Mexicans and women. This debate was hardly a "class act"—Kaine continually interrupted Pence, contesting his defense of Trump, and at times both candidates were talking over each other. Kaine's rudeness and Pence's soft-spoken demeanor translated into positive response to Pence as a reasonable and capable choice for running mate. Nearly everyone declared Pence the victor. In the final analysis, most political scientists believe that the vice presidential debates have very little, if any, impact on the outcome of the national election.

## Presidential Primary Debates

While presidential primary debates never match the importance or audience level that the presidential debates achieve, they have provided an early opportunity for voters to take measure of their party's candidates who seek the nomination. There have been numerous primary debates that provided an occasion for memorable moments. Drawing from David Jackson's review of primary debate moments (*USA Today*, August 2, 2015), some of these moments include interaction between successful politicians and others who faded into near oblivion:

On March 5, 1972, in Durham, New Hampshire, front-runner Edmund Muskie faced challengers George McGovern, Vance Hartke, Sam Yorty, and Ned Coll, a young man who had founded Revitalization Corps, an antipoverty group. Coll held up a rubber rat during a discussion of urban problems and proclaimed, "This is the real problem." Muskie, who had been on the ticket with Hubert Humphrey four years earlier, won the New Hampshire primary the next day, and McGovern went on to win the Democratic nomination, only to be trounced by Nixon in the general election.

On February 23, 1980, in Nashua, New Hampshire, Republicans George H. W. Bush and Ronald Reagan met for a debate—a debate that Bush sought to be conducted with Reagan alone. Reagan's campaign financed the debate and at the last minute opted to include the other Republican candidates. When the moderator called for cutting off Reagan's microphone, the candidate from California issued a stern warning that became a famous phrase: "I'm paying for this microphone, Mr. Green." Eventually, Reagan won the nomination, named Bush as his running mate, and then won the general election by defeating incumbent Jimmy Carter.

On March 11, 1984, in Atlanta, Democratic favorite Walter Mondale, the former vice president, was challenged by Senator Gary Hart. Hart supposedly had "new ideas," but Mondale felt the ideas were lacking specificity and made effective use of a popular Wendy's hamburger commercial: "When I hear your new ideas, I'm reminded of that ad, 'where's the beef?'" Mondale won the nomination, placed a woman (Geraldine Ferraro) on the ticket as running mate, but lost the general election in a landslide to President Reagan.

On March 15, 1992, in Chicago, Bill Clinton was leading the nomination race, and challenger Jerry Brown brought up allegations about the Arkansas law firm in which Hillary Clinton served as a partner. Clinton gave a stern warning: "Jerry, I don't care what you say about me...but you ought to be ashamed of yourself for jumping on my wife." Clinton won the nomination and the presidency, and later Jerry Brown became governor of California. Hillary Clinton, of course, was slated to be a lightning rod for scrutiny and controversy for the next quarter century.

On February 15, 2000, in Columbia, South Carolina, the commercial break in a debate between Republicans George W. Bush and John McCain occasioned a tense moment. Bush backers had already brutally attacked McCain in political ads. When Bush seemed to offer an olive branch with an extended hand and request an end to the acrimony, McCain cited some of the unkind attacks on him and his family. Bush then said he had nothing to do with the attacks. McCain shot back, "Don't give me that s***, and take your hands off me." Bush won the state's primary, the Republican nomination, and the general election. McCain won the nomination in 2008.

On January 5, 2008, in Manchester, New Hampshire, Barack Obama and Hillary Clinton were the leading Democrats in the primary debate and, in fact, their battle continued until the primary season had ended. A questioner asked Clinton a question about her questionable "likability," and she replied jokingly, "Well, that hurts my feelings...but I'll try to go on." Obama injected, "You're likable enough, Hillary," but the backhanded compliment was not well received. Obama won the presidency; Hillary Clinton served as his secretary of state.

On November 9, 2011, in Rochester, Michigan, Rick Perry, governor of Texas, was considered a major threat to the front-runner Mitt Romney, former governor of Massachusetts. At one moment in the debate, Governor Perry announced there were "three agencies of government when I get there that are gone: Commerce, Education and the...what's the third one there?....Let's see..." Some opponents attempted to cue him with suggestions, but Perry eventually conceded, "The third one...I can't....sorry... Oops." People laughed. Perry looked most human and modest in his memory lapse. Reviewers called it a "meltdown" from which Perry never recovered.

On August 6, 2015, Fox News Network hosted the first presidential primary debate among Republican candidates for the 2016 nomination. The field of aspirants was so large that Fox used popularity polls to narrow the number of debaters in prime time to ten men. The only woman among Republican candidates seeking nomination was relegated to an early round of "happy hour" or "kids' table" debate that some also jokingly called the "junior varsity" team. These seven declared candidates, who did not poll well enough to make the "varsity team," debated the same issues in a time slot prior to prime time. One dominant issue seemed to capture a huge slice of media attention—how would billionaire businessman Donald Trump fare in the midst of nine seasoned politicians seeking the nomination? Going into the first debate, Trump enjoyed a lead in the polls over all other Republican candidates. He never relinquished that lead.

This event turned out to be the most-watched presidential primary debate in history, and it nabbed a higher rating than the women's soccer World Cup final championship game and the NBA Finals. A record-setting twenty-four million people tuned in for the political clash—the highest ranked non-sports cable release of all time and the highest-rated broadcast in the network's twenty-year history. Whether seeking entertainment or insight into the candidates, likely no viewers were totally disappointed. Sparks flew between the only female moderator, Megyn Kelly, and Trump when Kelly questioned the celebrity billionaire about insulting comments he had uttered about women. This was the very first question of the night. Trump was on the defensive and seemed totally unprepared to answer the question, and he continued to berate Kelly in subsequent days for what he contended was an unfair, belligerent line of questioning. Fellow Republican challengers were openly unsparing in criticizing his attitude toward women in general and toward specific individuals, but nothing seemed to slow the Trump momentum toward the Republican nomination, secured in July 2016. Perhaps no one on the stage that night nor anyone sitting in the audience would have wagered that Donald Trump would win his party's nomination, much less the presidency!

## TED Talks

One of the most creative ways that ideas have been advanced by modern electronic technology, undoubtedly reaching the largest possible worldwide audiences in history, is called simply TED Talks. TED is an acronym for "Technology, Entertainment, Design." This global set of conferences is run by the private non-profit Sapling Foundation and the intricate program has been advanced under the slogan "Ideas Worth Spreading." The significant ideas are presented in brief addresses from expert speakers on topics related to education, business, science, technology, entertainment, as well as other general subjects. The central idea is for speakers to present a great idea in eighteen minutes or less.

TED Talks was founded in 1984 and has sponsored an annual conference series since 1996. The main TED conference is held annually in Vancouver, Canada, but there are smaller conferences held around the globe. The mission statement emphasizes the value of education and critical thinking: "We believe passionately in the power of ideas to change attitudes, lives, and ultimately the world." The speakers come from a wide range of nations and cultures, and they address a wide range of topics within science and culture. Some of the issues are addressed through story-telling. Among the former speakers: Bill Clinton, Al Gore, Madeleine Albright, Jimmy Carter, Jane Goodall, Gordon Brown, Billy Graham, Richard Dawkins, Richard Stallman, Bill Gates, Bono, Mike Rowe, and many Nobel Prize winners. In 2012 the online viewership topped one billion times worldwide.

Obviously, public speaking in the United States has come a long way since the days of the New England town meeting and the Lincoln-Douglas debates where audiences were comparatively small, local in nature, and gathered in small assemblies with only stenographic recording of remarks. TED Talks represents the wave of the future, and the future is now: international topics and issues; international speakers; and electronic accessibility at the listener's convenience.

By June 2015 over two thousand TED Talks had been posted and the program has moved into various forms of communication outreach. The most popular talks have included the following: Ken Robinson, "Do Schools Kill Creativity?"; Ann Cuddy, "Your Body Language Shapes who You Are"; Simon Sinck, "How Great Leaders Inspire Action"; Brene' Brown, "The Power of Vulnerability"; Tony Robbins, "Why We Do What We Do"; Dan Pink, "The Puzzle of Motivation"; Cameron Russell, "Looks Aren't Everything—Believe Me, I'm a Model"; Susan Cain, "The Power of Introverts"; Pamela Meyer, "How to Spot a Liar"; Shawn Achor, "The Happy Secret to Better Work"; David Gallo, "Underwater Astonishments"; Dan Gilbert, "The Surprising Science of Happiness"; Julian Treasure, "How to Speak so that People Want to Listen"; Elizabeth Gilbert, "Your Elusive Creative Genius"; David Blaine, "How I Held My Breath for Seventeen Minutes"; Keith Barry, "Brain Magic"; and Kelly McGonigal, "How to Make Stress Your Friend."

One critic, Nathan Heller, notes that TED Talks has enjoyed a strong connection with Silicon Valley. Many new electronic devices intended to appeal to consumers have been introduced and promoted in the Talks. The popular speakers tend to be high achievers in public life and, as Heller points out, most TED Talks "share a strong narrative and a polished theatrical style" (*New Yorker*, July 1, 2012). Many of the speakers provide good role models in public speaking for today's college and university students.

Clearly, the history of this nation's political and cultural life is replete with various venues and strategies for reaching the general public with public addresses designed to inform, persuade, inspire, and even entertain. And the electronic era has exponentially widened and multiplied these opportunities for reaching wider audiences. The future of rhetoric and public address looks bright, though we must always remember that while rhetoric and public address can advance the causes of truth, knowledge, and justice, such rhetoric can also perpetrate great harm and serve the purposes of evil.

# 3. Honored Guests–Top Speeches by World Leaders Presented in the United States

A number of outstanding world leaders have visited the United States, especially in the past half century or so when overseas travel has become much easier, and delivered speeches to a wide audience. We cite here only some of the most important public addresses presented on American soil by foreign dignitaries.

## Winston Churchill, "Sinews of Peace" Address, at Westminster College, March 5, 1946

As World War II came to an end, new tensions arose between the Soviet Union and the Western democracies. The Soviets had been an ally to those democracies in the fight against Hitler and Nazism, but immediately after surrender of both the Germans and Japanese they began to make moves to add new territory to their sphere on political domination and control. These tensions were all part of what came to be known as the Cold War, and it brought much consternation to Western world leaders, especially British Prime Minister Winston Churchill and American leaders such as President Truman and Secretary of State Dean Acheson.

In the context of such tension, Winston Churchill was invited to address at audience at Missouri's Westminster College. The small town of Fulton, population seven thousand, was jammed with forty thousand visitors to see the British leader. For the festive occasion Churchill had prepared something more than a mere commencement address. He had prepared a bombshell—a realistic assessment of mounting post-war tensions between two blocs of nations. No other speech in recent history stirred such a torrent of controversy and criticism. The speech is best known for its use of a metaphor that became such a widely-known and frequently-used figure of speech—perhaps the best known metaphor in American political history: "Iron Curtain." Churchill declared: "From Stetin in the Baltic to Trieste in the Adriatic an 'Iron Curtain' has descended across the continent. Behind that line lie all the capitals of the ancient states of Central and Eastern Europe—Warsaw, Berlin, Prague, Vienna, Budapest, Belgrade, Bucharest and Sofia. All these famous cities and the populations around them lie in what I must call the Soviet sphere, and all are subject, in one form or another, not only to Soviet influence but to a very high and in some cases increasing measure of control from Moscow."

The "Iron Curtain" metaphor gained popularity as a short-hand reference to the division of Europe as the Cold War intensified. The phrase also symbolized the ideological conflict and physical boundary dividing Europe into two separate areas and spheres of influence—a boundary that was staunchly maintained from the end of World War II in 1945 until the end of the Cold War in 1991. In actuality, the Iron Curtain was a series of border defenses and boundary checkpoints between the countries of Europe in the middle of the continent—on the east side of the curtain were countries connected to, and influenced by, the Soviet Union and on the west side were free nations that developed their own international and economic alliances. The most notable border was marked by the Berlin Wall and its Checkpoint Charley served as a symbol of the Iron Curtain. That famous Berlin Wall was later to become the physical setting for notable speeches by American Presidents John Kennedy and Ronald Reagan.

The origin of the metaphor "Iron Curtain" might be questioned. Churchill had first used the phrase in a telegram to President Truman in May 12, 1945. Then he used it again in a speech to the British House of Commons on August 16, 1945. Some authors, including G. K. Chesterton, had used the phrase before Churchill employed it, and even Joseph Goebbels, German Minister of Propaganda during the war, is said to have used it. Regardless, Churchill's use of the metaphor in his Missouri oration solidified its place in the American political vocabulary. "Iron Curtain" became a euphemism for boundaries—physical and ideological—between communist and capitalist nation-states. Outside of history books and history classes, the metaphor is not heard so much today.

## Margaret Thatcher, Address to Congress, February 20, 1985

The longest-serving British prime minister addressed Congress in 1985, with House Speaker Tip O'Neill presiding, and generally embraced President Ronald Reagan's policies. Thatcher began her speech by noting one of her predecessors, Winston Churchill, had already addressed the U. S. Congress three times, but that he had the advantage of an American mother, thus "ties of blood" with an American audience.

The Prime Minister's speech was a kind of celebration of forty years of peace in Europe, an achievement for which she gave American political and military leadership credit. "America has been the principal architect of peace in Europe which has lasted forty years," she declared. There was a great deal of history in this address in order to provide a backdrop for current policy recommendations. Thatcher endorsed the American president's space-based missile defense research plan and insisted that Western political leaders "must talk to the Soviets for we have one overriding interest in common—that never again should there be a conflict between our peoples."

At the conclusion of her speech, Thatcher quoted the eloquent peroration of Abraham Lincoln's Second Inaugural Address: "With malice toward none and charity toward all." Afterward, the British Prime Minister said her speech to Congress was "one of the most moving occasions of my life," *The New York Times* reported.

## Corazon Aquino, Address to Congress, September 18, 1986

The first female president of the Philippines received a warm reception by the members of Congress as requested help to "build a new home for democracy." Corazon Aquino was the widow of a beloved opposition leader, addressing Congress just months after she led the "People Power" revolution that ousted Dictator Ferdinand Marcos. The soft-spoken leader wore her trademark yellow—the color of the People Power movement—as did also several American congressional legislators to demonstrate solidarity. Aquino died in 2009 and her son, Benigno Aquino III, became president of the Philippines.

## Benazir Bhutto, Address to Congress, June 7, 1989

Benazir Bhutto (1953–2007) was the eleventh prime minister of Pakistan, serving two non-consecutive terms, 1988-90 and 1993-96. She served as the first female leader of a Muslim nation, and yet many of her roots were in the U. S., having graduated from Radcliffe College at Harvard University. While prime minister, she waged tough rhetorical opposition to her domestic rivals and neighboring India. She was charged with corruption and went into exile in Dubai in 1999; while in exile, she gave lectures in the U. S. In this address to Congress, Bhutto praised the U. S. for its "unwavering support" for democracy. She pledged that Pakistan would not develop a nuclear weapon and would crack down on the opium industry. Sadly, she was assassinated on December 27, 2007, upon her return to her native country after years in exile and after leaving a political rally, two weeks before the general election in which she was the leading candidate.

## Benazir Bhutto, Harvard Commencement Address, June, 1989

The speech to the Harvard graduating class and their guests was entitled "Democratic Nations Must Unite," and it expanded some of the same themes as expounded before Congress. Bhutto spoke as an alumnus and graduate of the Harvard class of 1973, and she was awarded an honorary degree. She quoted poet-philosopher Iqbal: "'Life is reduced to a rivulet under dictatorship. But in freedom it becomes a boundless ocean.'" This is true in Pakistan, and on every continent on earth. Let all of us who believe in freedom join together for the preservation of liberty. My message is, democratic nations unite." The speaker noted that the greatest export from the U. S. was not inventions or products or other commodities: "Your greatest export is an idea."

## Nelson Mandela, Addresses to Congress, June 26, 1990 and October 6, 1994

The South African anti-apartheid leader was the first private black citizen to address Congress in 1990, just months after he was released from prison after twenty-seven years of incarceration. "Let us keep our arms locked together so that we form a solid phalanx against racism," he implored. In 1994 Mandela returned as South Africa's first black president. He acknowledged his country had long been divided by apartheid, and pleaded for a multi-racial democracy and peace. "Our people demand democracy. Our country, which continues to bleed and suffer pain, needs democracy," Mandela declared. "We fight for and visualize a future in which all shall, without regard to race, color, creed or sex, have the right to vote and to be voted into all elective organs of state." He urged Americans to look beyond their national borders and take the lead in creating a world of democracy, peace and prosperity. "Once you set out on this road," Mandela said, "no one will need to be encouraged to follow." Mandela died in 2013 at age ninety-five. President Obama traveled to South Africa to present a tribute and eulogy at Mandela's memorial service.

## Queen Elizabeth II, Address to Congress, May 16, 1991

Queen Elizabeth's speech in Congress was the first address presented to this august body by a British monarch. The Queen spoke warmly of the spirit of cooperation between the United States and Great Britain, and she was interrupted several times by applause. At one point she poked fun at herself with a reference to her face being obscured when she made remarks earlier in the day at the White House: "I do hope you can see me today," she joked.

## Boris Yeltsin, Address to Congress, June 17, 1992

Yeltsin was the first democratically elected president of Russia, and his speech redefined the relationship between his nation and the United States. He pledged to bring democracy and a market economy to Russia. Communism "has collapsed never to rise again. I am here to assure you, we will not let it rise again in our land," he declared. The speaker also vowed "there will be no more lies—ever!" Yeltsin died at age seventy-six in 2007.

## Tony Blair, Address to Congress, July 17, 2003

Tony Blair was the eloquent and charismatic British prime minister and the strongest ally of George W. Bush's "coalition of the willing" in the decision to invade and attack Iraq. Blair's speech was delivered amidst a fierce debate about the validity of an intelligence report that was the justification for the war in Iraq. Blair added credibility to Bush's controversial decision to invade Iraq. "Every fiber of instinct and conviction I have" supported the idea that the U. S. and Great Britain were correct about Saddam Hussein. Blair cautioned that "history will not forgive" world leaders who do not address the rise of terrorism and weapons of mass destruction. Despite skepticism about the wisdom of war, members from both parties cheered Blair, who assured them, "We will be with you in this fight for liberty." The Prime Minister left office in 2007, though today his legacy is questioned by critics who claim he misled the British people about the Iraq War.

## Nouri Al-Maliki, Address to Congress, July 26, 2006

The Prime Minister of Iraq addressed Congress a day after he and President George W. Bush signed a new security plan for Baghdad. Al-Malaki insisted that Iraq could be trusted on the front lines in the war against international terror. "This is a battle between true Islam, for which a person's liberty and rights constitute essential cornerstones, and terrorism, which wraps itself in a fake Islamic cloak." Some Democrats chose to boycott the speech, in part because al-Maliki had not condemned Hezbollah militants that were in conflict with Israel. Al-Maliki resigned in 2014, having spent eight turbulent years in office with the support, but not always the respect, of American political leaders.

## Angela Merkel, Address to Congress, November 3, 2009

German Chancellor Angela Merkel addressed Congress a week before the twentieth anniversary of the fall of the Berlin Wall. The Chancellor noted several crucially important issues of mutual concern to Germany and the U.S.—Middle East peace, Iran's nuclear weapons development, and climate change—and challenged American lawmakers to unite with Germany in confronting these challenges boldly. "We are able to tear down walls of today," the Chancellor declared, by "creating prosperity and justice. And it means protecting our planet."

## Malada Yousafzai, Address to the United Nations, July 12, 2013

When Malada Yousafzai was introduced to the United Nations at the first Youth Takeover of the U. N., she received a standing ovation. With adoration understandable and merited, the young woman who was celebrating her birthday was also given the podium to share the lessons of her incredible, and some would say miraculous, story. Yousafzai had survived being shot in the left side of her forehead by the Taliban, recovered from the wound, and then continued her efforts to enhance educational opportunities for Pakistani young women.

This address was actually her first speech since being attacked by the Taliban in Pakistan on October 9, 2012. The focus of her speech, covered by major news networks, was women's rights and girls' education in the Middle East, because, as Yousafzai pointed out, females are the ones suffering most under oppressive rule in the Middle East. And while she addressed the U. N. Youth Assembly, there were many adults in attendance, some of whom wiped tears from their eyes as she expressed gratitude for the love demonstrated for her and the support for her mission. The friends with her during the attack were also shot. "They thought that the bullets would silence us. But they failed…Nothing changed in my life but this: weakness, fear, and hopelessness died. Strength, power, and courage were born."

Yousafzai said that she learned compassion from the prophet Muhammad, Jesus, and Buddha. Her tone was one of optimism. As she ended a powerful speech that captured rapt attention of the entire, culturally diverse audience, she declared: "One child, one teacher, one pen, and one book can change the world." Yousafzai won the Nobel Peace Prize at age seventeen. In 2015 she opened a school in Lebanon for Syrian refugee girls. In January 2017 she issued a statement on President Trump's executive order on refugees: "I am heart-broken today that President Trump is closing the door on children, mothers, and fathers fleeing violence and war."

## Benjamin Netanyahu, Addresses to Congress, July 10, 1996; May 24, 2011; and March 3, 2015

The 2015 speech by the Prime Minister of Israel was the most significant and controversial of the three addresses by Netanyahu. The speech got more advance discussion prior to delivery than most speeches to Congress receive after delivery. "Never so much has been written about a speech that hasn't been given," the Prime Minister declared the day before its presentation.

The whole occasion was rife with international intrigue and politics and at the center of the controversy was a difference in policy between President Obama and Netanyahu in handling Iran's capability of developing nuclear weapons. Netanyahu presented an eloquent case for Iran's threat to Israel's survival. The speech was interrupted on numerous points by thunderous applause from the audience and several standing ovations. On the other hand, many Congressional Democrats joined the President, the Vice President, and the Secretary of State in boycotting the speech because of their perception the speech was more about Israeli politics than international affairs; the rift was deepened when Speaker of the House John Boehner invited the Israeli Prime Minister to speak without consulting the President.

Netanyahu's "fiery speech" made the claim that the deal President Obama was leading in Geneva negotiations "doesn't block Iran's path to the bomb; it paves Iran's path to the bomb. So why would anyone make this deal?" With the Prime Minister making a grand entry, shaking hands with Congressional leaders, receiving much partisan applause, and introducing a special guest (in this case, Holocaust survivor Elie Wiesel, winner of the Nobel Peace Prize, in the visitors' gallery), the whole occasion was like a Presidential State of the Union Address. Incidentally, **Mohammad Reza Shah Pahlavi**, Shah of Iran, addressed Congress on April 12, 1962. He was deposed in 1979. No Iranian leader has addressed a joint session since.

## Shinzo Abe, Address to Congress, April 29, 2015

Prime Minister of Japan Shinzo Abe (AH-beh) delivered the first address to a joint session of Congress by a Japanese leader, and he stood by previous leaders' apologies for his nation's World War II abuses. He also expressed "eternal condolences" for the American lives lost fighting Japan in the war. "On behalf of Japan and the Japanese people, I offer with profound respect my eternal condolences to the souls of all American people that were lost during World War II," Abe declared. "Our actions brought suffering to the peoples in Asian countries. We must not avert our eyes from that," Abe confessed. "I will uphold the views expressed by the previous prime ministers in this regard. History is harsh. What's done cannot be undone," Abe said. The speaker received repeated standing ovations from the members of Congress. Watching from the gallery was Caroline Kennedy, U. S. Ambassador to Japan.

## Pope Francis, Address to Congress, September 24, 2015

In the first ever public address by a pontiff to a special joint session of the U. S. Congress, Pope Francis implored a divided legislature—and the U. S. nation—to "confront every form of polarization" in seeking solutions to society's most pressing problems. In the address, lasting one hour and delivered in English in a slow and deliberate tone, the Pope urged lawmakers to take action to welcome immigrants, protect the environment, abolish the death penalty, and reduce economic inequality. Francis' message challenged some Republican positions on those issues, especially immigration, that had divided both Congress as well as the party's candidates who were already campaigning for the primaries. Speaking of the large number of immigrants and refugees, the Pope counseled that "we must not be taken aback by their numbers but rather view them as persons, seeing their faces and listening to their stories, trying to respond as best we can to their situation."

Francis's address was clearly adapted to his audience, which welcomed him with warmth and excitement that is rare in the nation's Capital. As in other addresses, Francis smiled throughout and displayed a gentle and calm demeanor. "His rhetoric was softer than what he often employs on these issues—language that has earned him particular criticism in the U. S." reported three writers for the *Wall Street Journal* (September 25, 2015, p. 1). The Pope appealed to the foreign heritage of most of his listeners, identifying himself as the "son of immigrants, knowing that many of you are also descended from immigrants." He made a softer call for proper stewardship of the environment and omitted any specifics. He made a general reference to "concern for the family, which is threatened, perhaps as never before, from within and without." The Pope did not act on the requests of Republicans and many church leaders to speak more boldly on issues such as homosexuality and abortion.

The address must be rated as highly effective and successful. For certain, the Argentine Pope's popularity was high even before he traveled to the U. S. The speech was an occasion for a rare demonstration of bipartisanship in the Capitol, especially with one-third of lawmakers who are Roman Catholic. House Speaker John Boehner did not hide his feelings when Pope Francis spoke, often wiping tears from his eyes. Democratic House Minority Leader Nancy Pelosi seemed equally emotional, beaming throughout the address and jumping to her feet to applaud him. There was a festive atmosphere for the speech which had been long anticipated, and the enthusiastic lawmakers, usually the ones eager to speak, now listened quietly, determined to hear and ponder every word.

Another brief address was offered on a balcony in the nation's Capital wherein the Pope spoke in his native Spanish and asked the crowd for their prayers, adding that nonbelievers were welcome to send him "good wishes." He then closed with a benediction in English: "God bless America." The Pope then flew to New York where he presided over a service at St. Patrick's Cathedral, and, on Friday of that week, addressed the United Nations General Assembly.

## Other Notable Addresses by World Leaders

Notable world leaders have addressed American audiences in various settings, as noted with Churchill's commencement speech at a small college in Missouri, but the joint session of Congress provides the most impressive and visible venue for an address of significance. Joint meetings have been a favorite venue for foreign leaders, and one hundred and ten foreigners (along with a handful of Americans, most being early space-age astronauts) have addressed these Congressional sessions.

A list kept by the U. S. House Historian's Office shows King Kalakaua of Hawaii was the first world leader to address a joint meeting of Congress, in 1874. The ones previously cited are surely among the most significant. And yet there are others whose appearances before Congress stand out: Prince Heinrich of Prussia (Feb. 27, 1902); Winston Churchill, Prime Minister of the United Kingdom (May 19, 1943); Clement Atlee, Prime Minister of the United Kingdom (Nov. 13, 1945); Miguel Valdes, President of Mexico (May 1, 1947); Enrico Dutra, President of Brazil (May 19, 1949); Juliana, Queen of the Netherlands (Apr. 3, 1952); Hailie Selassie, Emperor of Ethiopia (May 28, 1954); Syngman Rhee, President of South Korea (July 28, 1954); Ngo Dinh Diem, President of South Vietnam (May 9, 1957); Charles de Gaulle, President of France (Apr. 25, 1960); Ferdinand Marcos, President of the Philippines (Sept. 15, 1966); Anwar El Sadat, President of Egypt (Nov. 5, 1975); Yitzhak Rabin, Prime Minister of Israel (Jan. 28, 1976); Pierre Trudeau, Prime Minister of Canada (Feb. 22, 1977); Menachin Begin, Prime Minister of Israel (Sept. 18, 1978); Hussein, King of Jordan (July 20, 1994); Shimon Peres, Prime Minister of Israel (Dec. 12, 1995).

The manifest conclusion to draw from this study is that the United States plays such a vital role in the contemporary world that foreign leaders seek to enhance their own standing and the standing of the nations they represent by presenting speeches to select American audiences.

# 4. Tragic Eloquence—Top Speeches by Native Americans

Most of the speeches we know that were delivered by Native Americans were presented as pleas to European-based people who wanted to deprive them of their land and other rights of self-determination. For five hundred years, Native American orators addressed conflicts and encounters with the French, Spanish, Dutch, British, and the "Americans"—their aggression, presumptions, policies, and influence. In the minds of Indian orators, their speeches and appeals were religious communication or moral suasion, though they likely would never have used those terms. Of course, American natives have been blessed by leaders among their nations and tribes who delivered messages long before there was European contact. Perhaps the greatest Native American speeches have disappeared with the deaths of the speakers and their listeners.

Our listing here only uses a rough chronological pattern and does not presume to be a complete listing or to rank the speeches in order of importance. Native Americans, like other ancient and indigenous peoples, belonged to oral cultures. These cultures depended on public speaking as a necessary, practical art, yet it was not deemed feasible or even possible to transcribe exact texts of the speeches. Texts that we possess of natives' speeches are typically based on translation and reconstruction of the orations by white men. Frequently we do not know the exact date on which a speech was delivered. Consider also that there is no official title to such addresses, thus a meaningful phrase in the speech is often selected for the title.

## Red Jacket, "We Are Owners of this Land," 1791

In 1791 President George Washington sent emissaries to pressure the Iroquois into submitting to U. S. government wishes on land and on neutrality in times of any war between the new U. S. nation and any other nation. Seneca leader Sacoyewatha, better known as Red Jacket (c. 1751–1830), was the premiere speaker in the tradition of Iroquois oratory. He was also, perhaps, the greatest orator in Native American history. Unlike other well-known native leaders, Red Jacket was not a warrior. In speaking of deity, he used the term "Great Ruler" and "Great Spirit." In speaking of George Washington, he used the term "the Chief Warrior of the United States." Red Jacket could speak English, but was determined not to speak English in public. His native name Otetiani meant "Always ready" or "He is prepared."

## Red Jacket, "We Never Argue About Religion," 1805

Red Jacket was an Iroquois chief who spoke to Boston Missionary society representatives who were seeking to perform missionary work among the Iroquois in upstate New York. Red Jacket began his address by making reference to "the Great Spirit" who willed that they should meet together, then he repeated what the Christian missionary had taught them: "You say that you are sent to instruct us how to worship the Great Spirit agreeably to his mind, and if we do not take hold of the religion which you white people teach, we shall be unhappy hereafter. You say that you are right and we are lost. How do we know this to be true?" Red Jacket asked. "We understand that your religion is written in a book. If it was intended for us as well as for you, why has not the Great Spirit given it to us; and not only to us, but why did he not give our forefathers the knowledge of that book, with the means of understanding it rightly? We only know what you tell us about it. How shall we know when to believe, being so often deceived by the white people?"

Red Jacket continued to reason with the Christian missionaries, noting that "if there is but one way to worship and serve the Great Spirit, if there is but one religion, why do you white people differ so much about it? Why do not all agree, as you can all read the book?....We never quarrel about religion." Even the most evangelistic Christians must concede the cogency of Red Jacket's argument and draw insight on how missionaries are received in a non-Christian culture.

## Tecumseh, "Sleep No Longer, O Choctaws and Chickasaws," September 1811

As a wise man and brave leader, Tecumseh (1768–1813) was respected by Native Americans and feared by whites as a man who used persuasive oratory to rally his people to fight. He was fully dedicated and relentless in an attempt to organize a confederacy of resistance to American encroachment on Native American lands. Tecumseh embarked on a speaking and organizing campaign that took him from Indiana to Florida, to Missouri, to the Plains, and even into Canada in a valiant effort to effect a union of Indian tribes. Despite his persuasive skills and personal charisma, he was not always successful.

Tecumseh typically appealed to the courage of the natives. He would remind his people of the past where tribes had all but disappeared at the hands of "white intruders and tyrants...[who were determined]...to enslave us." "Sleep no longer, O Choctaws and Chickasaws, in false security and delusive hopes," he appealed. "Our broad domains are fast escaping from our grasp. Every year our white intruders become more greedy, exacting, oppressive and overbearing." Tecumseh would end his speeches with an appeal: "I now call on you, brave Choctaws and Chickasaws, to assist in the just cause of liberating our race from the grasp of our faithless invaders and heartless oppressors. The white usurpation in our common country must be stopped, or we, its rightful owners, be forever destroyed and wiped out as a race of people...Haste to the relief of our common cause."

## Speckled Snake, "The Land You Live on is Not Yours," c. 1830

Chief Speckled Snake was a Cherokee who heard President Andrew Jackson offering friendship to the Cherokee nation and other Indians, but who also told the Indians, "The land you live on is not yours; go beyond the Mississippi, there is game; there you may remain while the grass grows or the water runs." Speckled Snake's speech is filled with biting sarcasm and irony as he acknowledges that "we have heard the talk of our great father; it is very kind. He says he loves his red children."

The chief cites some history of how other tribes had given white men their land, only to be run off again. The speaker, addressing his council, notes the irony of "our great father" claiming to "love his red children" and then telling them they must "move a little further, lest I should, by accident, tread on you." Speckled Snake seemed to use the ultimate statement in sarcasm when he asked about President Jackson: "Will not our great father come there also? He loves his red children, and his tongue is not forked." The traumatic and heart-breaking journey of hundreds of miles became known as "the Trail of Tears."

## Chief Seattle, "Concession and Swan Song," December 1854

Chief Seattle led six Indian tribes in the Pacific Northwest. He was a wise and learned man, who realized white settlers had increased in population and military might. Thus he decided, sadly, his people should accept the federal government's offer to move to a reservation rather than to fight a war of resistance they surely would lose. The chief's audience was composed of the territorial governor, white settlers, and about one thousand Indians. Governor Isaac I. Stevens had returned from Washington with the mandate for buying the Indians' lands and establishing reservations. On this historic occasion, the oration was delivered on the site that would become the city of Seattle.

Chief Seattle could be eloquent. Speaking of the "white man," he notes that "your time of decay may be distant, but it will surely come," as there is "common destiny. We may be brothers after all, we will see." The Chief says "I think my people will accept it and will retire to the reservation you offer them. Then we will dwell apart in peace."

Chief Seattle's speeches always were built on the premise of respect for the land and all of nature. "Every part of this soil is sacred in the estimation of my people," he declared. "Every hillside, every plan and grove, has been hallowed by some sad or happy event in days long vanquished."

## Young Joseph, "I Am Tired of Fighting," October 5, 1877

The story of Joseph, the father, and his son, Young Joseph can be traced as far back as the Lewis and Clark expedition that reached the Columbia River in the fall of 1805. The Nez Perces Indians were welcoming and kind to the American explorers and assisted them on their journey, and they pursued peaceful relations with incoming European settlers, even establishing trade agreements. However, more and more immigrants and miners overran the Indian Territory. Old Joseph refused to sign a new treaty because it was the homeland of his people. Before death, the father made his son promise never to sell the homeland. Young Joseph came under tremendous pressure to break that promise. As settlers moved in, tensions and even violence broke out. Then the U. S. military was summoned to fight the Nez Perces.

Young Joseph (c. 1840–1904) persuaded his people to move rather than go to war with white Americans. The Indians had lost so many horses and their children were hungry, they were defeated and demoralized. The surrender speech of Young Joseph was reported by Lieutenant Charles Erskin Wood and it is considered one of the most famous Native American speeches. "I am tired of fighting," Young Joseph declares. He then speaks of so many old and young men who were killed in fighting and how "the little children are freezing to death" and concedes he may find his children "among the dead." "Hear me my chiefs! I am tired. My heart is sick and sad. From where the sun now stands, I will fight no more forever."

Indeed, this oration is an example of tragic eloquence that expressed the pain and futility of fighting and killing. It caught the attention of many white people. (See more information on this speech in the main section of 101 speeches in this book.)

## Young Joseph, "An Indian's Views of Indian Affairs," January 1879

Young Joseph was invited to Washington, D. C., in January 1879, and presented a speech that described his tribe's history and recent fights with the U. S. Army. The speech is highly personal. Joseph tells of the moral laws and rules he was taught and by which his people tried to live. In adapting to his audience, he states: "The first white men of your people who came to our country were named Lewis and Clark. They also brought many things that our people had never seen. They talked straight, and our people gave them a great feast, as a proof that their hearts were friendly."

The address is lengthy. It reviews interaction between his tribal people and U. S. citizens, and the painful wars that occurred. In his peroration, Joseph is eloquent: "When I think of our condition, my heart is heavy. I see men of my race treated as outlaws and driven from country to country or shot down like animals," he laments. "Let me be a free man—free to travel, free to stop, free to work, free to trade where I choose, free to choose my own heart teachers, free to follow the religion of my fathers," he appeals. "Whenever the white man treats the Indian as they treat each other, then we will have no more wars. We shall all be alike—brothers of one father and one mother, with one sky above us and one country around us, and one government for all. Then the Great Spirit Chief who rules above will smile upon this land…For this time the Indian race are waiting and praying."

## Clyde Warrior, "We Are Not Free," February 2, 1967

There was a "Red Power" movement in the late 1960s and early 70s. The starting point was likely the dramatic takeover in 1969 of Alcatraz Island by Native American students. The takeover of the Bureau of Indian Affairs (BIA) in Washington, the siege at Wounded Knee in 1973, and other confrontations between Indian leaders and white officials gained attention for the American Indian Movement (AIM). In a sense, the entire nation was in turmoil over social justice issues during this period, the time of Vietnam conflict and racial and ethnic clashes in general.

Clyde Warrior (1939–1968), born in Oklahoma Indian territory, was an important leader and compelling speaker in this movement. As a teenager, he had traveled Indian country as a pow wow dancer. He was passionate about the Indian people, especially youth, rejecting white images of them and taking pride in their Indian heritage and values. As an eloquent Indian speaker, he advocated taking direct action to effect change.

In 1967 Warrior delivered a statement and testimony before the President's National Advisory Commission on Rural Poverty. The young Indian leader speaks of his upbringing by Indian grandparents, of the great "material deprivation" experienced by old people and yet "feeling rich because they were free." "They were rich in things of the spirit, but if there is one thing that characterizes Indian life today it is poverty of the sprit. We still have human passions and depth of feeling," Warrior declares, "but we are poor in spirit because we are not free—free in the most basic sense of the word…We do not make choices. Our choices are made for us; we are the poor." Warrior eloquently speaks of the plight of young Indian people and "forced assimilation and directed acculturated programs." His lament and appeal are moving and poignant.

## Russell Means, "In the Belly of the Monster," September 20, 1977

Russell Means (b. 1939) has become one of the best-known defenders of the rights of native peoples in the U. S. and world-wide. He was one of the founders of the American Indian Movement (AIM), which gained national notoriety in 1973 in its seventy-one day occupation of Wounded Knee. Though many tribes rallied to support the occupation, there was armed assault from a tribal government and the U. S. Government. During the controversial occupation, Means spoke about the revival of the famed Ghost Dance.

While both an actor and an author, Means is also an orator. In this speech, he addressed United Nations affiliates and members of the Human Rights Commission in Geneva, Switzerland. "We are the people who live in the belly of the monster," Means declared. "Every country in the Western Hemisphere follows the lead of the monster. I come not to turn the other cheek. We have turned it now for almost five hundred years." Means concluded his remarks: "Someone once said you can tell the power of a country by the oppression its people will tolerate. No longer are we going to tolerate the monster."

## Albert Bender, "Democrats Can't Be People's Party and Praise Jackson," November 3, 2015

Albert Bender is a Native American and historian, author, speaker, and community activist, especially for Native American causes. In this address, presented in editorial form in the *Tennessean* for a Middle Tennessee audience, Bender responds to the chairwoman of the Tennessee Democratic Party, who praised Andrew Jackson "because he captured the imagination of the American people." Bender offered a clear counter to this claim: "[Jackson] captured the imagination of racist white people who imagined an America without Indians, an America where there was no place for Native Americans." Registering his discomfort with the term "White House," Bender noted that this a "residence in which Native Americans were not welcome." As for Jackson, "he is reviled by American Indians across the country."

To Democrats and to Middle Tennesseans, Andrew Jackson is typically viewed in a positive light, even if they know very little about the president nicknamed "Old Hickory." To Bender, "Jackson carried out the most murderous removal campaign against Native Americans—Cherokees, Creeks, Choctaws, Chickasaws, and Seminoles—in U. S. history. He was directly responsible for the hideous, agonizing deaths of tens of thousands of Native Americans, beginning with the Creek War of 1813-14."

Bender cites other Jackson atrocities against American natives, including abuse of Creek women that were sold into slavery, and Indian children being starved and murdered in captivity, and orphaned children often taken off battlefields from the bodies of their dead mothers as "trophies." Finally, of course, Jackson signed the Indian Removal Bill of May 30, 1830, that led to forcible relocation of many Native American men, women, children, and elderly. Few under the age of six or over the age of sixty survived the hideous march of death that has been called "the Cherokee Trail of Tears."

In this address, Bender closes with some of the strongest name-calling against one of the nation's best-known presidents: Andrew Jackson is "racist monster," "racist devil incarnate, and "early-day American Hitler whose deadly legacy for American Indians remains extant to this very day." Clearly, Bender delivered a passionate message for mainstream Americans which surely challenged their understanding of early American history.

Manifestly, there is a rich legacy of Native American oratory that must not be lost or forsaken in the study of American history.

# 5. Preaching the Word–Top Sermons by American Preachers

Our study has surveyed political, reform, legislative, and even legal speaking that has both shaped and reflected the American political and social culture. Since we are studying American oratory, and since religious speaking has influenced the American society and culture as much or more as other kinds of speeches, it seems most appropriate at least to cite some of the top sermons in American history.

Looking for some depth and variety in the nature of religious messaging, including the entertainment media as well as speaking from American minority religious leaders? In an unashamed commercial, I recommend the author's own study, *From Pilgrim Pulpit to the Electronic Era: The Varieties of American Religious Communication* (Westbow Press, 2014). Religious messages have been presented millions of times on our continent. The listing below reflects a choice about the sermons that seemed to matter most. Not all "top sermons" by American preachers can be cited, and, yes, there is a bias here toward Christian sermons. In some cases, the sermons are more representative of a larger body of work, and some were repeated numerous times.

Incidentally, some names are not on this list because it is difficult to find one single sermon that stands out above all the rest. For example, George Whitefield deserves mention. Though ordained in the Church of England in 1739, he made several trips to the American colonies and his fervent preaching was the major catalyst for the Great Awakening that occurred between 1739 and 1745, beginning in New England, then moving to the Middle Colonies, and, to a lesser extent, South Carolina and Georgia. He preached to large audiences in the larger cities of the colonies (Boston, New York, Philadelphia, and Charleston), stirred many conversions, and is responsible for starting a new revivalist tradition by preaching outdoors, an act disdained by many established church leaders. Returning emotionalism to evangelical faith and homiletic practice, Whitefield even impressed the quintessential skeptic Benjamin Franklin, who estimated the revivalist could be heard and understood by an audience as large as 30,000, because of the voice of the preacher as well as the reverence and silence of the listeners. Whitefield made little attempt at depth of reasoning with his audience, and, in a sense, is the first in a line of famous American evangelists who effectively addressed large audiences with the same kind of simplicity and emotional appeal—Charles Finney, Dwight Moody, Billy Sunday, and Billy Graham.

## John Winthrop, "Model of Christian Charity," 1630

John Winthrop (1588–1649) was a lawyer and political leader, who served as Massachusetts' governor the first two decades of the colony's history. Though not formally a minister, civil authorities were expected to provide spiritual leadership. Manifestly, in this colonial enterprise there was no separation of church and state. Therefore, the governor delivered messages that were clearly a mix of politics and religion.

This sermon was Winthrop's best known message and was delivered in 1630, and American folklore has the message being presented aboard the flagship *Arbella* after departure from Southhampton, England. Truth is, portions of this message were undoubtedly delivered on numerous occasions, both by sea and on land. Winthrop noted in his admonition that many may come to America for wealth, but that was not the reason the people on the *Arbella* had ventured their lives: "We have drawn up indentures with the Almighty and if we succeed we will be rewarded." The Governor urged these Puritan pioneers to take seriously all biblical injunctions. "[We must] follow the counsel of Micah, to do justly, to love mercy, to walk humbly with our God. For this end, we must be knit together in this work as one man," the Governor counseled. Appeals were then made to brotherly affection, mutual support, bearing one another's burdens, laboring and suffering together, keeping unity and bonds of peace. And the end result? "We shall find that the God of Israel is among us, when ten of us shall be able to resist a thousand of our enemies...for we must consider that we shall be as a city upon a hill, the eyes of all people are upon us."

That well known metaphor, "city on a hill," drawn deeply from biblical terminology, captured for Winthrop and all Puritans in the new land the chief mission for which they had risked their lives and fortunes. The theme has been adduced numerous times by other preachers in other eras of our history.

## Jonathan Edwards, "Sinners in the Hands of an Angry God," 1741

Jonathan Edwards (1703–1758), the preacher who did more than anyone else to inaugurate the Great Awakening, was both student and scholar. He studied Latin, Greek, and Hebrew and was first in his class as a graduate at Yale in 1720. Edwards could have pursued several careers, but had a passion for God and spiritual matters. He was definitely an astute theologian and philosopher, as well as a defender of Puritan Calvinism and eloquent opponent of Arminianism (conditional election, unlimited atonement, partial depravity—all terms likely unknown to most contemporary readers and listeners).

"Sinners in the Hands of an Angry God" is Edwards' best known sermon, and this stirring message was based on the brief text in Deuteronomy 33: 35—"Their foot shall slide in due time." The sermon was delivered to the rural congregation at Enfield, Connecticut (then included in Massachusetts), on July 8, 1741, and has been repeated in American pulpits in one form or another; the text of the sermon has been published and printed in many anthologies and other books. Edwards was an intellectual who expounded Scripture, yet by today's standards of popular preaching he would likely be viewed as boring. Edwards' God is absolutely sovereign and human beings must be absolutely obedient to God. This preacher was effective in using imagery to depict the wrath of God. Some historians of American religion believe that this giant of the colonial pulpit was the most profound and systematic theologian that America ever produced. (Incidentally, if Edwards' preaching inaugurated the Great Awakening, then the revivalist preaching of George Whitefield, who traveled from colony to colony and drew the largest crowds of any preacher, gave the Awakening its greatest impetus.)

## Lyman Beecher, "Six Sermons on Intemperance," 1828

Lyman Beecher (1775–1863) was a prominent advocate of religious awakening in the early nineteenth century. As a Presbyterian minister, he addressed a number of reform issues, including temperance; he also served as president of Lane Theological Seminary. Beecher, the father of thirteen children, several of whom were gifted speakers and advocates for social justice, delivered a series of lectures on temperance in 1828. He was also the co-founder of the American Temperance Society. He insisted that the consumption of alcohol threatened not only the moral but also the economic and political fiber of the United States. "But of all the ways to hell, which the feet of deluded mortals tread," Beecher exclaimed, "that of the intemperate is the most dreary and terrific."

## Charles G. Finney, "What a Revival Is," 1835

Charles Finney (1792–1875) began organizing revival meetings in upstate New York in the 1820s, and he became the leading evangelist/revivalist of the early nineteenth century. This period was known as the Second Great Awakening. Finney was also concerned about reforming the American society. As a strong advocate of mainstream Protestant revivalism, he founded Oberlin College on the Ohio frontier to train ministers who would continue to energize this revivalist spirit. In this sermon, Finney expounded upon the values of spiritual revival in a Christian society.

## Theodore Parker, "Transient and Permanent in Christianity," May 19, 1841

Theodore Parker (1810–1860) was a studious intellectual Boston Unitarian preacher whose church audiences were the second largest in the nation after those of Henry Ward Beecher in Brooklyn. Though not as powerful in oratorical delivery, he was profound in thought and earnestness. His views on liberal Christianity evolved as he studied and presented lessons. Parker is best known for this sermon, "Transient and Permanent in Christianity," presented in 1841 at the Haws Place Church in Boston, in which he elaborates on the faith of Unitarians. His basic point is that there is so much merit and direction in Christian moral teaching that such doctrine did not need validation from miracle stories. In his view, Jesus Christ was the greatest man who ever lived, but he was not God. This sermon enhanced the Unitarian movement and is widely published.

## Ralph Waldo Emerson, "The Lord's Supper," September 9, 1832

This sermon, delivered September 9, 1832, is perhaps the most significant sermon in the diverse career of philosopher and minister Ralph Waldo Emerson (1803–1882). This reformer preached before liberal, intellectually elite audiences as well as any other speaker. In his sermons and essays, he seemed to struggle with doubts, confusion, and uncertainties, and, along with the tragic death of his first wife, with intellectual and emotional turmoil. Soon he became embroiled in a dispute over the administration of the Lord's Supper. He refused to preside over the ritual and explains his reasons and his doubts in this famous sermon.

## Russell Conwell, "Acres of Diamonds," 1861 and afterward

Whether "Acres of Diamonds" should be considered more as a lecture or an actual sermon, the message was delivered thousands of times by Russell Conwell (1843–1925), a Baptist preacher, and earned immense financial profits. While other speakers were earning a hundred dollars a week and paying their own expenses, Conwell was demanding two hundred dollars for a single lecture. He delivered this best known lecture for the first time in a small Methodist church in Westfield, Massachusetts, in 1861, and then subsequently presented it up to two hundred times for the next fifty years. Conwell was totally immersed in a speaking career, going for months in the summer into various states and presenting a lecture every night and a sermon on Sunday.

Conwell was a large man who displayed considerable physical vitality when delivering a speech. If we label "Acres of Diamonds" a sermon, then it was certainly counter to sermonic themes heard in most churches. Most preachers were likely to tell the congregants that, with the apostle Paul, the love of money was the root of all evil and that wealth was unnecessary. By contrast, Conwell proclaimed the value, even the duty, of gaining wealth, and then he argued that getting rich is not difficult for those who put their minds and energies toward that goal. Of course, he would soften the tone of such a strong premise by pointing out that the money earned should be devoted to charitable uses, and that he himself had donated his earnings to the education of poor boys.

Other the years, the lecture was essentially the same, though there were minor "tweaks" from year to year. The speaker often rambled, and he even admitted that he "often breaks all rules of oratory, departs from the precepts of rhetoric." Yet he remained immensely popular. Overall, this speech was a collection of stories, each one illustrating the speaker's central idea: There is a way to get rich. The basic story was about Ali Hafed, who sold his farm filled with "Acres of Diamonds" to travel the world over in a vain search for the precious stones. Piety and poverty, Conwell assured his listeners, could not dwell in the same person. Additionally, there is wealth all around us and we may not be noticing it and can lose that golden opportunity to access it. The appeal of the lesson, apart from the speaker's delivery, lay in the fact that this is what listeners of that era, characterized by hard work and low wages for millions of farmers and industrial laborers, most wanted to hear. And coming from a Baptist minister it could seem like a message from God.

Russell Conwell founded Temple University with the profits he earned from this single sermon/lecture. The "gospel of wealth and health" has continued to be presented by preachers in modern times, especially in the "electronic church" by popular television preachers.

## Billy Sunday, "The Booze Sermon"

William Ashley Sunday (1862–1935) was his real name, and he played professional baseball in Chicago before turning down a contract with a good salary in order to become an evangelist. Being in better physical shape than most other preachers, he became known for his "acrobatic preaching" and with dramatic sermons that invited sinners to "hit the sawdust trail." Sunday drew large audiences and developed a national reputation. Like Dwight L. Moody, Sunday was never ordained; neither was identified with a denomination, and neither had much knowledge or interest in the academic study of theology. Both preachers were making trial runs at mass evangelism, later perfected by Billy Graham in the electronic era. Sunday had a passion about preaching on social ills, and perhaps abolition was his most important issue. Versions of this sermon were preached for many years in many venues and pulpits.

## Harry Emerson Fosdick, "Shall the Fundamentalists Win?" May 21, 1922

Harry Fosdick (1878–1969) served as a long-time preacher at the Riverside Church in New York City, a setting in which he preached to overflow crowds, waiting lines, and an even larger radio audience. Perhaps his major contribution to American religious experience was adapting Christianity to the findings of modern biblical criticism. This passion led him on a path of rhetorical war with fundamentalists of the mid-1920s. Delivered May 1922, the famous sermon, "Shall the Fundamentalists Win?", stirred passion on all sides as Fosdick attempted to distinguish between fundamentalists, conservatives, and liberals. This thoughtful preacher decried fundamentalist efforts to draw lines of fellowship that excluded Christian thinkers who attempt to reconcile faith with modern science.

## Martin Luther King, Jr., "Loving Your Enemies"

In this sermon, printed in his little volume of sermons entitled *Strength to Love*, Dr. King preaches one of the main themes of his ministry: Hatred must be overcome by the power of love, and reconciliation occurs only when we recognize the good in everyone. Versions of this sermon were delivered in many venues, both in pulpits and reform platforms. Such love may not seem practical, King concedes, but living according to "practical" principles has proven at times to be disastrous. And the great irony, he concludes, is that the Christian way of love is more practical than the alternative.

## Billy Graham, "Salvation Through Jesus"

William Franklin Graham (born 1918 in North Carolina) is his real name and he has been America's most popular preacher of the twentieth century Likely he has preached to bigger audiences and more people in the U. S. and worldwide than any other preacher. The title above has been the continuing story line for nearly all sermons delivered by the Reverend Billy Graham, as millions call him. The basic theme has been delivered thousands of times: God created us, God instructed us as to what is good and beautiful and what is wrong and sinful, fallen humanity invariably chooses to sin and depart from God, then God in his abundant grace sends us his Son Jesus to bring us back to the Father, and listeners can be totally forgiven of their sins and restored to fellowship with the Father by believing that Jesus is God's Son and committing their lives to him.

Graham has enjoyed a long evangelistic career that has reached millions. Blessed with a dynamic speaking voice, and always holding a Bible and often declaring "the Bible says….," he has avoided controversial themes that have divided the Christian community and expounded basic spiritual themes with clear language and simple illustrations. His *ethos*, or credibility, has been one of his strongest traits as a public speaker. Graham's appeals have evoked thousands and thousands of visible responses. This evangelist has often acknowledged that he has preached on the assertion in John 3:16 more than on any other passage in the Bible. He has contended that this passage is "a miniature Bible" which contains the Bible's unchanging and relevant message that is applicable to all persons in every nation and culture.

## Billy Graham, "Mystery of Evil," April 24, 1995

Another Graham sermon that deserves to be in this listing is entitled "Mystery of Evil." The sermon was delivered on the occasion of a prayer service on April 24, 1995, that honored the victims of the horrific Oklahoma City bombing that occurred five days earlier. That bombing at the Alfred P. Murrah Federal Building was the worse act of domestic violence up to that point in our nation's history, killing 167 people, including nineteen children.

What would lead a young Gulf War veteran to commit such a callous, evil act? And why must innocent people suffer such unspeakable loss and pain? These questions provided the context for the sermon. "We come together here today not only to pray and forgive and love," the evangelist soberly began his sermon, "but to say to those who masterminded this cruel plot and to those who carried it out that the spirit of this city and this nation will not be defeated." Graham referenced the Old Testament character Job who wrestled with the same issue of evil many centuries earlier and quoted the New Testament as saying evil is a "mystery" and that "Satan is very real and he has great power." Graham also quoted Jesus in the Sermon on the Mount: "Blessed are those who mourn, for they shall be comforted." Then he closed his sermon: "My prayer for you today is that you will feel the loving arms of God wrapped around you and will know in your heart that He will never forsake you as you trust him. God bless Oklahoma!"

## Jeremiah A. Wright, "Confusing God and Government," 2008

Jeremiah Wright stirred much controversy with this sermon, more popularly known by a title deemed offensive by many Christians ("God Damn America"). Indeed, the sermon stirred much discussion and controversy in the 2008 presidential election because Wright had been preacher and friend of candidate Barack Obama for several years. The candidate felt compelled to dissociate himself from his former pastor, because Wright's views seemed extreme to a large segment of the voting public.

This listing has been the citation of only a few sermons that impacted American history, and there are surely readers who would select one or more other sermons to add to this list. Some contemporary preachers, such as Rick Warren and Max Lucado (just to name two among many), are known more for their books of sermons and lessons than their individual oral presentations. We acknowledge this listing contains preachers exclusively from the Christian tradition, yet some outstanding messages have been presented by Jewish and Islamic speakers as well as from leaders and teachers in other religious and spiritual traditions. In our history, millions and millions of sermons and other religious and spiritual messages have been presented by speakers who sought to make a difference in the lives of their listeners.

# 6. Hall Of Shame—Something Less Than Rhetorical Excellence

The American democratic experiment has provided the setting for many noble and stirring rhetorical efforts, to be sure, but also the setting for speeches that served only to diminish the best in the American spirit and experience. Irresponsible and dangerous rhetoric merits denunciation and criticism, for sure. Yet we study such rhetoric because it provides understanding of our past and also because our study serves as warning signs of negative rhetoric to look out for in the future. Yes, we remember some of the good, the bad, and the ugly so that we can learn from them. Some speeches or speech campaigns may, perhaps, at least merit preservation only as artifacts of a cultural mindset that no longer serves the national interest. Finally, some of the speeches might be preserved simply to bring a smile and a sense of relief that we, as a nation, have moved past such fear and ignorance.

## The Achilles Heel of Democracy

Many students in their first class of American history or American government find it most surprising that the Founding Fathers were not so enthused by the concept of democracy. Yes, the Founders wanted the new nation to be "a government of laws and not men," and, yes, they were opposed to monarchy and other arbitrary rule. Yet the idea of a "pure democracy" seemed an unworkable and dangerous risk. And why?

An answer may be found in *Federalist* number ten which counseled that citizens could be vulnerable to demagogues who exploit fear and ignorance: "Men of factious tempers, of local prejudices, or of sinister designs may by intrigue, by corruption, or by other means, first obtain the suffrages, and then betray the interests, of the people." And while democracy is, indeed, conceived by most as the best form of government, there can be moments in history when democracy fails to meet the needs and best interests of political society as a whole. The ever-present possibility of a demagogue gaining power and wreaking havoc in a political society and even beyond, as did Hitler of Germany in the 1930s and 40s, is indeed the Achilles heel of a democracy.

The demagogue, which originally meant a leader of the common people [from the Greek: *demos*, people, and *agogos*, leader] now is better defined as a person who stirs negative emotions among members of his or her audience, exciting and exploiting those emotions and prejudices for the purpose of winning them over in order to gain power. Negative emotions or conditions that are exploited most surely include fear (even paranoia), anger, pain, ignorance, prejudice, and hatred (even bigotry). The demagogue attempts control of others. The most dangerous demagogues are the ones with a huge, national stage and are the most adept at media manipulation and propaganda techniques. The demagogue usually opposes rational deliberation and dialogue and urges immediate, perhaps even violent, action to address a national crisis. The demagogue will label all those who disagree and those who urge caution, moderation, and a thoughtful deliberation that considers all the complexities of the crisis, as being both weak and ineffectual.

Experience with demagogues goes back to ancient Greece, and thinkers such as Socrates, Plato, and Aristotle were deeply concerned about demagogic power in a political society. In ancient Athens some demagogues appealed to lower, less educated classes of citizens. Aristotle called platform speakers who shouted "gadflies," and he found them both annoying and destructive. "Revolutions in democracies are generally caused by the intemperance of demagogues," this classical philosopher warned. The demagogue is typically an orator, often actually, quite an effective orator. And why an orator? It seems unimaginable that a demagogue could influence large segments of population simply by writing books, articles, or opinion pieces. The demagogue must exploit the dynamics of a live, emotional, public speaking situation with an immediate audience facing the speaker.

The connotation and context for demagoguery have changed somewhat over the centuries: The label is slightly gentler than "fascist" and more dignified than "buffoon," though, indeed, a demagogue might be either or both. We may think of a fist-pounding, finger-pointing, boisterous public speaker as archetypical demagogue, but with today's electronic and instant communication of television, Internet, Twitter, and other means of mass and instant media connection, then, styles and opportunities for demagoguery have been reshaped and multiplied. The demagogue can stay in constant, daily contact with devoted followers and susceptible masses waiting to be swayed by having their fears and prejudices validated and their hopes for a simple, pain-free solution confirmed.

We are not saying here that every unethical speaker who gained an audience was a demagogue. And it seems important to realize there are different degrees of demagoguery and different levels of danger that it poses. There are times in which even highly respected political leaders have lapsed into making demagogic statements in the heat of a close campaign. There are times in which a political leader was highly demagogic early in one's career and more statesmanlike later in that career (Richard Nixon comes to mind here). Democratic leaders may be viewed as speaking on a continuum from being less demagogic to highly demagogic. One citizen's "demagogic threat to American democracy" may be another's "populist hero." An old maxim comes to mind: "Democracy is a device that ensures we shall be governed no better than we deserve."

Our nation has produced its fair share of demagogues, propagandists, and wilfully ignorant influence-peddlers. There is no way to know how many political speakers have mounted a stage and spouted their prejudiced views but had so little understanding of our history or our Constitution. Neither is there any way to know how many preachers have been ignorant of historical-critical methodology in interpreting Scripture and simply pulled verses out of biblical context to support their own prejudices and pet causes.

No way complete listing can be compiled of all rhetorical efforts in our history that never should have been expended or that rendered a disservice to the nation. In this chapter we provide merely a sampling of less than reputable rhetorical presentations, though hundreds more could have at least been cited. There is a certain "art" in knowing how to exploit fear and crisis, some have succeeded where others have failed. In a dangerous world or time of national crisis, fear is both natural and inevitable. Cynically exploiting that angst is an "art," albeit, perhaps, a perverse one.

The following shameful rhetorical efforts are listed in no particular order, although we begin this little essay by referencing one of the most dangerous and despicable demagogues in the American experience, and we close by referencing one of the most contemporary and best known demagogues.

## Senator Joseph McCarthy's Wheeling, West Virginia, Speech (February 9, 1950) and his rhetorical campaign of questioning the patriotism of a wide range of Americans.

Joseph McCarthy (1908–1957), who had entered national politics under the guise of a battle-hardened combat veteran ("Tailgunner Joe") and had enjoyed a meteoric rise to the U. S. Senate in 1946, found a new cause he could exploit: "The Great Fear" of communism as a worldwide conspiracy. During the 1940s and 50s, Americans were indeed becoming increasingly worried by the actions of the Soviet Union and the meaning of China's fall to communist leadership so rapidly after World War II. Could the United States eventually fall to the communists as part of a worldwide conspiracy? And might America's most vital institutions be infiltrated by people who were either communists or harbored communist sympathies? If so, then, the United States might fall from insidious forces *within* the nation rather than by losing a war with the Soviets and other communists. The paranoia was widespread and McCarthy knew how to exploit it.

In the provocative speech to the Wheeling Women's Republican Club, Senator McCarthy accused President Truman's State Department with employing hundreds of known communists. McCarthy was not a great orator, but he definitely knew how to stir an audience. The speaker held up a piece of paper exclaiming: "I have here in my hand a list of two hundred and five people that were known to the Secretary of State as being members of the Communist Party and who, nevertheless, are still working and shaping the policy of the State Department." The audience gasped, but the speaker never called out the names. (In the following days, the 205 Communists changed quickly to fifty-seven, eighty-one, and then to 116.) People rightly feared the future, according to the speaker, "not because our only powerful potential enemy has sent men to invade our shores, but rather because of the traitorous actions of those who have been treated so well by this nation." People in this camp, according to McCarthy, included Secretary of State Dean Acheson and his predecessor, General George C. Marshall. The speech was reported nationally, and the nation likewise was stunned.

From this speech, McCarthy's career took flight. The Senator had suddenly become famous and, through the next four years, spearheaded a crusade to root out Communists in government and from other positions of power. McCarthy pointed fingers and leveled charges. The lack of clarity and lack of evidence seemed not to bother this crusader. He gained chairmanship of the powerful Senate Subcommittee on Governmental Operations and, from that post, launched investigations of the Voice of America broadcasting service and the U. S. Army Signal Corps. McCarthy's supporters may have seen the Senator on a crusade; others, who were alarmed at the tactics, considered the tirade to be a witch hunt.

McCarthy was aided in his witch hunt by a ruthless and unprincipled young lawyer named Roy Cohn, who was instrumental in one of the most highly publicized phases of the witch hunt—the investigation of Communist influence in the Hollywood film industry. In one committee session, McCarthy quizzed the famed musician Aaron Copland about his past relationships with the composer Hanns Eisler, a German communist, though Coplan turned out to be a difficult witness who cleverly deflected questions from the Senator. In all the committee hearings, some names were cited and those who failed to "cooperate" with the committee and those who stood accused were blacklisted—consequentially no studio or organization would hire them.

McCarthy rarely tried to substantiate his charges. He could be vague and reckless. He took aim at some perfectly legal organizations and affiliations, and he was a master of innuendo. Some of his ideas, such as ludicrously calling George Marshall, then serving as secretary of defense, an agent of Communism. The absence of fact or concrete evidence never slowed McCarthy. His personal crudeness rendered him a media star, but eventually such crudeness undermined him. In the nationally televised Army-McCarthy hearings (1954), viewers saw first-hand McCarthy's bullying strategy and heard the Army's lawyer, Joseph Welch, ask the Senator directly a poignant and unforgettable question: "Have you no decency?"

The end came quickly. McCarthy's "favorable" ratings plummeted. The U. S. Senate finally voted sixty-seven to twenty-two in December 1954 to condemn McCarthy for conduct "unbecoming a member of the Senate." For our purposes here as students of rhetoric, we may see Joseph McCarthy as the poster child for demagoguery. This demagogue knew how to exploit fear for his own political power and personal ego. True, there have been a number of demagogues in American history who used public speaking to advance their careers, but none so "effective" and reckless than Senator Joseph McCarthy. How appropriate that this populist-style demagoguery within the American political culture still bears his name—"McCarthyism!"

McCarthy's influence plummeted disgracefully as rapidly as it had risen. Overtaken by the alcoholism that had always dogged him, he died in 1957 at the age of forty-nine.

# Andrew Jackson Applauds the Removal Act—Second Annual Address to Congress (December 6, 1830)

*Humanity has often wept over the fate of the aborigines of this country, and Philanthropy has been long busily employed in devising means to avert it, but its progress has never for a moment been arrested, and one by one many powerful tribes disappeared from the earth... Nor is there anything in this which, upon comprehensive view of the general interests of the human race, is to be regretted. Philanthropy could not wish to see this continent restored to the condition in which it was found by our forefathers. What good man would prefer a country covered with forests and ranged by a few thousand savages to our extensive Republic, studded with cities, towns and prosperous farms, embellished with all the improvements which art can devise or industry execute, occupied by more than 12,000,000 happy people, and filled with all the blessings of liberty, civilization, and religion?*

Andrew Jackson (1767-1845) hailed from Tennessee and is given much credit for being a popular president, a political leader who favored states' rights but only within a perpetual and inviolable union. When he entered office, there was a crisis between frontier whites and native peoples of the eastern woodlands. In the old Southwest, 60,000 Cherokees, Creeks, Chickasaws, Choctaws, and Seminoles (considered the Five Civilized Tribes) were still living on their ancestral grounds, with tenure guaranteed by federal treaties that, by inference, recognized them as sovereign peoples. Conflict continued to brew, especially in Georgia where Cherokees declared themselves a republic with its own constitution, government, courts, and police. The Georgia legislature declared the Cherokee law null and void, thus heightening the tension.

In his first annual message, delivered December 8, 1829, President Andrew Jackson outlined his Indian policy and called on Congress to enact legislation that would remove eastern Indians to the region west of the Mississippi. In 1830 John Marshall's Supreme Court ruled in *Cherokee Nation v. Georgia* that the Cherokees could not sue the state because they were not a sovereign people but "domestic dependent nations," thus depending on the federal government. In *Worcester v. Georgia*, the Supreme Court ruled Georgia's extension of state law over Cherokee land was unconstitutional. Jackson ignored the law and reportedly snubbed the Chief Justice: "John Marshall has made his decision; now let him enforce it." Jackson already had a reputation, won during the Creek War of 1813-14, as an Indian fighter. In Jackson's political philosophy, the individual states had sovereign rights over the Indian country within their borders, thus the right to command compliance by Indian peoples.

The passage quoted above comes from Jackson's second State of the Union Address, after the passage of the Indian Removal Act. The President takes pride in the unveiling of his removal policy, extols its virtues, and predicts its success for all concerned. Jackson assumed that it was inevitable and good that white civilization would occupy and rule all of North America, and that the history and culture of the Native Americans would eventually end. The President is anxious for a speedy conclusion. The proceedings (removal) will go well, he assures his opponents, encouraging everyone to join in the "humane" task of convincing the recalcitrant tribes to retreat for their own good.

President Jackson speaks of "the wandering savage" and then engages in an orgy of self-congratulation: "Rightly considered, the policy of the general government toward the red man is not only liberal, but generous. He is unwilling to submit to the laws of the states and mingle with their population. To save him from this alternative, or perhaps utter annihilation, the general government kindly offers him a new home, and proposes to pay the whole expense of his removal and settlement."

This self-righteousness and these assumptions are indeed offensive to modern sensibilities, and they were offensive to many Americans at the time. Yet Jackson and most of his contemporaries considered removal the best and most humane solution to the Native American "problem." Hollywood seems to have left the impression with many that the great Indian wars came in the Old West during the latter nineteenth century, a time for the old "cowboy and Indian" days. While the killing, land theft, and enslavement began with the first European contact with the "New World," these cultural crimes reached their nadir with this federal policy under President Jackson. In 1838, the U. S. Army marched 18,000 Cherokee men, women, and children of Georgia, along with their animals and whatever they could carry, out of their home territory and into Oklahoma. At least four thousand—most of them old or very young—died on the march. This arduous route and horrific journey constituted the Trail of Tears.

*Postscript*: In April 2016 the federal government announced that Andrew Jackson would be booted to the back of the twenty-dollar bill in U. S. currency to make room for Harriet Tubman, a black anti-slavery activist. Tubman was a former slave who helped scores of other slaves escape to freedom, and she also worked as a union spy during the Civil War. Critics of this change in U. S. currency deemed this to be a bow to "political correctness" and argued that Jackson's views on slavery and Indians "fell within the mainstream of American thinking" at that time.

## The Southern Fire-eaters—Extremist Spokesmen for the Old South

Before the Civil War, Southern spokesmen found their purpose in defending the thesis that the states below the Mason-Dixon Line were commissioned both by God and fate to perpetuate a very special way of life that included political traditions, inequality, inequity, and social class. That case was never made more cogently than by John C. Calhoun, especially in his Senate speeches on various pieces of legislation. As compromises seemed both ineffective and more and more unlikely, emotions on both sides, North and South, became more heated. Southern leadership at all levels, political and religious, increasingly felt their traditions and institutions were being threatened. During U. S. Senate debate in 1850, Henry Clay, a wise and understanding compromise leader, pointed out "the North is contending for a mere abstraction, while with the people of the South it is a principle involving their property....their prosperity and peace."

Secession was carried out in a wave of emotionalism. There were speakers for the Old South who were reasonable and moderate in their discussions. There were other speakers who were so rabid in their oratory and so uncompromising in their positions that they became known as the Fire-Eaters. These secessionists were extremists, and the term "Fire-Eater" as an opprobrium seems to have become more popular following an appearance of Robert Barnwell Rhett and William Lowndes Yancey at a meeting in Macon, Georgia, on August 22, 1850.

After June 1850, in which a Southern convention representing nine states met in Nashville, Tennessee, the Fire-Eaters declared themselves in favor of secession if any compromise measures proposed by Henry Clay and Stephen Douglas were passed in the U. S. Senate. The Fire-Eaters were ready to secede at that time. Then, they were ready to use any rhetorical and propaganda strategy they could devise to sway the Southern population toward secession. They used various devices to appeal to the emotions of Southern rural residents, such as alarming telegrams from Washington, misrepresentations of Lincoln and his party, stump speaking and parades, and, above all, the public branding of reasonable, sensible speakers who opposed their designs as "submissionists." For the next fifteen years, 1850 until the end of the Civil War, fiery orators inflamed the electorate. Even the pulpit was employed to bring people over to the secessionist cause. The Fire-Eaters poured so much emotion into the delicate situation that they could not view the election of Abraham Lincoln to the national presidency with reasonable perspective or common sense.

Fire-Eaters used their public speaking as a tool to exploit fears and acrimonious feelings in their sympathetic audiences. Clearly, they were demagogues. They advanced misrepresentations and misconceptions of Northern leaders and citizenry. They misrepresented both the president and Northern U. S. senators. And the Southern audience was "ripe" for this kind of exploitation. Though most Southerners were not big slaveholders, most believed that the existence of slavery was essential to the economy of the region. Fire-Eaters convinced the majority that the institution of slavery and the plantation system, and, indeed, the entire Southern way of life, was in jeopardy and that the North was set on destroying Southern economy and institutions. "Amalgamation" (racial integration) was a big fear and theme in the Fire-Eating oratory.

There were many Fire-Eating orators. Some were preachers who used the pulpit to make a biblical justification for slavery. Others were political Fire-Eaters who argued the "compact theory"—the U. S. Constitution was a compact between the states, not an instrument of the people (Lincoln's view) and that each state may judge whether an act of Congress is applicable to its own situation or its best interests (Calhoun's view). In time, the more extreme Fire-Eaters developed another defense of slavery and the Southern way of life—slavery is a positive good intended to provide benevolent care, education, and religious faith to a class of people who cannot provide those blessings for themselves.

There were hundreds of Fire-Eating orators, both political and religious, and the four leading ones were:

1.  Edmund Ruffin, the old man from Virginia, who had the "honor" of firing the first shot at Fort Sumter. Though not an eloquent speaker, he spoke at every opportunity available. He kept a diary in which he expressed "unmitigated hatred...to the Yankee race." Outraged over the outcome of the war, he shot himself to death on June 18, 1865.

2.  John A. Quitman of Mississippi, who was elected governor of the state and then to the U. S. House in 1850.

3.  Robert Barnwell Rhett, from South Carolina, who came to be known as the "father of secession." Rhett attended the 1850 Nashville convention and departed from the event with fervent determination to speak and write for secession and against the Union. He was both austere and arrogant, and he agitated through the pages of the Charleston *Mercury*.

4.  William Lowndes Yancey has been called "the orator of secession." Year after year he spoke at scores of mass meetings, usually held outdoors. As a natural orator, Yancey was eloquent and moderate. He even spoke at the Cooper Union in his campaign for Breckinridge in 1860, convincing the New York audience that he was more reasonable and moderate than was expected of the "representative Fire-Eater." Yancey argued that slavery was imposed on the South by greedy New England slave traders and that it persisted in the South

due to" climate and economy." Furthermore, slaves were the happiest of laborers to be found anywhere ("These glorious sons of toil"—a term used in his New York speech). Yancey was clearly the most skilled and effective public speaker in defense of the Old South.

The Fire-Eaters' rhetoric and arguments were successful in the short-run. They convinced Southern political leaders and legislators to secede from the Union. The new Confederacy adopted most of the Fire-Eater platform for a new constitution. Through the years of their thousands upon thousands of speeches and sermons, they spoke fervently, with only slight variations, on the same theme: The South must resist unconstitutional exploitation or suffer the irretrievable loss of its way of life. As orators, they were sincere, earnest, unrelenting, and persistent. Were they wise, prudent, intelligent, understanding, and patient? History shows they were on the wrong side—both morally and politically—in this national debate. They, along with John Calhoun, Jefferson Davis, and other Southerners, had devoted their hearts and energies to the defense of the least defensible of American institutions.

The Fire-Eaters' effectiveness as speakers emerged from their commitment, their intensity, their sacrifices, and their courage. This group of orators would have been considered much more effective by both historians and rhetorical critics if the secession of the South had been successful and many positive virtues and constructive changes emerged within the new nation, the Confederacy. Indeed, the "fathers of secession" would have been honored and eulogized as the "fathers of their nation."

## William Jennings Bryan, Prosecutor at the Scopes "Monkey" Trial, Dayton, Tennessee (July, 1925)

For nearly forty years, William Jennings Bryan contributed an influential voice to every major political issue before the American people of his generation. Never mind that he was nominated and yet defeated for president three times. Truth is, he was progressive and ahead of his time on nearly every important issue—his ideas on the gold standard, progressive taxation, and anti-imperialism have been vindicated by history. Bryan was a pious man, but in his religious views he was not so progressive. After retirement from politics, Bryan lent his enormous influence to defending Bible literalism and

Christian fundamentalism. He worked to establish anti-evolution laws in states all over the country.

In a test case of Tennessee's new anti-evolution law, John Thomas Scopes was placed on trial for violating that law and the Great Commoner agreed to be prosecutor. Clarence Darrow, one of the nation's greatest criminal lawyers, could not resist an offer to defend Scopes. For Darrow, it was an opportunity to attack one of his long-time bogies—organized religion. The trial, thus, attracted national attention and many newspaper reporters.

Darrow assembled an illustrious group of biologists, geologists, educators, and other learned witnesses to testify to how modern science could be harmonized with Holy Scripture. Yet Bryan saw the Bible as the final word on any topic, called such testimony "pseudo-scientific," and pled successfully for the testimony to be irrelevant to guilt or innocence of John Scopes.

When the star witnesses were not allowed to offer testimony, Darrow asked if Bryan would consent to become a witness as an expert on the Bible. This provided the setting for one of the most amazing court scenes in Anglo-Saxon legal history. The Great Commoner confidently took the seat, fanning himself in a hot July courtroom, head raised in assurance that this was a great opportunity to witness God's eternal truth.

Though Bryan's testimony would not be considered a single oration, it was indeed the essence of a number of speeches he had made to various audiences and church groups since leaving politics. His most popular lecture on the circuit was entitled "The Prince of Peace." Many of the clever sayings in this courtroom had been offered previously in speeches and sermons, declarations such as: "I don't care about the ages of rocks, but only about the Rock of Ages." Darrow concentrated on Bryan's literal interpretation of the Scriptures, asking questions about biblical narratives (Joshua making the sun stand still, the great flood; Jonah and the whale), and Bryan defended a literal interpretation of the Bible saying he not only believed the whale swallowed Jonah but that Jonah could swallow a whale had God wanted him to do so. One of the interesting quotes from Bryan: "I do not think of things I don't think about."

Historians of American religion generally concur that Christian fundamentalism reached its death knell with Bryan's testimony, that this was a watershed event in the history of religion in the U. S. Many contend there were scholarly conservative religious professors who would have represented the orthodox Christian faith with far greater credibility and authenticity and less distraction and lampooning. Bryan died five days after the trial in Chattanooga.

## Edward Everett, The Gettysburg Address, November 19, 1863

Yes, the title may have caught the reader's attention. Edward Everett (1794–1865) occupied several positions of high responsibility—congressman, governor of Massachusetts, minister in England, president of Harvard, secretary of state, and U. S. senator. He was renowned as a speaker and appeared before all kinds of audiences. His most famous address was on George Washington, first delivered on February 22, 1856, and then repeated to all kinds of audiences. Like other speakers of his generation, the long-winded Everett could present speeches that were stem-winders.

Let's be clear: Everett deserves no shame or criticism whatever, but is discussed here because of the oration for which he is best remembered—Everett's "keynote" address at Gettysburg on November 19, 1863, the occasion for which President Abraham Lincoln was, belatedly, asked to offer "a few appropriate remarks." Everett's speech was envisioned by ceremony committee as being the highlight of the occasion, perhaps even a speech filled with memorable lines. As it turned out, precious few people have even heard about this speech. Can anyone even quote one line or figurative expression from this speech?

The Gettysburg battlefield and cemetery dedication constituted the setting for two speeches—one speech lasting two hours, the other one lasting two minutes. One speech has been often quoted, even memorized by school children for many decades. The other speech has been largely forgotten, even if anyone were aware it had ever been delivered (and certainly no lines from the longer oration have been memorized or quoted).

Thus Everett's contribution to the field of American public address is to serve as a negative example of verbose emptiness on an occasion rendered immortal by the sublime eloquence within succinctness of the Lincoln classic. Truly, Abraham Lincoln said more in two minutes than Everett in two hours.

Everett deserves credit as one of the few who instantly recognized the greatness of Lincoln's rhetoric. And the President, replying to his note of congratulations, justly remarked: "In our respective parts yesterday, you could not have been excused to make a short address, nor I a long one."

## Father Charles E. Coughlin, Anti-Semitism Broadcasting (1930s)

No one speech or radio broadcast stands out as the "best one" to feature here, yet Fr. Charles E. Coughlin (1891–1979) richly merits inclusion into this Hall of Shame for his many broadcast messages that were essentially anti-Semitist in content and supportive of both Adolph Hitler and Benito Mussolini in the early years of World War II.

To place in broader perspective: Jewish leaders and speakers have always found it necessary to address anti-Semitism, a major doctrine of discrimination that had its own spokesmen. No matter what speakers spread anti-Semite doctrine, the message was basically the same—the Jew is an inferior, conniving outsider who cannot be trusted to be fair or honest.

This heresy grew more widespread in the twentieth century with the stress of world wars and economic depression, and there were several American anti-Semite spokesmen. The most prominent, ironically enough, was a religious communicator, a Roman Catholic priest named Charles E. Coughlin, pastor of the Shrine of the Little Flower in Royal Oak, Michigan. Coughlin's main audience was not the farmers—to whom George Winrod and Gerald L. K. Smith had aimed their anti-Semite rhetoric—but rather the industrial workers (Royal Oak is located in the greater Detroit area where many industrial workers lived).

Coughlin had taken to the radio airwaves as a supporter of Franklin D. Roosevelt and the New Deal in the 1930s, but after building a national audience soon turned to preaching anti-Semitism. He was the most influential U. S. Roman Catholic priest of the 1930s, and he used both the spoken and the published word to spread his demagogic propaganda. His broadcast messages were more about political and economic topics than religious ones. The renegade priest with a national pulpit impugned American Jews' character and patriotism. His message of suspicion and accusation was easily received among the industrial unemployed throughout the country, who entertained little hope of returning to their jobs during economic depression. Coughlin's demagoguery continued to place Jewish people in this nation more at risk for all kinds of suspicion, violence, and discrimination. In time, his influence faded and he was hardly known by most Americans at the time of his death.

# Huey "The Kingfish" Long, "Share Our Wealth" Populist (1930s)

People in Louisiana either loved or hated Huey Pierce Long (1893–1935)—he was simply that polarizing. And he used the power of rhetoric to stir audiences in his home state and then around the country. Long was the fortieth governor of Louisiana, serving from 1928 to 1932, and then served as U. S. senator from 1932 till his assassination in 1935.

Within months after taking office in 1933, Franklin D. Roosevelt was confronted by a number of political rivals, yet none gave the President such deep concern as Louisiana's Huey Long. At the Democratic convention in Chicago in 1932, Long had been one of the leaders of the Roosevelt supporters, and his support was a key ingredient in Roosevelt's nomination. Long then attempted to influence, if not control, the new president, but in time referred to him as "the same old Frank." Long disliked the proposals of the "Hundred Days" and became contemptuous of Roosevelt and the well-educated urban New Deal reformers. Using the barb of ridicule against Roosevelt and his policymakers, Long hoped to win national power by convincing the general public that reform forces were shielding a national ruling class that held a monopoly of wealth which restricted the well-being of ordinary people.

Long was a shrewd operator and a thoroughly professional politician. He possessed the intelligence, ambition, and financial support that were requisite for national success but he had even more—extravagant rhetorical skills, a gift for political theater, and a sense for what people wanted. His demagoguery rendered him extremist, though he spoke in familiar terms of American populism, clowning his way into the national limelight. He wore pongee suits with orchid-colored silk ties, brown and white sport shoes, and striped straw hats. He womanized openly, swilled whiskey in the finest bars, swaggered his way around Washington, and, snubbing political correctness, exuded contempt for the national political establishment of "high hats" who looked down their noses at his kind of people. He took special delight in the nickname "Kingfish," a name borrowed from the popular radio serial "Amos 'n Andy." Though shrewd and intelligent, he sometimes cultivated the impression that he was something less than bright. He lampooned serious social and political thinkers of his day.

Huey Long was a populist with leftward leaning. He argued not merely for curtailing the working day but for shortening the working year. He proposed plowed land could be turned into golf courses. He declared every man could become a king. When he came to Washington, he defied the ordinary protocol and dignity expected. As a senator seeking and gaining national attention, the Kingfish had become an international figure who was challenging Roosevelt for the center of the stage.

In January 1934 Long, who had advocated massive redistribution of wealth for many years, founded a national political organization with its slogan "Share Our Wealth." The national organizer was Gerald L.K. Smith, the shrill Shreveport minister. The program went through several versions, but, in essence, it called for liquidation of all personal fortunes above a certain amount and giving to every family enough to buy a home, an automobile and a radio; senior citizens would receive pensions and worthy young men would be sent to college. Additionally, there would be levying of a steeply progressive income tax, vast public works spending, a shortened work week, a national minimum wage, a balanced farm program, and immediate cash payments of bonuses.

Share Our Wealth had an immense attraction. By February 1935, Long claimed more than 27,000 clubs and a mailing list of over 7,500,000 persons. While he was certainly popular in the South, he attracted live audiences in the thousands even in Northern states; he reached out to discontented farmers in the prairie states. Long certainly gave Democratic leaders severe fright. Roosevelt considered Long to be his chief threat to re-election in 1936. There was concern that Long, failing to get the nomination of his party, would draw millions of votes on a third-party ticket in 1936. And Long could have drawn enough votes away from main-line Democrats to throw the election victory to the Republican nominee.

Long was a gifted and flamboyant orator who spoke passionately in all kinds of venues—outdoor platforms, lecture halls, and national radio. In 1935 Long stepped up his national radio appearances. One of his radio speeches is rated by *American Rhetoric* as one of the top one hundred speeches of the twentieth century (delivered nationwide on March 7, 1935), in which the speaker argued there was no real difference between FDR and his predecessor, Herbert Hoover. Long boldly pressed his attack, indicting more than simply the Roosevelt policies but also the President's character. The broadcasts elicited more than a hundred thousand letters of support—a national audience was being awakened.

Great as his following was, Long was forced to share the limelight with another demagogic orator, the Reverend Charles Coughlin, priest of the parish of Royal Oak, Michigan, who also used radio broadcasting to reach the masses. A third important challenger to Roosevelt from the left was Dr. Francis Townsend, who seemed to speak for the discontents who lived in Western states. Indeed, the winds of discontent fanned by Long, Coughlin, and Townsend swept across the entire nation, and especially into the streets of industrial America.

The Democratic establishment, including Roosevelt, considered Long to be brilliant and dangerous. As with other demagogues, the logic and financial arithmetic of Long's proposals were unworkable. Yet some historians grudgingly give demagogues their due, in this case arguing that without the likes of Huey Long and Father Coughlin then there would not have been a genuine New Deal that embraced some of the proposals for which Long and his followers contended. Later, at times, Roosevelt seemed to "fight fire with fire" by imitating some of the demagogues' most confrontational rhetoric. And yet, like Lincoln, Roosevelt used rhetoric to speak to the "better angels" of American citizens' nature. Long had stirred general fascination and intrigue, but Roosevelt elicited general respect and admiration.

Would there have been a third party challenge in 1936 that would have fractured the American political system? FDR had successfully engineered employment and security legislation through Congress that had battened down the New Deal against these challengers from the left. Yet, we shall never know for certain. The saga of Huey P. Long came to an abrupt end. In September 1935 Long fell to assassin's bullets in the marble corridor of the Louisiana Capitol at Baton Rouge. After lingering for nearly two days, passing in and out of consciousness and wondering why he was shot, he died on September 10. His reported last words were "God, don't let me die! I have so much to do!"

## George Wallace, Gubernatorial Inaugural Address (January 14, 1963)

*I draw the line in the dust and toss the gauntlet before the feet of tyranny...and I say... segregation today...segregation tomorrow...segregation forever.*

A short, dark-haired, outspoken man made his mark on the state of Alabama and is even depicted in the movie *Forrest Gump* and referenced in Lynyrd Skynyrd's hit song, "Sweet Home, Alabama." A native of the state, George Wallace (1919–1998) achieved four gubernatorial terms across three decades, serving 1963-67; 1971-79; 1983-87. His wife Lurleen was even elected once as governor and surrogate for the politician who could not succeed himself. Wallace became known nationally when he made a symbolic opposition to the University of Alabama being desegregated and then in running for president four times, three times as Democrat and once as stand-bearer for the American Independent Party (1968).

Wallace first ran for governor in 1958, taking moderate positions and talking about state issues such as education and welfare. He was defeated for being too timid in his support for racial segregation. Wallace then vowed, in his own words, never to be "out-niggered" again. At that point, Wallace sold his soul to the devil, according to some biographers. He adopted a staunchly segregationist platform and gained the prize—he easily won the 1962 gubernatorial race. During the Inaugural ceremony, while he emphasized the importance of states' rights, he clearly affirmed commitment to racial segregation.

In the Inauguration Address, Wallace began by quoting General Robert E. Lee, ever the great hero of the old Confederate states and subsequent Confederate heritage. "Today I have stood where once Jefferson Davis stood, and took an oath to my people," Wallace proudly declared early in the address. "It is very appropriate then that from this cradle of the Confederacy, this very heart of the great Anglo-Saxon Southland, that today we sound the drum for freedom as have our generations of forebears before us have done, time and time again through history. Let us rise to the call of freedom-loving blood that is in us and send our answer to the tyranny that clanks its chains upon the South. In the name of the greatest people that have ever trod this earth…." Then, at this point, the new governor made a bold assertion of his position for which he is long remembered: "I draw the line in the dust and toss the gauntlet before the feet of tyranny, and I say Segregation now! Segregation tomorrow! Segregation forever!"

On June 11, 1963, when President John F. Kennedy sent one hundred members of the Alabama National Guard to escort two black students, Vivian Malone and James Hood, seeking to register at the University of Alabama, Governor Wallace symbolically blocked the doorway for a few moments to make his point about segregation and states' rights. Then he peacefully stepped aside. Wallace was a significant factor in the Southern vote tally in the 1968 presidential election, as he appealed to millions of alienated white voters—he carried five Southern states and won almost ten million popular votes.

George Wallace was known for stirring crowds with his oratory, which included name-calling and ridicule. To him, U. S. foreign aid was "money poured down a rat hole" by federal authorities who were "little pinkos." The appointed federal judges kept their heads in the clouds and were nothing but "pointy-headed intellectuals" out of touch with the real regional and local needs. Wallace joined millions of white Southerners in their distaste for the youth protest movement, and in speeches would often claim there were two four-letter words "that hippies do not like— 'w-o-r-k' and 's-o-a-p.'" He often condemned the concept of what he called "forced busing"—a federal court-issued plan for effecting racial balance in public schools. One of his favorite lines is that, on matters of race and desegregation, "There's not a dime's worth of difference between the Republicans and the Democrats."

In the 1972 primary election season, an assassination attempt on his life in Laurel, Maryland, left him paralyzed, and he used a wheel chair for the remainder of his life. His health degenerated with the passing of years. Before his death, Wallace confessed he had been wrong on race, that his views were part of the "old South," and he apologized to African-Americans for his earlier segregationist views, and even appointed some blacks to state office positions. In retrospect, most rhetorical critics would surely label him as demagogue—his voice was a roar of defiance.

On the other hand, more generously, those more sympathetic to his fascinating political career will call him foremost a populist, much in the tradition of William Jennings Bryan and other American populists who spoke up for millions who felt they were never heard by the elites in power. Despite all the sound and fury of Wallace's rhetoric over the years, little changed for the good in terms of welfare, education, and standard of living for the people in his home state. Fairly or unfairly, the Donald Trump of 2015-16 has been compared to George Wallace of the 1960s and 70s.

## Spiro Agnew and Polarizing Rhetoric of the Nixon Years

Spiro Agnew was the thirty-ninth vice president of the United States. Most Americans had not heard of him until Richard Nixon selected him as running mate for the 1968 presidential election. The governor of Maryland looked tough on the issue of "law and order," and he came from a traditionally Democratic state. The late 60s in the United States was a volatile time. The Vietnam War seemed the biggest issue around which many other concerns revolved, including the rise of youthful protest, urban unrest (fueled largely by a sense of social injustice), and the hippie movement. Nixon, Agnew, and most conservatives were concerned that lawless and even peaceful protesters did not represent majority thinking. While Nixon spoke of "the great silent majority," Spiro Agnew seemed to become its chief antagonist and spokesperson.

Though Agnew did not rant and rave in public speaking, his speeches were considered "fiery" and they certainly had contributed to the political and cultural polarization of this time. Agnew became one of the most visible vice presidents in modern American history. "The mature and sensitive people of this country," he proclaimed at a 1969 dinner speech to fellow Republicans, "must realize that their freedom of protest is being exploited by avowed anarchists and communists who detest everything about this country and want to destroy it."

Agnew did raise some good questions about the power and influence of the national media, but his *ethos* (credibility) was so weakened in the eyes of those he was attempting to convince by the perceived prejudice and insensitivity of the speaker. In the 1968 campaign, Agnew dropped a few ethnic slurs, speaking of "Pollacks" and calling one reporter a "fat Jap." Reminiscent of the tactics of Joe McCarthy, Agnew labeled Democratic nominee Hubert Humphrey "squishy soft on communism." The Republican candidates almost exclusively campaigned in the suburbs of large cities, as explained by Agnew: "If you've seen one slum, you've seen them all."

The greatest part of Agnew's dubious legacy for American rhetoric would be his memorable labeling and name-calling, often in alliteration. Four days after a massive anti-war protest in October 1969, the Vice President began firing away at a divergent range of enemies: "A spirit of national masochism prevails, encouraged by an effete corporation of impudent snobs who characterize themselves as intellectuals." People who promote peace demonstrations were "ideological eunuchs." Two weeks later he noted the national press was "a tiny and closed fraternity of privileged men" who engaged in "instant analysis and querulous criticism." He denounced opponents of Nixonian policies as "radic-libs," "nattering nabobs of negativism" and "hopeless hypochondriacs of history." He lamented that a "paralyzing permissive philosophy pervades every policy they [anti-war demonstrators] espouse." Two other Agnew phrases: "vicars of vacillation" and "pusillanimous pussyfooters."

Agnew's divisive, polarizing rhetoric was even more colorful than that of George Wallace, perhaps because he seemed more sophisticated and educated. His targets were numerous: anti-war protesters, first and foremost, but then opponents of school prayer, hippies, advocates of school busing, radical feminists, counter-culturalists, assertive blacks, spoiled university students, and intellectuals. Of course, many in that great silent majority loved the aggressive and divisive rhetoric, perhaps the most acerbic in the postwar political history. Some polls ranked him high in national "Most Admired Men" polling, just below Nixon himself and evangelist Billy Graham. Thousands bought a specially designed Agnew watch and wore it in support of the controversial vice president.

In time, however, the demagogic Humpty Dumpty had a great and rapid fall. Agnew accepted a plea-bargain arrangement to avoid prosecution for having accepted illegal kickbacks while he served in Maryland politics. Acting under the twenty-fifth amendment (ratified only in 1967), Nixon appointed, and both houses of Congress confirmed, Representative Gerald Ford of Michigan, a Republican Party stalwart with a reputation of great integrity, as the new vice president. And nearly everyone, Republican and Democrat alike, sighed with great relief.

At his death, the *New York Times* called him "Nixon's hatchet man" as well as "the tart-tongued political combatant." The *Times* declared Agnew to be "a classic practitioner of the hatchet-man role often assigned to a vice president." Yet Agnew was praised by Patrick Buchanan for "raw political courage" in serving as "the voice for the silent majority." Agnew watches can still be purchased on line.

## Colin Powell, Address to the United Nations Security Council, February 5, 2003

In late 2002 and early 2003, President George W. Bush seemed clearly to be advocating the invasion of Iraq, a decision that would involve a major investment of human resources and revenue. In fact, because it would be an act of war against a nation that had not attacked the U. S., Bush needed to win support for such an invasion. The nation had been reeling from the shock and losses of 9/11, and there was concern about future terrorist activity. The first president George Bush (George Herbert Walker Bush) had taken on Saddam Hussein in the Gulf War a decade earlier, and U. S. forces achieved a rapid victory in completing the objective of driving Iraqi military forces out of Kuwait. Now, the second George Bush was encountering some skepticism and outright opposition to another war in the Middle East, and he found it necessary to paint Iraq's dictator Saddam Hussein as a dangerous, evil man with both the potential and desire to attack the U. S. homeland.

Perhaps the most convincing, single rhetorical effort in this campaign for American support for this invasion was the speech of acting Secretary of State Colin Powell (b. 1937) to the plenary session of the U. N. Security Council and to a wider television audience. As a successful and greatly revered American statesman and retired four-star

U. S. Army General and a commander in the Persian Gulf War, perhaps no one possessed greater *ethos* (source credibility) in addressing the issue than Colin Powell. He was, and remains, almost unsurpassed as a man of integrity and honor, a true American hero. This speech is placed in a chapter on "rhetorical shame" because of how the address was used by his commander-in-chief to support an untenable decision—a decision that many historians and current generation political leaders consider the most disastrous foreign policy decision in American history.

The General contended the U. S. and other Western nations had no real choice but to act militarily. "The U. S. will not and cannot run that risk to the American people. Leaving Saddam Hussein in possession of weapons of mass destruction for a few more months or years is not an option, not in a post-September 11 world," Powell asserted. Drawing from what turned out to be flawed or manufactured evidence from the C. I. A., Powell also cited Hussein's possession of mobile biological weapon facilities and connections to al-Qaeda. Then warned the U. N. that any failure of the Security Council to support the invasion would place the Council "in danger of irrelevance." As he closed the speech, the General made a final appeal: "We must not shrink from whatever is ahead of us. We must not fail in our duty and our responsibility to the citizens of our countries that are represented by this body."

The speech received such positive reviews. Many journalists and the general U. S. public extolled Powell for a "masterful performance," considering that his arguments and evidence were "irrefutable" and that George W. Bush's case for going to war seemed rock-solid indeed. Yet, here is a case where the consequences were major. No one address, not even from the President, had more influence on Congressional support. Ten years later? So many recriminations, so much second-guessing, so much finger-pointing, so many excuses, and so many U. S. senators, including Hillary Clinton (a senator from New York at the time), trying to explain why they voted to support the U. S. invasion of Iraq in 2003!

As for the speaker ten years later, the former secretary of state blamed himself for not trusting his instincts and for making what proved to be false assertions to the U. N. about Iraq's possession of weapons of mass destruction and any Iraqi connection to al-Qaeda. "A failure will always be attached to me and my U. N. presentation," Powell said. "I am mostly mad at myself for not having smelled the problem. My instincts failed me."

## Fred Phelps and Hateful Rhetoric from Westboro Baptist Church

Observers have quipped that Westboro Baptist Church is neither "Baptist" nor "church" but, as once led by Fred Phelps (b. 1929), pastor from 1954 till his death on March 19, 2014, it was center to ugly and hateful rhetorical abuse against LGBT people, Jews, and politicians. Phelps and Westboro were probably best known for their anti-gay protests at military funerals, celebrity funerals, and other public events. The protesters carried signs that set new "lows" in terms of disrespect and bad taste, if not bordering on blasphemy—"Thank God for Dead Soldiers" and "God Hates Fags" were two of the messages on signs and banners. Seeking national media publicity, Phelps gained it

Phelps also won a legal battle. Though his rhetoric was offensive and tasteless to the ultimate degree, the Supreme Court ruled in *Snyder v. Phelps* that Westboro's protests and messages were protected free speech. His speeches and sermons contended that President Obama is the "anti-Christ." When Phelps died, *Time* (March 20, 2014) presented an obituary entitled "Good Riddance, Fred Phelps," and called him a "colossal jerk" who had "a deeply disagreeable personality" and who was "unpleasant and despicable" as "an angry, bigoted man who thrived on conflict." The pathetic reality, however, is that Phelps might have enjoyed that obituary because, once again, it gave him more publicity in the national media. What a sad and deplorable abuse of public speaking and human language!

## Sarah Palin, Campaigning and Entertaining, 2008 – 2016

Sarah Palin arrived on the American scene thanks to candidate John McCain and being selected by him as running mate on the 2008 Republican ticket. Such was the rapid jumpstart of a unique public career for the former Alaska governor. Though she currently weaves in and out of public view, she retains a solid core of devotees and she still seeks to be relevant. Even when Palin is delivering a serious political or campaign speech, it is typically entertaining.

In her endorsement for Donald Trump's nomination to the Republican Party presidential candidacy in early 2016, Palin, with almost inimitable high-pitched and shrill voice, strung together a series of phrases and rhyming words (now dubbed Palinisms) that seemed clever at the time but left supporters, even Trump himself, puzzled as to what exactly she was saying. That endorsement speech, as well as a few other Palin remarks, has been described as meandering, patriotic, sarcastic, fiery, and blustery; and Palin has been "credited" with spawning a new series of idiosyncratic expressions and brain-ticking locutions, even coining a few new words along the way. Little wonder that the Tina Fay depiction of Palin on *Saturday Night Live* skits is so hilarious and popular with viewers.

Do we need some examples of unique Palin syntax and stylistic chicanery? From the Trump endorsement speech: "Well, look, we're made and we've been had. They need to get used to it [presumably get used to rhetorical revenge]." Speaking of conflict in Middle Eastern nations: "Let them duke it out and let Allah sort it out." And speaking of Trump in a way that inserts a little religion: "He is from the private sector, not a politician. Can I get a 'Hallelujah'?"

Less entertaining are the speech occasions in which Palin allowed herself to play the role of a demagogue, exploiting fear and ignorance in her audience. One example: In the 2008 presidential campaign, Palin claimed that Democratic candidate Obama was largely an unknown, mysterious person—despite the fact Obama had granted scores of interviews to the national press.

Palin could commend herself for being courageous and forthright. At one fundraiser during the 2008 campaign, she declared: "There does come a time when you have to take the gloves off and that time is right now." On October 4, Palin accused Obama of regarding America as "so imperfect that he's palling around with the terrorists who would target their own country." The audience would gasp in shock, unaware that the "evidence" for this claim was a Chicago community board association with Bill Ayers, who was once a student radical and a founder of the 1960s radical group known as the Weathermen at a time Obama was only a young boy.

Yet even now, Palin can charm and entertain audiences and sell books based on her own Tea Party version of the body politick and what the voters need to do in order to right the ship of state. Her endorsement of Donald Trump for the Republican nomination was simply the latest version of word plays, rhymes, quips, and confusing claims and statements with more likely to come.


## Donald Trump, Republican Primary Campaign, 2015-16

One of the most astounding and surprising developments in the race for the presidency in the 2016 election was the rise and media dominance of billionaire, real estate mogul, and reality television personality Donald Trump. True, millions of Americans had heard of Donald Trump before 2015. They knew about Trump Towers and they knew about his reality television show, "The Apprentice." Yet who could have imagined Trump as a serious candidate for president of the United States?

As a serious candidate, Donald Trump seemed to break all the conventional rules for serious, respectful campaigning. He could use the word "stupid" in describing political leaders in Washington and voters in state primaries who consider other candidates besides himself, and he could label the policies of Obama and Clinton "disastrous." He could ridicule a woman's personal appearance (candidate Carly Florina), imitate and mock a disabled reporter covering his campaign, denigrate the service of a famous POW hero (long-time senator and 2008 Republican presidential candidate John McCain), come up with a negative nickname for every major political opponent, or cite FDR's wartime roundup of immigrants as a wise precedent for his own proposal of banning all Muslims entry into the U.S.A. until the government "can figure out what the hell is going on." He could use words and terms that some take as vulgar, and he could imply publicly that one female network anchor had given him unfair questioning because she was experiencing her menstrual cycle during the time of the debate.

Some academic political scientists expressed astonishment at the Trump phenomenon as did ordinary rank-and-file party members. How could some candidate so extravagantly wealthy, so arrogant, so prejudiced, and so insensitive, then succeed in the national political arena? "No one has an explanation for this phenomenon, and I am no different," stated one political scientist.

Trump seemed to jumpstart his campaign by voicing a complaint about Central American illegal immigrants crossing the border to enter the U. S. He spoke of them as murderers, thieves, and rapists, with a kind of afterthought that "some of them are good people, I assume." That sound bite was the first of many that kept Trump in the spotlight. Then, in November 2015, Trump offered his serious proposal to ban Muslim immigrants from entering the U. S. The proposal brought a firestorm of protest and negative criticism from political leaders and candidates in both parties, but Trump's standing in the polls inched even higher. In time, he was dubbed the "Teflon candidate" because no complaint or criticism against any outlandish comment or proposal seemed to stick—nothing he could say went over the line. Trump seemed to have given voice to an angry, alienated group of GOP voters that felt it needed a voice that previously had not been heard and will not be easily placated if another candidate besides Trump is nominated.

Was (and is) Donald Trump a demagogue instead of a statesman? To this author, the answer can only be affirmative. Consider the Trump style of demagogy. There were few speeches of substance. Often speeches that incorporated substantive issues would begin with a personal defense or personal attacks against his accusers. Late in his campaign, Trump defended himself against women who accused him of unwanted sexual advances and, in one serious speech, he pledged to file a lawsuit against them. Most public appearances and campaign speeches were best known, not for incisive policy analysis, but for the speaker's opinion of himself and for piercing, personal attacks on other candidates of either party. Trump could be a master of retaliation; once criticized or called a name, the reply was even more venomous. The Republican candidate called his Democratic opponent Hillary Clinton so many insulting names; to listen to Trump, Secretary Clinton was a "liar," "crooked," "criminal," and "utter disaster" as both public servant and wife. And Barack Obama was often called by Trump "the worst president in our nation's history."

The demagogue can be overly-simplistic in solutions or scapegoat another person or group for a national problem. Both Muslims and Hispanics in general were scapegoated for domestic and international terrorism and domestic crime and unemployment, respectively. The solution, as simplistic as the analysis: Ban Muslims from entering the country and build a giant wall to keep illegal immigrants out of the country. Too many citizens wear ready for a "quick fix" to the nation's problems, and found it refreshing that a candidate does not come from the Washington establishment, speaks his mind in an unfiltered and unscripted way, is spontaneous, eschews political correctness, and talks about "making America great again."

As year 2016 arrived, serious political analysts were viewing the Trump campaign as a continuing raucous, attention-grabbing, disruptive, compelling, discombobulating, media-obsessed, oxygen-hogging presence that entirely overshadowed both the Republican and the Democratic primary races for the nomination. Despite the criticism and fear he stirred, Trump was nominated by the Republican National Convention as the standard-bearer, the nominee for president. Thus he has become the most successful demagogue in American history. Almost every week of the general campaign, Trump uttered an unscripted declaration of one kind or another that created controversy and attention, and, often as not, offended a certain segment of the population. After several women in Trump's past stepped forward to accuse the candidate of sexual harassment and even sexual assault, his public statements and speeches seemed to become more absurdly dangerous. Trump described himself as a victim of conspiracy between the

Clintons and "liberal media," that the charges were false and "total lies," that President Obama is "totally incompetent," that the nation was headed toward a disastrous decline or complete destruction, and that he alone was the only person who could be the nation's "savior." Speaking of his "compulsive boastfulness" and "self-admiration," respected columnist George Will asked rhetorically, "Is there a disagreeable human trait that Trump does not have?" Many questioned not only Trump's personal moral character but also his mental and emotional health.

As the general election approached and Donald Trump seemed slowly to drop in the polls, the candidate continued his presidential bid in the same manner he began it: provocative, defiant, and oblivious to campaign norms, conventional wisdom, and advice of experts. His advisers seemed to have no success getting him to moderate his tone in order to reach out to independents, undecided, and swing voters. On the cable network shows, his surrogates and representatives spent much time and deployed twisted logical strategies to explain and "normalize" their candidate. By persistently calling his opponent "a liar" and accusing her of running "a very sleazy campaign" and announcing the election was "rigged against him," the Republican candidate seemed only to "gin" up his own hard-core supporters. One pundit observed that Trump was like a bull trying to make sure as many teacups as possible are shattered before he leaves the china shop.

As a nominee for the nation's highest office, Trump had to be taken seriously. Indeed, a demagogue might be elected or might simply relish being a permanent spoiler and spectacle who never has to go to work actually to solve the nation's woes that were exploited for selfish political gain. Little wonder centuries ago that Plato feared democracy and contended in his ideal republic that a nation-state should be governed by philosopher-kings. How interesting will be the way various future historians describe this volatile period in our history!

*Postscript:* To put this analysis in perspective, all of the above content was written prior to Election Day, November 8, 2016. Perhaps with perspective of time, and a fair chance for the new president to perform and serve the American people, much of this analysis could be rendered incorrect and/or unfair. There should be many months in office for the new president to "pivot" (a word used often in the 2016 campaign) away from a demagogic strategy and move toward a respectful, statesmanlike style of leadership that unites and heals.

Millions of Americans were surprised, even shocked, that Donald Trump pulled one of the greatest and most unlikely election upsets in the nation's history. So many citizens were elated and relieved and so many other citizens were disappointed and heart-broken.

While Secretary Clinton received almost three million more popular votes, Trump won the all-important electoral count by a 306 to 232 margin. The strengths and weaknesses of each major candidate, the role of rhetoric and advertising, the role of the news media, as well as the role of unexpected events and developments during the campaign (such as Russian hacking into Democratic party emails and allowing their release in order to influence the election returns), may all be factored into the election outcome—and they will surely be analyzed and debated in the years to come when strong emotion has subsided and more perspective is possible!

# 7. Missing the Cut–American Speakers Not Quite Making the List of 101 Top Speeches, Yet Deserving Honorable Mention

Those who have given study and thought to great American speakers will surely disagree with any listing of who was, and is, among the best and with any listing of the most important speeches in our nation's history. The following are some speakers worthy of mention. Perhaps some should have been cited earlier. Rather than ranking them according to who is best and most effective, their names and a brief discussion about their lives and oratory will be cited chronologically.

## Alexander Hamilton (1757–1804)

Born in the British West Indies, Alexander Hamilton immigrated to the New York colony in 1773, attended King's College (now Columbia University), and became a fervent advocate of the patriot cause. He earned a reputation as one of the young heroes of the American Revolution. He studied law, becoming a member of the bar in New York City. With political wisdom and insight, Hamilton saw the major inadequacies of the Articles of Confederation and felt the new nation was in a desperate situation. As a member of the New York State Assembly, he often rose to debate. His area of specialty was finance and taxation. He was one of a select group of fifty-five delegates who assembled at Independence Hall in Philadelphia on May 25, 1787, for revision of the Articles. The end result of this convention, of course, was the drafting of an entirely new Constitution, and Hamilton earned his place in history by influencing its ultimate ratification. He had authored a major section of the *Federalist Papers* and made speeches to contend for the values of the new Constitution and a new and more powerful national government.

Hamilton had a reputation for brilliance and eloquence, though, unlike other speakers in this volume, one does not point to individual, stand-alone orations that are remembered for greatness. On June 18, 1787, at the Constitutional Convention, the record shows he delivered an impressive five-hour address. Gouverneur Morris declared it to be the greatest speech he ever heard. As a speaker, he made a strong appeal to logic and reason. As he stood to speak, Hamilton, though not tall, was a handsome and well-built man with deep-set blue eyes, who could deliver a speech with directness and energy. His best speeches were often delivered in a debate. Though mostly a forensic and legislative speaker, Hamilton delivered a moving eulogy on behalf of Major General Nathaniel Greene, perhaps second only to George Washington in public esteem as military general; the eulogy was delivered on July 4, 1789.

Though a controversial figure even in his time, Hamilton was a highly influential leader among the Federalists that gave shape to the government in the earliest months of the nation's history under the new Constitution. President Washington appointed him as the first secretary of the treasury, a position he held from 1789 to 1795, and he interpreted the Constitution broadly and invested national political leaders with implied powers. Standing in opposition to Madison and Jefferson, Hamilton advocated the necessity of a strong national government and he distrusted the masses whom, he contended "seldom judge or determine right." Some see an irony in this position: Hamilton was the lone Founding Father who came from real poverty, born illegitimate, and then orphaned in the West Indies. While this life story would have doomed him to obscurity in any other nation, only in the new American nation could Hamilton become one of that nation's most powerful and influential political leaders.

Hamilton's career as a public leader and orator were cut short, dying at age forty-seven after being mortally wounded during a duel with Aaron Burr. A brilliant mind and tactical strategist was lost, though his lasting influence on American government and society continues. As an aside, Alexander Hamilton was the principal author of George Washington's significant "Farewell Address" as well as some other addresses presented by the first president.

In modern times, beginning with the 2015-16 Broadway season, Alexander Hamilton has received a major boost in public relations by the highly acclaimed and award-winning Broadway musical show about his life and thinking as one of the nation's Founders. This popular show simply named *Hamilton* is a rap and hip-hop retelling of heroism and plotting by Hamilton, George Washington, Thomas Jefferson, and others during the American Revolution is based on the acclaimed biography of Hamilton by Ron Chernow.

# Thomas Hart Benton (1782–1858)

When we think of the early national period, the names Clay, Calhoun, and Webster come to mind, and each of these three senators were effective thinkers and orators. Yet, the work of Thomas Hart Benton was just as important as any of his colleagues. His family lived in Tennessee, south of Nashville, and he was admitted to the Williamson County bar in 1806 and he served one term in the state senate. After serving under Jackson in 1812, he moved to St. Louis in 1815 where he practiced law and worked for Missouri statehood. He was elected U. S. senator in 1820 and served five terms (until 1850).

Benton made numerous speeches. Jacksonian democracy was at the heart of the majority of his public addresses. Late in his career he gave speeches in ceremonial and educational settings. He was a defender of Jeffersonian ideals all the way. He knew and respected history and could build strong arguments for his proposition, though one weakness was his tendency either to be angry or sound angry in some of his argumentation. Nonetheless, he commanded respectful attention for his energy and fervor and the cogency of his case.

Benton was a Westerner all the way, devoted to both the Union and to westward expansion. He gave speeches that advocated any legislation and policies that promoted the West: direct presidential elections, termination of the U. S. Bank, hard money, a central railroad, free public lands, and a staunch defense of the Union. Benton was an early disciple of Manifest Destiny. He believed great things could happen out West and argued for distribution of unoccupied land as rapidly as possible to those who could make new land ownership beneficial for the greater good. Benton's views on western lands were at the heart of a dispute that occasioned the great legislative debate between Robert Hayne and Daniel Webster. Webster's replies to Hayne have been celebrated as some of the greatest oratory in early national American history.

With such a long career in the Senate, Thomas Hart Benton addressed a changing set of issues. Interestingly, Benton argued in speeches against U. S. expansion into Texas, claiming that Mexico's claim to Texas through the Spanish settlement of Texas was one hundred years prior to the U. S. claim to Texas through the French settlement of the Louisiana Territory. He also announced he would not support the expansion of slavery into the new western territories. Because his views were not always popular, his rhetoric became defensive argumentation. As a politician, he deserves recognition with the mention of Calhoun, Webster, and Clay. In so many ways he was ahead of his time.

## Edward Everett (1794–1865)

In the study of American public address, Edward Everett is genuine irony—a man who held so many distinguished public positions, presented many speeches and lectures, and yet is hardly remembered today and is not considered among the nation's great orators! Among the positions he held: pulpit minister of the largest church in Boston, congressman, governor of Massachusetts, minister to England, president of Harvard, secretary of state, and U. S. senator. Everett was a gentleman and a scholar. Ralph Waldo Emerson thought of him as "the greatest American orator" of his time. He was a great public advocate both for democracy and higher education. He gave public lectures on ancient history even before the lyceum movement began. He spoke often at July Fourth celebrations. His speeches were always well prepared and contained a wealth of historical information.

To Everett, who joined the Whig Party, America was a chosen nation that is guided by Divine Providence and still imbued with a divine mission. Despite the fact that Everett delivered many speeches, who can name a great oration or any other public address that he delivered? Perhaps the best known speech Everett delivered is one known for its presentation at Gettysburg when Lincoln delivered a far briefer speech that is, indeed, so well-known and honored (see the previous chapter).

Everett was known for excellence in ceremonial speaking, thus little wonder he was a first choice to deliver the main address at the dedication of the battlefield at Gettysburg. Besides effective delivery, he possessed a gift for eloquent language and imagery. On December 22, 1824, the speaker delivered a ceremonial address at Plymouth Rock. In typical stylistic flourish, he depicted the harrowing ordeal for the pilgrim passengers crossing the mighty Atlantic on the *Mayflower*, "driven in fury before the raging tempest, on the high and giddy waves. The awful voice of the storm howls through the rigging. The laboring masts seem straining from their base; the dismal sound of the pumps is heard; the ship leaps, as it were, madly from billow to billow." And then the orator described the troubles that these pilgrim immigrants encountered after a safe landing had been accomplished.

Everett's first speech in Congress was delivered on March 9, 1825. The address was long and painstakingly prepared. This was a stressful assignment for the speaker as the issue of the Constitution and slavery was woven into almost every important Congressional address. Admitting that the Constitution was less than ideal and had been crafted through compromises, the speaker declared: "Sir, I do not think it perfect, but it is good enough for me." Everett, though opposed to slavery, called for "conciliatory forbearance" on that subject when heatedly discussed. On February 8, 1854, as senator from Massachusetts, he spoke about ninety minutes in a crowded Senate chamber on the Kansas-Nebraska bill. Yet he found the controversy over slavery to be so distasteful that he resigned his seat in 1855 and for the next decade appeared before the public only in the role of a special orator—a role in which he likely had no superiors!

Everett's most famous address honored George Washington, delivered first on February 22, 1856, and then repeated to various other audiences. The speech was used to raise funds for The Ladies Mount Vernon Association that intended to purchase Washington's estate and convert it into a national memorial. And, of course, there is the oration that is often remembered though never quoted, the one alongside Lincoln at Gettysburg on November 19, 1863. There were seventeen governors who composed the committee that planned the Gettysburg national cemetery occasion, and they unanimously concurred that Everett was their first choice for speaker. The event was originally set for a day in October, but in deference to Everett's request for more preparation time, bad weather was risked to delay the occasion for another month just to be certain Everett could accept the invitation.

Everett labored to prepare a memorable speech worthy of the occasion and of his reputation as the nation's premier ceremonial speaker. His speech was a plea for reconciliation between the North and South. Even with some substantial deletions from his main text, the address was two hours in length. Yet speaking of the North and South, he dared to use the word "one community," an expression almost unheard of at that time of crisis. "The bonds that unite us as one people—a substantial community of origin, language, belief, and law—these bonds of union are a perennial force and energy, while the causes of alienation are imaginary, factitious, and transient," the orator proclaimed. "The heart of people North and South is for Union....The weary masses of the people are yearning to see the dear old flag again floating upon their Capitols."

Everett's last major speech was presented three weeks prior to the 1864 election. Despite earlier reservations about Lincoln, Everett now strongly favored his re-election. Ironically, it was the first and only time this honorable public servant actually presented a stump speech. Like all previous ceremonial speeches and public lectures, one underlying reality became evident—Edward Everett loved the Union and wanted it preserved.

## William Lownes Yancey (1814–1863)

Along with Robert Barnwell Rhett, William Yancey was the leading oratorical figure and spokesman in the old South for secession. Born in Georgia, his family moved to South Carolina, but then as a young man he moved to Alabama where he fully immersed himself into the plantation system. Later he studied law and then went into politics. Originally, Yancey supported President Van Buren, spoke respectfully of the Union and the Constitution, yet argued that the interests of the South must always be the priority of his beloved region. After a brief stint in state politics, he was elected to the U. S. House of Representatives in 1844 and, despite winning re-election, resigned in 1846. He then devoted himself to a career of public advocacy of the rights of Southern states.

Yancey was a popular speaker and highly effective in his extemporaneous style, coming to be known as "the Charles James Fox of America." Thousands heard him speak each year. He spoke with passion and undoubtedly was perceived as a man of integrity and sincerity. We do not have manuscripts of his speeches, yet we know he influenced audiences and we know the positions he advocated. He went to the Democratic National Convention at Charleston in 1860 to block the nomination of Stephen A. Douglas for president and to steer the platform in a direction of total support for Southern rights. At that time, and for decades to follow, Southern rights were seen as "states' rights." One writer called him the "Orator of Southern Constitutional Rights." In his rhetoric, he claimed slaveholders did not wish to break up the Union. Indeed, he popularized the political philosophy of John Calhoun.

Though highly effective in addressing a live audience, Yancey has been considered the prototype of a demagogue, stirring passions of fear and distrust for personal political gain. He contended that slavery was imposed on the South by the greed of New England slave traders and that it had grown due to the "climate and economy" of the region in which it must be retained—the beloved South! With Yancey's speaking reputation, he was invited to speak to Northern audiences, once addressing the prestigious Cooper Institute, on October 10, during the 1860 campaign, and also at Boston's Faneuil Hall. Speaking to large audiences, he indeed earned his reputation as "the orator of secession," and in the North he was known as "the Prince of Fire-eaters."

Yancey advanced the argument that the North had forced the South into disunion and that the election of Lincoln had culminated in disaster and "awful calamity." After secession, the new Confederacy "honored" his rhetorical skills by sending him on a diplomatic mission to London, though his attempts to get British support for the rebel cause were unsuccessful. He continued to make speeches for the Confederate cause and served in the Confederate Senate, where he made speeches in support of President Jefferson Davis. Nonetheless, while hailed in his beloved region, Yancey was spokesman for a lost cause, and he died a painful death of an internal infection shortly after the Battle of Gettysburg. He was thus spared witnessing the collapse and surrender of his beloved Confederacy to the Union forces. One rhetorical critic, Rexford Mitchell (in the Brigance series, Vol. 2, p. 748), concludes his study by declaring that "if the South had been victorious, tradition might have made him the Patrick Henry of the Confederacy."

## Stephen A. Douglas (1813–1861)

History has not been so kind to Stephen A. Douglas. Were it not for Lincoln, the rhetoric of this prominent senator from Illinois would have placed him amidst our top 101 speakers and speeches. Douglas was a reasonable man. He worked hard at peaceful solutions to the nation's problems. He believed in democratic solutions and compromise in order to save the Union. And, but for division within the Democratic Party in 1860, he would have been elected president and Lincoln might have been little more than a paragraph or two in U. S. history survey textbooks, known simply as someone who debated Douglas and ran for president and was defeated.

Douglas's career was remarkable. Though born in New York, he moved to Illinois and was a prairie politician, a stump speaker for his causes and ideas. He had served as a schoolmaster, state attorney, legislator, secretary of state, justice of the Illinois Supreme Court, representative to the U. S. Congress for three terms, a prominent U. S. senator for sixteen years, chairman of U. S. Committee on Territories that brought in a dozen new territories and states, and, at last, Democratic nominee for U. S. president. In all these roles, Douglas presented thousands of speeches on the stump throughout the nation and hundreds of other speeches in committee meetings and the general sessions of both houses of Congress.

Short in stature (5' 2"), he acquired the nickname of "Little Giant," and his success as a politician was intricately linked with his ability to persuade an audience. His friends considered him highly persuasive and effective, and his enemies dismissed his rhetorical efforts as coming from a sophist and a trickster. General consensus holds that the campaign for the Illinois senate seat in 1858, the occasion for debating the new politician in the state, was the most important in his career.

The 1850s was a decade of change. Americans were interested in going westward. Antislavery sentiment was growing in most of the Northern states, including Illinois. The number of churches doubled during the decade. Educational opportunities began to multiply. There was interest in reform. And there was an increased interest in politics. People were willing to travel at some distance to hear political debates and speeches. In Illinois there was division over slavery, with antislavery sentiment growing, especially in the northern part of the state. The old Whig Party was dying and the Republican Party was rising. Lincoln was a state politician who had served one term in the U. S. House, but otherwise not considered to be a very successful politico. When Douglas and Lincoln met for debate in that famous 1858 state campaign, the issue most debated was the former's "popular sovereignty." The Republican stand on slavery was to accept it where it was established, but "no more slave territory."

As a speaker, Douglas spoke extemporaneously. The source of his ideas seems to be his own experience and observation. Douglas was a loyal member of the Democratic Party, this commitment being a ruling principle of his political life. He studied the slavery issue carefully and at no time did he declare himself in favor of the extension of this institution, but he understood the South and contended for that section's constitutional rights to maintain slavery as part of its economic system. Popular sovereignty, the rhetorical theme for which Douglas is best known, seemed both truly democratic and expedient.

Both friends and political opponents recognized Douglas' speech delivery as highly effective. He used a staccato style of presentation and his voice had strong carrying power, so important in the age before electronic amplification. Here was a speaker who had strong and positive *ethos* all over his home state of Illinois. His speaking was indeed effective. To be sure, he was a gifted orator. His arguments were basically sincere and consistent. He loved the Union and did not want to see it split by sectional rivalry. He made speeches for all kinds of legislation, perhaps none better known than the Kansas-Nebraska bill.

While winning the Democratic nomination in 1860, the nation and his own party had become even more divided, and a new political leader from his own state had risen to national prominence. After the March 1861 presidential inauguration, the nation was hearing a new voice. With only a few circumstances being different, Douglas might have been standing where Lincoln stood, and, ironically, might have seen his duty and policies in the same way. One man rose in history, despite the fact his time in office seemed tragically aborted, and the other man quietly and immediately walked into the shadows of national life and soon passed away.

## Jefferson Davis (1808–1889)

Jefferson Davis, president of the Confederacy, has hardly been appreciated in modern times nor was he much appreciated in his own time. He was falsely accused, placed in prison and in chains, denied pardon, and stripped of his citizenship. As for his ideology, Davis and John Calhoun could have been blood brothers, each believing that slavery was justified as a merciful strategy to provide a good life for African-Americans, who, incidentally, by God's creation order were inferior to the white race. Both believed that slaves were property and, as such, deserved to be protected by law as any other kind of property is safeguarded. Both believed the Constitution was a compact between the states and that every state possessed a legal and moral right to withdraw from the compact (or the Union) at any time it deemed state welfare was not being protected.

Davis was also an orator with considerable skill before an audience. After the death of Calhoun in 1850, he then became the acknowledged leader and leading advocate for the Southern cause in the U. S. Senate. Davis himself was a slaveholder with over one hundred slaves and generally was a humane master, guarding his household against mistreatment. He often delivered lectures in the U. S. Senate, typically taking aim against the views of senators favoring abolition, such as William Seward.

As a speaker, Davis traveled to New England, the very heart of abolitionist sentiment, in the fall of 1858 where he defended the system of slavery and attempted to assuage fears of Northerners about Southern intentions. On this lecture tour, Davis spoke at Boston's famed Faneuil Hall and New York's Palace Garden. His last extended speech in the U. S. was delivered on January 10, 1861, an address in which, with war clouds hanging over a divided nation, Davis claimed to "have striven unsuccessfully to avert the catastrophe which now impends over the country." On his way from Washington to Montgomery to join the convention of Southern states to inaugurate the new Confederacy, Davis delivered twenty-five speeches and all were conciliatory in tone—in fact, Davis was not a fire-eating disunionist and his rhetoric often demonstrated a warm and positive tone.

In February 1861, in Montgomery, Alabama, Davis was inaugurated as president of the Confederacy and, a year later, was inaugurated again when the capital was moved to Richmond, Virginia. The basic theme of his addresses, then, was that the South wanted peaceful co-existence with the North but must be prepared to fight and sacrifice for its freedom. His speeches as president of the Confederacy do not appear to have been a strategic factor one way or the other among peoples of the South. After the war, Davis was most reluctant to return to a lecture platform, though he did deliver a few ceremonial speeches.

Jefferson Davis lived another quarter century past the ending of the Civil War, and those years may have been anti-climactic to the reputation he established as the younger and then middle-aged man—a political leader with good intentions and excellent skills but ensnared in circumstances that made him the chief defender (after John Calhoun) of the most evil and indefensible of American institutions.

## Lucius Quintus Cincinnatus Lamar (1825–1893)

Though born in Georgia, Lucius Q. C. Lamar established his reputation as a Mississippian: teacher, attorney, representative and senator to the U. S. Congress, cabinet member, and associate justice of the U. S. Supreme Court. In all these roles he was an intelligent and persuasive public speaker, renowned more for his keen, analytical mind and ability to state complex concepts in simple and understandable language than for a powerful delivery. In 1861 Lamar resigned from the U. S. Congress after the secession of Mississippi in order to serve the Confederacy, himself being a passionate defender of Southern institutions, even an active secessionist to safeguard those traditions. In 1873 Lamar returned to his place in the U. S. Congress to become the most influential public voice from the South. He was a man of courage and conviction.

Lamar held the strong conviction after the Civil War that the South must accept the unalterable outcome of the war and must convince the North that its acceptance of the outcome was complete and that a reconciliation between the sections was imperative. Yet, how might this political leader achieve this purpose? The opportunity came with the unexpected death of one of the South's bitterest enemies, Senator Charles Sumner, the Massachusetts abolitionist leader, a founder of the Republican Party, and an architect of Radical Reconstruction. Sumner died on March 11, 1874.

This eloquent eulogy for Sumner was Lamar's most important speech in a long and varied political career. It was a delicate speaking situation. The speaker's purpose was to demonstrate and pledge good will and cooperation with the North, but also in a manner that did not stir a negative reaction among Southern citizens. Lamar acknowledged the pain and devastation of the South yet gave credit to the North for "magnanimous emotions." With simplicity and sincerity, the eulogist praised Sumner as a great man who possessed an "all-controlling love for freedom." He labeled Sumner a "self-sacrificing hero." And then he concluded with a sentimental yet effective admonition: "My countrymen! Know one another, and you will love one another."

The impact of Lamar's speech was huge, being reprinted in newspapers throughout the nation and receiving fulsome praise in the both North and the South. The young editor for the Atlanta *Constitution*, Henry Grady, himself a spokesman for "the New South," gave the speech great praise. Lamar had achieved his purpose. This address was just one contributing factor that brought Reconstruction to an end three years later. Lamar served effectively in the U. S. Congress and then on the Supreme Court, but his legacy is that of an orator and advocate of reconciliation. And his life and career gave clear evidence that an intelligent and sincere person can change one's mind and rise to national greatness.

## Lucy Stone (1818–1893)

The best-known women orators of the nineteenth century were typically immersed in reform campaigns of the era. Their contribution has been largely their passionate advocacy and agitation for causes they believed in rather than individual political achievement.

There were many minor female figures out there on the platform, women such as "Yelling Mary" Lease of Kansas, who advised farmers to "raise more hell than corn," Carrie Nation, who chopped up saloons with a hatchet, and Antoinette Brown, a Quaker preacher. There was a wide range of causes. In Salt Lake City a group of women challenged the Mormon practice of plural marriages. Women ran homes for other women who had unwanted pregnancy or needed shelter and sanctuary from abusive relationships or were even escaping a polygamous marriage. Like other social reform movements, women's reform work in general during this later national period possessed a strong missionary strain.

The chief concern of women reformers was suffrage, the right to vote. The nation actually faced two components of the debate about suffrage and the issues were discussed and debated simultaneously. One was a debate over black suffrage. Also, since the end of the Civil War, a small group of abolitionists had sought to enhance women's rights.

In 1866 the U. S. Congress debated the Fourteenth Amendment that called for "equal protection," and this spurred women's rights advocates into efforts to link their cause, too, with civil rights. Some Radical Republicans and reformers could not see voting rights for blacks and voting rights for women sharing the same urgency. Frederick Douglass, though a long-time women's rights advocate, argued that women had many ways of linking themselves to the ruling power of the land, but that black Americans had none. Women's rights leaders such as Elizabeth Cady Stanton and Susan Anthony, speaking on their own behalf, fervently disagreed.

Lucy Stone came from a very traditional farm family where her father was clearly boss and who worked his girls as hard as he drove himself. After reading the divine command in Genesis that woman's desire should be for the man "and he shall rule over thee," then young Lucy determined never to marry, but to pursue education. She was twenty-five when she finally entered Oberlin, the only college that would admit women. She formed the first debating society for college women and enrolled in a rhetoric class. Later she practiced her rhetoric at the Young Ladies Association. When she graduated, she announced she was devoting her speaking skills to plead the cause for the slaves and "for suffering humanity everywhere." Therefore, she began her public speaking career immediately after college graduation, giving her first women's rights speech at her brother's church in Massachusetts in 1850.

Stone became one of the late nineteenth century's most eloquent women speakers and her chief cause was also women's suffrage. She traveled extensively in the U. S. doing reform speaking and also delivered speeches in Canada. Her main themes were justice and equality. Her application of those abstract principles pointed out that women had been cheapened, handicapped, and violated without having the right to vote. Despite a clear and prophetic denunciation of inequality and a forthright and direct manner, Stone was ladylike, modest, sweet, and kind in her public demeanor. Even facing hostile audiences, her manner remained controlled and calm. She did not attack males, but rather praised the ones who were attempting to help women's equality. Stone founded the American Woman Suffrage Association, which welcomed men as well as women, and she established *The Woman's Journal* as a vehicle of communication. Incidentally, Stone did marry a Henry Blackwell, and the marriage rites included a pledge not to obey the husband and that she, as bride and future wife, would keep her maiden (birth) name.

# Mark Twain (1835–1910)

One might wonder how on earth Mark Twain would be placed in a book on American oratory. He is given little, if any, attention in books on the history of rhetoric and public speaking. He is not considered a major orator or skilled persuader. He is known mostly for his craft in writing humorous and entertaining fiction about life along the Mississippi River. His place in the annals of American literature is well established. Yet the man born Samuel Clemens in 1835 established a stronger reputation as a speaker in his own day than he is known for in contemporary times. And out of his success as a speaker he developed the public persona as Mark Twain. (Interestingly, Twain was late in receiving credit for his craftsmanship in fiction.) Twain's first public speech was presented in Keokuk, Iowa, on January 17, 1856, at a meeting of the Typothetae, an association of master printers who celebrated their craft annually on the birthday of Benjamin Franklin, the patron of all printers. Twain soon had those assembled doubling over in laughter—such was the beginning of a long speaking career!

Samuel Langhorne Clemens was born in the little town of Florida, Missouri, and grew up near the banks of the Mississippi River. His formal education ended when, as an early adolescent, his father died. As a young man he served as an apprentice journalist for his brother Orion, then later as apprentice and pilot on the Mississippi River, an experience that brought him into contact with all kinds of interesting characters. He failed as a silver miner, but succeeded as a journalist, eventually winding up in San Francisco. Out West he was fascinated by various professional humorists, the best known being Artemus Ward. He enjoyed travel, and venturing overseas was a rather unusual experience for most Americans of the nineteenth century, so he loved sharing his perspective on these experiences by writing about them. Yet it was life on the big river that stirred his creative juices the most. Returning to Hannibal and the mighty Mississippi River, he was moved to write a series of articles about his old steamboating days for the *Atlantic Monthly*, then these writings were adapted and elaborated for his literary masterpieces: *Tom Sawyer* (1876), *Life on the Mississippi* (1883), and *The Adventures of Huckleberry Finn* (1885). Nonetheless, it was on the lecture platform that Twain first earned his fame.

Twain's debut as a professional speaker began in San Francisco on October 2, 1866, with a public lecture on the Sandwich Islands, the name for the Hawaiian Islands at that time. The speaker had made a journalistic tour of the islands, had written some letters about his travels, and then decided to develop his skills at lecturing. Despite misgivings

and anxiety about public speaking, he rented the city's largest venue for the occasion and
then put out an announcement that read simply: "Admission one dollar; doors open at
half past seven, the trouble begins at eight." At 8:00 P.M., Twain walked out and faced
his first audience of any size, but later reported in his *Autobiography* the feeling of anxiety
that is so typical of many speakers: "The fright which pervaded me from head to foot
was paralyzing. It lasted two minutes and was as bitter as death; the memory of it is
indestructible but it had its compensations, for it made me immune from timidity before
audiences for all time to come." Actually, it was an audience of considerable size as the
house was filled. Twain spoke about those beautiful islands, mentioned the American
missionaries there, and spoke of "the absurd customs and characteristics of the natives"
and also referenced "a den of wild beasts." The evening was a success for an inexperienced
speaker launching a professional speaking career.

Twain was gratified at this opening event. He felt confident enough to attempt the
same lecture again; this time there were 1,500 in the audience. The journalist-turned-
public speaker began to earn more money than he had ever made in his life. The humorist
then began a lecture tour of northern California and western Nevada, delivering sixteen
lectures along his route. Encouraged by his success in the late 1860s, he was willing
to work with James Redpath, a lecture circuit manager and organizer of the Boston
Lyceum Bureau. Under Redpath's management, Twain was booked to speak at venues
in Pennsylvania, Massachusetts, Rhode Island, Connecticut, New Jersey, and at New
York's famed Cooper Institute where Lincoln and other famous Americans had been
granted a forum. He sometimes expressed surprise at how lecture halls were filled, even
crowded at times onto the stage, to hear his lectures. The more he repeated the stories,
the more fun he seemed to have, and there was never a need for manuscript or notes. The
humorist once quipped he could remember anything, whether it ever happened or not.

Despite comments about stage fright, Twain seemed to love public speaking. His
stories about adventures of life on the Mississippi River and in traveling were edited oral
versions of content he had written for publication. Though he hated the discomforts of
a rigid travel schedule and being away from his family, he loved the stimulus of a live
audience. He even established his own publishing firm, Webster and Company, but that
firm failed leaving Twain debts of $80,000, a considerable sum in the 1890s. Thus, the
writer turned again to public speaking and lecturing, and in 1894 decided a round-the-
world lecture tour would be interesting and stimulating. Indeed, it was all that and
more—he returned a year later with debts substantially paid.

What was Twain like on stage and/or behind a podium? His style did not haphazardly develop. He gave careful thought to technique, and even wrote an insightful essay, "How to Tell a Story." And he was influenced by humorists he had heard and studied, such as Artemus Ward, whose specialty was satirizing the Mormons, and Henry Shaw, *a.k.a.* Josh Billings, who spun down-home, common-sense philosophy in the form of dialogue humor. Twain believed timing to be strategically important and emphasized what might be called the "pregnant pause." Talking slowly, with a Southern drawl, he would carefully calculate the time for a long pause. "The right word may be effective," Twain often said, "but no word was ever as effective as a rightly timed pause." He would tell his stories deadpan, sometimes with a hint of sadness and sorrow. His facial expressions were telling. When the men and women in his audience roared in laughter, he could act surprised as though he had not anticipated such audience delight. While he lectured, he would puff on a cigar, pausing at just the right moment to either light it or take a draw off the burley product, letting the words he had just uttered to sink in.

Twain spoke the language of the people in his audience. He possessed high *ethos* as a man who could speak in the vernacular style of his listeners and, if not exactly promoting high moral character, could convince them he was dispensing extraordinary common sense. He had a feel for the audience and instinctively adapted himself to each audience. Sometimes Twain did not want or need an introduction, and could just walk out and begin his monologue.

By the 1870s Mark Twain was known from coast to coast. His marriage to Olivia Langdon in 1870 took him off the circuit for one year, but he soon returned. He toured in Europe during the decade of the 70s, speaking and reading before more than thirty audiences in London, Liverpool, and Leicester. In most cases, he would read selections from his writings rather than giving a lecture. He then took a few years off from touring and lecturing, doing more writing, and then embarked on a world tour in 1895 to 1896—indeed, a formidable undertaking in American lecturing during the era. The speaker began in Cleveland in July 1895, made his way through Michigan, Minnesota, Montana, Washington, Oregon and then to Vancouver, British Columbia, from which he sailed to Australia. Twain found public speaking exhilarating. "Lecturing is gymnastics, chest-expander, medicine, mind healer, blues destroyer, all in one," he wrote to the *San Francisco Examiner* in August 1885; "I am twice as well as I was when I started out. I have gained nine pounds in twenty eight days, and expect to weigh six hundred before January. I have not had a blue day in all the twenty-eight."

Twain lectured, then, in many diverse cities among diverse cultures and audiences: from Australia (eight weeks) to New Zealand (six weeks), India (eight weeks), Ceylon,

Mauritius, and South Africa (seven weeks), and then sailing back to England. There were scores of lectures, and many days aboard a ship; likely there was much talking, if not formal public speeches, on board the ship. Often he wearied of lecturing, but he saw lecturing as a means of livelihood and also increasingly as a way to market his writing. His last speech was a commencement address at a females' college in Baltimore in June 1909, and during his lifetime he presented almost one thousand lectures and public addresses.

The amazing feat was how well Twain related to his audiences, how they easily enjoyed his humor, yet also perceived him as a man who understood their culture and was sincerely aware of human suffering. One of his best quotes: "Kindness is the language which the deaf can hear and the blind can see." Whether in the USA or abroad, audiences perceived Mark Twain as a man of humor, but at deeper levels, a man of practical wisdom whose knowledge did not come from advanced textbooks but from daily experience. Twain knew his audience wanted to leave the lecture hall having learned something, and he did not disappoint. Some of his most famous homespun quotes will live for future generations. One of the most relevant Twain quotes for speech classes: "There are only two types of speakers in the world: the nervous and the liars." And then one more: "It usually takes me three weeks to prepare a good impromptu speech."

Mark Twain was truly one of the most skilled and successful masters of the professional lecture platform. He was admired as speaker by so many of his contemporaries. In its simplicity, his skill was disarming, yet Twain possessed distinguished appearance (thick white hair in old age and a flickering smile), magnetism, and charm. Despite the fact that *Tom Sawyer* still remains one of those classic books assigned to American school children, perhaps we need to remember Twain as much or more as a public speaker than as a writer. And gratitude is owed actor Hal Holbrook for demonstrating authentically Twain's conversational style of public speaking and dramatizing the relevance of his ideas on a range of subjects to this contemporary generation.

## Eugene Victor Debs (1855–1926)

Born in Terre Haute, Indiana, Eugene Debs worked for the railroad as a boy of just fourteen years of age, becoming a locomotive fireman within a few years. He rose rapidly as a labor organizer and leader within the Brotherhood of Locomotive Firemen and, then, in 1893, founded the American Railway Union, an industrial union of all railroad workers. As president of the new union, the ARU won a number of bargaining victories though it engaged in a disastrous 1894 strike against the Pullman Car Company (President Grover Cleveland sent troops to Chicago to break up the strike). Debs was sentenced to six months in prison for violating a court injunction. Spending time reading socialist literature while in confinement, he emerged from incarceration as a believer in the class struggle. In 1898 Debs founded the Socialist Party of America, and he ran and campaigned in 1900 as the Socialist candidate for president.

Debs ran for president four more times. In 1904 he polled some 400,000 votes. The following year he teamed with rival socialist Daniel DeLeon and mineworkers' leader "Big Bill" Haywood to found the Industrial Workers of the World (the IWW), deemed a radical organization at the time as it sought to organize all workers, regardless of trade or industry, into one large union. Debs was the Socialist Party candidate again in 1908, receiving around 420,000 votes. In a strong 1912 presidential field with President Taft, Theodore Roosevelt, and Woodrow Wilson also on the ballot, Debs polled about six percent of the vote, around 900,000 votes.

During his career, Debs delivered thousands of speeches and his writings for the publications *Appeal to Reason* and the *International Socialist Review* reached wider audiences than the orations. When released from jail he would deliver a speech explaining his actions and discuss the concepts of freedom, liberty, and power in a democratic state. Other speeches were delivered on trade unionism. Keep in mind this was an era in which the majority of Americans feared and opposed organization of unskilled laborers. Another group of speeches concerned Debs' role as a candidate in the Socialist Party.

Debs and other Socialists opposed the U. S. entry into the Great War in 1917. His scathing rhetoric criticized the Woodrow Wilson administration for leading the nation into war. The federal government was already monitoring Debs' activity as a Socialist, but when he presented a forthright, scathing speech criticizing support for the war effort in a 1918 Canton, Ohio, appearance, he was arrested and convicted for violating the Espionage Act of 1917 and was charged with sedition.

In this trial Debs was permitted to present a plea, and thus he delivered a moving appeal. This Canton address, presented on June 16, 1918, was devoted to pacifism, liberty, and socialism. Debs reflected on his boyhood and the blessings of living in America—the beauty, the natural resources, the richest and most fertile soil, marvelous productive machinery, and millions of eager workers. He then explained the basic thesis of socialism and the common sense of "common property of all, democratically administered in the interest of all."

"I am opposing a social order in which it is possible for one man who does absolutely nothing that is useful to amass a fortune of hundreds of millions of dollars, while millions of men and women who work all the days of their lives secure barely enough for a wretched existence!" he exclaimed. The speaker continued to extol the virtues of socialism and the making of common cause, and he cast a vision of a future in which "we shall have universal commonwealth—the harmonious cooperation of every nation with every other nation on earth." After the speech, the judge sentenced him to ten years in prison. As a presidential candidate in 1920, though still in federal prison, Debs garnered his highest total of votes (915,000).

As a speaker, Eugene Debs spoke eloquently for a minority of American citizens. His rhetorical success demonstrated the power of an idea, even though not an idea held by the majority, still an idea (and an ideal, too) that served several purposes: enriching the American public dialogue during the onset of the Great Depression; explaining the system of socialism; and explaining the vulnerabilities of capitalism. American Socialist presidential candidates have generally not polled high numbers, but the rise of Bernie Sanders, Independent and Socialist from Vermont, in the 2016 Democratic presidential primary marked an uptick in interest and enthusiasm for socialist ideals. Sanders stirred great enthusiasm among the Millennial Generation. Perhaps both Debs and Sanders have been a little ahead of their time.

## Hubert H. Humphrey (1911–1978)

Hubert Horatio Humphrey devoted his life to public service. He was a scholar; a reform mayor of Minneapolis who worked to eliminate discrimination in city employment; a civil rights spokesman at whatever speaking venue was available to him; the first Democratic senator from Minnesota; the sponsor of many progressive legislative proposals (often under leadership of John F. Kennedy, for example: Nuclear Test Ban Treaty, Peace Corps, and the 1964 Civil Rights Act); Senate leader and Democratic party whip; the vice president under Lyndon B. Johnson; an indefatigable party campaigner who sought the presidency in 1960, 1968, and 1972; and Democratic nominee for president in 1968.

In all these roles, Humphrey's success and effectiveness as a progressive national public servant and political leader enabled him to wield great influence and keep his name before the American public for a generation during some of the most volatile times in our nation's history. The fact that Humphrey was defeated by Richard Nixon in a close 1968 election has, perhaps, significantly diminished his stature and influence when compared with the likes of Eisenhower, Kennedy, Johnson, and Nixon. Nonetheless, he won the respect of friend and political foe alike as a good and honorable man in public service and political life.

Humphrey delivered thousands of speeches during his long career. He was, along with Stevenson and Kennedy, one of the leading Democratic orators of his generation. He had strong *ethos*, or source credibility, with all audiences. He often spoke of his goal in public speaking as being a teacher who is enthused about his subject, elevating the level of political thinking in America. He spoke with passion and exuberance about progressive issues. Clearly, for Senator Humphrey, civil rights was the most important issue among many progressive causes.

Could we select one of his speeches as being the best? One possibility would be Humphrey's civil rights speech to the 1948 Democratic National Convention, sometimes titled "The Sunshine of Human Rights." The issue at that convention was whether the Democrats would adopt a progressive civil rights plank that would be similar to the one adopted by the Republicans at their national convention. During that era, the Southern wing of the Democratic Party wielded much power that was used in vetoing progressive legislature, contending ingenuously that states' rights trumped national legislation in such matters as racial equality. Yet Humphrey, then mayor of Minneapolis, led a group of Northern liberals in the fight for the party platform including a statement that supported the "basic and fundamental rights" of equal opportunity of employment and full political participation. The struggle was a challenging one.

Humphrey gained permission to address the delegates. What he stated in this brief speech was echoed in many career speeches. He first commended "the courageous trailblazing of two great Democratic presidents: Franklin Roosevelt and Harry Truman." "Sure, we're here as Democrats. But, my good friends, we are here as Americans," the speaker reminded the delegates; "this is far more than a party matter." After urging that "there can be [no] compromise on the guarantees of civil rights," the speaker made a final appeal: "To those who say we are rushing this issue of civil rights, I say to them we are a hundred and seventy-two years late. To those who say this civil rights program is an infringement on states' rights, I say this: The time has arrived in America for the Democratic Party to get out of the shadows of states' rights and to walk forthrightly into the bright sunshine of human rights...I ask the Democratic Party to march down the highroad of progressive democracy."

The impact of this address: Humphrey's plank on civil rights was adopted.

Pandemonium broke out on the floor. Three days later, disgruntled Southern Democrats bolted the Party and formed their own States' Rights Democratic Party, commonly nicknamed the Dixiecrats, nominating Strom Thurmond as standard bearer. A most surprising political phenomenon occurred in the general election—though the Democrats were split three ways, incumbent Harry Truman squeaked out a victory!

## Eugene McCarthy (1916–2005) and George McGovern (1922–2012)

The story of David and Goliath is known to almost everyone in Western culture, and it provides a fascinating parallel to the story of Eugene McCarthy, relatively little-known senator from Minnesota in 1967, and President Lyndon B. Johnson, who was facing re-election in 1968. McCarthy was opposed to the war in Vietnam and began delivering speeches against it. Encouraged by other opponents of the war, McCarthy entered the race for the 1968 Democratic Party nomination for president. Ordinarily, it would seem unthinkable for a little-known senator to challenge an incumbent president within his own party—but these were no ordinary times!

McCarthy was not a dynamic, spell-binding orator. His delivery was low-key and rather ordinary, if not touching the regrettable realm of boring. Yet the Minnesota senator was courageously vocal in his criticism of President Johnson in early 1968. The key to his rhetorical influence was in the power of his ideas and the compelling nature of his central thesis. In his speeches, McCarthy advocated a swift end to the war through an immediate withdrawal of American forces. He articulated the idea there was a "deepening moral crisis" in the nation with the rejection of the political system by many citizens and a sense of "helplessness" he hoped to alleviate. McCarthy drew a nice mix of audiences at his campaign stops, though younger supporters composed his chief audience. Yet listeners came from all ages and walks of life. He addressed crowds of thousands at various university campuses. "No nation has a right to destroy a nation, with the rationale of 'nation building,'" he declared before many audiences.

The importance of the New Hampshire primary should never be under-estimated. Though Johnson actually beat McCarthy in this primary, the Senator did win forty-two percent of the vote, an especially strong showing that led Senator Robert F. Kennedy, New York Democrat, to enter the race. With both McCarthy and Kennedy, a brother of the late president, making compelling and forthright speeches against the sitting president, Johnson decided to retire from his position at the end of his term of office and not seek reelection.

Year 1968 was a tumultuous one. Tragically, Robert Kennedy was assassinated at the end of the primary season when his candidacy was gaining strength. Vice President Hubert Humphrey was seen as the "stand-in" for Johnson, and his policies and organization possessed too much strength for McCarthy to overcome. McCarthy, therefore, narrowly lost to Humphrey at the convention amidst the protests inside the arena and riots outside on the streets of Chicago.

The public speaking and rhetorical arguments of Eugene McCarthy, it could be argued, made a difference in the candidate who was elected president in 1968, and it gave voice to millions of Americans who were disillusioned with what seemed unending, pointless, and expensive warfare. Meantime, domestically the issues of social justice and race relations were demanding attention and action.

Another little known senator, this one from a small state, rose to national prominence four years later on the power of rhetorical expression of ideas about war, the Vietnam War in particular. Senator George McGovern of South Dakota came to the upper chamber in 1963 and served the next eighteen years. While a liberal on most political issues of the day, it was McGovern's staunch opposition to the war in Vietnam for which he is best known and remembered. The Senator sought every legislative and every rhetorical means of ending the war—by making speeches to educate the public and by the McGovern-Hatfield Amendment!

In 1972 McGovern's grass-roots campaign gave him opportunity to speak out against the war in the primaries. He won the Democratic nomination, in part by taking advantage of new rules requiring more women and minority delegates at the convention—rules written by a commission that McGovern co-chaired. McGovern capitalized on support by antiwar activists and reform liberals, but his speeches inspired thousands of students to go door-to-door campaigning for him. His position was immediate withdrawal from the Vietnam War in exchange for the return of American POWs, offering amnesty for draft evaders who had departed the country, and then ultimately a reduction in defense spending.

The Democratic National Convention was a fiasco at times. Yes, McGovern had won the nomination and a minority of American liberals were ecstatically happy. Yet the vice presidential selection process was a disaster that plagued the campaign before it ever got started (several prominent Democrats turned down the chance to be running mate after Senator Tom Eagleton made a quick exit from the slate). On the final night of the convention, procedural wrangling over both a new party charter and a running mate delayed the schedule. McGovern's moving acceptance speech, "Come Home, America," was not delivered until three o'clock in the morning, reducing the television audience from an expected seventy million to around fifteen million.

The outcome of the 1972 election was never in doubt. Here was a progressive senator from a small state, advocating liberal ideas that could be interpreted as "surrender" to the Communists in North Vietnam, and up against an incumbent president who was basking in the glow of his recent, historic visit to China. Insult was added to injury when the "Democrats for Nixon" campaign was started. McGovern campaigned vigorously and while many election campaigns give birth to memorable lines, perhaps it was simply three words at a campaign stop in Battle Creek, Michigan, on November 2, that summed up the candidate's fatigue and exhaustion. At this rally, a Nixon admirer kept heckling the candidate. McGovern then motioned the heckler to come closer and he leaned in and told the heckler in a lower voice: "Kiss my ass." The incident was heard by a reporter and publicized nationally. And it actually helped humanize the candidate, showing he had some passion. In the general election on November 7, the McGovern-Sargent Shriver ticket suffered a 61 to 37 percent defeat to President Richard Nixon, with a humiliating Electoral College loss of 520 to 17.

McGovern continued to make speeches and teach history after the embarrassing loss. He taught as a professor of history for one year at the University of New Orleans. He was able to relate his campaign misadventures in a self-deprecating way, such as saying at the 1973 Gridiron Dinner, "For many years I wanted to run for the presidency in the worst possible way—and last year I sure did!" Nonetheless, history has been kind to both Eugene McCarthy and George McGovern. Their campaign speeches gave hope to millions that peace objectives were alive and well and that intelligent citizens should not be disparaged for seeking an immediate end to the misbegotten military adventure in Vietnam. Had their voices not been heard, how much more blood and national treasury would have been wasted?

Through public address and rhetoric, there are both outsiders and insiders (*i.e.*, of the Washington political structure) that gain national exposure and acceptance of their ideas. Besides McCarthy and McGovern, there are others: Wendell Willkie (1940); Ronald Reagan (1968, 1976); Jimmy Carter (1976); George H. W. Bush (1980); Gary Hart (1984, 1988); Jesse Jackson (1984, 1988); Pat Buchanan (1992); Ross Perot (1992); Bernie Sanders, Carly Fiorina, Ben Carson, and Donald Trump (2016). Obviously, some of these were winners and some losers.

# Caesar Chavez (1927–1993)

While the American labor movement has roots that go back to the late nineteenth century, most labor leaders considered it unlikely, if not impossible, to organize farmworkers into an effective union. Of course, there have been farmers' associations and "co-ops" for many generations, yet most of these organizations could not wield power similar to unions of craftsmen and even industrial workers. Caesar Chavez was raised in a migratory family during the Great Depression and learned first-hand the exploitation and poverty of farm workers. Living in California, Chavez knew that most farm workers were among the poorest of poor Americans; many were illiterate, indigent, and migratory. By contrast, the California agribusiness moguls possessed wealth and power. The labor-management situation seemed dismal.

Chavez received training in community organization. He read widely from both classical sources, such as St. Paul and Aquinas, as well as narrative accounts of U. S.-Mexican history. Having studied the lives of Jesus and Gandhi, he believed in nonviolence as a strategy for social justice. Through both public speaking and face-to-face, direct communication, Chavez, along with Dolores Huerta, created the National Farm Workers Organization in 1962 in Fresno that would later become the United Farm Workers. Chavez knew that effective public address was essential in organizing workers. He believed in drawing simple word pictures that attentive workers could understand.

Chavez' speaking and organizing activity brought national attention. He often spoke of revolution and the poor of every color being on the march to justice—"black, brown, red, everyone, whites included." He wisely linked the farm workers' cause with the Civil Rights Movement and its strategy of direct engagement and nonviolence. His style was to act aggressively but nonviolently. Of course, Martin Luther King was far better known than Chavez, but among Hispanics/Latinos this reformer earned total respect and credibility.

Chavez may have been the most effective labor leader of his generation. He definitely has become a major cultural and historical icon for the Hispanic community; many schools, streets, parks, and even some libraries have been named in his honor. In his speeches, he popularized a slogan, "Si, se puede [yes, one can]," and a version of this slogan ("Yes, we can!") was used by Barack Obama in his 2008 election campaign. In 1994 President Bill Clinton awarded Chavez posthumously the Presidential Medal of Freedom.

In his protest and organizing rhetoric, Chavez used speeches, letters, interviews, and proclamations. He could also employ nonverbal strategies such as marches and fasts. His Roman Catholic faith's religious language and icons infused his messages. In February 1968 Chavez began a twenty-five day fast as a strategy for reminding farm workers who were in the midst of a long strike against grape growers that violence was not the answer for bargaining success. The hunger strike did gain attention among the workers and also nationally. Chavez lost thirty-five pounds and was so weakened that he could hardly walk or perform menial tasks.

The occasion of Chavez's fast being ended was cause for celebration and worship. On March 10, eight to ten thousand people gathered at the Delano County Park to celebrate and hear Chavez's address. Senator Robert F. Kennedy flew to the event and sat next to Chavez to show his support for the workers' cause. Only thing, Chavez was too weak to stand and deliver the speech he had written for the occasion, so the document was read for him, first in Spanish, then in English. Chavez spoke of workers being family; he thanked them for their support during the fast; he explained that workers faced rich and powerful opponents, but these opponents were not invincible. "We are poor. Our allies are few. But we have something the rich do not own," Chavez admonished. "We have our own bodies and spirits and the justice of our cause as our weapons."

Chavez's theme was always social justice. He spoke in language that ordinary workers could understand. He had strong *ethos* because he could identify with the workers and their families, having lived and worked as did they. Yet a strong spiritual current, informed by the Catholic faith, ran throughout his rhetoric. The peroration of the 1968 address expressed the typical Chavez theme. "When we are really honest with ourselves we must admit that our lives are all that really belong to us. So, it's how we use our lives that determines what kind of men we are," the reformer turned preacher declared. "It is my deepest belief that only by giving our lives do we find life. I am convinced that the truest act of courage, the strongest act of manliness, is to sacrifice ourselves for others in a totally nonviolent struggle for justice. To be a man is to suffer for others. God help us to be men!"

## Shirley Chisholm (1924–2005)

"She was our Moses that opened the Red Sea for us!" Thus declared Robert E. Williams, president of the NAACP, as he looked back on the life of Shirley Chisholm, who was unique in many ways: the first African-American congresswoman, elected in 1968, and the first major party black candidate to make a bid for the U. S. presidency. She made that bid in 1972, a volatile time in American political life, especially with the war in Vietnam raging with no end in sight.

The idea of a candidate who was both African-American and female was something of a novelty for 1972, thus, not surprisingly, Chisholm worked hard to be recognized as a serious candidate. She stayed in the race until the time of the convention and received more than a hundred and fifty votes on the first ballot. (Actually, Chisholm was not the first female to run for the nomination to the nation's highest office; Margaret Chase Smith ran for the Republican nomination in 1964. While these facts may seem trivial to some, they become of relevance considering the successful run of Hillary Clinton for the Democratic nomination in 2016, a run that ended on Election Day, November 8.)

Chisholm was a product of New York education, having earned a Master's degree from Columbia University in elementary education. Though born in Brooklyn, as a young girl she and her young sister were sent to Barbados to be raised by a grandmother. That experience impacted Chisholm, and she always spoke with a West Indian accent. Her unique style of delivery commanded attention.

Chisholm served seven terms in the House as a representative of New York's Twelfth Congressional District. Clearly, she was intelligent and articulate. Her most highly acclaimed speech was delivered to the U. S. House of Representatives on August 10, 1970, in a rousing argument and plea for passage of the Equal Rights Amendment. She argued that discrimination against women was based on "outmoded views of society" and "prescientific beliefs about psychology and physiology," and she urged Congress to "sweep away those relics of the past and set future generations free of them." The amendment passed the House with only fifteen dissenting votes, then it was sent to the Senate where it was delayed, and then eventually the ERA died a slow death in the hands of state legislatures. This address is rated number ninety-one in Lucas and Medhurst's listing of the top one hundred speeches of the American twentieth century.

Shirley Chisholm was a small woman in physical size, but a formidable spokesperson for progressive causes in the nation. Her favorite slogan about herself—"Unbought and Unbossed"—was the title of her book and those words are inscribed on her vault. Those three words, perhaps, describe her public life best!

# Frank Church (1924–1984)

Few delegates to the U. S. Congress have understood and appreciated the power of effective public speaking more than Senator Frank Church from Idaho. As a bright youngster, Church studied history and politics, but he also studied and practiced good oratory. As a youth he would listen by radio to the speeches of his boyhood hero, Idaho Senator William Borah, a popular and influential Republican. He was a champion debater in high school, served in the military during World War II, then enrolled at Stanford University, where he was awarded the institution's highest debating prize.

Church completed a law degree also at Stanford, practiced law in Boise, and taught speech at the local college. As a young man of thirty-two, he dared to run in 1956 against an incumbent Republican senator, Herman Welker, and won easily though President Eisenhower carried the state in the national election by 60,000 votes. Political observers attributed this victory by the freshman senator to his oratorical skills and handsome physical appearance. In the Senate, serving from 1957 to 1981, Church focused on the area for which he had the strongest passion—foreign policy. He supported the U.N. and N.A.T.O., but he had strong reservations about U. S. involvement in revolution and change in developing, Third World, nations. He became a member of the Foreign Relations Committee, teaming with Chairman J. William Fulbright from Arkansas to address the conscience of Americans about the practical and moral implications of U. S. involvement in Third World nations.

Within the first four years of his service in the Senate, Church established a reputation as a skilled orator. Little wonder, then, the Idaho Senator was selected to deliver the keynote address at the 1960 Democratic National Convention in Los Angeles—the convention that nominated John F. Kennedy for president and also was addressed by such spokesmen as Lyndon Johnson, Adlai Stevenson, and Hubert Humphrey. Yet the cause for which Church rendered the greatest service to the nation was in educating and arousing the conscience of the American public about the use of American power in the developing world. In the mid-50s, Church began to argue eloquently against U. S. intervention in the internal affairs of other nations. He was among a small group of senators who became alarmed about our nation's increasing involvement in Southeast Asia, especially the conflict in Vietnam.

Church became a well-known national figure for his speeches and declarations that warned of unbearably costly involvement in Vietnam, and the dangers of over-extension in other nations and their revolutions around the globe. In fact, while there was a growing number of reformers and religious spokespersons speaking out against the war, Church became one of three U. S. senators best known for eloquent criticism and dissent against national policy in Southeast Asia (the other two being George McGovern and J. William Fulbright, all Democrats). He was co-author of two legislative efforts to curtail the Vietnam War (Cooper-Church Amendment, 1970, and Case-Church Amendment, 1973). His opposition to this war was courageous at a time when "silent majority Americans" felt dissent was unpatriotic, even disloyal. By contrast, Church declared in his public appearances that opposition to that war is "the highest form of patriotism—which is not the patriotism of conformity."

## Ann Richards (1933–2006)

As a politician who served as the forty-fifth governor of Texas, from 1991 to 1995, Ann Richards was a colorful, outspoken Democrat and feminist who was known for delivering speeches that zoomed straight to the point and were often filled with quotable one-liners. She was the first Texas female governor elected in her own right, though Ma Ferguson had been elected Texas governor twice as a proxy for her husband to continue his administration.

Richards' most famous speech was the Democratic National Convention keynote address at the 1988 convention (on July 18 in Atlanta). At the time of this address, she was Texas State Treasurer and virtually unknown outside the Lone Star State. This was an opportunity for Richards to introduce herself to the rest of the nation, and, with an attractive face, white hair, and Texas twang, she proceeded with unforgettable introduction. The address was highly critical of the Ronald Reagan administration and successor/Vice President George H. W. Bush, but her style possessed humor and down-home Texas charm. Mainly, the keynoter was remembered for her folksy colloquialism and playful scorn of Reagan and Bush and their policies. In debunking Bush's patrician heritage, Richards exclaimed: "Poor George. He can't help it—he was born with a silver foot in his mouth." The partisan audience roared in laughter.

In the introduction to the speech, Richards combines praise for women with pride in Texas political speaking: "Twelve years ago, Barbara Jordan, another Texas woman, made the keynote address to this convention, and two women in a hundred and sixty years is about par for the course. But if you give us a chance, we can perform. After all,

Ginger Rogers did everything that Fred Astaire did. She just did it backwards and in high heels."

Richards was frequently interrupted with applause and laughter. Lucas and Medhurst rank the address as number thirty-eight in their list of top one hundred speeches of the American twentieth century. One of Richards' daughters spoke on behalf of Hillary Clinton in the 2016 Democratic National Convention.

## Tom Brokaw (b. 1940)

As television journalist and long-time anchor and managing news editor at NBC Nightly News from 1982 to 2004, Tom Brokaw is clearly a well-known, reputable, knowledgeable and conversational communicator. True, he is not so much considered a dynamic public orator, but he merits honorable mention for being one of the nation's most familiar public voices, for effectively communicating the news (in his heyday he was part of a mighty triumvirate of news anchors alongside CBS' Dan Rather and ABC's Peter Jennings), and for a number of speeches he presented on special occasions, especially commencement addresses.

In his career Brokaw covered a number of highly important stories—the *Challenger* disaster, the tearing down of the Berlin Wall, Hurricane Andrew that hit South Florida, just to name a few. He speaks with great *ethos*, as did the late Walter Cronkite of CBS, having earned the respect of his colleagues and the general public. Cronkite was often thought of as the most trusted man in America, and it is possible to place Brokaw right at the top of that list of totally credible sources today. On the fateful morning of 9/11, Brokaw was called to the NBC studio to join Katie Couric and Matt Lauer, arriving at 9:30 A. M. and continuing on through that day of terrorism and panic that began in New York City and impacted the entire nation. After the collapse of the second tower, Brokaw stated to the nation: "This is war. This is a declaration and an execution of an attack against the United States."

In recent times, Brokaw is often sought for "on the air" opinions on truly significant political developments, such as the proceedings of the national political conventions. Yet, in sharing his personal story of fighting cancer, this native South Dakotan has impacted thousands of fellow citizens. His best-selling *The Greatest Generation* has been a source of information and inspiration to many readers who seek to capture the human side of World War II. He has won many awards and received a number of honorary degrees.

Brokaw has toured some of the battle sites of the Second World War and feels that such visits provided a "life-changing experience." His speeches and remarks in television commentary can be filled with memories laced with nostalgia. He has devoted himself to honoring and remembering the sacrifices of this "greatest generation" and urging the new generation of political leaders to take the same measure of wisdom and courage for our own time. Brokaw has spoken of lessons learned from two world wars with millions of casualties and a holocaust "in the heart of western civilization." "The long lesson?" he asked rhetorically when addressing the graduating class of Santa Fe College on May 15, 1999. "It is not enough to wire the world if you short-circuit the soul. It is not enough to probe the hostile environments of distant galaxies if we fail to resolve the climate of mindless violence, ethnic and racial hate here in the bosom of Mother Earth." As for "the greatest generation," Brokaw admitted its members were not perfect, that they were slow to recognize the equal place of women and other minorities, but "they never gave up," and in sacrificing their lives "they saved the world—nothing less!"

As Brokaw closed the speech, he offered brief exhortations: "Take care of your Mother. Mother Earth. Become color-blind. Hate hate. Fight violence. And take care of each other. You have a whole new century to shape. I envy you, but I want to stand aside now because you have work to do."

# Newt Gingrich (b. 1943)

Having been in national politics most of his adult life, Newt Gingrich has always tried, and been successful, at being a leader. Along the way, he has been controversial, outspoken, at times polarizing. Through it all, he has been a confident, intelligent, prepared, and forceful political communicator who has made hundreds of speeches and engaged in just as many interviews.

Clearly, Gingrich, the former Speaker of the House during the Bill Clinton administration, made his mark. Clashing with liberal and progressive Democrats, he brought a "hyperpartisan obstructionist" approach to Washington. He was known for an aggressive, combative style of Speaker leadership. To his credit, after the 1994 mid-term election he became the first Republican Speaker of the House in forty years. As co-author of the well-publicized "Contract with America," Gingrich seemed to establish himself as a proponent of balanced, conservative government. In reality, the Speaker was willing to shut down the federal government and become the leader of the anti-Bill

Clinton wave of the 90s. Conservative Republicans have sought his support. He was on the short list of vice residential possibilities for Donald Trump in 2016 and, though he was not selected, Gingrich made a strong and reasonable presentation at the national convention for the Republican ticket.

As for Gingrich's *ethos* as a public speaker, it remains as mixed as his polarizing image. On the one hand, his knowledge and experience gain wide respect. With his mop of white hair and long record of experience, Gingrich is seen by supporters as a veritable reservoir of policy knowledge and expertise, perhaps is thereby also viewed as knowing more than anyone else in Washington on an array of issues. On the other hand, some opponents picture Gingrich as hypocritical and demagogic, considering a less than sterling private life in contrast to his public advocacy of "family values" and condemnation of Clinton sex scandals. Critics see an ambitious politician who has presented "angry oratory" against the Democrats from the House floor, especially when C-SPAN cameras are rolling. A number of years remain to shape that image one way or the other. He gave a strong endorsement speech for Donald Trump at the 1916 convention and was considered to be on the "short list" as a candidate for vice president's slot on the ticket.

## Elizabeth Warren (b. 1949)

As the first woman elected to the U. S. Senate for Massachusetts, Elizabeth Warren has experienced a rapid rise on the national political scene. Several factors have contributed to this rise, but an important one is skill and energy in political oratory. Warren is highly educated and an intelligent member of the Senate, considered a scholar in bankruptcy law and consumer affairs. She is considered a populist and is popular among U. S. progressives. In the 2014 (mid-term) election cycle, she was a top Democratic fundraiser.

Warren is comfortable, energetic, and dynamic in public speaking. She received a prime time speaking appointment in the 2012 Democratic National Convention, and she was invited to deliver the keynote address on the opening evening of the 2016 Democratic National Convention held in Philadelphia. At that point, she had already campaigned energetically and made speaking appearances with Hillary Clinton, and many party regulars urged Warren be placed on the ticket as a running mate. As the campaign continued, Warren feuded with Republican nominee Donald Trump, who gave Warren even continued national attention by calling her "goofy," "Indian," and "Pocahontas"—terms that many considered insults and mockery of her Native American ancestry. Warren continued to speak directly and bluntly, at times with much sarcasm, with pointed criticism of Trump. She especially seemed to relish facetiously exploiting the label "Nasty Woman" that Trump had called Clinton in their last debate. Anything but boring, how entirely possible that some of Warren's best speeches are yet to be delivered!

Readers will think of other names that could be added to this list, and, just by watching the national political conventions, there is evidence that quite clearly a new generation of highly effective and passionate political orators is rising. The electronic era has ushered in a wide variety of media and strategies for delivering all kinds of messages to all kinds of audiences. The future will be fascinating, challenging, and possibly scary at times, too!

# Acknowledgments and Bibliographic Essay

The excerpts from the wide variety of speeches cited in this book were drawn from a variety of sources. Most of the texts for the speeches are located in internet sources, two of which are most important: *American Rhetoric.com* contains a listing of the top one hundred American speeches of the twentieth century, and *Presidentialrhetoric.com* is a highly valuable trove of the great speeches by American presidents with complete texts for many of them. At times, excerpts from more recent speeches were drawn simply from news reports of the occasion; I have often used *New York Times* and *Huffingtonpost.com*. In addition, I drew excerpts from former textbooks that I had adopted for classes in American public address and American political thought: A. Craig Baird, *American Public Addresses, 1740–1952* (McGraw-Hill, 1956); Diane Ravitch, *The American Reader: Words That Moved a Nation* (Second Edition, Harper Collins, 2000); William A. Linsey, *Speech Criticism: Methods and Materials* (Wm. C. Brown, 1968). Incidentally, Ravitch's *Reader*, a volume I have previously adopted as a supplementary text in teaching American political thought, was very useful in suggesting literary documents and addresses that are discussed in Part Three, Chapter One.

Additionally, I have drawn excerpts from *In Our Own Words: Extraordinary Speeches of the American Century*, edited by Senator Robert Torricelli and Andrew Carroll (Kodansha International, 1999), which contains a wide variety of speeches presented in the twentieth century as well as an excellent foreword essay by Doris Kearns Goodwin. For a wider variety of some two hundred speeches in world history, I recommend William Safire, *Lend Me Your Ears: Great Speeches in History* (W. W. Norton, 1992); Safire, himself a former speechwriter and language scholar, drew speeches from all categories of public address in world history. Two additional sources are James R. Andrews and David Zarefsky, editors, *Contemporary American Voices: Significant Speeches in American History, 1945 to Present* (Longman, 1987) and John Graham, editor, *Great American Speeches, 1898–1963: Texts and Studies* (Appleton-Century-Crofts, 1970). Philip S. Foner and Robert James Branham have edited a special volume, *Lift Every Voice: African-American Oratory, 1787-1900* (Tuscaloosa: University of Alabama, 1998) and Arthur

L. Smith has edited an insightful study, *Language, Communication, and Rhetoric in Black America* (New York: Harper and Row, 1972), that draws from the scholarship of over twenty-five different rhetorical critics. And finally, Ted Widmore, a former speech writer for President Bill Clinton, has edited two volumes of notable speeches: *American Speeches: Political Oratory from the Revolution to the Civil War*, Vol. 1, and *American Speeches: Political Oratory from Abraham Lincoln to Bill Clinton*, Vol. 2 (Library of America, 2006). Focusing on the twentieth century oratory, I highly recommend Stephen E. Lucas and Martin J. Medhurst, *Words of a Century: The Top 100 American Speeches, 1900–1999* (New York: Oxford University Press, 2009); obviously, there are many speech texts in this volume but the helpful part of this collection is an introduction to each speech that is more detailed than one finds in most collections; the speeches are ranked in the order that the author/editors believe are most important.

As for my discussion of some of these speeches, I simply drew from lecture notes in American history that I had compiled over the years; sources for those notes are sometimes long lost or in books donated to book sales. Of course, I injected my own opinion as any author should do, and, in this case, I heard many significant speeches beginning with the 1960s and 70s. The first truly significant speech I remember hearing and seeing at the moment of delivery was King's famous "I have a dream" address. For speeches before the 1970s, my lecture notes in American rhetoric were typically drawn from essays in the Brigance and Hochmuth series, *History and Criticism of American Public Address*, and Robert Oliver's one volume study, *History of Public Speaking in America*, both cited in my opening essay. Perhaps the one book I relied on most when in graduate school for ideas in rhetorical criticism, becoming almost a "Bible" for me in this field, was Lester Thonssen and A. Craig Baird's *Speech Criticism: The Development of Standards for Rhetorical Appraisal* (Ronald Press, 1948; there has been a subsequent revision with Waldo Braden). Two other works were avidly used: J. Jeffery Auer, editor, *Antislavery and Disunion, 1858 – 1861: Studies in the Rhetoric of Compromise and Conflict* (Harper and Row, 1963) and Waldo W. Braden, editor, *Oratory in the Old South, 1820 -1860* (Louisiana State University Press, 1970). As a young instructor in this field, one year I adopted DeWitt Holland, editor, *America in Controversy: History of American Public Address* (Wm. C. Brown, 1973).

In 1987 Bernard K. Duffy and Halford R. Ryan edited the first multi-volume set on American public address since the Brigance volumes of more than four decades earlier: *American Orators Before 1900: Critical Studies and Sources* (New York: Greenwood Press) with essays on fifty-five leading political, social, and religious speakers, and then a subsequent volume, *American Orators of the Twentieth Century: Critical Studies and Sources* (Greenwood Press) with essays on approximately sixty different influential public speakers. This two-volume series enlisted the research and writing of numerous authors for the various chapters and a brief bibliography along with a listing of that speaker's greatest speeches at the end of each chapter is helpful. A more recent study is James Perrin Warren's *Culture of Eloquence: Oratory and Reform in Antebellum America* (University Park: Pennsylvania State University, 1999). Another specialized collection is an edition by Rob Blaisdell, *Great Speeches by Native Americans* (Mineola, New York: Dover Publications, 2000); this little volume gave me ideas about some of the eloquent speeches of American natives. Incidentally, Iowa State University has archives of women's political communication. A more general yet quite scholarly and perhaps a bit academic for ordinary readers is an edition by Thomas W. Benson with foreword by Lewis Perry, *American Rhetoric: Context and Criticism* (Carbondale: Southern Illinois University Press, 1989); the readings herein seem primarily focused on colonial and early America years; you will likely find the most technical discussion of Patrick Henry's "Liberty or Death" speech as can be found anywhere or desired anywhere (at least among underclassmen). This collection deals with written rhetoric as well as spoken rhetoric.

In studying the rhetoric of the pre-Revolutionary period, I recommend Stephen Lucas, *Portents of Rebellion: Rhetoric and Revolution in Philadelphia, 1765-76* (Temple University Press, 1976). The author emphasizes linguistics in his study: "A choice of words is also a choice of worlds. Language plays a ubiquitous and powerful role in shaping political perceptions, values, and behaviors." Lucas also has an excellent essay in the above cited Benson edition, *American Rhetoric*, entitled "Justifying America" (pp. 67-130). This professor makes a number of interesting points: July 2 and not July Fourth was the day the Founders felt would be celebrated as the most glorious day in the new nation's history; the Founders did not see the Declaration as being any more sacred than any of the other sixteen state papers issued by the Continental Congress prior to 1776; the Declaration was a rhetorical effort within the ongoing dialectic with the mother country; every aspect of the Declaration was designed to create a favorable image of Congress and its actions; the claim of unanimity among the founders is a façade as some held some strong difference of opinion; the Preamble to the Constitution is a model of clear, concise, and simple statement (202 words) to inform others what the new government was all about.

One of the readings assigned in one of my graduate classes in history opened my mind to the idea of the Declaration of Independence as a rhetorical document: *A Casebook on the Declaration of Independence: Analysis of the Structure, Meaning, and Literary Worth of the Text*, edited by Robert Ginsberg (Thomas Y. Crowell Company, 1967). "The Declaration of Independence is the most widely known and influential secular document in the history of the world," declares the editor. "Conceived in the midst of a great argument over the rights of men, the obligations of the state, and the necessity of revolution, the Declaration has perennially been invoked on many subsequent occasions when these issues have been debated....and thus the Declaration remains contemporary and controversial, worthy of careful study by those who would understand human events and human ideals." (p. v). Ginsberg's own essay, "The Declaration as Rhetoric," acknowledges the value of studying this document from the historical, philosophical, and literary perspectives but it foremost must be studied as a piece of rhetoric: "The Declaration of Independence is primarily an effort made by certain men at a given moment to persuade other men to adopt special attitudes and courses of action" (p. 220). I doubt that I could have explained the concept of rhetorical criticism any better!

One of the topics treated in this book is the Chautauqua, an institution that began its life as a Sunday School assembly and then became a summer center for a variety of educational and cultural activities. Public speaking was the centerpiece for so many of these activities. An excellent and interesting volume on this topic that I enjoyed reading is Theodore Morrison's *Chautauqua: A Center for Education, Religion, and the Arts in America* (University of Chicago Press, 1974). The narrative is enriched by numerous historical photographs of speakers, performers, and audiences.

Virtually any material written by Kathleen Hall Jamieson and Karlyn Kohrs Campbell can be highly interesting and deeply valuable in the study of rhetoric and public address. Their study of presidential rhetoric, *Deeds Done in Words: Presidential Rhetoric and the Genres of Governance* (University of Chicago Press, 1990) deals with all kinds of speaking situations for the American president: Inaugural addresses; speeches of ascendant Vice Presidents; State of the Union addresses, veto messages, war rhetoric, rhetoric of impeachment, pardoning rhetoric; and farewell addresses. As one would expect, there are many historical allusions in the various chapters. The two authors also co-wrote *The Interplay of Influence: Mass Media and Their Publics in News, Advertising, Politics* (Two editions, Wadsworth Publishing Company, 1983 and 1988). One of the most interesting volumes that I have read in American rhetoric is Jamieson's *Eloquence in an Electronic Age: The Transformation of Political Speechmaking* (Oxford University Press, 1988); the book contains an interesting blend of historical illustration with anecdotes. Campbell is the author of a two-volume work on influential women orators entitled *Man*

*Cannot Speak for Her: Key Texts of the Early Feminists* (2 volumes, 1989) an anthology that represents a hundred years of feminist oratory. Two specialized volumes I read in graduate school for general background on American oratory: Robert L. Scott, *The Rhetoric of Black Power* (New York: Harper and Row, 1969) and Donald W. Zacharias (ed.), *In Pursuit of Peace: Speeches of the Sixties* (New York: Random House, 1970); this little volume in the "Issues and Spokesmen Series" dealt largely with addresses on the Vietnam War.

*The Handbook of Rhetoric and Public Address*, edited by Shawn J. Parry-Giles and J. Michael Hogan (Malden, MA: Wiley-Blackwell, 2010), presents seventeen essays in the field of rhetoric and public address. The essays are based on studies of several public speakers as well as the rhetoric of various reform movements. I especially enjoyed the first essay on the background of the academic study of American public address, especially in the past century. J. Michael Hogan has edited *Rhetoric and Community: Studies in Unity and Fragmentation* (University of South Carolina Press, 1998) that includes the editor's essay on "Rhetoric and Community" and then chapters by a dozen or so scholars in rhetoric and communication on topics related to rhetoric and race, gender, war, film, science, and community.

If one is seeking a general textbook on rhetoric, one that has depth and challenges students to do critical thinking regarding public speaking, then I would recommend Karlyn Campbell, Susan Huxman, and Thomas Burkholder's *The Rhetorical Act: Thinking, Speaking, and Writing Critically* (Fifth edition; Stamford, CT: Cengage Learning, 2015). This work draws amply from famous speeches in American history as a means of illustrating rhetorical theory. I have enjoyed using this book as a text in classes of Advanced Public Speaking.

# About the Author

Perry C. Cotham is Professor and Senior Lecturer in Communication Studies at Middle Tennessee State University. He earned both the M. A. and Ph. D. in Speech Communication, with a minor in U. S. History, from Detroit's Wayne State University. His doctoral dissertation focused on the rhetoric of the New Deal and World War II era.

Dr. Cotham has completed post-doctoral studies in religion at Vanderbilt University and in history, political science, and psychology at Middle Tennessee State. He has served as both full-time and adjunct professor in rhetoric and public address, history and political science, and philosophy and ethics at several colleges and universities, especially in the Nashville area: Lipscomb, Belmont, Nashville State, Tennessee State, and MTSU.

Cotham has written some twenty published books and many articles in the fields of history and political science, worldviews and religion, philosophy and ethics, and rhetoric and public address. His study of the Tennessee labor movement won the prestigious 1995 "Best Book" award from the Tennessee Historical Society and Tennessee Library Association. His two most recent books in the field of public speaking are: *From Pilgrim Pulpit to the Electronic Era: The Varieties of American Religious Communication* (Westbow Press, 2014) and *In Search of Rhetorical Excellence* (BlueDoor Publishing, 2015).

Cotham and wife, Glenda, enjoy three children and a number of grandchildren. He has an avid interest in all kinds of collegiate and professional sports and his hobbies include hiking and tennis.

Edwards Brothers Malloy
Ann Arbor MI. USA
August 25, 2017